STUDY GUIDE TO ACCOMPANY
BREALEY AND MYERS

PRINCIPLES OF CORPORATE FINANCE

THIRD EDITION

CHARLES A. D'AMBROSIO

Editor-in-Chief
Financial Analysts Journal
University of Washington

STEWART D. HODGES

Esmée Fairbairn Professor of Financial Management
School of Industrial and Business Studies
University of Warwick
Coventry CV4 7AL
England

McGraw-Hill Publishing Company

New York St. Louis San Francisco Auckland Bogotá
Caracas Hamburg Lisbon London Madrid Mexico Milan
Montreal New Delhi Oklahoma City Paris San Juan
São Paulo Singapore Sydney Tokyo Toronto

Study Guide to Accompany Brealey and Myers:

PRINCIPLES OF CORPORATE FINANCE

Third Edition

Copyright © 1988 by McGraw-Hill, Inc. All rights
reserved. Printed in the United States of America. Except as
permitted under the United States Copyright Act of 1976, no part
of this publication may be reproduced or distributed in any form
or by any means, or stored in a data base or retrieval system,
without the prior written permission of the publisher.

ISBN 0-07-007388-0

4 5 6 7 8 9 0 EDWEDW 9 3 2 1 0

CONTENTS

PREFACE

This Study Guide to *Principles of Corporate Finance* by Brealey and Myers will help you learn about finance as quickly and as easily as possible. The purpose of the Study Guide is to make you more proficient in the science and art of financial decision making. It helps you achieve this end in three ways.

1. *As an aid to reading the text.* The Study Guide sets the scene for each chapter by telling you how it relates to other chapters and what key ideas you should look for. Additional explanations and worked examples are provided to help deepen your understanding of particular points in the text.

2. *As a source of additional exercises.* The Study Guide provides both questions and answers.

3. *As an aid to reviewing for exams.* The summaries of each chapter and the lists of terms will help you to remember the main points. The summaries will help you to review what you have learned, either after you have studied a chapter or when you are preparing for an examination. As you study both the text and the Study Guide, always assume that you are the financial manager, keeping in mind his or her goals, perspective, and rationale for doing what he or she does.

STRUCTURE OF THE STUDY GUIDE

Each chapter of the Study Guide refers to the corresponding chapter of the text. Except for Chapter 36, each chapter contains the following sections:

INTRODUCTION
The short introduction gives a concise guide to what the chapter is about. It will help you to determine the gist of the chapter and understand how it fits in with any neighboring chapters that relate to it.

WHAT TO LOOK FOR
The second section, entitled "What to Look for in Chapter _____," will help you find your way through the detail of the corresponding chapter in the text. Special attention is paid to explaining the points that students most often find difficult. You will probably want to read these first two sections of the Study Guide *before* studying the corresponding chapter of the text.

WORKED EXAMPLES
Worked examples are provided depending on the nature of the chapter. They enhance the explanations presented earlier and give you a guide to the sorts of calculations you should be able to make after you have studied the chapter.

SUMMARY
The summary provides a concise synopsis of the chapter. Whereas you might read this before studying the chapter, it is wiser to use it to review what you have learned, either after reading the chapter or when preparing for an examination.

LIST OF TERMS

This section provides a list of the most important *new* terms that you will have encountered in reading the chapter. It is a good idea to check this list *immediately* after you finish reading a chapter. If you find that you have forgotten the meaning of a term, check it in the Glossary at the back of the text, or, if necessary, go back to the place in the chapter where it was introduced.

EXERCISES

The exercises take three main forms. The first set of exercises in each chapter are fill-in questions, which further check to determine whether you know what the new terms mean and how they are used. By filling in these exercises you will provide yourself with a chapter-by-chapter glossary of the most important terms. The second set of exercises consists of problems. These correspond broadly to the types of problems given as worked examples. Finally, a number of suggested essay questions are worth reading because they indicate the kinds of issues that you should be able to discuss after you have studied the chapter.

ANSWERS

Where it is possible to do so, we have provided answers to all the exercises other than the essay questions. In many cases, fairly complete solutions are given. Nevertheless, we urge you to make sure that you complete your answer before you succumb to the temptation to look at ours!

One point about our answers is in order. Many of the mathematical solutions were calculated either with a hand-held calculator or by computer. Consequently, some of your answers may differ from some of ours because the tables in the text's Appendix are rounded to three significant digits, whereas most hand-held calculators carry eight digits and computers carry more than that. The differences should not be great, however.

STARRED SECTIONS

Some parts of the summary and some problems are indicated by a star, or asterisk. As in the text, these are of unusual difficulty, and many students will want to omit them on a first reading. We hope that some of the starred problems will provide an interesting challenge even to more advanced students.

SOME TIPS

You should realize that authors of books work from outlines. The subject matter is broken down into very small parts, but never so small as to become burdensome. The first way to break down the subject matter is by chapters. So before studying the subject of corporate finance, look over the chapter headings in order to locate yourself in the milieu called financial decision making. You should know at the outset, for example, that firms make decisions on what investments to make and how to finance them. By perusing the chapter headings, the topics of financial decision making will be placed in perspective.

When you first tackle a chapter, employ the same process you used with respect to the entire book: examine the headings of each section and subsection of the chapter and simply page through the chapter. By so doing you will have a preview of events to come, and, as you study one section of the chapter, you will doubtless recall some of the other headings so that the one currently being studied will be placed in perspective relative to earlier ones.

Then study the chapter, section by section. After you have done that, go over the summary several times. Then go back over each of the headings and subheadings, stopping for a moment to recall what each contained. Finally, close the text and sit back and tell yourself, aloud if possible, the major points of the chapter.

This approach will reap you large benefits and enhance your understanding of the process of financial decision making; the rewards will be far in excess of the costs.

The same approach should be taken as you study the Study Guide, keeping in mind that the Study Guide *summarizes* most of the chapters of the text. As noted above, the format of the Study Guide is straightforward.

BON VOYAGE!

Not all students will use the Study Guide in exactly the same way. However you use it, we trust you will find it helpful, and we hope you will get as much knowledge and enjoyment from the text as we have. Good luck!

Charles A. D'Ambrosio
Stewart D. Hodges

CHAPTER 1
WHY FINANCE MATTERS

INTRODUCTION

This chapter, like the first chapter of many other large textbooks, is a brief introduction to the book. It is important because it sets the scene for what is to follow. The chapter answers the following three questions:

1. What kinds of problems occur in finance, and why are they interesting?
2. Who do we really mean when we talk about "the financial manager"?
3. What topics does the book cover and in what order?

WHAT TO LOOK FOR IN CHAPTER 1

Chapter 1 has three short sections corresponding to the three questions described above and an even shorter concluding section. The full meaning of Sections 1-1 and 1-3 will become apparent only as you progress through the whole book. In the meantime, look out for the following three major sets of problems faced by financial managers. First, in order to carry on business, companies spend money to purchase various *real assets* such as factories, plants, and machinery. Decisions regarding which specific assets to purchase (or invest in) are the company's *investment* decisions. Chapters 2 to 12 are concerned with investment decisions.

The second set of problems centers on ways to obtain money or credit. After all when a company wants to make an investment, it may first have to obtain cash in order to be able to do so. Financial managers raise money in various ways. For example, they may borrow money by signing a loan agreement with a bank or by selling debentures (long-term bonds). Alternatively, they may decide to raise additional money by issuing new shares of stock for cash. In both cases the company sells pieces of paper (called *financial assets*) whose value is based on its claims to the profitability of real assets. Decisions about how cash should be raised are *financing* decisions. Financing is dealt with in Chapters 13 to 26. Closely related to financing is the idea that a company can reduce the risks it is exposed to by hedging operations in the financial markets. This is also covered here.

The remaining chapters (27 to 36) are concerned with the third set of problems, a variety that involves *both* investment *and* financing decisions. These include the management of various forms of short-term borrowing and lending, financial planning, mergers, and international operations. The book concludes with a summary of what is known and what is still unknown in finance.

In sum, the financial manager's tasks are compartmentalized into investment decisions, financing decisions, and a combination of investment and financing decisions.

The Challenge of Financial Management: We have just sketched a few of the many decisions that financial managers have to make. But what criterion is to be applied to select the best decisions? Remember, legally the shareholders are the ultimate owners of the firm and the role of the manager is that of an agent acting on behalf of the owners. Therefore, the financial manager's duty is to make decisions that will benefit shareholders, that is, will increase the value of their stake in the firm. Of course, although the financial manager's main duty is to the shareholders, there are also obligations to creditors, employees, and society.

Because the prime concern is to try to increase shareholder value, it is hardly surprising that the theory and implications of how financial assets are valued play a key role in the text. They represent an exciting challenge to students and practitioners alike.

The text also stresses the importance of understanding how capital markets work. Capital markets are important to a financial manager for two reasons. First, a financial manager cannot understand how the values of financial assets are determined without knowing something about the markets in which they are traded. Second, a financial manager is often a direct participant in the capital markets. They provide a vehicle for raising money (and disbursing it), and for managing risk.

Both the text and the study guide provide the solid foundation of concepts and information on which sound financial decisions are based. You will build on this foundation with your own experience, talents, judgment, creativity, and initiative.

The Financial Manager: So far we have begged the question of precisely who we mean by the "financial manager." Section 1-2 of the chapter deals with that issue. Naturally a large number of managers in a firm may be involved in contributing to financial decisions. Any of these may justifiably be called a financial manager. Of course, some managers specialize in finance. Look out for the special role of the treasurer. In large companies there may be a controller as well as a treasurer. Look out for how their roles differ. Finally, bear in mind the importance of the board of directors. Directors are elected by shareholders (the ultimate owners of the company) and act as their representatives. The final decisions on dividend payments, public issues of securities, and the approval of major investment projects are made by the board of directors.

SUMMARY

Financial Decisions

Companies make *investment* decisions about which real assets to purchase.

They make *financing* decisions about how to raise cash.

The usual criterion for success is value. The shareholders are the ultimate owners of the firm, and managers act as their agents. The financial manager should make decisions that will *increase the value of the shareholders' stake in the firm.* (At the same time there is clearly a further duty to honor the firm's obligations to its creditors, its work force, and society at large.)

Four Aspects of the Financial Manager's Job

The financial manager's job cannot be learned just by reading a textbook. The text is no substitute for experience, although it supplies the conceptual foundation on which good financial decisions are based. Here are four challenges of the financial manager's job:

1. *Understanding capital markets:* The financial manager is an intermediary between the firm's operations and the capital markets in which the firm's securities are traded. Correct investment and financing decisions require an understanding of how capital markets work.
2. *Understanding value:* We can't expect to make financial decisions that will consistently increase the wealth of shareholders unless we understand how financial assets are valued. A large part of the text is devoted to explaining the theory of financial value and its implications.
3. *Understanding the effects of time and uncertainty:* Most investments do not repay themselves for some years, and their outcomes are often very uncertain. The financial manager must understand how the timing and uncertainty of future earnings affect the value of a prospective investment.

4. *Understanding people:* The financial manager needs the opinions and the cooperation of many people. Understanding how people tick is essential if damaging misunderstandings or conflicts of interest are to be avoided.

The Financial Manager

No one person is responsible for all the financial decisions described in the book. The term *financial manager* is used to refer to anyone responsible for a significant financial decision of a company.

The *treasurer* of a company is its principal financial manager. The treasurer is responsible for obtaining financing, managing relations with banks, making sure the company meets its obligations to its security holders, and generally managing the company's capital.

Large corporations may have a *controller* as well as a treasurer. The controller managers budgeting, accounting, and auditing, functions which involve inspecting to see that money is used efficiently. In the largest companies, the treasurer and controller may both report to a financial vice-president who acts as chief financial officer.

The power for ultimate financial decisions often rests with the board of directors, although the authority for approving small- or medium-sized investments is commonly delegated. Moreover, only the board has the legal power to declare a dividend or sanction a public issue of securities.

TOPICS COVERED IN THE BOOK

The following outline provides a key to the main sections of the book and to the main topics covered within each section.

MAIN SECTIONS	PART	CHAPTERS	TOPICS COVERED
Introduction	1	1	Why finance matters
The investment decision		2-6	How to value assets
	2	7-9	The link between risk and value
	3	10-12	Managing the investment process
The financing decision	4	13	Can securities be issued at a fair price?
		14-15	How are securities issued?
	5	16-19	Dividend policy and debt policy
	6	20-22	Options and their applications
	7	23-26	Valuing different kinds of debt Risk management
Financial planning	8	27-29	Performance measurement, financial planning and strategy
Short-term financing	9	30-32	Managing short-term assets and liabilities
Miscellaneous topics	10	33-35	Mergers (international) and pensions
Conclusions	11	36	What we do know and do not know about finance

You will find it useful to refer back to this outline as you progress through the book.

4

LIST OF TERMS

Bond
Capital budgeting
Capital market
Controller
Financial assets
Financing
Intangible assets

Investment
Real assets
Share
Stock
Tangible assets
Treasurer

EXERCISES

Fill-in Questions

1. A company's _REAL ASSETS_ consist of the tangible and intangible assets that it uses to carry on its business.
2. _TANGIBLE_ assets consist of physical assets such as factories, offices, plant, machinery, and equipment.
3. Trademarks, patents, and technical expertise are examples of _INTANGIBLE_ assets.
4. Stocks and bonds are pieces of paper that represent claims on real assets. They are called _FINANCIAL_ assets.
5. A corporate _BOND_ is a certificate which shows that money has been lent to a company.
6. A _SHARE_ (or _STOCK_) represents a claim to the ownership of a fraction of the company.
7. The purchase of an asset is a _INVESTMENT_ decision.
8. The firm's _CAPITAL BUDGETING_ decisions are concerned with which real investments should be undertaken.
9. The firm's _FINANCING_ decisions are concerned with how cash should be raised.
10. The markets in which financial assets are traded are called _CAPITAL_ markets.
11. The _TREASURER_ is the principal financial manager of the firm.
12. Large corporations may have a further financial executive, called a _CONTROLLER_, who is responsible for budgeting, accounting, and auditing.

Problems

1. Which of the following are investment decisions and which are financing decisions?
   a. Issuing common stock — B — a
   b. Developing a new product — B
   c. Buying a factory
   d. Paying a dividend to stockholders — a
   e. Borrowing from a bank — a
   f. Selling a warehouse — B
   g. Purchasing shares of another company — B

2. Which of the following are real assets and which are financial assets?
   a. A patent
   b. An office building leased by the company
   c. A debenture
   d. Raw materials inventory
   e. A lease
   f. A bank loan

Essay Questions

1. Describe the differences between each of the following:
   a. A tangible asset and intangible asset
   b. Investment and financing
   c. The treasurer and the controller

2. Explain what capital markets are and why financial managers need to understand them.

ANSWERS TO EXERCISES

Fill-in Questions

1. real assets
2. tangible
3. intangible
4. financial
5. bond
6. stock, share
7. investment
8. capital budgeting
9. financing
10. capital
11. treasurer
12. controller

Problems

1. a, d, and e are financing decisions; b, c, f, and g are investment decisions.

2. a, b, and d are real assets; c, e, and f are financial assets.

CHAPTER 2
PRESENT VALUE AND
THE OPPORTUNITY COST OF CAPITAL

INTRODUCTION

This chapter introduces the single most important idea in finance: *present value*. Most investments produce revenues at some later date. *Present value* tells us how much the prospect of future income is worth today after taking account of the time value of money. *Net present value* measure how much an investment will add to the value of the company because it is the amount by which the investment's present value exceeds its cost. By accepting positive net present value projects and rejecting negative net present value projects, financial managers will increase the value of the company. Such increases always serve the best interests of shareholders as long as they can buy and sell shares and other financial claims in an efficient capital market such as we have in the United States.

WHAT TO LOOK FOR IN CHAPTER 2

The value of an asset stems form the future cash flows it produces. *Present value* is the method we use to determine how much the prospect of a future cash flow is worth today.

Present Value: Present value is worth spending some time on because it is important; it tells us how much an investment is worth today, given its expected cash flows. Suppose you have an investment which is expected to pay $100 in 1 year. How much is it worth to you today? Well, it all depends. On what? On the return you expect to make on other investments of comparable risk. If comparable-risk investments offer a return of 10 percent, an investment of $90.91 (= $100/1.1) today also is expected to produce $100 in 1 year. Your original investment has a *present value* of $90.91. If it costs only $80, it has a *net present value* of $10.91 (= $90.91 – $80.00). It makes you better off by $10.91 relative to the alternative investments. Make sure you understand the meaning of return, present value, and net present value and that you can calculate each of them.

The Separation of Ownership and Management: Present value has important implications. How can the managers of a large company make decisions that will win the approval of *all* their stockholders (who may number thousands)? The answer is by using present value. When managers make an investment with a positive net present value, they can be certain that they are making every stockholder better off. The *capital market* makes it possible for individuals to postpone their consumption or bring it forward by lending or borrowing at the *capital market rate*. Investments with a return which is higher than the capital market rate make the stockholders better off. Investments with a lower return are inferior to investing directly in the capital market. The existence of the capital market makes it easy for management to be separated from ownership. Managers don't have to keep asking owners, "Would you like me to do this?" Instead they can ask themselves, "Does this investment offer more than the capital market rate?"

Finally, if you want to go deeper into the theory and the detailed assumptions which underlie these principles, you should study Section 2-2 of the chapter. This section is summarized in section 4 of our Summary.

6

WORKED EXAMPLE

The following numerical example illustrates the main ideas of the chapter. It shows how to calculate a return, a present value, and a net present value. It also illustrates why financial markets enable ownership and management to be separated, (the principle established by Irving Fisher in 1930).

PROBLEM: RETURN, NPV AND THE SEPARATION OF MANAGEMENT

A company has $20,000 to invest in a project which will pay back $23,000 in 1 year.
1. What return does the investment offer?
2. What are its PV and NPV if the capital market rate is 20 percent?
3. What are they if the capital market rate is 10 percent?
4. What difference does it make if the company has no cash currently available for this investment?
5. What difference does it make if some shareholders would prefer to consume more this year and less next year?

SOLUTION

1. $\text{Return} = \dfrac{\text{profit}}{\text{investment}} = \dfrac{\$23,000 - \$20,000}{\$20,000} = 15 \text{ percent.}$

2. $\text{Present value} = \dfrac{\$23,000}{1.2} = \$19,167.$

   $\text{Net present value} = \$19,167 - \$20,000 = -\$833.$

   The investment would make stockholders worse off. The company should either invest the $20,000 in the capital market to earn 20 percent or return the money to the stockholders for them to consume or reinvest.

3. Present value = $23,000/1.1 = $20,909.

   Net present value = $20,909 - $20,000 = $909.

   The investment will make the stockholders better off by $909.

4. It should make no difference to the investment decision. The company can borrow or issue more shares to raise the necessary capital.
5. It should make no difference to the company. Shareholders are free to sell some of their shares to increase their immediate consumption.

SUMMARY

1. **Why we need a theory of value**
   a. The aim of investment is to find assets that are worth more than they cost.
   b. When there is a good market, value = market price, *but* we still need to know *how* asset values are reached.
   c. The market for many kinds of assets is very thin.

2. **Present value**
   a. Calculation:

$$PV = \frac{C_1}{1+r}$$

$$NPV = PV - \text{cost of investment}$$
$$= C_0 + \frac{C_1}{1+r}$$

where C_0 = cash flow at time 0 (usually negative)
C_1 = cash flow at time 1
r = discount rate (= return offered by comparable investment alternatives)

   b. Why we discount:
   A dollar today is worth more than a dollar tomorrow.
   \$1 invested now is worth $\$1(1 + r)$ in a year's time.
   To get \$1 after a year I must invest $\$1/(1 + r)$ today.
   $\$C_1$ in a year's time is worth $\$C_1/(1 + r)$ today.

   c. Rates of return:
   Return = profit/investment. Investments with positive NPVs are those that offer a return that is higher than the discount rate. We may either (1) accept investments with positive NPVs or (2) accept investments with a return greater than their opportunity cost of capital.

3. **Separation of ownership and management**
   a. *Shareholders* want
   to increase their wealth,
   to choose when they consume,
   to choose what risks they take.
   b. An efficient *capital market* provides
   choice of when you consume,
   choice of what risks you take.
   c. *Financial managers*
   should accept all investments with positive NPVs
   because this adds to shareholder wealth.
   d. Irving Fisher (1930) discovered this fundamental principle.
   e. Other criteria: PV is also relevant where the interest of shareholder wealth has to be balanced against other, wider interests. It is in managers' long term interests to satisfy the requirements of their shareholders.

*4. **The underlying theory** (Section *2-2)
   a. The argument:
   The *capital market* enables people to lend or borrow.
   Lending postpones consumption, *borrowing* brings it forward.
   Investments giving less than the market rate are never worthwhile: it's better to lend.
   Investments giving more than the market rate should *always* be made: I can borrow (or sell securities) to leave my current consumption unchanged.
   b. The assumptions:
   Market rates can be used when the following conditions for a *perfect market* are satisfied:
   (1) No individual can influence prices.
   (2) Access to the market is free. Trading is costless.
   (3) Information about securities is freely available.
   (4) There are no distorting taxes.

A market is called *imperfect* when these assumptions fail. In an imperfect market shareholders may disagree about what discount rate the manager should use.

LIST OF TERMS

Discount factor   Present value (PV)
Net present value (NPV)   Return
Opportunity cost of capital   Separation

EXERCISES

Fill-in Questions

1. The current (discounted) value of a future cash flow is called its ___PV___.
2. A ___FV___ is the present value of a single dollar received at some future date.
3. ___RETURN___ is the profit from an investment expressed as a proportion of the initial outlay.
4. A future cash flow is multiplied by a ___DISCOUNT FACTOR___ to give its present value.
5. The existence of a capital market facilitates the ___SEPARATION___ of ownership and management.
6. The expected return from a comparable investment in bonds or shares represents the ___RISK___.
7. The ___NPV___ of an asset is the difference between its present value and its cost.
8. Financial managers will benefit the firm's stockholders if they maximize ___NPV___.

Problems

1. If a 1-year bill (which pays $1000 after 1 year) costs $920, what is (a) the 1-year rate of return, (b) the 1-year discount factor (DF)?

   $\frac{1000-920}{920} = .087$ 8.7%   DF = .92

2. Calculate the 1-year discount factors for discount rates of (a) 5 percent, (b) 15 percent, (c) 0 percent.

   a) = .9524   b) .8696   c) $\frac{1}{1+0}$ = 1

3. I get a 1-year student loan of $5000 at 3 percent interest instead of the 12 percent rate my bank would charge me. (a) How much money does that save me next year? (b) How much is that saving worth today?

   $450   401.8

4. I can buy a plot of land for $120,000, spend a further $120,000 to build a house on it, and I expect to sell if for $300,000 in a year's time. A similar risk investment would give me an expected return of 15 percent. (a) What is the expected return from my house building venture? (b) What is the PV of the house? (c) What is the NPV of the project?

5. A. Miser, Sr., has $20,000 to invest. He is considering two projects. Project A requires $10,000 and will pay $11,000 after a year. Project B also requires $10,000 but will only pay $10,700 after a year. What should he do if interest rates are (a) 6 percent, (b) 9 percent, (c) 12 percent?

6. B. Prodigal, Jr., has just $50 to his name. He is interested in spending as much money as possible as quickly as possible. He is interested in investment only as a way of increasing his disposable income. Faced with the same opportunities as Miser, Sr., in question 5, what should B. Prodigal, Jr., do? (Assume he can borrow to invest, but not to consume.)

10

*7. I see in *The Wall Street Journal* that I can buy No. 2 cotton at 59.2 cents per pound for immediate delivery, and that I can simultaneously contract to sell it at 65.8 cents in 12 months. (a) What return does this represent? (b) I also notice that I can get a return of 9.5 percent by investing in safe 1-year bonds. What do you think is the *least* I would have to pay for storage at the end of a year if I decided to buy and store the cotton?

8. Imagine an economy in which there are just three individuals, A, B, C. Each has money to invest and a number of possible investment projects, each of which would require $1000. A has $2000 to invest and has two projects that offer a return of 11 percent and one that offers 8 percent. B has $1000 to invest and has projects yielding 11 percent and 7 percent. C has $1000 to invest and has projects offering 15 and 12 percent. (a) What projects will be undertaken if there is no borrowing or lending? (b) If they do borrow and lend to each other, what projects will be undertaken and what will the interest rate be?

Essay Questions

1. Explain the meaning of net present value and why it is relevant to the financial manager.

2. "Many of our shareholders are retired and cannot afford to lose any of the value of their savings. That is why we demand a higher rate of return on our new investments than do many other companies." Discuss.

3. Explain how the existence of a financial market can benefit both consumers and businesspeople.

ANSWERS TO EXERCISES

Fill-in Questions

1. present value
2. discount factor
3. return
4. discount factor
5. separation
6. opportunity cost of capital
7. net present value
8. net present value

Problems

1. (a) $\frac{\text{Profit}}{\text{Investment}} = \frac{(1000-920)}{920} = \frac{80}{920} = 8.70\%$

   (b) $1/1.0870 = 0.9200$

2. (a) $1/1.05 = 0.9524$; (b) $1/1.15 = 0.8696$; (c) $1/1.00 = 1.0000$

3. (a) $450; (b) $401.79 after discounting at my 12 percent opportunity rate.

4. (a) $\frac{\text{Profit}}{\text{Investment}} = \frac{60,000}{240,000} = 25\%$;

   (b) PV = $300,000/1.15 = $260,870;
   (c) NPV = PV − Cost = $20,870

5. (a) Invest in both projects; (b) Invest in Project A only (and lend $10,000); (c) Invest in neither project (but lend $20,000 at 12%).

6. B. Prodigal will want to make precisely the same investment decisions as A. Miser.

7. (a) Return = (65.80 – 59.20)/59.20 = 11.15%; (b) A 9.5 percent return would be given by a net selling price of 59.20 x 1.095 = $64.82, so I must expect storage costs of at least (65.80 – 64.82) = $0.98.

8. (a) Always take those projects with the highest returns, all else the same. So A takes two 11 percent projects, B takes an 11 percent project, and C takes a 15 percent project. (b) C's 12 percent project will be undertaken instead of one of the 11 percent projects. The interest rate will be 11 percent.

CHAPTER 3
HOW TO CALCULATE PRESENT VALUES

INTRODUCTION

It is essential to master the technique for calculating present values described here. The present value of a single cash flow which will occur after a number of years is the basic building block. It enables us to work out the value of any stream of cash flows by adding together the present values of all the separate cash flows. We can often save a lot of time in these calculations by knowing the present values of three special types of cash-flow streams:

1. Perpetuity: a fixed payment each year forever.
2. Constant growth: payment increasing at a constant rate each year forever.
3. Annuity: a fixed payment each year for a limited number of years.

Make sure you try our own special method for working out present values on a calculator, which is described in the "What to Look for" sections below. It could save you a *lot of time* later on. The chapter also explains the difference between compound interest and simple interest, and the effect of different compounding intervals.

WHAT TO LOOK FOR IN CHAPTER 3

The emphasis in this chapter is on numerical problems. The best way to learn how to calculate present values is to practice. You can save time on the calculations by using a calculator, the tables in the appendices at the end of the text, or spread sheets for microcomputers. Use our problem 6 to compare the efficiency of the different methods.

Invested at an interest rate of r per year, $1 will grow to $$(1 + r)^t$ at the end of t years. Appendix Table 2 gives values of $(1 + r)^t$, the future value of $1.

The amount of money that must be invested today to produce $1 in t years' time is $$[1/(1 + r)]^t$. Appendix Table 1 gives values of this, the present value of $1. Appendix Table 1 makes it easy to calculate the net present value of any stream of cash flows. We often need to evaluate situations such as the following:

"An investment of $100 will produce $60 in 1 year's time, a further $50 after 2 years, and a final $40 in 3 years. What is the net present value of this investment if a return of 10 percent is required?"

The conventional form of calculation (shown below) is done in four steps:

1. Write down the column showing cash flows in each year.
2. Write down next to it the discount factors (from Appendix Table 1).
3. Multiply across.
4. Add up to get the net present value.

NET PRESENT VALUE CALCULATION

YEAR	CASH FLOW	DISCOUNT FACTORS (10%)	PRESENT VALUE
0	−100	1.000	−100.00
1	60	0.909	54.54
2	50	0.826	41.30
3	40	0.751	30.04
			NPV = 25.88

Present Values on a Calculator: With a calculator, the following "bottom-up" method of discounting a stream of cash flows is *much* quicker than the one described above and in the text. Instead of writing down a column of discount factors, we simply start with the last cash flow and discount back 1 year at a time, adding cash flows as we go. The calculation (shown below) is done in the following steps:

1. Write down the cash flows.
2. Enter the last cash flow as the value in the *last* year.
3. To obtain the value in the previous year, divide by $(1 + r)$ and add (across) the corresponding cash flow.
4. Repeat step 3 *up* the table until it is complete.

NPV ON A CALCULATOR

YEAR	CASH FLOW	VALUE IN EACH YEAR	HOW CALCULATED	
0	−100	25.92	(= 138.51/1.1 − 100)	↑
1	60	138.51	(= 86.36/1.1 + 60)	
2	50	86.36	(= 40.00/1.1 + 50)	
3	40	40.00	(= + 40)	

This shows that the net present value of the investment (its value in year 0) is $25.92. This calculation is actually more accurate than the previous one (which gave $25.88) because there is no rounding of discount factors. Before you start the calculation, put 1.1 (or in general, $1 + r$) in the memory of your calculator, if it has one, to save having to enter it each time.

There are even more efficient ways of finding the present values of cash flow streams which are constant (for a finite or infinite period) or which grow forever at a constant rate. Here are some tips on how to remember formulas for these three special types of cash flows.

Perpetuity: The text describes the rate of return on a perpetuity as equal to the interest rate (so $C/\text{PV} = r$). Alternatively, some students prefer to remember that the annual payment is just the principal value times the interest rate ($C = \text{PV} \times r$). Thought of this way, it is clear that we must wait until the *end* of the first year for the first payment. Either way, it is easy to rearrange to get $\text{PV} = C/r$.

Constant Growth: The constant-growth formula must simplify to $\text{PV} = C/r$ when $g = 0$. Since positive g must obviously *increase* PV, it is easy to remember that $\text{PV} = C/(r - g)$. (If you're not convinced, see problem 18 for a further exercise on this.)

Annuity: Think of a *t*-year annuity as a perpetuity minus another perpetuity which starts t years later. This makes it easy to write down the formula

$$PV = C \left[\frac{1}{r} - \frac{1}{r(1+r)^t} \right]$$

and impress your friends. Annuities are particularly useful and crop up in many situations and in different disguises. Students often find it difficult at first to recognize annuities or solve annuity problems. It is worthwhile spending a little extra time to master them. Problems 13 to 16 provide a range of exercises involving annuities, and Appendix Table 3 in the text provides a table of annuity present values.

WORKED EXAMPLES

Finally, before you start on the numerical exercises, you may find it helpful to work through the following examples.

PROBLEM 1: FUTURE VALUES

I invest $200 in a savings account where it earns interest at 6 percent. How much will my investment be worth (1) after 5 years, and (2) after 10 years?

SOLUTION

After 1 year I will have 200 x (1.06); after 2 years I will have 200 x $(1.06)^2$; and so on. Appendix Table 2 tabulates future values for various interest rates and time periods. I therefore have

1. After 5 years, future value = $200 x $(1.06)^5$ = $200 x 1.338 = $267.60.

2. After 10 years, future value = $200 x $(1.06)^{10}$ = $200 x 1.791 = $358.20.

[Notice that because the interest is compound (rather than simple) I received more interest in the second 5 years ($90.60 = 358.20 – 267.60) than in the first 5 years ($67.60 = 267.20 – 200).]

PROBLEM 2: PRESENT VALUE AND A PERPETUITY

My rich uncle wishes to create an endowment income of $2000 a year for his alma mater, but proposes that the first payment should not be made until 4 years' time. If he can invest at 8 percent, how much must he invest today to do this?

SOLUTION

The endowment is a *perpetuity*. We know that if the first payment were in 1 year's time, the value of the perpetuity would be

PV   = $2000/0.08 = $25,000

Because the perpetuity starts 3 years later, its value is

PV   = $25,000 x $1/1.08^3$ (Use Appendix Table 1 to find the value of
     = $25,000 x 0.794   this discount factor)
     = $19,850

PROBLEM 3: AN ANNUITY

I expect royalties from my latest book to pay me $300 a year for 4 years, starting in 1 year's time. What is their present value to me, if my opportunity cost of capital is 10 percent?

SOLUTION

$$PV = \$300 \times (\text{annuity factor: } t = 4, r = 10\%)$$
$$= \$300 \times 3.170 \text{ (from Appendix Table 3)}$$
$$= \$951$$

PROBLEM 4: SOLVING FOR A PAYMENT AMOUNT

I borrow $1000 at 10 percent interest. The capital and interest are to be repaid in four equal installments. Work out the size of my annual payments, and calculate the outstanding balance of my loan at the end of each year.

SOLUTION

My payments represent a 4-year annuity. The amount I borrow is the *present value* of this annuity. From Appendix Table 3, I know that I can borrow $3.170 if I pay $1 each year. To borrow $1000 I must therefore pay $1 × (1000/3.17) = $315.46 each year. We can now work out the loan balance year by year as follows:

YEAR	OPENING BALANCE	+	INTEREST AT 10%	−	ANNUAL PAYMENT	=	CLOSING BALANCE
1	1000.00		100.00		315.47		784.53
2	784.53		78.45		315.47		547.51
3	547.51		54.75		315.47		286.79
4	286.79		28.68		315.47		0.00

Note that the closing balance in year 4 comes to exactly zero, as it should.

SUMMARY

1. **Present value**
   a. Future values:
      $1 invested at an annual rate r will grow to $\$1(1 + r)$ at the end of 1 year, $\$1(1 + r)^2$ at the end of 2 years, and $\$1(1 + r)^t$ at the end of t years.
      Appendix Table 2 provides a table of values.
      The interest is *reinvested* each year: this is *compound interest*.
      Under *simple interest* (seldom used in finance) interest is not reinvested; so I get $\$1(1 + r)$, $\$1(1 + 2r), \ldots, \$1(1 + tr)$.

   b. Discount factors:
      To get $1 after t years I must invest $\$1[1/(1 + r)]^t$ today.
      $DF_t = 1/(1 + r)^t$ is the discount factor for year t cash flows.
      Appendix Table 1 provides a table of discount factors.

   c. Present values:
      PV of a cash flow C_t at the end of year $t = C_t /(1 + r)^t$.
      PVs can be *added*, just like the cost of items at a supermarket checkout. So, for an extended stream of cash flows,

$$PV = \frac{C_1}{(1+r)} + \frac{C_2}{(1+r)^2} + \ldots + \frac{C_t}{(1+r)^t}$$

NPV = PV of cash flows from investment - cost of investment.

*2. Term structure of interest rates

Sometimes we apply different interest rates to different time periods: $DF_1 = 1/(1 + r_1)$, $DF_2 = 1/(1 + r_2)^2$. A dollar to be received in year 2 must always be cheaper than \$1 in year 1. That is, DF_2 is less than DF_1. If this were not the case I would have a money machine. I could *borrow* DF_2 and lend DF_1 to cover the repayment. The remainder ($DF_2 - DF_1$) could be used to buy beer. Similarly, $DF_{t+1} \leq DF_t$ for any t.

3. Shortcuts

a. Perpetuity:

A perpetuity pays an amount C at the end of each year, forever.

$$PV = \frac{C}{(1+r)} + \frac{C}{(1+r)^2} + \frac{C}{(1+r)^3} \ldots$$

$$= C/r$$

(Remember: $r = C/PV$; so $C = r \times PV$ and $PV = C/r$.)

b. Constant-growth perpetuity:

$$PV = \frac{C_1}{(1+r)} + \frac{C_1(1+g)}{(1+r)^2} + \frac{C_1(1+g)^2}{(1+r)^3} \ldots$$

$$= C_1/(r - g)$$

(Remember: no growth with $g = 0$ gives the previous result.)

c. Annuity:

An annuity makes t equal payments C, at the end of years $1, 2, \ldots, t$.

$$PV = \frac{C}{(1+r)} + \frac{C}{(1+r)^2} + \frac{C}{(1+r)^3} + \ldots + \frac{C}{(1+r)^t}$$

$$PV = C \left[\frac{1}{r} - \frac{1}{r} \frac{1}{(1+r)^t} \right]$$

(Remember: this is a perpetuity *minus* a second perpetuity which starts t years after the first.)

Appendix Table 3 gives a PV of \$1 annuity $= \dfrac{1}{r} - \dfrac{1}{r} \cdot \dfrac{1}{(1+r)^t}$

Future value: \$1 received at the end of years $1, 2, \ldots, t$ has present value

$$\frac{1}{r} \left[1 - \frac{1}{(1+r)^t} \right]$$

Reinvested at interest rate r, it is worth $(1 + r)^t$ times as much by the end of year t. That is, it is worth: $\dfrac{1}{r} [(1+r)^t - 1]$

*4. **The compounding interval**
Compounding twice a year gives $(1 + r/2)^2$ after 1 year.
Compounding m times a year gives $(1 + r/m)^m$ after 1 year.
As m approaches infinity, $(1 + r/m)^m$ approaches $(2.718)^r$, which is e^r.
$1 invested at a continuously compounded rate of r grows to $\$e^r$ in 1 year, and to $\$e^{rt}$ in t years.
Appendix Table 4 gives values of e^{rt}.

5. **Summary of Tables in Appendices**
Appendix Table 1. Present value of $1 (discount factors) $= 1/(1 + r)^t$
Appendix Table 2. Future value of $1 $= (1 + r)^t$
Appendix Table 3. Present value of an annuity $= 1/r - \{1/[r(1 + r)^t]\}$
($1 at the end of each year for t years)
Appendix Table 4. Future values with continuous compounding e^{rt}
Appendix Table 5. Present value of an annuity received as a continuous stream. In this table r is an annually compounded rate. Continuously compounded rate $R = \log(1 + r)$, and $PV = 1/R[1 - e^{-Rt}]$.

LIST OF TERMS

Annuity	**Discount rate**
Compound interest	**Perpetuity**
*Continuously compounded rate of interest	**Simple interest**
Discounted-cash-flow (DCF) formula	***Term structure of interest rates**

EXERCISES

Fill-in Questions

1. _____ interest is calculated on the accumulated amount of the investment, with interest reinvested.
2. The formula for present value is also called the _____ formula.
3. The present value of a future cash flow is calculated by discounting it at the appropriate _____.
4. _____ interest is calculated on the initial investment only, without reinvestment of interest.
5. An asset that pays a fixed number of dollars a year for a limited number of years is called _____.
6. The _____ of interest rates explains why bonds that pay off in different years offer different returns.
7. An asset that pays a fixed number of dollars a year forever is called _____.

Problems

1. How much does $100 grow to after (a) 8 years at 6 percent interest, (b) 6 years at 8 percent interest?

2. I invest $50 at 7 percent interest. How much will my investment be worth (a) after 5 years, (b) after 10 years?

3. What is the value of $200 after 5 years invested at (a) 12 percent per year, (b) 3 percent per quarter, (c) 1 percent per month?

4. How long will it take $1 to double when it is invested at (a) 3 percent, (b) 5 percent, (c) 10 percent, (d) 12 percent, (e) 15 percent?

5. How much should I be prepared to pay for (a) $100 in 10 years' time at an interest rate of 10 percent, (b) $100 in 5 years' time at an interest rate of 21 percent?

6. An investment of $1000 will produce income of $270 a year for 5 years. Calculate its NPV at a discount rate of 10 percent by each of the following methods: (a) The conventional NPV method using separate discount factors. (b) Our hand calculator "bottom-up" method. (c) Using the annuity formula. (d) Using the table of annuity factors. Compare the efficiency of these methods.

7. An investment costing $2000 will produce cash flows of $700 in year 1, $700 in year 2, and $900 in year 3. Calculate its net present value at (a) zero, (b) 5 percent, (c) 10 percent (d) 15 percent discount rate.

8. I have savings amounting to $1200 and I expect to save an additional $600 next year. I need my savings to pay for school fees of $800 in 2 years' time and $900 in 3 years' time. How much can I afford to spend now on a stereo set if my savings will earn (a) 5 percent, (b) 7 percent, (c) 9 percent?

9. I will receive from my late uncle's estate $40 in 1 year's time and annually thereafter in perpetuity. What is the value of this perpetuity at an interest rate of (a) 8 percent, (b) 10 percent?

10. How much is the previous perpetuity worth if it begins in 5 years' time instead of 1?

11. I now discover that my uncle's will provides that I shall receive $40 in 1 year's time and that this amount is to be increased annually at a rate of 6 percent. What is the present value of this growing stream of income at an interest rate of (a) 8 percent, (b) 10 percent?

12. IBM's dividend is expected to be $3 next year. If the shareholders require a return of 15 percent and the current share price is $80, what rate of dividend growth must they be expecting?

13. At an 8 percent rate how much would the $40 a year income of problem 9 be worth if it lasts for only (a) 20 years, (b) 10 years?

14. My bank will lend me money at 12 percent interest. How much should they lend me if (a) I promise to make five annual payments of $300 starting in 1 year's time or (b) I make the first of five annual payments of $300 immediately?

15. I am saving for the deposit to buy a house. I have just invested $1500 and I expect to save a further $1500 at the end of each future year. If I invest my savings at 6 percent interest, how much will I have after (a) 3 years, (b) 5 years?

16. A store offers the following credit terms on a color television set "slashed" to a price of only $320: only $20 down and 18 monthly payments of $20. (a) Is this an attractive proposition if I can borrow at 1 percent per month? (b) What monthly interest rate is being charged? (c) What annual rate is being charged?

17. How much does $100 grow to at continuously compounded interest when invested for (a) 8 years at 6 percent, (b) 6 years at 8 percent? Compare your answer with that in problem 1.

*18. This problem will give you a simple way of deriving the constant-growth model $P = C/(r - g)$. Show that if C grows at the rate g, then so too must P. Use this to write down an expression for the return r over a single period. Then rearrange this expression to obtain the formula for P.

ANSWERS TO EXERCISES

Fill-in Questions

1. compound
2. discounted-cash-flow
3. discount rate
4. simple
5. an annuity
6. term structure
7. a perpetuity

Problems

1. (a) $100 \times (1.06)^8 = \$159.38$; (b) $100 \times (1.08)^6 = \$158.69$

2. (a) $50 \times (1.07)^5 = \$70.13$; (b) $50 \times (1.07)^{10} = \$98.36$

3. (a) $200 \times (1.12)^5 = \$352.47$; (b) $200 \times (1.03)^{20} = \$361.22$; (c) $200 \times (1.01)^{60} = \$363.34$

4. (a) 23.45; (b) 14.21; (c) 7.27; (d) 6.12; (e) 4.96 years

5. (a) $100 \times 1/(1.10)^{10} = \$38.55$; (b) $38.55 as before

6. (a)

YEAR	CASH FLOW	DF	PV
0	-1000	1.000	-1000.00
1	270	.909	245.43
2	270	.826	223.02
3	270	.751	202.77
4	270	.683	184.41
5	270	.621	167.67
			NPV = $ 23.30

(b)

YEAR	CASH FLOW	VALUE IN EACH YEAR
0	-1000	23.51 = NPV
1	270	1125.86
2	270	961.65
3	270	738.60
4	270	515.45
5	270	270.00

(c) $\text{NPV} = -1000 + 270 \times 1/0.10 \left(1 - \dfrac{1}{1.10^5}\right) = \$23.51$

(d) $\text{NPV} = -1000 + 270 \times 3.791 = \$23.57$

You should find that each method is quicker than the previous one. If not, then you're doing something wrong! The time it took Professor Hodges was (a) 90 seconds, (b) 50 seconds, (c) 40 seconds, (d) 25 seconds. What do your times look like? Make up a slightly different problem to keep it fair! The moral is clear. Use annuities and the special formulas when you can. Otherwise use our "bottom-up" method.

7. (a) \$300.00; (b) \$79.04; (c) –\$108.94; (d) –\$270.24

8. I can spend the present value of my savings *minus* the present value of my school fees: (a) \$268.35; (b) \$327.33 (c) \$382.15

9. (a) \$40/0.08 = \$500; (b) \$40/0.10 = \$400

10. (a) \$500 x $1/(1.08)^5$ = \$367.52; (b) \$400 x $1/(1.10)^5$ = \$273.20

11. (a) \$40/(0.08 – 0.06)= \$2000; (b) \$40/(0.10 – 0.06) = \$1000

12. $80 = 3/(0.15 - g)$, which gives $g = 11.25$ percent

13. (a) \$40 x (20-year annuity factor) = \$392.73; (b) \$40 x (10-year annuity factor) = \$268.40

14. (a) \$300 x (5-year annuity factor) = \$1081.43; (b) \$300 + \$300 x (4-year annuity factor) = \$1211.20

15. (a) PV = \$1500 x (1 + 3-year annuity factor) = \$5509.52.
    But we want future value = \$5509.52 x $(1.06)^3$ = \$6561.92.
    (b) \$10,462.98

16. (a) Present value cost is \$347.97, unattractive. (b) The monthly interest rate is that rate which gives the 18-period annuity of \$20 a present value of \$300. That is, which gives an 18-period annuity of \$1 a present value of \$15. From Appendix Table 3 we find that this is just under 2 percent per month. More exactly, it is 1.99 percent. (c) This is equivalent to an annual rate of $(1.01994)^{12}$ = 26.73 percent.

17. (a) \$161.60; (b) \$161.60 as before.

*18. Whatever time period we have reached, P is given by

$$P_0 = \frac{C_1}{1+r} + \frac{C_1(1+g)}{(1+r)^2} + \ldots$$

where C_1 is the value of the next cash flow to be received.
Since

$$\frac{P_0}{C_1} = \frac{1}{1+r} + \frac{(1+g)}{(1+r)^2} + \ldots$$

is a constant, it is clear the P_0 and C_1 must grow at the same rate g. This means that $P_1 = P_0(1 + g)$, so the return over one period is given by

$$r = \frac{P_1 + C_1 - P_0}{P_0} = \frac{C_1 + gP_0}{P_0}$$

which rearranges $\quad P_0\,(r - g) = C_1,$

and $\qquad P_0 = \dfrac{C_1}{r - g}$

CHAPTER 4
PRESENT VALUE OF BONDS AND STOCKS

INTRODUCTION

The present-value techniques developed in Chapters 2 and 3 enable us to understand the market prices of bonds and common stocks. In each case the value of the security is equal to the expected stream of cash payments discounted at the rate of return expected by investors. If we know the market price of a bond or a stock, we can estimate the rate of return investors require. Financial managers need to know about these rates in order to make correct investment and financing decisions.

Some companies reinvest a large proportion of their earnings in order to achieve rapid expansion. Others pay out most of their earnings as dividends and grow at a slower rate. A company's share price reflects the market's assessment of its opportunities for *profitable* growth. A company which is expected to make a lot of investments with positive NPVs can command a high market price relative to its current level of earnings. It will have a high price-earnings ratio (P/E ratio).

WHAT TO LOOK FOR IN CHAPTER 4

Our knowledge of present value doesn't mean that we can expect to make our fortunes speculating in stocks and bonds. However, it does help us to understand why various securities are priced as they are.

Bonds: The chapter starts by looking at the prices of bonds. Bonds are especially simple because everyone know what cash flows they promise to pay. A bond pays a regular stream of coupon payments until the date of its *maturity*, when it also pays off its *face value*. The price of a bond is simply the present value of the cash flows expected from it, discounted at the rate of return required by investors. Notice that the coupons form a constant annuity stream and the face value is a single future payment.

How can we tell what return investors require form bonds? By looking at the prices they pay for them. The present value of a bond's cash flow depends on what discount rate we use. The discount rate that makes the present value of the bond exactly equal to its price is called its *yield to maturity*. When we want to work out how much a bond is worth, it is usually helpful to calculate the yields to maturity of other similar bonds. To calculate the yield to maturity of a bond, we must try different discount rates until, by trial and error, we get the right one. Alternatively, special tables, calculators, and computer programs are available which give the yield directly.

Don't worry too much about the further complication of annual versus semiannual compounding. Most bonds make two coupon payments a year (i.e, a 6 percent coupon bond pays $30 every 6 months rather than a single payment of $60 every 12 months). Because of this, yields to maturity are usually quoted at an annual rate which is compounded semiannually. In other words, for a 2-year 6 percent coupon bond with a yield to maturity of 8 percent (i.e., 4 percent every 6 months):

$$\text{Bond price} = \frac{30}{1.04} + \frac{30}{1.04^2} + \frac{30}{1.04^3} + \frac{30}{1.04^4}$$

The true *annually compounded* rate is given by $1.04^2 - 1 = 8.16$ percent.

Stocks: The chapter describes three equivalent ways of viewing the price of a stock. These are

1. The present value of future dividends.
2. The present value of free cash flow.
3. The present value of current activities *plus* the present value of growth opportunities.

As before with bonds, we sometimes want to use the capitalization rate to calculate the value of the security, and we sometimes want to infer the capitalization rate from the price of the security.

Dividends and Free Cash Flow: The central idea here is that the price of a stock is its future dividends D_t discounted at the market capitalization rate r:

$$P = \sum_{t=1}^{\infty} \frac{D_t}{(1+r)^t}$$

Make sure you understand why this doesn't ignore the value of capital gains. Dividends are hard to forecast, as they depend on whatever dividend policy the company adopts. Instead, we may prefer to forecast the flow of cash that the activities of the company are likely to produce. (We add depreciation back to the earnings figure, and subtract any additional investment and increases in working capital.) The company can distribute this so-called *free cash flow* to the shareholders as dividends, and we can discount them to work out the value of the stock. In some situations we may expect dividends to increase at a constant rate g, and in this case we may use the constant-growth formula $P = D_1/(r - g)$.

Present Value of Growth Opportunities (PVGO): If the current level of earnings can be maintained without any new investment having to be made (and that is what earnings means), the price of the stock must be at least E_1/r. The price is exactly equal to E_1/r if all new investments have a zero net present value. Finally if there *are* growth opportunities with a positive NPV, this must be added, giving

$$P = (E_1/r) + \text{PVGO}$$

This relationship immediately implies that stocks with good prospects for profitable growth (large PVGO) have high P/E ratios. We must be careful to remember that PVGO represents more than just growth: it represents the net present value of future growth opportunities. Growth by itself is easy to achieve. By plowing back earnings a company will grow at the rate

$$g = \text{plowback ratio x ROE}$$

where ROE is the average return on equity of its new investments. But these investments will not have a positive NPV and will not give the company a positive PVGO unless their return is greater than the market capitalization rate.

See problem 2 of the worked examples for another numerical example, a bit like Fledgling Electronics, which illustrates the different viewpoints.

WORKED EXAMPLES

PROBLEM 1: BOND PRICES AND YIELDS
What is the price of a 15-year 8 percent coupon bond with a $100 face value if investors require a 12 percent return? What is its yield to maturity if its price is $78.43?

SOLUTION

$$\text{Price} = \$8 \times (\text{annuity factor: } t = 15, r = 12\%) + \$100 \times 1/1.12^{15},$$
$$= (\$8 \times 6.811) + (\$100 \times 0.1827)$$
$$= \$72.76$$

If the price is instead $78.43, the discount rate must be rather lower. By trial and error we find that this price is obtained by discounting at 11.0 percent. This is its yield to maturity.

PROBLEM 2: PRESENT VALUE OF GROWTH OPPORTUNITIES

Next year Penn, Inc., will have earnings per share of $4. The company is expected to continue to plow back 60 percent of its earnings into new investment projects with an average ROE of 20 percent. Its capitalization rate is estimated to be 16 percent. Calculate

1. The stock price.
2. The P/E ratio.
3. The PVGO.
4. Show directly the amounts of investment which produce PVGO.

SOLUTION

1. Next year's dividend = 0.4 x $4 = $1.60
   Growth of dividends = plowback ratio x ROE
   $$= 0.6 \times 20\% = 12\%$$
   $$\text{Price} = D_1/(r - g) = \$1.60/0.04 = \$40$$

2. $P/E_1 = 10$; so $P/E_0 = 11.2$, since earnings grow at 12 percent.
3. $\text{PVGO} = P - (E_1/r) = \$40 - (\$4/0.16) = \$15$
4. Plowback in year 1 amounts to 0.6 x $4 =$2.40. This earns 20 percent, i.e., $0.48 a year in perpetuity, which is worth $0.48/0.16 = $3.00. The NPV of this investment is $0.60. Further plowback leads to new NPVs increasing at 12 percent. PVGO = $0.60/(0.16 − 0.12) = $15 as before.

SUMMARY

1. **Bonds**

   If we know the return required from a bond, we can work out its price. For example, if a 10 percent return is required on a 3-year 6 percent coupon bond with a face value of $1000, its price is given by $PV = 60/1.10 + 60/1.10^2 + 1060/1.10^3 = \$900.53$.

   Conversely, if we know the price we can work out the return (by trial and error). So if the bond has a market price of $877.81, then since $877.81 = 60/1.11 + 60/1.11^2 + 1060/1.11^3$, it promises a return of 11 percent. This is its *yield to maturity*.

2. **The value of common stocks**

   The price of a stock today is the discounted value of the dividends expected in the next year plus its forecast price 1 year hence. That is,

   $$P_0 = \frac{DIV_1 + P_1}{1 + r}$$

   The expected return r is often called the *market capitalization rate*.

All securities in the same risk class are priced to offer the same expected return. (If one stock offered a higher return, everyone would rush to buy it, pushing its price up and the expected return down.)

The price expected next year depends on dividends and price the year after:

$$P_1 = \frac{DIV_2 + P_2}{1 + r}$$

Substituting this into the previous equation for P_0 gives

$$P_0 = \frac{DIV_1}{1 + r} + \frac{DIV_2 + P_2}{(1 + r)^2}$$

and repeating the process:

$$P_0 = \frac{DIV_1}{1 + r} + \frac{DIV_2}{(1 + r)^2} + \frac{DIV_3}{(1 + r)^3} + \ldots = \sum_{t = 1}^{\infty} \frac{DIV_t}{(1 + r)^t}$$

The value of a company's stock is therefore equal to the discounted stream of *all future dividends* paid on that existing stock. Future dividends expected on stock not yet issued are not included. Dividends are cash produced by the company and not reinvested, i.e., revenue minus costs and investment. Another word for this is free cash flow.

3. **The constant-growth model**
   If dividends are expected to grow at a constant rate g, then, as we saw in Chapter 3:

$$P_0 = \frac{DIV_1}{r - g} \qquad \text{(provided } g < r)$$

Conversely, the market capitalization rate r is the dividend yield plus the rate of dividend growth:

$$r = (DIV_1/P_0) + g$$

Companies can use this to estimate the return expected by their shareholder. The tricky part is to estimate g. One useful approach is to use

$$g = \text{plowback ratio} \ \times \ \text{return on equity}$$

4. **Setting electricity prices**
   The Federal Energy Regulatory Commission (FERC) sets prices for interstate sales of electric power. The price is supposed to provide a "fair" rate of return on the equity invested. The market capitalization rate r is this fair rate of return. So the FERC has to estimate r and then set prices to enable r to be achieved.

5. **Pitfalls for the unwary**
   a. Estimates of r may be inaccurate for a single stock. An average of estimates from a large sample of companies is usually better.
   b. High growth rates are usually short-lived, so the constant-growth model is inappropriate. Instead, work out the dividends expected during the period of high growth and use the constant-growth model to predict the price at the end of that period.
   c. No easy money. If you think that the market price of a stock is too high or too low, it may be because *you* have used poor dividend forecasts.

6. **The relation between stock price and earnings**
   Three cases are considered:
   a. All earnings are distributed as dividends which remain constant through time. The earnings-price ratio equals the capitalization rate as

   $$r = \frac{DIV_1}{P_0} = \frac{EPS_1}{P_0} \qquad \text{(EPS = earnings per share)}$$

   b. Some earnings are plowed back into new projects, but these have zero NPVs. Although DIV_1 is reduced, P_0 is unchanged, and in the short run earnings are unchanged. That is,

   $$r = \frac{EPS_1}{P_0} > \frac{DIV_1}{P_0}$$

   so the earnings-price ratio still equals the capitalization rate. In both these cases $P_0 = EPS_1/r$.

   c. It is more usual for a company to have some growth opportunities with positive NPVs. P_0 is increased by the present value of future growth opportunities PVGO; so

   $$P_0 = \frac{EPS_1}{r} + PVGO$$

   Rearranging gives

   $$\frac{EPS_1}{P_0} = r \left(1 - \frac{PVGO}{P_0} \right)$$

   so the earnings-price ratio is *less* than the capitalization rate. (PVGO is rarely negative, since firms can usually reject projects with negative NPVs.)

7. **Meaning of the P/E ratio**
   a. *Price-earnings ratios* are published along with stock price quotations in the newspaper. They do not give P_0/EPS_1 but are based on the most recent earnings announcements.
   b. Often high P/E ratio indicates that earnings are expected to rise; but it may just mean they are currently very low.
   c. The P/E ratio provides a useful yardstick for valuing companies whose stock is not traded publicly.
   d. A high P/E *does not* indicate a low capitalization rate.
   e. The EPS figure depends on the company's choice of accounting procedures and is unlikely to reflect the amount to money which could be paid out without affecting its capital value. The P/E ratio can therefore be very misleading, even for comparisons between similar companies.

*8. **Valuing a Business (Appendix)**
   a. Forecast Free Cash Flow. Cash flow may be negative in early years of rapid growth.
   b. Choice of horizon date. Free cash flows are estimated to some horizon date, perhaps 5 to 10 years away.
   c. Horizon Value.
      This may be estimated using the constant growth formula, but the value may be very sensitive to the assumptions.
   d. Other Comparisons.
      Cross check the horizon value against
      • P/E ratios
      • market to book ratios of similar companies.
      • Date at which PVGO disappears and P/E becomes $1/r$.

LIST OF TERMS

Coupon rate	Maturity date
Dividend yield	Payout ratio
Face value	P/E ratio
Free cash flow	Plowback ratio (retention ratio)
Growth stock	Return on equity (ROE)
Income stock	Semiannually compounded rate
Market capitalization rate	Yield to maturity (internal rate of return)

EXERCISES

Fill-in Questions

1. The _____ value of a bond is the amount of money that is repaid when the bond matures (usually $1000).
2. A bond's _____ is its interest payment, usually expressed as an annual percentage rate.
3. A bond must be repaid on its _____.
4. The _____ of a bond is the rate of return it offers if held to maturity.
5. Most U.S. Treasury bonds make _____ coupon payments per year and their yields are quoted as _____.
6. The _____ is the return that investors require from investment in a stock or bond.
7. Annual dividend per share/ share price = _____.
8. The proportion of earnings paid out as dividends is called the _____.
9. The proportion of earnings kept in the business is called the _____.
10. The _____ is the net profit of a company expressed as a proportion of the book value of the equity.
11. _____ stocks are held primarily for future capital gains.
12. _____ stocks are held primarily because they provide a regular income.
13. Cash which is generated by a company and not retained in the business is often known as _____.
14. A firm with good growth opportunities will usually have a high _____ ratio.

Problems

1. You are asked to put a value on a bond which promises eight annual coupon payments of $50 and will repay its face value of $1000 at the end of 8 years. You observe that other similar bonds have yields to maturity of 9 percent. How much is this bond worth?

2. You are offered the bond of problem 1 for a price of $755.50. What yield to maturity does this represent?

3. Your company has an issue of 7 percent debentures outstanding which mature in 17 years. They are currently being traded at a price of $829.10. (a) What is their yield to maturity? (b) What price would you expect to get for a new issue of 8.5 percent coupon 10-year debentures?

4. A U.S. Treasury bond has a 13 percent coupon and is quoted with a yield to maturity of 8 percent. (a) Calculate its correct price, given that it makes semiannual coupon payments, and the quoted yield is semiannually compounded. (b) Calculate the (incorrect) price that would have been obtained assuming annual payments and compounding.

5. Company X is expected to pay dividends of $5.50 a share in 1 years' time and $5.80 a share in 2 year's time, after which its stock is expected to sell at $91. If the market capitalization rate is 10 percent, what is the current stock price?

6. You forecast that ITT will pay a dividend of $2.40 next year and that dividends will in future grow at a rate of 9 percent a year. What price would you expect to see for ITT stock is the market capitalization rate if 15 percent?

7. If the price of ITT is $30, what market capitalization rate is implied by your forecasts of problem 6?

8. The price of UPP shares is $30 and next year's earnings are expected to be $3 a share. The current level of earnings can be maintained indefinitely with no new investment. What is the present value of growth opportunities if investors require a return of (a) 12 percent, or (b) 15 percent?

9. Company A retains 80 percent of its earnings and invests them at an average return on equity (ROE) of 10 percent. Company B retains only 20 percent of its earnings but invests them at an average ROE of 25 percent. Which company has the higher P/E ratio? (*Hint*: Assume each company has current earnings of $1, and work out its price for a number of values of the market capitalization rate.)

10. The current earnings of B & S Video are $2 a share, and it has just paid an annual dividend of 40¢. You forecast that the company will continue to plow back 80 percent of its earnings for the next 5 years and that both earnings and dividends will grow at 25 percent a year over that period. From year 5 on, you expect the payout ratio to be increased to 50 percent and that this will reduce the subsequent growth rate to 8 percent. If the capitalization rate for this stock is 15 percent, calculate (a) its price, (b) its price-earnings ratio, (c) the present value of its growth opportunities.

11. If the current price of B & S Video in problem 10 is $35, (a) what capitalization rate does this imply; (b) what is the present value of growth opportunities?

12. Look up Hewlett Packard's current stock price, earnings, and dividend payment. (a) If the capitalization rate is 9 percent above the 3-month Treasury bill rate, what (constant) rate of growth does this imply? (b) At the current retention rate what ROE would produce this rate of growth? (c) What is the present value of growth opportunities?

*13. The calculations for Hewlett Packard in problem 12 took no account of inflation. (a) If the capitalization rate is 9 percent in real terms, what rate of *real* growth does this imply? (b) What *real* ROE does this imply if current earnings can be sustained in *real* terms with no plowback? (c) What is the present value of growth opportunities?

*14. Derive the formula:

$$\frac{P}{E_1} = \frac{1}{r - (\text{plowback ratio/payout ratio})(\text{ROE} - r)}$$

from the constant-growth formula and the equation $g = \text{ROE} \times \text{plowback ratio}$, where ROE is the average return on equity on new investments and r is the capitalization rate.

15. Clutz Corp has made the following forecasts for the next eight years ($ millions):

Year	1	2	3	4	5	6	7	8
Asset value	32.00	39.20	47.00	60.80	68.40	75.30	79.80	84.60
Earnings	4.50	5.70	7.50	8.90	9.80	10.50	11.20	11.80
Net investment	7.20	7.80	13.70	7.70	6.90	4.50	4.80	5.10

Analysts have determined that the required rate of return on Clutz is 13 percent. A steady state is reached in year 6, and thereafter growth is expected to average 6 percent. Mature companies in this industry have an average P/E_1 ratio of 10.5 and a market to book value ratio of 1.35.

(a) Determine the annual free cash flows, and the present value of those occurring up to year 6.
(b) Estimate the year 6 horizon value, and the value of Clutz today, using the alternative methods of
(i) constant growth, (ii) the P/E ratio, and (iii) the market to book value ratio.

Essay Questions

1. What does the P/E ratio mean? Explain how it is possible for a low P/E stock to be expected to grow faster than a high P/E stock.

2. A company's earnings figure represents money which may in principle be distributed to shareholders. Explain why the stock price represents the present value of dividends rather than earnings.

3. "Some companies have a policy of retaining all earnings and never paying a dividend. Doesn't this invalidate the principle that the stock price equals the present value of future dividends?" Discuss.

4. What can you say about the effect of an increase in interest rates on the prices of (a) bonds, (b) stocks?

ANSWERS TO EXERCISES

Fill-in Questions

1. face
2. coupon
3. maturity date
4. yield to maturity
5. two, semiannually compounded rates
6. market capitalization rate
7. dividend yield
8. payout ratio
9. plowback ratio
10. return on equity
11. growth
12. income
13. free cash flow
14. price-earnings

Problems

1. $(50 \times 5.535) + (1000 \times 0.502) = \$778.61$

2. 9.50 percent

3. (a) 9% (gives $70 \times 8.544 + 1000 \times 0.231 = \$829.13$); (b) $85 \times 9.129 + 1000 \times 0.178 = \$954.36$

4. (a) \$129.13; 16 periods, 6.5 percent interest income, discounted at 4 percent; (b) \$128.73; 8 periods, 13 percent interest income, discounted at 8 percent.

5. $5.5/1.1 \times (5.8 + 91)/1.1^2 = \$85$

6. $2.40/(.15 - .09) = \$40$

7. $r = (2.40/30) + 0.09 = 0.17$ (i.e., 17 percent)

8. (a) $30 - (3/.12) = \$5$; (b) $30 - (3/.15) = \$10$

9. For company A, $g = 8\%$ and P/E $= (1.08 \times .20)/(r - 0.08)$
For company B, $g = 5\%$ and P/E $= (1.05 \times .60)/(r - 0.05)$. Company B's P/E is higher unless the capitalization rate is below about 9 percent.

10. Earnings and dividends over the next 6 years are as follows:

Year:	0	1	2	3	4	5	6
Earnings	\$2.00	\$2.50	\$3.125	\$3.906	\$4.883	\$6.104	\$6.592
Dividend	\$0.40	\$0.50	\$0.626	\$0.781	\$0.977	\$3.052	\$3.296

In year 5 it will be worth $3.296/.07 = \$47.09$, so discounting this and each year's dividends at 15 percent, we get (a) the current price is \$26.91; (b) P/E = 13.46; (c) $EPS_1/r = (\$2.5/.15) = \$16.67$; so PVGO = \$10.24.

11. (a) The capitalization rate r must satisfy:

$$35 = \frac{0.50}{(1+r)} + \frac{0.626}{(1+r)^2} + \frac{0.781}{(1+r)^3} + \frac{0.977}{(1+r)^4} + \frac{3.052 + 3.296/(r-0.08)}{(1+r)^5}$$

This gives $r = 13.57$ percent.

(b) $EPS_1/r = \$2.50/.1357 = \$18.42$, so PVGO = \$16.58.

15. (a) Free cash flow is simply earnings minus net investment:

Year	1	2	3	4	5	6	7	8
Free Cash Flow	-2.70	-2.10	-6.20	1.20	2.90	6.00	6.40	6.70

The present value (at 13 percent) of the first six cash flows is -\$3.14 million.

30

(b) (i) $P_6 = 6.40/(.13 - .06) = 91.43$, so $P_0 = \$40.78$ million.

(ii) $P_6 = 11.2 \times 10.5 = 117.60$, giving $P_0 = \$53.35$ million.

(iii) $P_6 = 101.66$, $P_0 = \$45.69$ million.

CHAPTER 5
WHY NET PRESENT VALUE LEADS TO
BETTER INVESTMENT DECISIONS
THAN OTHER CRITERIA

INTRODUCTION

Chapters 2 and 3 introduced the net present value (NPV) method for making capital budgeting decisions. In practice, companies often use other measures for evaluating investment projects. Four of the most commonly used are:

1. Payback (and discounted payback).
2. Average return on book value.
3. Internal rate of return (IRR).
4. Profitability index (or benefit-cost ratio).

Chapter 5 describes these methods and explains why they do not always give correct or even consistent decisions. These methods continue to be used despite the superiority of NPV; so *you need to know:*

1. How to calculate each measure.
2. Its major weaknesses.

This should equip you to argue convincingly against their use, or if you have to use them, you will at least be able to avoid their most dangerous pitfalls.

WHAT TO LOOK FOR IN CHAPTER 5

Review of NPV: The first section gives a straightforward review of the net present value method. Always remember that present values represent market values. The NPV of a project measures the amount by which it will increase the value of the company to its stockholders. Accepting a project with a positive NPV will make the stockholders better off by the amount of its NPV. With the NPV method fresh in your mind, you can compare the other methods against it. Any rule which can give different decisions from the NPV rule will not serve the best interests of the stockholders.

The Time Value of Money: Net present value takes account of the time value of money: that is, you are better off it you receive $1 today than if you have to wait a year to receive it. Look out for methods of investment appraisal which do not take account of the time value of money.

Mutually Exclusive Projects: Some methods appear to be similar to NPV in the sense that they use discounting and generally lead to the same accept-reject decisions as NPV. The internal rate of return and profitability index are examples of such methods. The problem with these methods is that they can easily give an incorrect ranking of projects and result in an incorrect choice from alternative projects. For example, project A may have a higher NPV than project B, and hence may be a better project. At the same time it may have a lower internal rate of return and so appear to be inferior under that criterion. If we can accept both projects, this may not matter. Unfortunately, projects are often mutually exclusive. That is, only one can be accepted because, for example, they would be built on the same site or compete for the same market. In this case it is not enough to know that they are both desirable projects; we must know which is better. Few of the alternatives to NPV are good at handling this situation.

Incremental Analysis: Unless we are using NPV, which always provides the correct answer, the only way to compare two such projects is as follows. If we accept project A, we will have to forgo the cash flow from project B. We therefore calculate the incremental cash-flow stream of project A's cash flow *minus* project B's cash flow. We thus analyze the effect of accepting project A rather than project B, or "project (A - B)" for short. If (A - B) appears worthwhile, A should be chosen in preference to B. If (A - B) is not worthwhile, then B should be chosen rather than A. Provided this method of incremental analysis is used, both the IRR and the profitability index methods generally give a correct comparison of mutually exclusive projects.

The Effect of Combining Projects: The use of this method of incremental analysis [evaluating (A - B)] avoids another common problem you should look out for. Capital budgeting methods other than NPV can lead to inconsistent decisions. Let us suppose that a decision is being taken as to whether to build factory A or factory B, and that there is also a proposal to build warehouse C, irrespective of which factory is built. In present value terms, if the NPV of factory A is greater than that of factory B, the factory-warehouse combination A + C will also have a higher NPV than the alternative of B + C. However, under some of the other criteria (such as payback and IRR) it is possible for the combination of factory A and the warehouse C to appear *worse* than B + C, even though by itself A appears better than B. In this case the ranking of A and B is changed by "packaging" the proposals with the proposal for warehouse C. The incremental approach avoids this inconsistency: when we calculate the cash flows of (A + C) minus those of (B + C), the C cash flows cancel out and the comparison is therefore exactly the same as we would make between A and B directly.

The following worked example illustrates how the different evaluation measures are calculated.

WORKED EXAMPLE

PROBLEM: SIX METHODS OF INVESTMENT APPRAISAL

The Multicash Corporation is considering an investment in new equipment costing $500,000. The equipment will be depreciated on a straight-line basis over 5 years, and it will have a zero salvage value at the end of that period. The equipment will produce annual cash operating revenues of $140,000 for 5 years. Multicash has a required rate of return for this project of 10 percent. There are no taxes. Calculate (1) average return on book, (2) payback, (3) NPV, (4) IRR, (5) profitability index, and (6) discounted payback for the project.

SOLUTION

First calculate the annual earnings and cash flows (figures in $1000s):

Operating revenues	140
Less depreciation	100
Profit	40
Cash flow	140

1. Average profit = 40,000
   Average book value of investment = $250,000
   Average return on book = 40/250 = 16 percent

2. Payback: the first 3 years generate cash flows amounting to 420, which is 80 short of payback. Payback is 3 + 80/140 = 3.6 years. Or 500/140 = 3.6 years.

3. Net present value:

	Amount	Discount Factor	PV
Year 0: initial investment	-500	1.000	-500.0
Years 1-5: after-tax cash flows	140	3.791	<u>530.7</u>
Net present value =			30.7

4. First calculate NPV at various discount rates:

$$\begin{aligned}
\text{NPV at 10 percent} &= 30.7 \\
\text{NPV at 11 percent} &= 17.4 \\
\text{NPV at 12 percent} &= 4.7 \\
\text{NPV at 13 percent} &= -7.6
\end{aligned}$$

Next, interpolating between 12 and 13 percent,

IRR = 12 percent + 4.7/(4.7 + 7.6) = 12.4 percent

Note: This shows the general trial-and-error method. In this example the IRR can be obtained more easily as the rate which gives a 5-year annuity factor of 500/140 = 3.57.

5. Profitability index = 530.7/500 = 1.061

6. NPV of cash flows in years 0 to 4 is -$56,200.
    NPV of cash flows in years 0 to 5 is $30,700. Discounted payback is between 4 and 5 years.
    Interpolating gives 4.6 years.

SUMMARY

1. **Review of net present value**
    a. Calculation:
        Forecast the incremental cash flows generated by the project.
        Determine the discount rate; this represents the opportunity cost of capital.
        Calculate the present value (PV) of the cash flows, by adding their discounted values.
        Calculate the NPV of the project, by subtracting the investment's initial cost, i.e., NPV = PV - initial investment.
    b. Decision rule:
        Accept projects with NPV greater than zero.
    c. Interpretation:
        The NPV indicates how much the value of the company (to its stockholders) will be changed if the project is accepted. The *discount* rate should be the market rate of return which stockholders can expect to earn by holding other securities with equivalent risk.
    d. Advantages:
        Correctly accounts for the time value of money.
        The NPV of a project is not affected by "packaging" it with another project.

2. **Payback period**
   a. Calculation:
   Number of years required for the sum of the cash flows to equal the initial investment.
   b. Decision rule:
   Accept projects with payback less than some specified period.
   c. Interpretation:
   Number of years required for the original cash investment to be returned (but without interest).
   Do not be misled into thinking that all cash flows after payback represent profit.
   d. Advantages:
   Simple to calculate.
   e. Disadvantages:
   Does not allow for the time value of money, since it gives equal weight to cash flows before the cutoff date. Ignores cash flows after the cutoff date. Can be inconsistent: the ranking of projects may be changed by "packaging" with other projects.
   To give the same decisions as NPV, different cutoff periods should be used for different projects, depending on the project life, the pattern of cash flows, and the risk of the project.

3. **Discounted Payback**
   a. Calculation:
   Same as for payback, but using the present values of cash flows.
   b. Decision rule:
   Same as for payback.
   c. Interpretation:
   Point at which project cash flows could be truncated (cut off) and still provide an acceptable return.
   d. Any project which has a discounted payback period has a positive NPV.
   e. No longer simple to calculate.
   Poor ranking of projects, and may be changed by "packaging".

4. **Average return on book value** [return on investment (ROI)]
   a. Calculation:

$$\text{ROI} = \frac{\text{average profit after depreciation and tax}}{\text{average book value of the asset}}$$

   b. Decision rule:
   Accept projects with ROI greater than the return on book value of the firm, or some external yardstick.
   c. Interpretation:
   Uses the company's average return on book value or other external yardstick as the sole criterion of profitability.
   This is extremely unlikely to maximize the returns of stockholders.
   d. Advantage:
   Fits in with accounting procedures used by firms.
   e. Disadvantages:
   Makes no allowance for the time value of money; gives too much weight to distant earnings.
   Uses accounting earnings rather than cash flows. It therefore depends on the choice of depreciation method and on other accounting conventions.
   Can give inconsistent ranking of projects; rankings may be altered by "packaging."
   Bears no relationship to the IRR or to the required rate of return in the market.

5. **Internal rate of return** (DCF rate of return)
   a. Calculation:

   IRR is the discount rate which makes NPV = 0.

   It is calculated by trial and error: calculate NPV for two or three discount rates and plot them on a graph. Use the graph to decide which discount rate to try next. Continue until sufficient accuracy has been obtained with the NPV close to zero.

   b. Decision rule:

   Accept projects with IRR greater than the opportunity cost of capital.

   c. Advantage:

   Gives the same accept-reject decisions as NPV for most projects other than mutually exclusive ones.

   d. Disadvantages:

   Can rank projects incorrectly, and the rankings may be changed by the "packaging" of the projects.

   But mutually exclusive projects can be compared correctly by calculating the IRR on the differences between their cash flows.

   Some projects give cash inflows followed by outflows, which amounts to borrowing. These should be accepted if their IRR is *less than* the hurdle rate.

   For projects whose cash flows change sign more than once: (1) it may not be obvious whether a high IRR is good or bad; (2) there may be several IRRs; and (3) there may be no IRRs.

   Does not allow different discount rates to be used for different time periods; i.e., no account can be taken of the term structure of interest rates.

6. **Profitability index** (or benefit cost ratio)
   a. Calculation:

   Profitability index = present value of net cash inflows/present value of net cash outflows
                        = PV/I = 1 + (NPV/I)

   where I = investment
   PV = present value
   NPV = net present value

   b. Decision rule:

   Accept projects with profitability index greater than 1.

   c. Advantages:

   Gives the same accept-reject decision as NPV for all projects other than mutually exclusive ones.

   Provides a method for ranking projects under capital rationing.

   d. Disadvantages:

   Can rank projects incorrectly, and the ranking may be changed by "packaging" projects together.

   But, mutually exclusive projects can be compared correctly using the difference between their cash flows.

7. **Other points**

   These methods are used by companies: if you *have* to use them, make sure you use them in the best possible way. For example, always compare mutually exclusive projects on the basis of the difference between their cash flows. Remember that it is the cash flows which determine the value of a project. Inadequate forecast of the cash flows can be far more disastrous than using the wrong appraisal technique. Cash-flow forecasts can be expensive and difficult to make. It is silly to waste them by using an inferior method of appraisal.

LIST OF TERMS

Average return on book (or book rate of return)   Internal rate of return
Benefit cost ratio   Mutually exclusive projects
Discounted-cash-flow rate of return   Payback period
Discounted Payback   Profitability index

EXERCISES

Fill-in Questions

1. The _____ is the length of time it takes an investment to repay its initial cost but without providing any return.
2. The _____ is the time beyond which cash flows could disappear and still leave the project with a positive net present value.
3. Average profit/average depreciated value of investment = _____.
4. The discount rate that gives a project a NPV of zero is called its_____.
5. When it is possible to accept only one of a number of competing projects, they are said to be _____.
6. The _____ rate of return is an alternative name for the internal rate of return.
7. The present value of a project divided by its initial cost is called its _____ or its _____ ratio.

Multiple Choice

Indicate which (if any) of the five measures of investment worth applies: net present value (NPV), payback (P), average return on book (AROBV), internal rate of return (IRR), or profitability index (PI):

	NPV	P	AROBV	IRR	PI

1. Puts too much weight on distant cash flows.
2. Depends on the scale of the project.
3. May have several values.
4. Gives the same accept-reject decisions as NPV on single projects.
5. Does not depend on the method of depreciation used for tax purposes.
6. Puts too little weight on distant cash flows.
7. Can use different required returns for different time periods.
8. Is the most complicated to calculate.

Problems

1. The Pratt Piston Company is considering an investment in a new plant which will entail an immediate capital expenditure of 2000 ($1000s). The plant is to be depreciated on a straight-line basis over 10 years and there will be no salvage value. Operating revenues (before depreciation and taxes) are expected to be 410 per year over the 10-year life of the plant. Assuming that the company has a required return of 12 percent for such an investment, calculate (a) average return on book, (b) the payback and discounted payback periods, (c) NPV, (d) IRR, (e) the profitability index. There are no taxes.

2. Rework problem 1 assuming that annual operating revenues will be 410 for the first 5 years and 320 for the following 5 years.

3. For each of the following four projects calculate the IRR, NPV, and profitability index at a 10 percent discount rate. Note how the rankings differ for each method.

	TIME PERIOD			
CASH FLOWS	0	1	2	3
Project A	-100			145
Project B	-100	115		
Project C	-100	230	-120	
Project D	- 45	20	20	20

4. An investment of $100 will produce a level stream of cash flows for T years. (a) Find what level of cash flow is necessary to produce an average return on book value of 8 percent (and also 16 percent), if $T = 5$ (and also if $T = 10$). (b) Find what level of cash flow is necessary to produce an IRR of 8 percent (and also of 16 percent), if $T = 5$ (and also if $T = 10$).

5. Thanet House Investments has an opportunity cost of capital of 13 percent. Which of the following projects should Thanet accept?

	CASH FLOWS ($1000s)				
PROJECT	C_0	C_1	C_2	C_3	IRR, %
A	-112	40	50	60	15
B	45	60	-70	-70	16
C	-100	-26	80	80	11
D	146	-70	-60	-50	12
E	-100	425	-576	252	20

6. Thanet House Investments is considering the following mutually exclusive investments:

	CASH FLOWS ($1000s)			
PROJECT	C_0	C_1	C_2	C_3
A	-400	220	310	
B	-400	130	190	260

Thanet's opportunity cost of capital is 13 percent. Calculate the NPV, IRR, and payback of the two projects. Why do the methods give different rankings? Which project should be chosen?

7. Thanet House Investment's opportunity cost of capital is still 13 percent. Thanet is now considering the following mutually exclusive investments:

| | CASH FLOWS ($1000s) | | | |
PROJECT	C_0	C_1	C_2	C_3
B	-400	130	190	260
C	-800	360	360	360

Calculate the NPV, IRR, and profitability index of the two investments. Which investment should be undertaken?

8. Beanstalk Enterprises expects to generate cash flows of $100,000 in year 1 and $200,000 in year 2. If they make an immediate investment of $35,000, they can expect to receive $190,000 in year 1 and $150,000 in year 2 instead. Beanstalk's opportunity cost of capital is 12 percent. Calculate the NPV and IRR of the proposed project. Why is the IRR a poor measure of the project's profitability?

9. Beanstalk Enterprises in problem 8 now finds that the cost of their proposed investment has risen form $35,000 to $42,000. Recalculate the NPV and IRR of the project. Why is the IRR a poor measure of the project's profitability?

Essay Questions

1. Describe four common methods of appraising capital investments. Discuss the advantages and disadvantages of each.

2. Describe carefully under what circumstances the IRR and NPV methods may imply different investment decisions.

3. Explain why comparing the IRRs of two mutually exclusive projects may lead to an incorrect decision. Describe the correct way to compare such projects using the IRR method.

*4. Explain how return on book differs from the DCF rate of return. Under what circumstances do they produce similar values?

ANSWERS TO EXERCISES

Fill-in Questions

1. payback period
2. discounted payback
3. average return on book
4. internal rate of return
5. mutually exclusive
6. discounted-cash-flow
7. profitability index; benefit cost

Multiple Choice

1.	AROBV	5.	none
2.	NPV	6.	P
3.	IRR	7.	NPV and PI
4.	PI	8.	IRR

Problems

1. Depreciation = 200; profit = 210; cash flow = 410. (a) AROBV = 210/1000 = 21%; (b) payback = 2000/410 = 4.88 years; discounted payback = 7.78 years. (NPVs are -128.9 and 36.7 for first 7 and 8 years' cash flows respectively.) (c) NPV = -2000 + 410 x 5.65 = 316.50 ($1000s); (d) annuity factor must equal 2000/410 = 4.878, giving IRR = 15.75%; (e) PI = 2316.50/2000 = 1.158.

2. (a) 16.5 percent; (b) 4.88 years; 8.74 years; (c) $132,500; (d) 13.7 percent; (e) 1.066

3.

PROJECT	NPV	IRR, %	PI
A	$8.94	13.18	1.089
B	$4.55	15.00	1.045
C	$9.91	-20.00; +50.00	1.099
D	$4.74	15.89	1.105

4.

REQUIRED CASH FLOWS UNDER	*T* = 5 YEARS r = 8%	r = 16%	*T* = 10 YEARS r = 8%	r = 16%
Return on book	$24.00	$28.00	$14.00	$18.00
IRR	$25.00	$30.50	$14.90	$20.70

IRR is more conservative because it takes account of the need to earn compound interest rather than simple interest.

5.

PROJECT	NPV
A	4.14
B	-5.24
C	-4.91
D	2.41
E	-0.34

Accept projects which have positive net present values, namely, A and D.

6.

PROJECT	NPV	IRR, %	PAYBACK, YEARS
A	37.47	19.73	1.58
B	44.04	18.68	2.31

Take the project which produces the higher net present value, project B.

7.

PROJECT	NPV	IRR, %	PI
B	44.04	18.68	1.11
C	50.01	16.65	1.06

Take C.

8. The incremental cash flows are -35, 90, -50 ($1000s). NPV = $5497; IRR = -18.81 percent and 75.95 percent. The two values provide totally different impressions of the project's profitability.

9. NPV = -$1503. The IRR does not exist; there is now no discount rate that will give this project a positive NPV.

CHAPTER 6
MAKING INVESTMENT DECISIONS
WITH THE NET PRESENT VALUE RULE

INTRODUCTION

Anyone making capital budgeting decisions will want to be familiar with the issues that are discussed here. The chapter considers the following three problems.

1. How to decide which items should be included in the cash-flow analysis. We need to work out how the after-tax (corporate) cash flow is changed by accepting the project.
2. How to evaluate investments which affect other activities or decisions of the firm. Sometimes, for example, we are forced to choose among alternative projects with different lives. It is pointless to compare the capital cost of a machine which lasts 10 years against that of one which lasts only 5 years. We can, however, compare them in terms of the annual rental (paid over the life of the machine), which has the same present value as the capital cost. This annual rental is called the equivalent annual cost.
3. How to choose investments so as to make the best use of limited capital, management time, or other scarce resources.

WHAT TO LOOK FOR IN CHAPTER 6

What to Discount: Sections 6-1 and 6-2 explain how to work out the incremental after-tax cash flows from a project and discount them. Notice that cash flow can be *very* different from the earnings figure that an accountant would calculate. First, while the accounting earnings for a period do relate to that period, they need not have been received in cash. For example, if I buy 100 grommets for $1 (cash) each, and I sell 40 of them at $1.50 each, I have a profit of $20 (= 40 x 50 cents). However, in cash terms I am still $40 out of pocket [= 100 – (40 x $1.50)]; and if I sold the grommets on credit, I am $100 out of pocket. A second, and even more important difference, is in the way capital items are treated in the accounts as separate and different from income. For example, suppose that I buy a small truck for $20,000 that produces $6000 a year for 5 years, and then falls apart. Accountants will regard $4000 a year as the return necessary if I am to recover my investment over the life of the truck. They deduct this amount (as depreciation) to arrive at the earnings figure of $2000 a year. Nevertheless it is still the cash flows of -$20,000 followed by +$6000 a year for 5 years that I should discount to evaluate the investment.

This constant (**straight-line**) depreciation is used to calculate the income that is reported to shareholders. When it comes to calculating my *taxable* income, however, I can usually use a different depreciation schedule which allows me to depreciate the asset more quickly. This is called **accelerated depreciation**. For example, for tax purposes I may be able to deduct the entire cost of my truck from my taxable income over a period of 3 years instead of 5. The effect of this type of arrangement is to reduce the present value (but not the total amount) of the taxes I have to pay, and it is designed to encourage investment. Watch out for the details of how accelerated depreciation works in practice.

It is often quite tricky to work out exactly which costs and benefits depend on a project's being accepted (which costs and benefits are incremental) and which do not. The best way to tell is to consider what will happen *with* the project and what will happen *without* the project. Whatever changes between the two cases is incremental to the decision.

Look out too for the correct way to treat inflation. The easiest way is to project cash flows in (nominal) future dollars (i.e., grossed up for inflation) and to discount them at a nominal (dollar) rate that is sufficiently high to offer a reasonable return above the inflation rate. If you prefer, you can discount real cash flows (in constant-base-year prices) at a real rate (which is the nominal rate deflated by the expected rate of inflation).

Project Interactions: Most capital budgeting investments affect other activities. For example, they may compete for land, factory space, the time of key managers, or the market for existing products of the company. Often, when one investment proposal is accepted, it means that other alternative proposals must be rejected, as, for example, when alternative sizes and locations are considered for a new plant. In making decisions of these kinds, it is essential to take a sufficiently broad view of net present value and to remember that the goal is to maximize the present value of the whole company.

Look out for decisions where there is a choice of project timing, location, or size. Look out too for the equivalent annual cost (EAC) technique. This technique is particularly useful for deciding among similar facilities (such as machines) with different lives, and for deciding on when an existing facility should be replaced. The third worked example illustrates the use of the EAC method.

Resource Limitations: Section 6-4 is rather less important than the earlier sections. There are two key ideas. First, when only a limited amount of funds is available for investment, we must get as much present value as possible for each dollar we invest. The way to do this is to pick the top-ranking project in terms of ratio of present value to investment. This ratio is our old friend (from Chapter 5) the profitability index. Second, where resource limitations are more complicated, we can often use a technique called linear programming (LP) to choose the combination of projects which gives the biggest NPV. Finally, bear in mind that most companies can raise large sums of money on fair terms if they want to. Budget constraints are often imposed to curb over-optimistic managers, or because of the problems which might be created by very rapid corporate growth.

WORKED EXAMPLES

PROBLEM 1: DEPRECIATION AND CASH FLOW
A company has:

> Net cash revenues of $300 (REV)
> Tax depreciation of $100 (DEP)
> So taxable earnings are $200 (REV – DEP)
> It pays tax at a tax rate of 40 percent (T)
> Calculate its cash flow (C).

SOLUTION

1. Cash flow = revenue – tax
   C = $300 – 0.4($300 – $100)   [REV – T(REV – DEP)]
      = $300 – $80 = $220

2. Cash flow = revenue after tax + depreciation tax shield
   C = $300(1 – 0.4) + 0.4 x $100   [REV(1 – T) +T(DEP)]
      = $180 – $40 = $220

3. Cash flow = earnings after tax + depreciation
   C = ($300 – $100)(1 – 0.4) + $100   [(REV – DEP)(1 – T) + DEP]
      = $120 + $100 = $220

The second of the methods in this example is usually the easiest one for capital budgeting. You just take off tax on the whole of the revenues and then add back the depreciation tax shield. Financial analysts often arrive at cash flow by the third method: they add back depreciation to after-tax earnings. Changes in working capital, etc., necessitate further adjustments.

PROBLEM 2: INFLATION: CORRECT AND INCORRECT TREATMENTS

Western Supermarkets is promoting a competition in which it will be giving away, in twelve months time, one hundred crates of groceries currently worth $1000 each. The nominal interest rate is ten percent and inflation is expected to be seven percent.

1. Calculate Western Supermarkets' cash flow in both real and nominal terms, and work out the real interest rate.

2. Show all possible combinations of using real or money cash flows with real or nominal interest rates to arrive at the present value of Western Supermarkets' liability. Indicate which combinations are correct and which are incorrect.

SOLUTION

1. The real cash flow is $100,000 in today's dollars. Since inflation is 7 percent, the nominal cash flow is $107,000. The real interest rate is given by

    $$1.10/1.07 - 1 = 2.8 \text{ percent.}$$

2. We use either the money cash flow and the nominal rate, or the real cash flow and the real rate. All other combinations are incorrect.

Discount at	Money Cash Flow $107,000	Real Cash Flow $100,000
Nominal Rate 1/1.10	$97,273 CORRECT	$90,909 INCORRECT
Real Rate 1/1.028	$104,082 INCORRECT	$97,273 CORRECT

PROBLEM 3: EQUIVALENT ANNUAL COST METHOD

Homemaker Inc. wishes to acquire a new retail outlet. The leases on two similar shops are up for sale. Shop A has a 7-year lease involving lease rental payments of $150,000 a year payable in advance. The lease can be acquired for $700,000. The lease on shop B has only 4 years to run. It can be acquired for $550,000, and it involves lease rentals of $100,000 a year payable in advance. Which of these shops is financially the more attractive if the opportunity cost of capital is 10 percent?

SOLUTION

Shop A involves an immediate payment of $850,000 followed by six annual payments of $150,000. Its present value (in $1000s) is therefore

$$850 + 150 \times (\text{annuity factor: } t = 6, r = 10\%) = 850 + (150 \times 4.355)$$
$$= \$1,503,000$$

44

Similarly the present value cost of shop B (in $1000s) is

$$650 + 100 \text{ x (annuity factor: } t = 3, r = 10\%) = 650 + (100 \text{ x } 2.487)$$
$$= \$899,000$$

We cannot compare these present values, though, for shop A provides a facility over a longer period of time than does shop B. We must translate the cost of each shop into an annual rental over the period of the lease. We can then compare the annual rentals.

What equivalent annual rental (EAC) on shop A (paid at the end of each year for 7 years) would have a present value cost of $1,503,000?

$$\text{EAC (shop A) x (annuity factor: } t = 7, r = 10\%) = \$1,503,000$$

$$\begin{aligned}\text{Clearly, EAC (shop A)} &= \$1,503,000/(\text{annuity factor: } t = 7, r = 10\%)\\ &= \$1,503,000/4.868\\ &= \$309,000\end{aligned}$$

Similarly, for shop B

$$\begin{aligned}\text{EAC (shop B)} &= \$899,000/(\text{annuity factor: } t = 4, r = 10\%)\\ &= \$899,000/3.170\\ &= \$284,000\end{aligned}$$

That is, the total cost of shop B is equivalent to payments of $284,000 at the end of each year for 4 years. This cost is cheaper than the corresponding annual cost of $309,000 for shop A.

SUMMARY

1 **What to discount**
   a. Only cash flow matters
      Calculate cash flows on an after-tax basis.
      The cash flows represent dividends which *could* be paid if the project were financed entirely with equity; so ignore any projected dividend or interest payments. Dividend and borrowing decisions will be analyzed separately.
      Depreciation is *not* a cash flow, but it does affect tax payments.
   b. Discount incremental cash flows
      With or without principal: incremental cash flows are the difference between the cash flows if the project is accepted and if it is not.
      Distinguish between average and incremental. A division which is very profitable may include some (marginal) projects that are unprofitable.
      Include incidental effects, such as benefits from the disposal of waste.
      Include working capital requirements.
      Sunk costs are irrelevant.
      Include opportunity costs.
      Beware of allocated costs and overhead.
   c. Treatment of inflation
      Discount rates are usually quoted in *nominal* terms.
      It is easiest to discount *nominal* (money) cash flows at a *nominal* discount rate.
      Instead, some companies prefer to project cash flows in *real* terms and discount them at a *real* rate of interest. If r_N is the nominal rate, r_I is inflation, and r_R is the real rate, then $1 + r_N = (1 + r_I)(1 + r_R)$; so the real rate is given by

$$r_R = \frac{1+r_N}{1+r_I} - 1$$

Never discount real cash flows at a nominal rate.

2. Methods of depreciation

Depreciation is important only because it reduces taxable income. Each year the tax saving is the depreciation allowance times the marginal tax rate.

Under the Modified Accelerated Cost Recovery System the tax depreciation allowed for an asset depends on which Recovery Period Class it belongs to. The following table summarizes the depreciation schedules.

TAX DEPRECIATION SCHEDULES BY RECOVERY PERIOD CLASS

YEAR	3-YEAR	5-YEAR	7-YEAR	10-YEAR	15-YEAR	20-YEAR
1	33.33	20.00	14.29	10.00	5.00	3.75
2	44.45	32.00	24.49	18.00	9.50	7.22
3	14.81	19.20	17.49	14.40	8.55	6.68
4	7.41	11.52	12.49	11.52	7.70	6.18
5		11.52	8.93	9.22	6.93	5.71
6		5.76	8.93	7.37	6.23	5.28
7			8.93	6.55	5.90	4.89
8			4.45	6.55	5.90	4.52
9				6.55	5.90	4.46
10				6.55	5.90	4.46
11				3.29	5.90	4.46
12					5.90	4.46
13					5.90	4.46
14					5.90	4.46
15					5.90	4.46
16					2.99	4.46
17-20						4.46
21						2.25

3. Project interactions

Most capital expenditures decisions involve choices of the kind: "either A or B but not both." The chapter gives five examples of how to maximize NPV subject to interactions of this kind.

a. Optimal timing of investment

The fact that a project has a positive NPV does not mean that it is best undertaken now; it may be even more valuable if undertaken at a later date. We must choose the date which gives the highest present value.

For example, if we can harvest a tract of timber immediately with a NPV of $10 million or in 5 years with a NPV then of $20 million, we must compare $10 million with $20 million$/(1 + r)^5$ and choose whichever is greater.

More generally we must maximize (net future value at t)$/(1 + r)^t$

b. Projects with different lives
    Mutually exclusive projects with different lives cannot be simply compared on the basis of
    NPV. To do so would ignore the value of a likely replacement project. We can compare the
    NPVs of chains of projects of equal length. We can compare projects' *equivalent annual cash
    flows* (see problem 3).

c. The replacement decision
    The capital cost of a new machine can be restated as an equivalent annual cost (EAC). Its
    optimal life is the one which minimizes its EAC.

    We can decide whether to replace an existing machine by comparing its cost for the next year
    (including the loss of salvage value over the year) against the EAC of the new machine; i.e.,
    replace if $C_1 + S_1 - (1 + r)S_0 > EAC$.

    Remember that these comparisons are based on simplistic assumptions. We can take account
    of inflation by doing the analysis in real terms. This still ignores other important considerations
    such as technical change.

d. The cost of excess capacity
    Increased utilization of a facility (such as a computer or a warehouse) may bring forward the
    dates of further expenditures.

e. Fluctuating load factors
    Consider different sizes of investment and choose the size which has the highest (positive)
    NPV. A new project may affect the value of other investments: sometimes we must work out
    detailed scenarios to unravel these effects.

4. **Limited resources**
    a. Capital rationing:
        With limited cash for investment the greatest NPV comes from accepting projects with the
        highest NPV per dollar of initial cost.

$$\text{Profitability index} \quad = \quad \frac{\text{present value}}{\text{investment}}$$

    provides an equivalent method of ranking. Positive NPV projects have a profitability index
    greater than 1.
    b. Drawbacks:
        This method may waste resources if the capital budget is not exactly satisfied.
        When more than one resource is rationed, a more complicated (linear programming) analysis is
        needed.
        The profitability index cannot cope with mutually exclusive projects or where one project is
        contingent on another.
        Capital constraints are often self-imposed to force divisions to focus on priorities and to weed
        out projects which stem from overoptimism.

LIST OF TERMS

Accelerated depreciation	**Real interest rate**
Capital rationing	**Straight-line depreciation**
Equivalent annual cost	**Recovery period class**
Linear programming	**Sunk costs**
Net working capital	**Tax depreciation**
Nominal interest rate	**Tax shield**

EXERCISES

Fill-in Questions

1. Costs that have occurred in the past and are irrecoverable are called _____.
2. Current assets minus current liabilities equals _____.
3. An interest rate expressed in dollars with no adjustment for inflation is called a _____ rate.
4. An interest rate adjusted for inflation so that it represents an increase in purchasing power is called a _____ interest rate.
5. Under _____ depreciation the deduction for depreciation is the same amount each year.
6. _____ depreciation is the general term for any depreciation method that provides larger deductions in the early years of the asset's life.
7. In order to work out the after tax cash flows from an investment we need to know what _____ is allowed, rather than how it is depreciated for accounting purposes.
8. The tax depreciation allowed for a particular asset depends on which _____ it belongs to.
9. The tax depreciation amount multiplied by the tax rate is called the depreciation _____.
10. The _____ of a piece of equipment is the constant annual charge which over the life of the equipment has the same present value cost as the equipment.
11. _____ refers to a situation in which a company has only limited funds available for investment.
12. We can sometimes find the most profitable combination of activities subject to a number of budget constraints (or other kinds of constraints) by using a technique called _____.

Problems

1. Galactic Engineering is considering an investment of $40 million in plant and machinery. This is expected to produce sales of $8 million in year 1, $16 million in year 2, and $24 million in year 3. Subsequent sales will increase at the expected inflation rate of 10 percent. The plant is expected to be scrapped after 8 years with a salvage value of $8 million. It is depreciated for tax purposes on a straight-line basis of $4 million per year. Operating costs are expected to be $7 million in year 1 and $12 million in year 2, and to increase at 10 percent for the remaining 6 years. Working capital requirements are negligible. Galactic Engineering pays tax at 46 percent. Calculate the expected cash flows in each year and the NPV of investment when the required rate of return is 21 percent.

2. Repeat the calculation of problem 1 doing the analysis in *real* instead of nominal terms. (Discount at the real rate of 10 percent.)

3. How does your analysis of problem 1 change, if the new plant qualifies for tax depreciation under the 5-year Recovery Period Class?

4. Octopus, Inc. is evaluating an investment project which will cost $40 million and generate taxable revenues of $11 million per year for 7 years. There will be no salvage value at the end of this period. Octopus is currently unsure whether the investment will belong to the 3-year, 5-year, or 7-year Recovery Period Class. Calculate the NPV of the project for each of these three possibilities. Octopus' tax rate is 34 percent and its required return is 15 percent.

5. Calculate the present values of the tax depreciation amounts allowed on 3, 5, 7, and 10 year Recovery Period Class assets at 0, 10 and 20 percent discount rates respectively. Comment on what you figures reveal.

6. An investment of $200,000 in a computer is expected to reduce costs by $40,000 a year in perpetuity. However, the prices of computers are predicted to fall at 10 percent a year for the next 5 years. When should the computer be purchased if the cost of capital is 13 percent?

7. The Sundowner Company must choose between two machines which perform exactly the same operations but have different lives. The two machines have the following costs:

YEAR	MACHINE A	MACHINE B
0	$30,000	$40,000
1	$5,000	$7,000
2	$5,000 + replace	$7,000
3		$7,000 + replace

Which is cheaper if the discount rate is 10 percent?

8. A machine costs $100,000. At the end of the first year $5000 must be spent on maintenance. Each year the cost of maintenance rises by 15 percent. How long should the machine be kept before it is scrapped if the opportunity cost of capital is 10 percent? (Assume the machine has a zero salvage value.)

9. XYZ Company is considering whether to replace an existing machine or to spend money on overhauling it. The replacement machine would cost $18,000 and would require maintenance of $1500 at the end of every year. At the end of 10 years it would have a scrap value of $2000 and would not be maintained. The existing machine requires increasing amounts of maintenance each year, and its salvage value is falling as shown below:

YEAR	MAINTENANCE COST	SALVAGE VALUE
0	$2000	$2500
1	$3000	$2000
2	$4000	$1500
3	$5000	$1000
4	$5000	none

If XYZ faces an opportunity cost of capital of 15 percent, when should it replace the machine?

10. The acceptance of a particular capital budgeting proposal will mean that a new computer costing $200,000 will be purchased in 1 year's time instead of in 3 year's time. This also implies that an extra computer programmer costing $30,000 a year must be hired in year 1 instead of year 3. Work out the present value cost of these two items when the opportunity cost of capital is 14 percent.

11. Unimagic is planning a new plant to make a consumer packaged good called Unibubble. The latest proposal is as follows: A plant with the capacity to produce 10 million units of Unibubble a year is to be constructed at a cost of $17 million. Sales of this amount will produce revenues of $15 million a year for 10 years, and the direct manufacturing costs are expected to run at $9 million a year. Unimagic pays corporate tax at 46 percent. It would depreciate the plant on a straight-line basis over 10 years, and it would have no salvage value at the end of that period.

    Mr. Johnson, the financial director, has figures that indicate that the investment offers an internal rate of return of about 20 percent. Since Unimagic's required rate of return for a project of this kind is 12 percent, he is strongly in favor of the proposal. Mr. Jackson, the production manager, agrees that the project is viable, but he would like to see the company build an even bigger plant. He points out that there are significant economies of scale in the costs of building a bigger plant. Within the capacity range of 7 to 13 million units per year, each additional 1 million units of capacity costs only $0.80 million, as against the average cost of $1.70 million per million units for the proposed plant. The operating costs would remain at $0.90 per unit. Mr. Smith, the marketing manager, also likes this idea. He reports that demand for Unibubble is very elastic, and he is sure that he can sell an extra 1 million units with only a very modest decrease in price from $1.50 to $1.45. Conversely, if they reduced the capacity and output of the proposed plant by 1 million units, they would still be able to increase the selling price only to $1.55. On the basis of these figures, what size of plant should Unimagic build?

12. Rank the following projects in order of desirability when the funds available for investment are limited. Which projects should be accepted when the company considering them has imposed a budget limit of $800,000?

PROJECT	INVESTMENT ($1000s)	NPV ($1000s)	IRR, %
1	100	8	13.9
2	400	43	14.4
3	300	25	16.0
4	200	23	14.1
5	200	21	16.1
6	200	19	15.7

*13. In 1986, sinking an oil well in the North Sea offered a real return of about 20 percent. The income accrues over a 10-year period in a level stream. Some critics have argued that for a well of this kind it would be better to leave the oil under the sea a little longer. Suppose that the real price of oil is expected to increase continuously at a rate of 4 percent a year and investors require a real rate of return of 8 percent. When would be the best date to sink the well?

Essay Questions

1. Describe carefully how you would decide what cash flows to include as incremental in a capital budgeting appraisal situation. Give a list of items that are commonly treated incorrectly and say how they should be treated.

2. "We always allocate a proportion of company overhead to a new project in relation to its payroll requirements. After all, in the long run there's no difference between average and marginal cost." Discuss.

3. Describe how to work out the economic life of a piece of machinery and how to decide when to replace an existing machine which performs the same function.

50

4. Explain how linear programming can be used to select capital investments under a variety of capital rationing and other kinds of constraints. Show how the profitability index provides the solution to one particular problem of this kind.

*5. Timber is a renewable resource; oil and other mineral reserves are not. Both the value of a tract of timber and the value of a known oil reserve increase with time. The costs of "harvesting" each stay relatively constant in real terms. Discuss how the problem of when to log a tract of timber (renewable resource) differs from the problem of when to exploit a known reserve of oil (nonrenewable resource) so as to maximize its value.

ANSWERS TO EXERCISES

Fill-in Questions

1. sunk costs
2. net working capital
3. nominal
4. real
5. straight-line
6. accelerated
7. tax depreciation
8. Recovery Period Class
9. tax shield
10. equivalent annual cost
11. capital rationing
12. linear programming

Problems

1. The cash flows in $1000s and PV calculation (using the "bottom-up" method described on p. 15) are:

YEAR	INVESTMENT & SALVAGE	DEPRECIATION TAX SAVINGS	NET AFTER-TAX OPERATING REVENUES	TOTAL CASH FLOW	VALUE IN EACH YEAR AT 21%
0	-40,000			-40,000	-11,567
1		1,360	660	2,020	34,403
2		1,360	2,640	4,000	39,184
3		1,360	7,128	8,488	42,573
4		1,360	7,841	9,201	41,242
5		1,360	8,625	9,985	38,770
6		1,360	9,487	10,847	34,830
7		1,360	10,436	11,796	29,019
8	8,000	1,360	11,480	20,840	20,840

This shows a negative NPV of -$11.567 million.

2. In real terms:

YEAR	INVESTMENT & SALVAGE	DEPRECIATION TAX SAVINGS	NET AFTER-TAX OPERATING REVENUES	TOTAL CASH FLOW	VALUE IN EACH YEAR AT 10%
0	-40,000			-40,000	-11,567
1		1,236	600	1,836	31,275
2		1,124	2,182	3,306	32,383
3		1,022	5,355	6,377	31,985
4		929	5,355	6,284	28,169
5		844	5,355	6,200	24,073
6		768	5,355	6,123	19,660
7		698	5,355	6,053	14,891
8	3,732	634	5,355	9,722	9,722

Again, we've used our "bottom-up" calculator method to do the discounting. This shows the same NPV of –$11.567 million as before.

3. The previous depreciation tax savings were worth $1360 x 3.726 = $5.067 million.

These are replaced by depreciation tax shields of the following:

YEAR	DEPRECIATION TAX SAVINGS	PRESENT VALUE AT 21%
0		7,687
1	2,720	9,301
2	4,352	7,963
3	2,611	4,370
4	1,567	2,128
5	1,567	679
6	783	-1,075
7	0	-2,248
8	-2,720	-2,720

The NPV becomes -11,567 – 5,067 + 7,687 = – $8,947, which is still unprofitable.

4. The following table shows the PVs in $1000s of the various component cash flows and the total NPV under the three methods.

	3-YEAR	5-YEAR	7-YEAR
Investment	-40,000	-40,000	-40,000
Depreciation tax shield	10,413	9,386	8,527
Net revenues	30,205	30,205	30,205
NPV	618	-409	-1,268

5. As a percentage of the depreciable investment we get:

DISCOUNT RATE	RECOVERY PERIOD CLASS			
	3-YEAR	5-YEAR	7-YEAR	10-YEAR
0	100.0	100.0	100.0	100.0
5	90.9	87.5	84.2	79.7
10	83.2	77.3	72.1	65.4
15	76.6	69.0	62.7	54.9

At a zero interest rate it is as if all assets could be written off for tax purposes immediately (expensed). At higher rates the tax depreciation is less generous, especially on the longer recovery period assets. NB. Multiply by the tax rate to get the tax shield.

6. The NPV of purchasing the computer after t years is $(-200{,}000 \times 0.90^t + 40{,}000/.13)/1.13^t$

   This expression takes its maximum value of $114,098 (over integer t) for $t = 2$ years.

7. Equivalent annual costs are $22,286 for machine A and $23,085 for machine B, so A is cheaper.

8.

YEARS KEPT	PV COST	ANNUITY FACTOR	EAC (= PV/ANN)
5	$119,459	3.791	$31,513
10	$149,192	6.145	$24,280
11	$155,974	6.495	$24,014
12	$163,063	6.814	$23,932
13	$170,475	7.103	$23,999

The EAC is minimized by keeping the machine 12 years.

9. The equivalent annual cost of the new machine is $4,914.2. The costs of each year's operation of the old machine (adjusted to the end of each year) are given below:

YEARS	COST OF OPERATION	HOW CALCULATED
1	$3,175	(2000 + 2500) x 1.15 – 2000
2	$4,250	(3000 + 2000) x 1.15 – 1500
3	$5,325	(4000 + 1500) x 1.15 – 1000
4	$6,900	(5000 + 1000) x 1.15

The machine should be replaced after 2 years.

10. Present value cost of change in computer timing = $40,444.
    Present value cost of extra programmer = $49,400.

11. Net present value at various plant sizes is as follows:

Capacity (million units)	8	9	10	11
NPV ($ million)	5.689	5.859	5.725	5.286

The capacity of 9 million units has the highest NPV.

12. The ranking of projects according to their profitability index is : 4, 2, 5, 6, 3, 1. With a budget limit of $800,000, projects 2, 4, and 5 should be accepted.

13. To give a real return of 20 percent, an investment of $100 must produce 10 years' real income of $23.85 per year. At an 8 percent real rate this has a present value of $160.05 and a NPV of $60.05. If we decide to defer the investment to year t, its NPV is: $[160.05 \times (1.04)^t - 100]/(1.08)^t$

This has a maximum value of $64.60 when the investment is made after 6 years, that is, in 1992.

CHAPTER 7
INTRODUCTION TO RISK AND RETURN
IN CAPITAL BUDGETING

INTRODUCTION

Most people agree that risk is a bad thing and that a safe dollar is worth more than a risky one. Investors expect a higher rate of return from a risky investment than they do from a safe investment. This basic principle was introduced back in Chapter 2, but it was not developed in any detail there. Chapters 7, 8, and 9 form a single unit which deals with what we mean by risk, and how it affects the opportunity cost of capital for a project.

Chapter 7 is an introduction to how we measure risk, and to the relationship between risk and return. When I buy a 6-month Treasury bill, I know exactly what return I will get over the next 6 months: it is riskless. On the other hand, if I hold a portfolio of common stocks, such as Standard & Poor's Composite Index of 500 stocks, my return is quite unpredictable. To compensate me for this risk, I can expect to earn a higher return, on average, than from holding Treasury bills. The variation of past returns on Standard & Poor's Index gives some idea of just how unpredictable they are. We can use statistical measures (like the standard deviation) to describe this variability.

Individual stocks are even more risky than Standard & Poor's Index. Diversification (holding a lot of different stocks) provides a way of reducing risk. Unfortunately there is some risk that you can never diversify away. This undiversifiable risk stems from economy-wide perils that threaten all businesses; it is called *market risk*. The risk a security adds to a well-diversified portfolio depends on its market risk, which we measure by its *beta*. Finally, this leads us to the punch line of the chapter: the capital asset pricing model. We find that the extra return (or *risk premium*) that a security has to offer, because it is risky, is proportional to the security's beta value.

With this outline established, Chapters 8 and 9 fill in some further important details. Chapter 8 puts the theory on firmer foundations, and Chapter 9 explains how it can be used to find the appropriate discount rate to use in evaluating an investment project.

WHAT TO LOOK FOR IN CHAPTER 7

This chapter develops the concept of risk in a precise way. It is mostly concerned with the risks faced by individual investors holding portfolios of securities. This builds toward Chapter 9, which describes how corporate financial managers should take account of risk when they make capital budgeting decisions. Managers of corporations act on behalf of their stockholders. They want to see the price of their company's shares as high as possible: this will make the stockholders as well off as possible. It is logical to begin by examining risk from the stockholder's point of view, and then to move on to the implications for companies.

There are four key ideas that you should find in this chapter. The first is that Treasury bills and the market portfolio of common stocks provide two useful benchmarks of risk and return. We will often refer to these benchmarks when we assess the risk and expected return of an investment. The second idea concerns the effects of diversification. Shareholders can, and do, reduce their risk very significantly by diversification. The risk that matters to them is therefore the market risk that each security adds to a diversified portfolio.

55

We measure this market risk as the security's beta. Beta measures the sensitivity of the return on the security to the return on the market. Beta is important because of the third key idea, the capital asset pricing model (CAPM), which tells us that it is a security's beta which determines the return investors expect from it. Finally, the fourth idea is that of value additivity. The value of a project does not depend on how well its returns mesh with the returns on other activities of the company. This is because the shareholders can diversify directly to obtain whatever benefits of diversification are available. They are unlikely to accept lower returns in order to have a corporate manager diversify for them.

Statistics: You will find this chapter quite easy if you already know some elementary statistics. The text gives all the necessary definitions, but you may want to refresh your memory from a statistics textbook. It will help if you are familiar with the terms variance, standard deviation, and covariance, and if you have already met a normal distribution.

Risk: The idea of risk is a familiar one. It means that there are a number of possible outcomes (which are not equally desirable), and we cannot be certain which one will occur. The return on a portfolio of common stocks cannot be predicted with any accuracy. It is risky. The use of statistics helps us to analyze this type of risk in a precise way. The spread of past returns gives a good indication of the range of uncertainty about future returns. This spread is best measured by the standard deviation or the variance.

The standard deviation of the annual returns on Standard & Poor's Index is about 21 percent. That's quite a lot of risk. It accounts for why (over the last 60 years) common stocks have on average earned about 8 percent more than Treasury bills (which are virtually riskless). These two numbers (21 and 8 percent) are useful ones to remember.

Diversification: The standard deviation of an individual stock is generally much higher than for the market as a whole. In fact it is usually about double (35 to 40 percent). The risk in a diversified portfolio is lower than for a single security because the returns of different stocks do not move perfectly together. Diversification is an important concept with powerful implications. When we hold many stocks, the risks which are *unique* to each one tend to cancel each other out, as they are largely unconnected. Some risks, though, stem from uncertainty about factors which affect the whole of the market. This *market* risk cannot be eliminated by diversification: it must be borne by investors, and the investors can expect to earn a higher return for bearing it.

Beta: The contribution a security makes to the risk of a well diversified portfolio depends on how sensitive it is to market movements. The average stock return will tend to move up 5 percent when the market moves up 5 percent. Of course, sometimes it will go up more than the market and sometimes it will go up less than the market. On average, though, it goes up (and down) one for one with the market. This means its beta is 1. A stock that is more sensitive to market movements might tend to move twice as far (10 percent) in response to a market rise of 5 percent. Conversely, it would tend to fall 10 percent if the market fell 5 percent. This stock is twice as sensitive as the average and its beta is 2.

The beta of a portfolio is just an average of the betas of the stocks included in it (weighted according to their value in the portfolio). In other words, if a portfolio consists 60 percent of stocks with betas of 0.8 and 40 percent of stocks with betas of 1.2, the beta of the portfolio is 0.6 x 0.8 + 0.4 x 1.2 = 0.96. When a portfolio is well diversified, the amount of unique risk it contains is negligible. In this case the standard deviation of the portfolio is just its beta multiplied by the standard deviation of the return on the market portfolio. This makes beta an important number. Beta measures how much a stock contributes to the risk of a well-diversified portfolio. Its return must compensate for this risk. And so we arrive at the CAPM.

56

WORKED EXAMPLES

PROBLEM 1: INVESTMENT OPPORTUNITIES LIE ON A LINE

An investor, Mr. Richards, has $100 to invest. He can invest in a risky portfolio S of equities which has an expected return of 14 percent and a standard deviation of 20 percent. He can also lend or borrow risk-free at 6 percent interest. Show how he can construct a portfolio with standard deviations of (a) 10 percent or (b) 30 percent. Work out the expected returns on these portfolios. Show that these four investment opportunities lie on a straight line.

SOLUTION

To halve the standard deviation of the risky investment, S, Mr. Richards must halve the amount he puts into it. Instead of investing $100 in S, he would have to invest $50 in S and the remaining $50 at the risk-free rate. Similarly, to increase the standard deviation from 20 to 30 percent, he must increase his investment in S from $100 to $150 by borrowing $50 at 6 percent interest. The expected returns and standard deviations from these portfolios are given in the table below. The table also shows the returns that will be obtained one standard deviation above or below the expected value; this is a useful check that the standard deviations are correct.

	INVESTMENT	EXPECTED RETURN	STANDARD DEVIATION	EXPECTED RETURN *PLUS* ONE STANDARD DEVIATION	EXPECTED RETURN *MINUS* ONE STANDARD DEVIATION
S:	$100 in S	$14	$20	$34	- $6
r_f:	$100 in r_f	6	0	6	6
a:	$50 in S	7	10	17	- 3
	+50 in r_f	3	0	3	3
	$100 total	$10	$10	$20	$0
b:	$150 in S	$21	$30	$51	- $9
	-50 in r_f	- 3	0	- 3	- 3
	$100 total	$18	$30	$48	-$12

It is now clear that each additional 10 percent standard deviation earns an additional expected return of 4 percent. The investment opportunities plot on the straight line shown below.

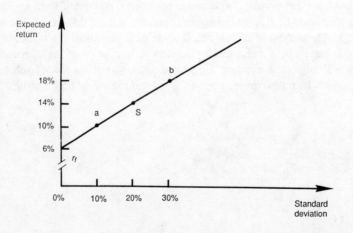

PROBLEM 2: CAPM

The Treasury bill rate is 7 percent and the expected return on the market portfolio is 15 percent.

1. What is the risk premium on the market?

2. What is the required rate of return on an investment with a beta of 1.25?

3. If the market expects a return of 11 percent from XTC Leisure, Inc., what is its beta?

4. If an investment with a beta of 1.5 offers an expected return of 20 percent, does it have a positive NPV?

SOLUTION

1. The risk premium on the market is the difference between the expected return on the market portfolio and the Treasury bill rate. In this example it is 15 percent – 7 percent = 8 percent.

2. The expected return on any investment is given by expected return = risk-free rate + (beta x market risk premium). For a beta of 1.25 this gives

$$
\begin{aligned}
\text{Expected return} \ &= 7 + (1.25 \times 8) \\
&= 7 + 10 \\
&= 17 \text{ percent}
\end{aligned}
$$

3. An expected return of 11 percent represents a risk premium of 4 percent. Since this premium is beta times the market premium of 8 percent, beta must be 0.5. In general, beta = risk premium on stock divided by risk premium on market.

4. An investment with a beta of 1.5 has a required rate of return of 7 + (1.5 x 8) = 19 percent. This investment has an expected return of 20 percent; so its NPV is positive.

SUMMARY

Portfolio Risk and Return: A *risky* portfolio in one in which a *variety* of different returns is possible. We can measure the past variation in returns by their *variance*, the expected value of $(\tilde{r} - r)^2$, where $\tilde{r} =$ actual return and $r =$ expected return, and which in turn equals $[1/(N-1)]$ x sum of squared deviations from average. Risk is also measured by the *standard deviation*, the square root of the variance.

Note that the variance is easier to calculate, but the standard deviation is easier to interpret.

Note also that for a normal distribution 68 percent of returns are within 1 standard deviation of the average, and 95 percent of returns are within 2 standard deviations of the average.

The variation of past returns is a good guide to the uncertainty of future returns. However, because of this variation, we need to measure average returns over long periods of time. Historical risk and average return from various securities were:

| | AVERAGE ANNUAL RETURN, % | | STANDARD |
	NOMINAL	REAL	DEVIATION, %
Common stocks			
(Standard & Poor's 500)	12.0	8.8	21.2
Long-term corporate bonds	5.1	2.1	8.3
Long-term governments bonds	4.4	1.4	8.2
Treasury bills	3.5	0.4	3.4

Note that returns include cash payments and capital gains; the figures refer to the period 1926-1985 (Ibbotson Associates); Treasury bills give a very low real return (0.4%); the average nominal risk premium on common stocks was 8.4 percent; and the standard deviation of Standard & Poor's 500 was higher than average in 1926-1945, lower than average on 1946-1985.

The standard deviation of the returns on a single stock is usually much higher than for the market portfolio (for example, 35.4 percent for Digital Equipment). Diversification reduces variability, it can roughly halve the standard deviation of portfolio returns.

Unique risk stems from perils unique to an individual company. It can be eliminated by diversification. *Market risk* stems from economy-wide perils that threaten many companies. It cannot be eliminated by diversification.

The Effect of Individual Stocks on Portfolio Risk: The risk of a well-diversified portfolio depends on the *market risk* of the securities included in the portfolio. *Beta* (β) measures the market risk of a stock as its sensitivity to market movements. Stocks with beta greater than 1 are usually sensitive to market movements. Stocks with beta less than 1 are usually insensitive to market movements.

The beta of a portfolio is the weighted average of the beta of the securities included in it. That is, $\beta_p = x_1\beta_1 + x_2\beta_2 + \ldots + x_N\beta_N$. The standard deviation of a well-diversified portfolio is its beta times the standard deviation of the market portfolio. A diversified portfolio of high beta stocks is therefore more risky than a diversified portfolio of low beta stocks. Beta is important because it determines the expected return that investors require:

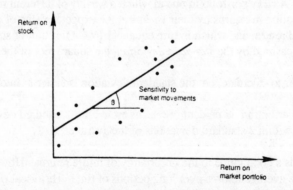

Diversification and Value Additivity: Diversification is good for individual investors. But because investors can diversify by holding a variety of stocks, they have no reason to pay more for the stocks of companies which are already diversified, nor should they pay less. As a result, the value of a project does not depend on how its returns mesh with the returns from other activities of the company which undertakes it. If the capital market establishes a value PV(A) for asset A, and PV(B) for asset B, the market value of a firm that holds only these two assets is

$$PV(AB) = PV(A) + PV(B)$$

This is the *value-additivity principle*.

It fits nicely with our ideas from the CAPM. Suppose we combine two projects A and B into a single new project AB. Then both the expected return and beta of AB are a weighted average of the individual expected returns and betas. [The weights are PV(A)/PV(AB) and PV(B)/PV(AB).] As a result, if A and B both lie on the market line, so too must AB. If you're not sure about this, try problem 4.

LIST OF TERMS

Beta (β)
Capital asset pricing model
Diversification
Expected market return (r_m)
Market portfolio
Market return ($\bar{r}_m$)
Market risk
Market risk premium ($r_m - r_f$)

Risk-free rate of return(r_f)
Security market line
Standard deviation (σ)
Unique risk
Value additivity
Variability
Variance (σ^2)

EXERCISES

Fill-in Questions

1. Standard & Poor's Composite Index is often regarded as the _____ portfolio.
2. The average annual _____ between 1926 and 1985 was 12.0 percent.
3. Diversification cannot eliminate risk entirely because stocks have _____.
4. Diversification reduces _____.
5. The difference between the _____ and the risk-free rate is called the market _____.
6. The risks of investing in common stocks can be reduced by _____.
7. Projects with the same risks as Standard & Poor's 500 Index should be evaluated with a discount rate equal to the _____ plus the normal risk premium for the market portfolio.
8. Over the last 50 years the average annual _____ of the return on the market portfolio has been about 21 percent.
9. The _____ of the market as a whole is 1.0.
10. The _____ is the square of the standard deviation.
11. _____ measures the risk a stock adds to a well-diversified portfolio.
12. The model which relates expected return to risk (measured in terms of beta) is called the _____.
13. According to the CAPM, the expected returns from all investments must plot along the _____ line.
14. The capital asset pricing model implies that the risk premium from any stock is equal to its beta multiplied by the _____.
15. The principle of _____ means that PV(AB) = PV(A) + PV(B). It implies that firms cannot expect to increase their value by just diversifying.

Problems

1. A firm is considering a new machine which costs $24,000 and which will directly save a net cash amount of $10,000 each year for 3 years. The firm has no other projects to consider. The funds would be obtained by selling Treasury bills, currently yielding 9 percent, which are owned by the firm. Assuming that the risk of this project is the same as that of the market portfolio, should the firm purchase the machine? (Use a historical average for the market risk premium).

2. A portfolio of stocks has risks similar to a portfolio consisting 30 percent of treasury bills and 70 percent of Standard & Poor's Index. The Treasury bill rate is 10 percent, and you expect a normal risk premium of 9 percent on Standard & Poor's Index. What return would you expect from the portfolio of stocks?

3. Your investment will give a return of either -10 or +30 percent (a) Calculate the expected return and the standard deviation of return if these outcomes are equally likely. (b) Calculate them if there is a 0.6 probability of the -10 percent return and a 0.4 probability of the +30 percent return.

4. A portfolio consists of the following stocks:

STOCK	PERCENTAGE OF PORTFOLIO	EXPECTED RETURN, %	BETA
Stock A	10	18	0.9
Stock B	30	22	1.3
Stock C	25	24	1.5
Stock D	20	17	0.8
Stock E	15	21	1.2

Calculate the expected return and the beta of this portfolio.

5. The diagram below shows the effect of diversification. Fill in the appropriate words for the labels at A, B, C, and D.

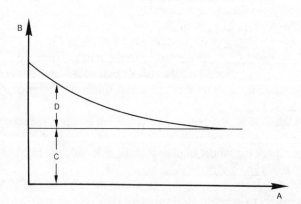

6. What are the betas of the following stocks?

STOCK	EXPECTED RETURN, %, IF MARKET RETURN IS -10%	EXPECTED RETURN, %, IF MARKET RETURN IS 20%
A	-13	20
B	- 7	17
C	- 9	21
D	-17	25

7. Calculate the expected returns on stocks with the following betas: (a) 0.5, (b) 1.0, (c) 2.0. Take the risk-free rate to be 9 percent and the expected return on the market portfolio to be 18 percent.

8. If stock Z has a beta of 0.8 and an expected return of 16 percent, and stock Y has a beta of 1.5 and an expected return of 23 percent, what must be (a) the expected return on the market; and (b) the risk-free rate of return, to be consistent with the capital asset pricing model?

9. What do you estimate are the expected returns investors require today for stocks with (a) beta of 0.5, and (b) betas of 1.5?

10. The capital asset pricing model is often stated in the alternative form:

$$r = \alpha + \beta r_m$$

where r is the expected return on a stock and r_m is the expected return on the market. (a) If α is zero, what must beta be? (b) What must α be if beta equals 2? (c) What must α be if beta equals zero? (d) Give a general expression for α.

Essay Questions

1. Describe how diversification can reduce the risk in an investment portfolio. Why can risk only be reduced and not eliminated in this way?

2. Describe what is meant by the beta of a stock. Why is a stock's beta more important than its standard deviation?

3. Describe what sort of characteristics are likely to be possessed by a company with a high standard deviation but a low beta.

4. Stockholders of publicly quoted companies do not benefit from corporate diversification, since they can diversify for themselves. Discuss under what conditions (if any) this principle extends to the case of a privately held company which is 100 percent owned by a single individual.

ANSWERS TO EXERCISES

Fill-in Questions

1. market
2. market return
3. market risk

4. unique risk
5. expected market return; risk premium
6. diversification
7. risk-free rate
8. standard deviation
9. beta
10. variance
11. beta
12. capital asset pricing model
13. security market
14. market risk premium
15. value additivity

Problems

1. Discount rate = risk-free rate + risk premium

$$= 9 \text{ percent} + 8.4 \text{ percent}$$
$$= 17.4 \text{ percent}$$

Net present value = $2046.60; reject the project

2. 16.3 percent

3. (a) Expected return: 10 percent; standard deviation of expected return: 20 percent;
   (b) expected return: 6 percent; standard deviation of expected return: 19.6 percent

4. Expected return: 20.95 percent; beta: 1.195

5. A: number of securities; B: portfolio standard deviation; C: market risk; D: unique risk

6. A: 1.1; B: 0.8; C: 1.0; D: 1.4

7. (a) 13.5 percent; (b) 18 percent; (c) 27 percent

8. (a) 18 percent; (b) 8 percent

9. (a) Treasury bill rate plus 4.2 percent; (b) Treasury bill rate plus 12.6 percent

10. (a) 1; (b) $-r_f$; (c) r_f; (d) $\alpha = (1 - \beta) r_f$

CHAPTER 8
MORE ABOUT THE RELATIONSHIP
BETWEEN RISK AND RETURN

INTRODUCTION

This chapter continues the development of the ideas introduced in Chapter 7. By considering how individual investors should choose sensible portfolios, it succeeds in putting the capital asset pricing model on firmer foundations.

WHAT TO LOOK FOR IN CHAPTER 8

This chapter builds on the ideas about risk and return that were introduced in Chapter 7. Make sure you remember what standard deviations and betas are before you start Chapter 8. The capital asset pricing model is developed in three stages.

Efficient Portfolios: The first stage is the idea of efficient portfolios. This is quite an easy concept to grasp. Most investors want a high expected return and prefer a low standard deviation of return. Portfolios that give the highest possible return for a given standard deviation are called *efficient*. Investors need only consider efficient portfolios, for all other portfolios give them a poor deal.

You may wonder if it's reasonable to assume that an investor can choose between portfolios solely on the basis of their expected return and standard deviations. The answer to this is that it usually *is* a reasonable assumption. Every portfolio has a different probability distribution of possible future returns, and the investor has to choose between them. In most cases the investor can reasonably regard the future return from any portfolio as coming from a normal distribution. This means that the whole distribution of possible returns is completely defined by the expected return and the standard deviation, so they are the *only* two measures which the investor need consider.

The chapter describes how the expected return and standard deviation of a portfolio may be calculated from the characteristics of the individual stocks. It also describes how we can calculate the risk a particular stock adds to an incompletely diversified portfolio. Our last worked example will give you an opportunity to review these calculations. If these seem rather too complicated for your taste, the chapter also gives the following useful rule of thumb guide to the benefits of diversification. The variance of a portfolio consisting of equal holdings on N stocks is equal to

$$\text{Average covariance} + (1/N)(\text{average variance - average covariance})$$

Typically, the average variance of annual returns on individual stocks is about 1500, and the average covariance between pairs of stocks is about 400. As N becomes large, the variance of the portfolio returns comes down toward the average covariance of 400. The standard deviation of the returns from a portfolio is simple the square root of their variance.

The Opportunity Set: The second stage in the argument is to introduce the possibility of lending or borrowing at a single risk-free rate, r_f. The effect of this is to present the investor with investment opportunities whose expected returns and standard deviations plot along a straight line. The portfolios along this line represent combinations of lending or borrowing with investment in a single risky portfolio S.

The investor's job can be *separated* into two parts: first to choose the best (risky) portfolio of stocks S, and second to combine it with the right amount of lending or borrowing to adjust its risk. In a competitive market there is no reason to concentrate portfolios in particular stocks, and we can identify S as the market portfolio.

The Capital Asset Pricing Model: In the final stage of the argument, the standard deviation is replaced by beta in a relationship for expected return which holds for all stocks. Remember that the *characteristic line* of a stock shows how its return depends on the return on the market index. The slope of this line is the stock's beta. The *security market line* (or *market line* for short) shows how expected return depends on beta (under the CAPM). In order to lie on the security market line, a stock with a given ß must have an expected risk premium of exactly $ß(r_m - r_f)$.

No stock can lie below the market line if it is to be as attractive as a combination of the market portfolio plus lending and borrowing. When any two stocks (such as P and Q below) are combined, the portfolio they form is on the straight line between them (e.g., at R). The combination of all stocks together has to be the market portfolio, and not some point above it. The only way this can happen is if *all* the stocks individually lie on the market line.

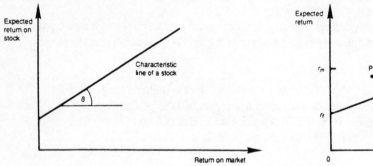 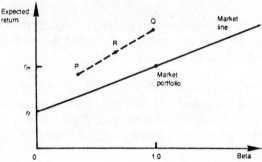

WORKED EXAMPLES

PROBLEM 1: EXPECTED RETURN AND RISK OF A PORTFOLIO
Calculate the standard deviation and expected return for the portfolio given below and work out how each stock contributes to the portfolio's risk.

| STOCK | PERCENTAGE HELD | EXPECTED RETURN, % | STANDARD DEVIATION | CORRELATIONS BETWEEN STOCKS | | |
				STOCK 1	STOCK 2	STOCK 3
Stock 1	50	10	20	1.0	0.5	0.3
Stock 2	30	15	30	0.5	1.0	0.1
Stock 3	20	20	40	0.3	0.1	1.0

SOLUTION
To work out the standard deviations of a portfolio we need information on the covariances between stocks. In this example we are given the *correlations* between stocks. We can work out the covariances σ_{ij} from the standard deviations σ_i and the correlations ρ_{ij} as $\sigma_{ij} = \sigma_i\sigma_j\rho_{ij}$. This gives the following table of covariances:

STOCK	STOCK 1	STOCK 2	STOCK 3		S 1	S 2	S 3
Stock 1	20 x 20 x 1.0	20 x 30 x 0.5	20 x 40 x 0.3	=	400	300	240
Stock 2	30 x 20 x 0.5	30 x 30 x 1.0	30 x 40 x 0.1	=	300	900	120
Stock 3	40 x 20 x 0.3	40 x 30 x 0.1	40 x 40 x 1.0	=	240	120	1600

Notice that this table is symmetric about the diagonal (that is, $\sigma_{12} = \sigma_{21}$, $\sigma_{13} = \sigma_{31}$, etc.). This symmetry is also preserved when we calculate the variance of portfolio returns using a similar table:

Portfolio variance =

$$
\begin{aligned}
&0.5 \times 0.5 \times 400 + 0.5 \times 0.3 \times 300 + 0.5 \times 0.2 \times 240 && = 100 + 45 + 24 \\
&+ 0.3 \times 0.5 \times 300 + 0.3 \times 0.3 \times 900 + 0.3 \times 0.2 \times 120 && + 45 + 81 + 7.2 \\
&+ 0.2 \times 0.5 \times 240 + 0.2 \times 0.3 \times 120 + 0.2 \times 0.2 \times 1600 && + 24 + 7.2 + 64
\end{aligned}
$$

$$= 169 + 133.2 + 95.2 \qquad\qquad = 397.4$$

Since the variance of the portfolio's returns is 397.4, its standard deviation is just the square root of this, which is 19.9 percent.

The expected return on the portfolio is the weighted average:

$$0.5 \times 10 + 0.3 \times 15 + 0.2 \times 20 = 13.5 \text{ percent}$$

The sum of each row in the variance calculation shows how much each stock contributes to the total variance, i.e., $169 + 133.2 + 95.2 = 397.4$. To get the proportional contribution of each stock to the variance we must divide each by the percentage held and the portfolio's variance. This gives

$$
\begin{aligned}
\beta_1 &= \sigma_{1p}/\sigma^2_p = 169/(0.5 \times 397.4) &= 0.85 \\
\beta_2 &= \sigma_{2p}/\sigma^2_p = 133.2/(0.3 \times 397.4) &= 1.12 \\
\beta_3 &= \sigma_{3p}/\sigma^2_p = 95.2/(0.2 \times 397.4) &= 1.20
\end{aligned}
$$

(Note that these are betas with respect to this portfolio and not the market.)

PROBLEM 2: EFFICIENT PORTFOLIOS UNDER BORROWING AND LENDING
Portfolios A, B, and C have the following expected returns and standard deviations:

PORTFOLIO	EXPECTED RETURN	STANDARD DEVIATION
A	19%	30%
B	16%	20%
C	13%	15%

Over what range of values of the risk-free interest rate might each one be an efficient portfolio?

66

SOLUTION
The line AB meets the vertical axis at 10 percent. The line BC meets it at 4 percent.

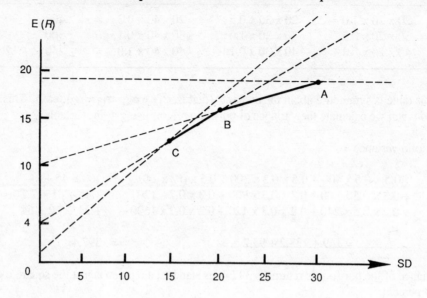

The figure shows clearly that:

Portfolio A can only be efficient for an interest rate above 10 percent: otherwise it is dominated by B or C plus borrowing.

Portfolio B can only be efficient for interest rates between 4 percent and 10 percent: otherwise it is dominated by A plus lending or by C plus borrowing.

Portfolio C can only be efficient for an interest rate below 4 percent: otherwise it is dominated by A or B plus lending.

SUMMARY

Portfolio Theory

Expected Returns and Standard Deviation: The returns on stocks over short periods of time conform closely to the bell-shaped normal distribution. A normal distribution is completely defined by two numbers: its expected value and its standard deviation. It is therefore reasonable to assume that investors will choose between portfolios on the basis of their expected return and the standard deviation of return, This much we know: *all* investors want high expected returns; and *all* investors who dislike uncertainty want a low standard deviation.

Efficient Portfolios: Portfolios which give the lowest possible standard deviation for a given expected return are called *efficient portfolios*. Markowitz introduced the idea of efficient portfolios in 1952, and he showed how they can be calculated by a method called *quadratic programming*.

How to Calculate the Expected Return and Risk: The *expected return* from holding a portfolio of stocks is a weighted average of the expected returns on the individual stocks. Expected portfolio return $r_p = x_1 r_1 + x_2 r_2 + \ldots + x_N r_N$, where x_1 = proportion of portfolio in stock 1, r_1 = expected return on stock 1, etc.

We *cannot* calculate the standard deviation of portfolio returns as a weighted average of the individual standard deviations (unless they are perfectly correlated). Rather

$$\text{Portfolio variance} = x_1^2\sigma_1^2 + x_1x_2\sigma_{12} + \ldots + x_1x_N\sigma_{1N}$$

$$+ x_2x_1\sigma_{21} + x_2^2\sigma_2^2 + \ldots + x_2x_N\sigma_{2N}$$

$$+ x_Nx_1\sigma_{N1} + x_Nx_2\sigma_{N2} + \ldots + x_N^2\sigma_N^2$$

Where σ_1^2 = variance of stock 1 (σ_1 is its standard deviation)

σ_{12} = covariance between stock 1 and stock 2

$= \sigma_1\sigma_2\rho_{12}$, where ρ_{12} is the correlation between stock 1 and stock 2

Where there are N equal-sized holdings (so $x_t = 1/N$),

$$\text{Portfolio variance} = (1/N)^2 [N \times \text{average variance} + (N^2 - N) \times \text{average covariance}]$$

$$= \text{average covariance} + 1/N \times [\text{average variance - covariance}]$$

A Security's Contribution to Portfolio Risk: From the top row f the portfolio variance calculation:

$$\text{Stock 1's contribution to risk} = + x_1(x_1\sigma_1^2 + x_2\sigma_{12} + \ldots + x_N\sigma_{1N})$$

$$= x_1\sigma_1 p$$

$$\text{Proportionate contribution to risk} = \frac{x_1\sigma_1 p}{\sigma p^2}$$

where $\sigma_1 p$ is its covariance with the portfolio, and σp^2 is the variance of the portfolio.

$\sigma_i p/\sigma p^2$ is the sensitivity of stock 1 to changes in portfolio value. Since $\sigma_{iM}/\sigma_M^2 = $ beta, beta measures a stock's contribution to the risk of the market portfolio.

Borrowing and Lending: We suppose investors can borrow or lend at a single riskless rate r_f. The following graph applies:

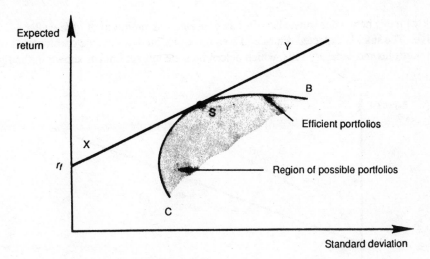

The key concepts are:

1. Combinations of portfolio *S* and lending (along *XS*), and of portfolio *S* and borrowing (along *SY*) are now preferred to other efficient portfolios (along *CSB*).

2. The composition of the portfolio *S* of common stocks does not depend on the investor's attitude toward risk.

3. Investors who are the most willing to bear risk invest farthest to the right along the line *XY*.

4. In a competitive market every investor will hold the same portfolio *S*, so *S* is the market portfolio!

5. This makes the CAPM easy to understand since a stock's beta measures its contribution to the risk of everybody's portfolio!

Capital Asset Pricing Model

The Logic of the CAPM:

1. An investor can construct a portfolio with any given beta and no unique risk by investing a proportion ß in the market portfolio and $(1 - ß)$ in Treasury bills. This portfolio has expected return

$$r = r_m ß + (1 - ß) r_f$$

$$= r_f + ß(r_m - r_f)$$

Its expected risk premium is

$$r - r_f = ß(r_m - r_f)$$

Any such portfolio lies on the security market line.

2. A stock with this beta value must also offer an expected risk premium of *at least* $ß(r_m - r_f)$ to be attractive. The stock's expected return and beta must plot on or above the combination of the market portfolio and Treasury bills, which determines the market line, as shown in the figure below.

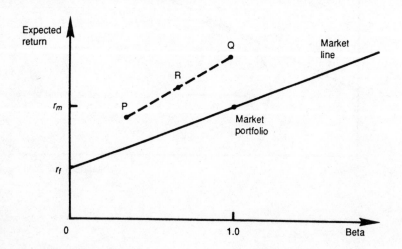

3. Adding all stocks together gives the market portfolio. No stock can have a risk premium *greater* than $\beta(r_m - r_f)$, for this would make the market risk premium greater than $(r_m - r_f)$.

4. The above argument shows that the risk premium for any stock must be at least $\beta(r_m - r_f)$, but no greater. That is,

$$r_m - r_f = \beta(r_m - r_f) \quad \text{for every stock}$$

Limitations of the CAPM: As with any model, the CAPM is a simplified statement of reality. Most people agree however, that: (1) investors require some extra return for taking on risk, and (2) investors are principally concerned with risk they cannot eliminate by diversification.

Empirical Tests of the CAPM: As with all models, the CAPM has been tested for its correspondence with reality. Remember, however, the CAPM is a theory about *expected* returns. We can only measure *actual* returns. This makes it difficult to test. Nonetheless, Fama and Macbeth grouped all New York Stock Exchange stocks into 20 portfolios with different betas. The estimated betas of these portfolios gave a partial explanation of their average returns over a subsequent 5-year period. This evidence is broadly consistent with the CAPM. But one major pitfall remains: the market portfolio should include all risky investments; most market indexes are only a sample of common stocks.

Assumptions of the CAPM: The CAPM captures these ideas in a conveniently simple way. But there are four important assumptions behind the CAPM.

1. Investors are only interested in the expected return and standard deviation of their investments. This implies that they will be content to invest in a mixture of Treasury bills and the market portfolio.

2. The return from Treasury bills is assumed to be risk-free. This ignores the risk of uncertain inflation.

3. Borrowing costs are the same as lending costs.

4. Generality of the CAPM: as long as investors are content to hold a limited number of benchmark portfolios, the expected return on any stock can be expressed in terms of the expected returns on these benchmarks.

*Arbitrage Pricing Theory: If each stock's return depends on several factors:

$$\text{Return} = a + b_1 \text{ (factor 1)} + b_2 \text{ (factor 2)} + \ldots$$

then its risk premium depends on the factor weights:

$$\text{Risk premium} = \text{expected } (r - r_f)$$

$$= b_1 \times \text{premium}_1 + b_2 \times \text{premium}_2 + \ldots$$

Ross (1976) showed that (given his assumptions) this relationship is necessary to present arbitrage opportunities occurring in the market.

LIST OF TERMS

Arbitrage   Expected risk premium
Arbitrage Pricing Theory   Markowitz
Characteristic line   Normal distribution
Correlation   Portfolio selection
Covariance   Quadratic programming
Efficient portfolios   Standard deviation
Expected return

EXERCISES

Fill-in Questions

1. When measured over fairly short time periods, the rates of return on almost any stock conform closely to a _____ distribution.

2. A portfolio which gives the highest expected return for a given standard deviation is called an

   _____.

3. _____ programming can be used to calculate efficient portfolios.

4. The idea of efficient portfolios was first described by _____ in 1952 in a famous paper on _____.

5. A normal distribution is completely defined by the _____ and the

   _____.

6. The variability of a well-diversified portfolio depends almost entirely on the average _____ between individual stocks.

7. The covariance between two stocks is the product of their standard deviations and the _____ coefficient between them.

8. The difference between the expected return on a stock and the risk-free rate is its

   _____.

9. The _____ line of stock shows how its expected return is affected by the return on the market portfolio.

*10. The simultaneous sale and purchase of equivalent securities for an immediate profit is called

   _____.

*11. The _____ holds that the risk premium on any asset is linearly related to its exposure to each of a number of risky factors.

Problems

1. Which one of each of the following pairs of portfolios would an investor be most likely to choose:
   a. Portfolio A: expected return 14 percent, variance 400.
      Portfolio B: expected return 13 percent, variance 441.
   b. Portfolio J: expected return 20 percent, variance 529.
      Portfolio K: expected return 20 percent, variance 400.
   c. Portfolio R: expected return 8 percent, variance 225.
      Portfolio S: expected return 9 percent, variance 225.
   d. Portfolio X: expected return 12 percent, variance 380.
      Portfolio Y: expected return 15 percent, variance 460.

2. Label the important features (A to G) of this diagram:

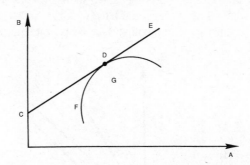

3. Your broker is urging you to invest in one of three portfolios on which the returns are expected to be: Portfolio A; 12 percent, portfolio B: 16 percent, Portfolio C: 20 percent. You believe these estimates, but you also have sufficient data to calculate the betas of the portfolios with confidence. You find the betas are 0.5 for A, 1.1 for B, and 2.0 for C. Which portfolio is best and why?

4. The average variance of the annual returns from a typical stock is about 1500 and its average covariance with other stocks is about 400. Work out what this implies for the standard deviation of returns from: (a) a fully diversified portfolio, (b) a portfolio of 64 stocks, (c) a portfolio of 16 stocks, (d) a portfolio of 4 stocks. Assume equal-sized holdings of each stock.

*5. You hold a portfolio of 16 stocks, each of which has a variance of 1500 and a covariance of 400 with the other stocks. One stock comprises 25 percent of your portfolio, and the other stocks are held in equal amounts of 5 percent each. (a) What is the standard deviation of your portfolio? (b) How many stocks held in equal amounts would give approximately the same standard deviation?

*6. Two stocks have standard deviations of 10 and 30 percent. A portfolio consisting of these stocks held in equal proportions has a standard deviation of 16 percent. (a) Guess how correlated the two stocks are, and (b) calculate the coefficient of correlation between them.

7. Stock A has an expected return of 15 percent and a standard deviation of 30 percent. Stock B has an expected return of 17.5 percent and a standard deviation of 35 percent. The correlation between them is 0.3. (a) Calculate the expected return and the standard deviation of the following four portfolios:

PORTFOLIO	PERCENTAGE IN A	PERCENTAGE IN B
1	20	80
2	40	60
3	60	40
4	80	20

(b) If the risk-free rate is 8 percent, which one of these four portfolios is the best?

8. Can a security have a negative expected rate of return and still be correctly priced? What sort of beta would it have?

72

9. The following diagram shows several characteristic lines. Name the line that goes with each of the investments listed. (a) Standard & Poor's Index, (b) short-term government securities, (c) a high-beta stock, (d) a stock which is negatively correlated with the market, and (e) a mutual fund whose performance is not sufficiently good to recoup all the costs of its transactions.

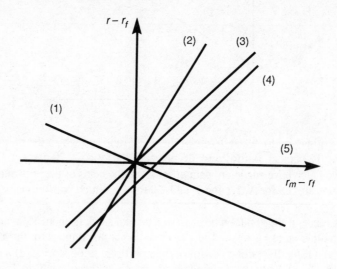

Essay Questions

1. Describe the concept of efficient portfolios. What assumptions does it rest on?

2. Some investors are prepared to take bigger risks than others. Explain why they still may all be content to invest in the same portfolio of common stocks.

3. Explain the difference between a stock's characteristic line and the market line.

4. Explain why the expected return on any security depends solely on its sensitivity to market movements and is unaffected by its unique risk.

ANSWERS TO EXERCISES

Fill-in Questions

1. normal
2. efficient portfolio
3. quadratic
4. Markowitz; portfolio selection
5. expected return; standard deviation
6. covariance
7. correlation
8. expected risk premium
9. characteristic
10. arbitrage
11. arbitrage pricing theory

Problems

1. (a) A; (b) K; (c) S; (d) One cannot tell unless the investor's utility function--how she feels about the trade-off between risk and expected return--is known.

2. *A* is the standard deviation of expected returns; *B* is expected returns; *C* is the risk-free rate of return; *D* is the market portfolio; *E* is the capital market line; *F* is the set of efficient portfolios; and *G* is the feasible set of portfolios.

3. Portfolio B seems to offer the best value. If we combine 60 percent of A with 40 percent of C, we obtain a portfolio with the same beta as B, but with an expected return of only 15.2 percent.

4. Variance = $400 + 1100/N$, giving standard deviations of (a) 20 percent; (b) 20.43 percent; (c) 21.65 percent; (d) 25.98 percent.

5. (a) Variance = 510, giving standard deviation = 22.58 percent. (b) We want to find N such that $400 + 1100/N = 510$, so $N = 10$.

6. (b) Variance = $256 = 250 + 150\rho$, so $\rho = 0.04$.

7. (a)

PORTFOLIO	EXPECTED RETURN, %	STANDARD DEVIATION, %	EXCESS RETURN PER UNIT OF RISK
1	17.0	30.34	0.2966
2	16.5	27.13	0.3133
3	16.0	25.91	0.3088
4	15.5	26.94	0.2784

(b) Portfolio 2, because the excess return per unit of risk is greatest. The numbers are derived in this way: $(r_p - r_f)/\sigma_p$, where r_p is the expected return on the portfolio, r_f is the risk-free rate of return, and σ_p is the standard deviation of the portfolio.

8. Yes, provided its marginal contribution to the portfolio is overall positive. How can that be? By having a negative beta, of all things. Negative betas are to be prized because the stocks that have them are negatively correlated with the market and almost all other stocks. Negatively correlated stocks tend to reduce portfolio risk considerably. If stocks with negative betas also have negative expected returns, chances are the reduction in portfolio risk is expected to be greater than the reduction in portfolio expected return, thereby rendering them attractive investments.

9. (a) 3; (b) 5; (c) 2; (d) 1; (e) 4

CHAPTER 9
CAPITAL BUDGETING AND THE CAPITAL
ASSET PRICING MODEL

INTRODUCTION

Chapter 9 applies the theory of risk and return, developed in Chapters 7 and 8, to the practical problem of measuring the opportunity cost of capital for an investment project. The return required on a project depends on the nature of the project, rather than on which company undertakes it. Nevertheless, we may still want to know what return is expected from the securities of a company: from this we can work out what return is required from projects whose risks are similar to those of the company's existing business. Riskier projects should have a higher cutoff rate, and safer projects a lower cutoff rate.

To work out the expected return on a company's stock, we estimate its beta. It is often best to calculate the beta for a group of similar companies instead of for a single company. To get the required rate of return on the investment in an average project, we must take into account any borrowings of the company: these will have increased the beta of the company's stock. Finally, the general nature of a new project is sufficient to tell us something about its probable riskiness. The projects which are most likely to have high betas and high required rates of return are the ones whose earnings are cyclical (depend on the state of the business cycle) or which have high fixed costs.

WHAT TO LOOK FOR IN CHAPTER 9

The Cost of Capital: The first section of Chapter 9 describes an apparent paradox. Many companies estimate the rate of return required by investors in their securities and use this "company cost of capital" as the discount rate for evaluating new projects. Different companies have different costs of capital and would therefore use different discount rates even for identical projects. However, we also know that as long as the cash flows from a project don't depend on which company owns it, then neither does its value. A given project is worth the same amount to all firms, and all firms should apply the same required rate of return in appraising it. The correct discount rate for a capital investment project depends solely on the risks associated with that project and not on which company happens to undertake it.

Why then do we describe how to estimate the cost of capital *of a company* if the cost of capital for a project is something different? The answer to this is that *we don't have* a way to estimate the required return on a project directly, and so we have to make do with a second best approach. Once we know what return security holders require a company to earn on its total assets, this tells us what return is required on a typical investment by the company. Clearly a higher return will be required from projects with higher systematic risk (beta) than is typical. Conversely, a lower return will be required on less risky projects.

Estimating Beta for a Project: We saw in the last two chapters that the required rate of return for a project depends on its systematic risk, and that this is measured by its beta. The problem of choosing a suitable discount rate for a project therefore amounts to working out what sort of beta it has. We cannot do this directly (as individual investment projects don't have prices quoted daily on the New York Stock Exchange); so we must do the best we can by looking at the betas of companies.

74

The beta of a company's stock measures how its price responds to market movements. You could estimate this beta by plotting monthly returns on the stock against monthly returns on the market index, and fitting a line through the scatter of points. The slope of this line gives you the beta of the stock. Alternatively you can just go to a published "beta book" and look up someone else's estimate. "Beta books" are published regularly by a number of brokerage and advisory services. The Merrill Lynch one described in the chapter is fairly typical of the sort of information you can get from such services.

The beta book gives an estimate of the beta of every stock that has traded regularly, and it gives some other information as well. The most useful of this additional information is probably the column giving the standard error of beta. We can never know exactly what the "true" beta of a stock is. We can only estimate what it appears to be from its price behavior in the past. Our estimates could never be perfect even if betas never changed through time (which they do). The standard error tells us how much confidence we can put in a particular estimate. For example, the estimated beta of Diebold Inc. is 0.72 and its standard error is 0.26. This means that if the true beta really is 0.72, then two-thirds of the time we should have expected to have estimated a beta within plus or minus 0.26 of this, i.e., between 0.46 and 0.98. Similarly 95 percent of the time we should have estimated beta within plus or minus two standard errors, i.e., between 0.20 and 1.24. We cannot even be entirely confident that its beta is less than one.

As you see, the standard error of the beta of a single company can be uncomfortably high. This is because a lot of its price movements are unrelated to the movements of the market as a whole. There is a broad scatter of points around the line we have to fit to estimate beta, and so we cannot be very confident as to exactly what the slope of this line ought to be. Fortunately, we can estimate the beta of an entire industry with much more precision than we can estimate the beta of an individual stock. The errors in our estimates for individual companies tend to cancel themselves out. If we average the betas of N stocks to get the beta of a particular industry sector, then as a rule of thumb we will have to multiply the standard error by a factor of about $1/\sqrt{N}$. For example, if we took 50 stocks with standard errors of their betas of 0.21, the standard error of the average beta would be only about $0.21/\sqrt{50} = 0.03$. In most cases, then, a beta calculated for an industry group will provide a more accurate yardstick for the beta of a project than could be obtained by looking at a single company.

Adjusting Beta for Borrowing: One further problem remains. The betas we have described so far measure the risk of a company's shares. However, what we want to measure is the risk of its assets, which may be financed by debt as well as by equity (shares). In other words, since the value of the company's assets must equal that of its liabilities, we can write (in terms of market values)

Value of assets = value of equity + value of debt.

If the value of the assets is divided between shareholders and debtholders, the risk of the assets must also be divided between them. Remember that betas can be averaged in a very simple way. If I invest two-thirds of my portfolio in a stock with a beta of 1.2 and I invest the other third in a stock with a beta of 0.3, the beta of my portfolio is

$$(2/3 \times 1.2) + (1/3 \times 0.3) = 0.9$$

We can regard the beta of the company's assets in a similar way. The assets are partly equity and partly debt, and the beta of the assets is an average of the beta of the equity and the beta of the debt (weighted according to their market values). Thus:

$$\beta_{assets} = \beta_{equity} \times \frac{equity}{debt + equity} + \beta_{debt} \times \frac{debt}{debt + equity}$$

The beta of debt is usually very close to zero; so a company with high-beta shares may have low-beta assets (and a low cost of capital) if it has a lot of debt. It is therefore quite important to be able to make this adjustment when working out required rates of return. The worked example provides a further illustration of the procedure.

Estimating Beta Without a Beta Book: The third section of the chapter discusses how to estimate the beta (and hence the discount rate) for a project, when price data for estimating beta are unavailable. This involves an understanding of what determines whether a particular asset has a high or a low beta. Remember here to distinguish between systematic and unique risk. The question is not simply what makes an asset's future earnings uncertain. What matters is the extent to which abnormally low earnings are likely to coincide with low earnings in the economy as a whole. For example, the returns from the shares of gold mines are very risky, but they tend to fair remarkably well when everything else is doing badly, a fact born out by the classic market report on the radio newscast: "Gold drifted lower today, because of the absence of bad news." Gold stocks have low betas. On the other hand, companies with cyclical earnings, which are strongly dependent on the state of the business cycle, tend to have high betas. When a company has a high beta, this usually means that its earnings are very variable. This is often the case with companies that have high fixed costs. The high level of fixed costs produces a leverage effect which makes profits particularly vulnerable: a small percentage change in revenues will produce a much larger percentage change in profits. Companies with high fixed costs (often called high operating leverage) tend to have high betas.

Another Look At Discounted Cash Flow: The earlier parts of the chapter have concentrated on how we may estimate the beta of a project. Once we know this beta, we normally use it to calculate the project's opportunity cost of capital by means of our capital asset pricing model formula:

$$r = r_f + \beta(r_m - r_f)$$

The expected cash flows C_t are then discounted at this rate to give the project's net present value:

$$NPV = \sum_{t=0}^{r} \frac{C_t}{(1+r)^t}$$

This final section of the chapter reveals an alternative method of taking the risk of a project into account in evaluating it. Instead of adding a risk premium to the risk-free rate, as long as we make appropriate adjustments to the cash flows, we may discount at the risk-free rate. Given any uncertain cash flow C_t, there must be some fixed cash flow which investors find equally attractive. This is called a certainty-equivalent cash flow CEQ_t. If we replace expected cash flows by the corresponding certainty equivalents, we can discount at the risk-free rate. The Appendix shows how this approach can also be derived from the capital asset pricing model.

Comparison of the two methods reveals that the earlier procedure implies risk increases at a constant rate as you look further out into the future: a constant r is consistent with your more distant forecasts being less certain than your near ones. A constant r is therefore *not* appropriate when much more uncertainty will be encountered in some periods than others.

WORKED EXAMPLE

PROBLEM: ADJUSTING BETA FOR FINANCIAL LEVERAGE
You want to know the cost of capital of your construction company. You find that the average beta of a group of similar construction companies is 1.32 and that their average debt-equity ratio is 0.20. Your company has a debt-equity ratio of 0.30. If the risk-free rate is 12 percent and the expected risk premium on the market portfolio is 9 percent, what is:

1. The required return on the assets of the company?
2. The required return on the shares of the company?

SOLUTION

1. The average beta of the shares of the other construction companies is 1.32 but, because of their financial leverage (debt), this overstates the beta of their assets. We know that

$$\beta_{assets} = \beta_{equity} \; x \; \frac{equity}{debt + equity} \; + \; \beta_{debt} \; x \; \frac{debt}{debt + equity}$$

So if $\beta_{debt} = 0$ (which is likely, at least as an approximation), then

$$\beta_{assets} = 1.32 \; x \; 1/1.2 = 1.10$$

The required rate of return on the *assets* (i.e., the cost of capital of the firm) is therefore 12 percent + (1.1 x 9 percent) = 21.9 percent.

2. Rearranging the earlier equation and assuming $\beta_{debt} = 0$, we have

$$\beta_{equity} = \beta_{assets} \; x \; \frac{debt + equity}{equity}$$

For your construction company this gives

$$\beta_{equity} = 1.1 \; x \; 1.3 = 1.43$$

The required rate of return on the *shares* of your company is therefore

$$12 \; percent + (1.43 \; x \; 9 \; percent) \; = \; 24.87 \; percent$$

SUMMARY

The Company Cost of Capital: Many companies discount cash flows at the company's cost of capital, that is, at the rate of return required by investors on its securities. The true cost of capital depends on the use to which the capital is put. The discount rate should depend on the beta of the project and is determined by $r = r_f + \beta(r_m - r_f)$. The use of a single discount rate for all projects means that too many high-risk projects (and too few low-risk ones) will be accepted. We need to be able to estimate the betas of individual projects. This is a difficult problem, but one that won't go away.

Measuring Beta: The beta of a stock can be estimated by fitting a line through its (monthly) rates of return plotted against the corresponding returns on the market index. The slope of the line is the stock's beta. The line may be fitted by least-squares regression analysis.

Betas estimated in one period, however, are imperfect guides to the future, because the actual beta may change through time and there is an estimation error. Beta estimates are not exact; so fine distinctions between stocks are not possible. The errors tend to cancel out when you estimate the beta of a portfolio: the betas of portfolios can be estimated much more accurately than the betas of individual stocks.

Some brokerage and advisory services publish estimates of beta and other statistical information. For example, the Merrill Lynch "beta book" provides:

1. Beta: the regression-analysis estimate of beta.
2. Alpha: the intercept of the fitted regression line.
3. *R* squared: the proportion of the variance of price changes explained by market movements.
4. Residual standard deviation: the standard deviation of the unique risk of the stock.

5. Standard errors of beta and alpha: measures of the probable accuracy of these estimates.
6. Adjusted beta: the earlier estimate adjusted to take account of the effect of estimation errors.

The beta of a portfolio of stocks drawn from a single *industry* is easier to estimate than the beta of a single company. This *industry beta* can provide a useful estimate of the cost of capital for a *division* of a company. The beta of a company is an average of the betas of its various divisions, weighted by their importance.

Adjustment for Financial Leverage: Financial leverage (company borrowing) increases the risk of the common stock. It also increases its expected return. Consequently, the beta of a company's assets is a weighted average of the betas of its securities:

$$\beta_{asset} = \beta_{debt} \left(\frac{debt}{debt + equity} \right) + \beta_{equity} \left(\frac{equity}{debt + equity} \right)$$

It is the asset beta that is relevant to assessing the risk of a capital investment project. The beta of debt is usually very close to zero, which means that:

$$\beta_{asset} = \frac{equity}{debt + equity} \beta_{equity}$$

$$\beta_{equity} = \frac{debt + equity}{equity} \beta_{asset}$$

Choosing a Discount Rate Without a Beta Book: Rather than add fudge factors indiscriminately for any type of risk, it is better to use fundamental considerations to get a rough estimate of beta. No completely satisfactory explanatory theory of betas exists. Although stock or industry betas may be estimated directly they provide only a rough guide to the typical risk in various businesses. Both earnings cyclicity and high operating leverage tend to produce high betas.

Cyclical firms, whose earnings are strongly dependent on the state of the business cycle, tend to have high betas. Variability of earnings can be due to unique risk. A strong relationship between a firm's earnings and aggregate earnings means high market risk. The *accounting beta* or the *cash-flow beta* can be used to measure this.

The cash flow of a company with high fixed costs is very sensitive to changes in revenues, and the company is said to have high *operating leverage*. With financial leverage the fixed costs of debt increase the risk of the operating cash flows and make the asset beta higher:

$$\beta_{asset} = \beta_{revenue} \frac{PV(asset) + PV(fixed\ costs)}{PV(asset)}$$

*Certainty Equivalent Cash Flows: We usually evaluate projects by calculating the NPV of their expected cash flows, which are discounted at a risk-adjusted rate derived from the capital asset pricing model. That is,

$$NPV = \sum_{t=0}^{T} \frac{C_t}{(1+r)^t}$$

where $r = r_f + \beta(r_m - r_f)$

This procedure would be incorrect for a project whose beta is expected to vary through time.

The certain cash flow CEQ_t is the *certainty equivalent* of an uncertain cash flow C_t (which occurs on the same date) if investors are indifferent as to which they receive. Since CEQ_t is certain, it can be discounted at the appropriate risk-free rate; so

$$NPV = \sum_{t=0}^{T} \frac{CEQ_t}{(1+r_f)^t}$$

The certainty equivalent CEQ_t is some fraction a_t of the expected cash flow C_t. The two methods must give the same present value; so

$$NPV = \sum_{t=0}^{T} \frac{CEQ_t}{(1+r_f)^t} = \sum_{t=0}^{T} \frac{C_t}{(1+r)^t}$$

$$= \sum_{t=0}^{T} \frac{C_t}{(1+r_f)^t} \frac{(1+r_f)^t}{(1+r)^t}$$

so $CEQ_t = a_t C_t$

with $a_t = \left(\frac{1+r_f}{1+r} \right)$

By using a constant risk-adjusted discount rate, the manager is assuming that the risk borne per period will be constant. This is appropriate when risk is resolved at a steady rate through time. It implies a larger deduction for risk from late cash flows than from early ones.

It is incorrect to use a constant risk-adjusted discount rate when most of the project's risk is resolved *either* very *early* in the project, *or* very *late* in the project. Take the Vegetron example in which most of the information arrives *during the first year*. The investment of $125,000 will be worth $0 or $1.5 million at the end of a year. Return over the first year will be -100 or +1200 percent. In subsequent years the risk is "normal." Discounting at a constant risk-adjusted rate would have made this project look unattractive. And in the shipowner example, the investment of $100,000 is expected to be worth $138,000 in 2 years' time, which represents an annual compound return of 17.5 percent for 2 years. At the end of the first year the investment is worth $105,000; so its expected return over the second year is 31.4 percent.

LIST OF TERMS

Accounting beta

Alpha

Business risk

Cash flow beta

Certainty equivalent

Company cost of capital

Cyclical

Financial leverage

Financial risk

Industry beta

Operating leverage

Project beta

Residual standard deviation

Risk adjusted rate

EXERCISES

Fill-in Questions

1. The use of the company _____ as a discount rate ignores differences in the risk of projects.
2. The discount rate for evaluating a capital budgeting proposal should be derived from the _____ beta.
3. _____ measures the average rate of price appreciation on a stock in the past, when investors in the market as a whole earned nothing.
4. The _____ of a stock is a measure of its unique risk.
5. When a company raises debt finance, it increases the _____ risk borne by its shareholders.
6. The cost of capital depends on the _____ risk of the firm's investments.
7. Financial risk is produced by _____.
8. Companies with high fixed costs have high _____.
9. A firm whose revenues and earnings are strongly dependent on the state of the business cycle is said to be a _____ firm.
10. We can measure the strength of the relationship between a firm's earnings and the aggregate earnings on real assets by estimating either its _____ beta or its _____.
11. Instead of discounting the expected value of a cash flow, we may discount its _____ at the risk-free rate.
12. The beta of a portfolio of stocks drawn from a single industry is called an _____.

Problems

1. A firm is considering the following projects:

PROJECT	BETA	EXPECTED RETURN, %
A	0.5	12
B	0.8	13
C	1.2	18
D	1.6	19

(a) Which projects have a higher expected return than the firm's 15 percent cost of capital? (b) Which projects should be accepted? (c) Which projects would be accepted or rejected incorrectly on the basis of the cost of capital as a hurdle rate? The Treasury bill rate is 8 percent and the expected market premium is 7 percent.

2. Development Corp America (DVP) has the following characteristics:

Adjusted beta	1.33
Alpha	-0.56% per month
R squared	0.30
Residual standard deviation	9.54% per month

(a) How much did DVP tend to go up in a month in an unchanged market? (b) How much did DVP tend to go up in a month when the market went up 10 percent? (c) How likely would it be for the price of DVP to fall in a month in which the market went up 10 percent? (d) What economic reasons can you give to explain why this company's beta is so high?

3. The following table shows the returns on a mutual fund against the corresponding returns on the market portfolio in successive quarters:

RETURN ON MUTUAL FUND MARKET

QUARTER	1	2	3	4	5	6	7	8	9
	8.9	-3.3	-4.4	7.3	2.1	-6.4	4.9	8.7	1.4
	10.1	-4.3	-5.6	8.2	2.1	-7.9	5.4	9.8	1.2

Plot a graph of these returns and estimate alpha and beta for the fund.

4. Acetate, Inc. has common stock with a market value of $20 million and debt of $10 million. The current Treasury bill rate is 10 percent and the expected market risk premium is also 10 percent. A plot of the returns on the stock against the market returns shows a scatter of points through which a line can be fitted with a slope of 45°. (a) What is Acetate's financial leverage? (b) What is the beta of Acetate's stock? (c) What is the beta of Acetate's assets?

5. Acetate, Inc., of problem 4, now decides to invest in $10 million of additional assets which are similar to its existing assets. It decides to finance this investment by borrowing a further $10 million of debt. (a) What is the beta of the additional assets? (b) What discount rate should be used for these additional assets? (c) What is the beta of Acetate's stock after the debt issue?

6. The market value of the shares of Astrofab Corp. is currently $24 million and their beta is 1.4. Astrofab has a nominal $6 million of 8 percent coupon debentures outstanding which mature in 7 years. These debentures have a beta of 0.1, and they currently yield 10 percent. What is the beta of Astrofab's assets?

7. Other things being equal, which company (from each of the following pairs) do you think should be using the higher discount rate in its capital budgeting: (a) (1) a steel company, (2) a brewing company; (b) (1) a manufacturer of recreational vehicles, (2) a mining company; (c) (1) a company with high operating leverage, (2) a company with high financial leverage; (d) (1) a manufacturer of office equipment, (2) an electric utility company.

*8. A project is expected to generate net cash flows of $1000 in each of years 1 and 2. Its beta will be 1.5 throughout its life. The risk-free interest rate is 10 percent and the expectd return on the market is 18 percent. Calculate (a) the present value of the cash flows, (b) the certainty equivalents of the cash flows, and (c) the ratios of the certainty equivalents to the expected cash flows, (i.e., a_1 and a_2).

*9. Business Aids, Ltd., is investing $2 million in equipment and promotion to launch a new product. Virtually all the uncertainty about the success of this product will be resolved by the end of the first year. Its success depends critically on the climate for business as a whole. The Dow Jones Industrial Average (DJI) stands at 945 as the investment is about to be made, and Business Aids predicts that its net cash flow in year 1 from this product will be 600 ($1000s) less than the level of the index in 12 months' time. They expect this income to amount to $500,000, and whatever income they get in year 1 will continue unchanged for the following 4 years (making 5 years in all). Assuming that the risk-free rates to all maturities are 10 percent, what is the net present value of this project? What is its expected return over the first year? (Ignore the effects of dividends on the return of the DJI.)

Essay Questions

1. Write a short memorandum describing why you think companies can benefit from using the capital asset pricing model to set cutoff criteria for new investment projects.

2. Your company uses the DCF rate of return to appraise new investment projects in the following way: Projects with payback less than 3 years are accepted if their DCF rate of return exceeds 12 percent. Projects with payaback longer than 3 years are accepted if their DCF rate of return exceeds 16 percent. Discuss the advantages and disadvantages of this rule.

3. Describe how you would calculate the cost of capital of a company by estimating its beta.

4. Describe some of the characteristics that tend to be associated with companies whose shares have high betas.

5. Explain the difference between the use of risk-adjusted discount rates and certainty-equivalent cash flows. Give an example of a situation where you think the certainty-equivalent method is preferable.

ANSWER TO EXERCISES

Fill-in Questions

1. cost of capital
2. project
3. alpha
4. residual standard deviation
5. financial
6. business
7. financial leverage
8. operating leverage
9. cyclical
10. accounting; cash-flow beta
11. certainty equivalent
12. industry beta

Problems

1. (a) C, D; (b) A, C; (c) A incorrectly rejected; D incorrectly accepted

2. (a) -0.56 percent; (b) r = -0.56 percent + (10 percent x 1.33) = 12.74 percent; (c) About 9 chances in 100, because a zero return corresponds to 1.34 residual standard deviations below the mean predicted return. The chances of getting a return *lower* than 1.34 standard deviations are about 9 percent. (d) Chances are its earnings are highly cyclical, i.e, they depend crucially on the state of the U.S. economy.

3. The actual alpha is 0.34 and the beta is 0.85, which is roughly what the "eyeballed" graph (Figure 9-1) tells us. The correlation in rates of return is almost perfectly positive, as is obvious from the fit of the scatter to the line. The computed correlation coefficient is 0.999989. We invented this one to make it easy for you!

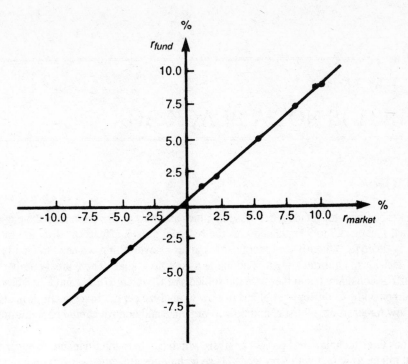

4. (a) 1/3;   (b) 1;   (c) 0.67, assuming beta of debt is zero

5. (a) 0.67;   (b) 16.7 percent;   (c) 1.33

6. Value of debt: market price per bond x 6000 bonds = $902.63 x 6000 = $5,415,790

    Value of equity: $24 million

    Total market value of firm   = value of debt + value of equity
                                 = $5,415,790 + $24,000,000
                                 = $29,415,790

$$\beta_{assets} = \beta_{debt} \left(\frac{debt}{debt + equity} \right) + \beta_{equity} \left(\frac{debt}{debt + equity} \right)$$

$$= 0.1 \left(\frac{\$5,415,790}{\$29,415,790} \right) + 1.4 \left(\frac{\$24,000,000}{\$29,415,790} \right)$$

$$= 1.1607$$

7. (a) 1;   (b) 1;   (c) 1;   (d) 1

8. (a) Using r = 10 percent + (18 percent – 10 percent) 1.5 = 22 percent, PV = $1491.53; (b) Certainty-equivalent cash flows are $901.64 and $812.95; (c) a_1 = 1.1/1.22 = 0.9016 and a_2 = 0.8130.

9. The cash flow in year 1 equals the DJI minus $600,000. Such a cash flow could have been obtained by investing $945,000 in the DJI and by borrowing the present value of $600,000 (i.e., $600,000/1.1) in order to create the $600,000 deduction. The overall investment necessary to do this is $945,000 – ($600,000/1.1) = $399,545, which represents the present value of the first cash flow. Because the interest rate is 10 percent, the certainty-equivalent cash flow is 1.1 x $399,545 = $439,500. This certainty-equivalent cash flow applies in all 5 years, so discounting the $439,500 annuity at 10 percent results in a present value of the cash inflows of $439,500 x 3.791 = $1,666,145 and an NPV of $1,666,145 – $2,000,000 = -$333,856.

CHAPTER 10
A PROJECT IS NOT A BLACK BOX

INTRODUCTION

Chapters 2 to 6 described how to calculate net present values and how to use them to make capital budgeting decisions. Chapters 7 to 9 explained how the risk of a project affects the discount rate that should be used to evaluate it. You might expect that this gives us everything we need to enable us to make capital budgeting decisions. Unfortunately it is not quite as simple as that. There are a number of practical issues that must still be considered, and these are the subjects of Chapters 10, 11, and 12. These three chapters are concerned with the difficult problems of how to analyze capital investment projects, how to ensure that cash-flow forecasts are realistic, and how to organize and control capital expenditures.

Chapter 10 describes three techniques of project analysis which can help the financial manager to think clearly about what might go wrong with a project. These techniques are called sensitivity analysis (which includes break-even analysis as a special case), Monte Carlo simulation, and decision trees.

WHAT TO LOOK FOR IN CHAPTER 10

The general theme of this chapter is given (surprise!) by its title: "A Project is not a black box." If projects *were* black boxes (so we couldn't find out what went on inside them), we would be quite happy to hear our financial manager say: "Well, I put this money in here, and wait a bit, and then if I'm lucky I get so much more out at the other end." Of course, the world isn't like that: we *can* find out what will determine a project's success or failure, and it is part of the financial manager's job to know. The financial manager doesn't simply take a set of cash-flow forecasts out of a convenient file, choose a discount rate, and crank out a net present value. He or she must think about where those cash flows came from, and what can go wrong with them. This chapter describes three important techniques for getting to grips with the key factors that determine the success of a project. Of these, by far the most important is the first one: sensitivity analysis.

Sensitivity Analysis: The idea of sensitivity analysis is an easy one. The NPV of a project was arrived at by combining a number of different forecasts to arrive at after-tax cash flows. The forecasts might include such things as the size of the *total* market for the product, our share of that market, the price we will get for our product, and the amounts of all the various costs involved in producing and distributing it. We can't be sure what the outcome will be for any of these variables. What we can do is work out how much difference it makes if any of these forecasts turns out to be wrong. Each of the forecasts is varied in turn, first to a more optimistic value and second to a more pessimistic one. All the other forecasts are kept unchanged at their original values. The NPV of the project is recalculated under these different assumptions and the results are set out in a table such as the one below, which represents part of Table 10-2 of the text.

	NET PRESENT VALUE ($000,000)		
VARIABLE ALTERED	PESSIMISTIC	EXPECTED	OPTIMISTIC
Market size	11	34	57
Market share	-104	34	173
Unit price	-42	34	50
Unit variable cost	-150	34	111
Fixed cost	4	34	65

Stop and look at this table. What does it show? Clearly, we will have a disaster on our hands if the pessimistic values of the unit variable cost or the market share are realized. On the other hand, it seems to be relatively less important to have an accurate assessment of the total market size or of the project's fixed costs. That's all very well, you may say, but how can the manager benefit from having this information? The answer is that it points out the potential "weak links" in the project, and the manager can now consider actions that might strengthen them. For example, it may be worth investing in a further market survey to reduce the uncertainty about market share: a pessimistic survey would allow the project to be abandoned before any massive expenditure was incurred. Perhaps a different advertising campaign would bolster market share. At the very least management is alerted to the importance of keeping a sharp eye on what happens to market share. Similarly, it is alerted to the crucial nature of its variable costs. Perhaps the uncertainty about these can be reduced by hedging in commodity futures markets, or by an additional design study.

Break-Even Analysis: The manager is likely to want to know how low the expected level of sales will have to be before the NPV of the project falls to zero and the project has no value to the firm. Break-even analysis provides the answer. In the example we looked at just now, the assumptions of the base case were of a NPV of $34 million from sales of 100,000 units. The sensitivity analysis showed that subtracting 10,000 units of sales (by reducing the total market size by 10 percent) reduced the NPV by $23 million (from $34 million to $11 million). To reduce the NPV from $34 million to zero would therefore take a reduction in sales of 34 ÷ 23 x 10,000 = 15,000 units. The break-even level of sales must be 100,000 − 15,000 = 85,000 units.

Notice, though, that many companies calculate break-even on a rather *different basis*: as the level of sales that gives a zero accounting profit. In the example above, accounting profits are made when sales exceed 60,000 units. This level of sales would be *very* unsatisfactory. In fact our sensitivity analysis tells us that if we expect sales at this level, the NPV of the project is $34 million − [$23 million x (40,000/10,000)] = -$58 million.

Scenario Analysis: One drawback to sensitivity analysis is that the company is likely to have to accept a low unit price *just when* its volume of sales is lowest. In other words, altering the variables one at a time ignores the fact that they are usually interrelated. One way around this problem is to look at how the project would fare under a number of different plausible scenarios of the future. Forecasts are made for *all variables* so as to be consistent with a particular view of the world. In the text, for example, the forecasters are asked to consider the effects of an immediate 20 percent rise in the price of oil, and the NPV of the project is recalculated on the resulting assumptions.

Monte Carlo Simulation: Monte Carlo simulation (or simulation for short) may be regarded as a logical extension of the idea of scenario analysis. In scenario analysis we look at a small number of specially chosen scenarios. In simulation we generate a large number of possible scenarios as they might occur if we could keep on winding back time and starting again. This usually involves a computer. The forecaster must specify probability distributions for all the factors that affect the success of the project. The computer then generates random numbers (this is its way of rolling dice) to produce a value for each factor. This provides one scenario, which has been selected as a random sample from the continuum of possibilities. The "dice rolling" procedure is then repeated a large number of times to build up a complete picture of what may happen to the project.

That is the broad outline, but you need to know more about some of the details. As an example, suppose that we give the computer instructions on how to generate plausible forecasting errors for the market size. In a given simulation the computer may then decide that market size is 10 percent higher than the expected value; so it adds 10 percent to this to get the "actual" market size for that simulation. We can do the same thing for the unit price and all the other key variables. Notice, though, that in order to take account of interrelationships, these too have to be specified to the computer. For example, we might decide that a 10 percent increase in market size results on average in a 3 percent increase in the unit price. In this case we could tell the computer to calculate the forecasting error for the price as

$$\text{Percentage error in unit price} \;=\; 0.3 \times \text{percentage error in market size} \;+\; \text{randomly generated error}$$

Look for the three stages involved in simulation. First, we must choose the best form of equations to model the cash flows of the project. Second, we must specify the probability distributions of all the error terms. Finally, we must run the simulations and assess the results. Look at the distributions of cash flows given in Figure 10-5 of the text. These are part of the results of a simulation analysis, and they provide information both about the expected (average) cash flows and about how far they are likely to deviate from their averages. Notice that the average cash flow is different from what you might have expected from the average unit sales and the average profit per unit. This is because the interrelationship between unit sales and unit price means that the average level of revenues (unit sales times unit price) *is not equal to* the average unit sales times the average unit price. One of the advantages of simulation is that it is able to take account of these kinds of effects. Its disadvantage is that it can be costly and difficult to implement.

We now have better estimates of expected cash flows; so the NPV can be calculated more accurately. We also have an accurate picture of how uncertain the cash flows are. If we like, we can even obtain a probability distribution for the IRR of the project over its life. Beware, though, of so-called probability distributions of NPV. Even though the results of a project are uncertain, the project still has only one value in the marketplace today. Since the NPV of the project represents the difference between its value and its cost, *there can only be one NPV*.

Decision Trees: The final technique described in the chapter is the use of decision trees. Look at the decision tree in our second worked example. As time elapses we can make various decisions, and various events may occur over which we have no control. The decision tree provides a way to represent these different possibilities so that we can be sure that the decisions we make today take proper account of what we can do in the future. A project is more likely to be worth undertaking if we can bail out of it later if things go wrong, than if we can't.

The key point about analyzing a decision tree is that you have to work out what the best decisions will be at the second stage before you can choose the best first-stage decision. The process of working back through the decision tree from the future to the present is sometimes called rolling back the decision tree.

WORKED EXAMPLES

PROBLEM 1: SENSITIVITY ANALYSIS

The following forecasts have been prepared for a new investment of $20 million with an 8-year life:

	PESSIMISTIC	EXPECTED	OPTIMISTIC
Market size	60,000	90,000	140,000
Market share, %	25	30	35
Unit price	$750	$800	$875
Unit variable cost	$500	$400	$350
Fixed cost	7	4	3.5

You use straight-line depreciation, pay tax at 34 percent, and have an opportunity cost of capital of 14 percent. Calculate the NPV of this project and conduct a sensitivity analysis. What are the principal uncertainties of the project?

SOLUTION

The first step is to calculate the annual cash flows from the project for the base case (the expected values). These may be calculated as shown in the following table:

DESCRIPTION	HOW CALCULATED	VALUE ($000,000)
1. Revenues	(90,000 x 0.30 x $800)	21.600
2. Variable cost	(90,000 x 0.30 x $400)	10.800
3. Fixed cost	($4,000,000)	4.000
4. Depreciation	($20,000,000/8)	2.500
5. Pretax profit	(Item 1 – items 2 + 3 + 4)	4.300
6. Tax	(Item 5 x 0.34)	1.462
7. Net profit	(Item 5 – item 6)	2.838
8. Net cash flow	(Item 7 + item 4)	5.338

This level of cash flow occurs for each of the 8 years of the project. The present value of an 8-year $1 annuity is 4.639 at 14 percent. The NPV of the project is therefore given by

$$\text{NPV} = \$5,338,000 \times 4.639 - \$20,000,000 = \$4,762,000$$

Now that the base case has been completed, the next step is to alter the forecasts one at a time to their optimistic and pessimistic values. The easiest way to do this is to work out how much each change affects the net cash flow, and then use the annuity factor as before to work out the NPV. For example, the optimistic value of the market size increases the pretax revenues by 50,000 x 0.30 x ($800 – $400) = $6 million; so it increases the (after-tax) net cash flow by $6 million x 0.66 = 3.96 million, to $9.298 million. The NPV now becomes

$$\text{NPV} = \$9,298,000 \times 4.639 - \$20,000,000 = \$23,132,000$$

The following table shows the net cash flows and NPVs corresponding to the pessimistic and optimistic forecasts for each of the variables. Calculations such as these are relatively easily automated on a spreadsheet.

	NET CASH FLOW ($000,000)		NPV ($000,000)	
FORECAST OF	PESSIMISTIC	OPTIMISTIC	PESSIMISTIC	OPTIMISTIC
Market size	2.96	9.30	-6.26	23.13
Market share	4.15	6.53	-0.75	10.27
Unit price	4.45	6.67	0.63	10.96
Unit variable cost	3.56	6.23	-3.50	8.90
Fixed cost	3.36	5.67	-4.42	6.29

The table clearly shows that the most crucial variable is the total market size. Both the fixed and variable costs also need watching, while market share and unit price seem less likely to cause serious problems.

PROBLEM 2: A DECISION TREE

Forest Products is evaluating a possible investment in a new plant costing $1000. By the end of a year they will know whether cash flows will be $140 a year in perpetuity or only $50 a year, but in either case the first cash flow will not occur until year 2. Alternatively, they would be able to sell their plant in year 1 for $700 ($800, if things go well). They assess a 60 percent chance that the project will turn out well and a 40 percent chance it will turn out badly. Their opportunity cost of funds is 10 percent. What should they do?

SOLUTION

Everything points to a decision tree! It is drawn below.

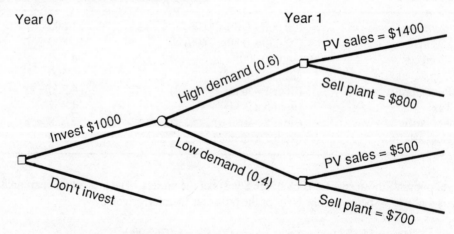

If things go well, the cash flows of $140 in perpetuity starting in year 2 will be worth $140/0.1 = $1400 in year 1. If things go badly, the cash flows will be worth $50/0.1 = $500 in year 1.

To analyze the decision tree we work backwards from the most distant branches of the tree. At the decision branch points, marked with squares, we make decisions. At the uncertainty ones, marked with circles, we calculate expected values. So if things go well (high demand), we will decide to continue with the plant at a value of $1400 in year 1. However, if things go badly (low demand), we will prefer to sell it for $700 rather than wait for cash flows worth only $500.

We can now take the expected value at the uncertainty branch point by weighting each of the possible outcomes by its probability:

(Expected value in year 1) = $1400 x 0.6 + $700 x 0.4 = $1120

Finally, we have to choose at the very first branch point whether to make the investment. If we invest we have a NPV of -$1000 + $1120/1.1 = $18.2. If we don't invest we have nothing; so we decide to go ahead. It is worth noting that without the possibility of selling the plant for $700, this investment would have been unattractive. Its expected year 1 value would have been $1040 giving it a NPV of -$54.5.

SUMMARY

Sensitivity Analysis: This chapter covered three important techniques to evaluate investment projects more thoroughly. First was *sensitivity analysis*, whose purpose is to calculate the effect of misestimating each factor that goes in NPV calculations. The method for accomplishing this is to identify the key variables that determine the success of the project, such as sales volume, fixed cost, unit variable cost, and selling price. Taking one variable at a time and replacing its expected value with both an optimistic and a pessimistic estimate, cash flows and NPVs are recalculated. In this way financial managers can identify those variables which affect NPV most. Research to reduce the uncertainty of those variables, as well as other, overlooked factors, may then be in order. The *value* of this *information* is worthwhile, however, only if the expected value of the information exceeds its cost, calculated thus:

Expected value of information =   sum of (PV of change in CF due to
                                                    new information x probability of that change)

Note that information that cannot affect any decisions is valueless.

The strength of sensitivity analysis lies in its ability to highlight key variables and key assumptions, to expose inconsistencies, and to identify where additional information is worthwhile.

Sensitivity analysis is limited, however, because of the subjectivity of the optimistic and pessimistic forecasts and because it ignores interrelationships among variables.

Scenario Analysis: One way to overcome the problem of interrelated variables is to present *scenarios*. Rather than alter variables one at a time, alternative scenarios are employed where, for each scenario, values are given to every variable to be consistent with one particular realization of the future.

Break-Even Analysis: Break-even analysis is a variation of sensitivity analysis and is used to determine how low sales can go before the NPV becomes negative. We do this by working out *either* what level of sales will equate the PVs of inflows and outflows *or* (equivalently) what level of sales will equate the annual cash inflow to the equivalent annual cost of the investment (investment/annuity factor). Break-even is often calculated as the sales level needed to give a zero accounting profit. This is misleading, as a zero accounting profit is really a big loss: it indicates a failure to earn *any* return on capital, and that represents a loss equal to the opportunity cost of capital.

Monte Carlo Simulation: The second technique employed to evaluate projects is *Monte Carlo simulation*, itself really an extension of scenario analysis except that a computer is used to generate a large number of possible outcomes for a project. Three stages produce the desired results:

1. Establish equations to model the cash flows of the project. These must reflect any interdependencies among variables.
2. Specify the probabilities of forecast errors of different magnitudes for each variable.
3. Sample outcomes. The computer samples from the distribution of forecast errors, calculates the cash flows, and records them. This is repeated a large number of times until an accurate picture of the distribution of possible outcomes has been built up.

As with all models, Monte Carlo simulation has its good and bad points. On the positive side, simulation forces explicit specification of interdependencies, such as, for example, that sales and margins move together. It can be used also to explore possible modifications to a project.

On the negative side, simulation can be time-consuming and expensive. Realism means complexity; building the model may have to be delegated, and this can diminish its credibility to the decision maker. It may replace one "black box" with another.

Beyond these points a common misuse of simulation arises when it is used to obtain distributions of "NPVs," which are calculated by discounting at the risk-free rate. The object is to avoid prejudging the risk of the project, which is reflected in the spread of the distribution. This practice is dangerous because:

1. "NPVs" calculated in this way no longer represent market values of the project.
2. The distribution does not give the information which would be needed to work out the market value of the project.
3. The method ignores the investor's ability to diversify.
4. It offends the value-additivity principle.
5. Distributions of IRRs are more useful.

Decision Trees: The third and final technique employed to evaluate investment projects is decision trees. They are used to analyze a sequence of different possible uncertain events and decisions through time.

To draw a decision tree, branches from points marked with squares (□) are used to denote different possible decisions. Branches from points marked with circles (○) denote different possible outcomes (with their probabilities often indicated in brackets).

To analyze a decision tree, calculate the expected values of the most distant branches first. "Roll back" to the immediate decision by accepting the best decision at each of the later stages. (See problem 2 of our worked examples.)

Decision trees are valuable because they display the links between today's and tomorrow's decisions. Moreover, they force implicit assumptions to be expressed. Decision trees are limited, however, because they very quickly become unmanageably complex. They also treat risk incorrectly.

LIST OF TERMS

Abandonment value	Probability
Break-even analysis	Project analysis
Decision tree	Scenario
Monte Carlo simulation	Sensitivity analysis

EXERCISES

Fill-in Questions

1. Sensitivity analysis, simulation, and decision trees are three different forms of
_____ analysis.
2. _____ enables the manager to see the effect of errors in forecasting sales, costs, etc. on the value of an investment project.
3. The analysis of a project under different _____ gives us a way to do a kind of sensitivity analysis which takes the interrelationships among variables into account.

4. _____ analysis tells the manager how low sales can go without making the project unprofitable.
5. The method of modeling the uncertainty about the level of sales and other important aspects of a project in order to discover the likelihood of various possible outcomes arising is called

   _____.
6. Sequential decisions can be analyzed by constructing a _____.
7. One of the difficulties of using a decision tree or simulation is that it becomes necessary to specify the _____ of different future outcomes.
8. The problem of whether to terminate a project before the end of its normal economic life is called the _____ problem.

Problems

1. Colorful Creams Cosmetics Corporation (CCCC) is considering an investment of $500,000 in a new plant for producing fluorescent disco makeup. The plant, which has an expected life of 4 years, has a maximum capacity of 700,000 units per year, and sales are expected to be 85 percent of this in each of the 4 successive years of production. Fixed costs are $200,000 per year and variable costs are $1.20 per unit produced. The product will be sold at a unit price of $2. The plant will be depreciated straight-line over 4 years, and it is expected to have a zero salvage value. The required rate of return on the project is 15 percent, and the corporation tax rate is 34 percent.
   a. Calculate the NPV of this project under the assumptions given above.
   b. Calculate how sensitive the NPV of the project is to variation in the level of sales, the unit price, the unit variable cost, and the level of fixed costs.
   c. CCCC is uncertain how to price its new product. What price would give a zero NPV?

2. In the investment project of problem 1 calculate what level of sales would give break-even in terms of (a) zero NPV, (b) zero accounting profit.

3. In problem 1, CCCC estimated that the annual sales would be 595,000 units, but there is some chance that the sales level will be inadequate to justify the capital expenditure. By commissioning a market survey, CCCC can hope to reduce this risk. CCCC's marketing department has some experience with such surveys. They estimate that there is a 20 percent chance that the survey will change the forecast sales to 500,000 or less, in which case the project would not be worth undertaking. If this does not occur (the remaining 80 percent of the time), they would expect the sales forecast to be revised upward to 640,000 units. What is the maximum amount that CCCC should be prepared to pay for a survey of this kind?

4. CCCC has another investment project with the following characteristics:

   Cost of investment, $800,000
   Expected sales volume, 21,000 units per year for 7 years
   Unit price, $150
   Unit variable cost, $120
   Annual fixed costs, $400,000
   Life of investment, 7 years (zero salvage value)
   Tax rate, 34 percent
   Required rate of return, 17 percent
   Calculate the NPV of this investment and perform a sensitivity analysis (use straight-line depreciation).

5. Analyze the project of problem 1 under the following two scenarios:

	PESSIMISTIC SCENARIO	OPTIMISTIC SCENARIO
Sales volume	Expected value -20%	Expected value +10%
Unit price	Expected value -10%	Expected value +20%
Variable cost	Expected value +10%	Expected value -5%
Fixed cost	Expected value +10%	Expected value -5%

6. Analyze the project of problem 4 under the scenarios described in problem 5.

*7. In problem 3, the first year of operation would give CCCC the same information as their market survey. After that year, if things go badly (with expected sales of 415,000 units), they can abandon the project to obtain a salvage value of $400,000 (less $8,500 tax) by selling the plant to another company. What value does the market survey have in the light of this option to abandon the project after it has been started?

8. The Transatlantic Toffee Company has to decide what size of new plant to build. A large plant will provide economies of scale but is also likely to lead to a reduced selling price. The capital costs and annual fixed and variable operating costs for different sizes of plant are as follows:

CAPACITY (MILLION UNITS)	INVESTMENT REQUIRED ($000,000)	ANNUAL FIXED COST ($1000s)	UNIT VARIABLE COST ($)
0.4	1.0	200	2.00
0.6	1.4	270	1.95
0.8	1.7	330	1.90

Transatlantic will discover how the market is receiving their product after the first year of operation. In the meantime they assess the prospects of being able to obtain various unit prices for their product at different levels of output as follows:

QUANTITY SOLD (MILLION UNITS)	UNIT PRICE($)	
	FAVORABLE	UNFAVORABLE
0.4	3.05	2.60
0.6	2.90	2.45
0.8	2.75	2.30

The two possible market conditions are thought to be equally likely. After the first year Transatlantic can adjust to the market conditions. They can build an additional $400,000 unit plant. Alternatively, they can reduce the capacity of a larger plant by 200,000 units, which will realize $150,000 immediately and reduce the annual fixed costs by $40,000. In this case the advantages of the lower variable cost are retained. The company has a required rate of return of 10 percent and does not pay any corporate taxes. The plants have an indefinite life. Draw a decision tree and work out what decisions Transatlantic should take.

Essay Questions

1. Describe the technique of sensitivity analysis as applied to the appraisal of capital investment projects. What reservations do you have about its usefulness?

2. Describe how to calculate the break-even point for a capital investment project. Why is it misleading to calculate break-even in terms of accounting profit?

3. "You can prove anything with figures, can't you? I may be old-fashioned but I don't see the point in all this sensitivity analysis stuff. As I see it, the job of the manager is to see that the forecasts are achieved. All this fiddling about is just a waste of time." Give a measured response to this statement.

4. Work out and describe in detail how you would produce and use a Monte Carlo simulation model to represent the purely financial aspects of buying a house instead of renting one. Assume you know you will be forced to sell it in order to relocate in a few years. Bear in mind the initial outlay costs, the various running costs (interest on the loan, taxes, repairs, insurance, heating), and the potential gain or loss on selling. Assume realistic values for these. Make sure to build appropriate interrelationships between variables into the model where necessary.

5. "What possible use to us," said the Ancient and Venerable Comptroller, "is a technique that pulls numbers out of a hat and adds them together? Sure! There are risks in this business, but we expect our managers to know what they're doing: if they don't, then they're out. It's all a matter of judgment, and there's nothing random about that." Is this a valid criticism of Monte Carlo simulation? How would you respond to this argument?

6. A decision must be taken whether to launch a new product immediately or subject it to further market research or abandon the idea altogether. Your boss has heard that decision trees can help with this kind of problem. Write a report on how a decision tree might be used in this situation. Make sure that you describe what sort of information you would need to apply this in practice, and how it would used.

ANSWERS TO EXERCISES

Fill-in Questions

1. project
2. sensitivity analysis
3. scenarios
4. break-even
5. Monte Carlo simulation
6. decision tree
7. probabilities
8. abandonment value

Problems

1.

    a.   The following table derives the cash flows and NPV for the base case and also for the pessimistic and optimistic scenarios of problem 5.

ITEM		YEARS 1 TO 4		
(IN $1000S)	YEAR 0	EXPECTED	PESSIMISTIC	OPTIMISTIC
Investment	-500			
Revenue		1190.0	856.8	1570.8
Variable cost		714.0	628.3	746.1
Fixed cost		200.0	220.0	190.0
Depreciation		125.0	125.0	125.0
Pretax profit		151.0	-116.5	509.7
Tax		51.3	-39.6	173.3
Net profit		99.7	-76.9	336.4
Net cash flow		224.7	48.1	461.4
NPV at 15%		141.4	-362.7	817.2

    b.   The next table shows how given changes in sales, variable cost, unit price, and fixed cost affect the net cash flows and the NPV. The final column also shows the levels which give break-even (i.e., zero NPV):

SENSITIVITY TO CHANGE OF	EFFECT ON CASH FLOW	EFFECT ON NPV	BREAK-EVEN LEVEL
100,000 sales (units)	52.8	150.74	501,200
10 cents variable cost	-39.27	-112.12	$1.33
10 cents unit price	39.27	112.12	$1.87
$10,000 fixed cost	-6.60	-18.84	$275,050

    c.   The final column indicates that a price of $1.87 gives a zero NPV.

2.

    a.   The final column of the previous table also shows that the level of sales required for break-even in terms of zero NPV is 501,200 units per year.

    b.   The base case gave a pretax profit of $151,000 at sales of 595,000. Each unit reduction in sales reduces pretax profits by $0.80; so sales will have to fall by 151,000/0.80 = 188,750 to eliminate profits entirely. That is, break-even sales are 406,000.

3. Without the extra information, the value of the project is its usual NPV of $141,400. With the information, there is a 20 percent chance of a zero NPV and an 80 percent chance of $209,230. The expected new NPV is equal to $167,380 minus the cost of the information; so the information must be worth $25,980.

4.

ITEM		YEARS 1 TO 7		
(IN $100S)	YEAR 0	EXPECTED	PESSIMISTIC	OPTIMISTIC
Investment	-800			
Revenue		3150.0	2268.0	4158.0
Variable cost		2520.0	2217.6	2633.4
Fixed cost		400.0	440.0	380.0
Depreciation		114.3	114.3	114.3
Profit before tax		115.7	-503.9	1030.3
Tax		39.3	-171.3	350.3
Profit after tax		76.4	-332.6	680.0
Cash flow		190.7	-218.3	794.3
NPV at 17%		-52.2	-1656.2	2315.5

The sensitivity analysis looks as follows:

SENSITIVITY TO CHANGE OF	EFFECT ON CASH FLOW	EFFECT ON NPV	BREAK-EVEN LEVEL
1000 unit sales	19.8	77.66	21,670
$1 variable cost	-13.9	-54.36	$119.0
$1 unit price	13.9	54.36	$151.0
$10,000 fixed cost	-6.6	-25.89	$379.8

5. See the answer to problem 1.

6. See the answer to problem 4.

7. Without the abandonment option, we found in problem 3 that the project had a NPV of $167,380 less the cost of the survey, or $141,400 without the survey. This gave the survey a value of $25,980.

With the abandonment option, there is now a 20 percent chance of abandoning at a NPV of -$46,852. This is calculated as follows: the expected first year sales of 415,000 will give cash flow of $129.62 and there will be $400,000 less $8,500 tax from selling the plant. This makes an expected $521,120/1.15 – $500,000 = -$46,852. There is also an 80 percent chance of $209,230. Combining the two figures, we find that the abandonment option increases the NPV of the project to $158,000. This reduces the value of the survey information to $9,380.

8. The following decision tree indicates that Transatlantic Toffee should build the 0.6 million unit plant, which has a NPV of $318,000 as compared with $300,000 for the 0.4 million plant and $295,000 for the 0.8 million one. All figures on the tree are shown in $1000s.

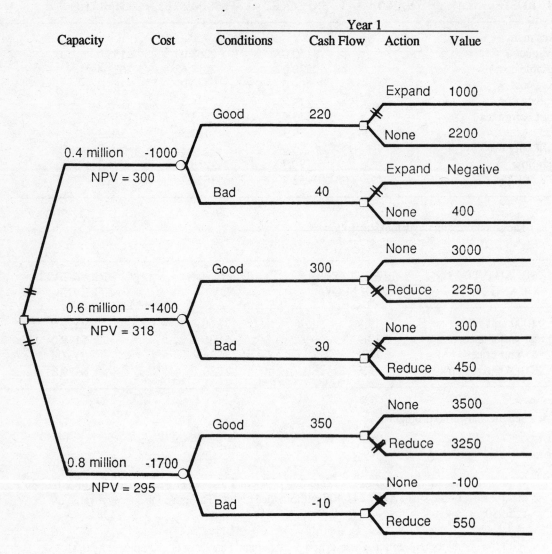

CHAPTER 11
WHERE POSITIVE NET PRESENT
VALUES COME FROM

INTRODUCTION

No matter how much we know about the theory of making capital budgeting decisions, we will end up making bad decisions if our forecasts of cash flows turn out badly. Chapter 11 tells us how we can ensure that these forecasts are as good as it is possible to make them. The first part of the chapter deals with some general issues concerning forecasts of any kind. Forecasts may on average be too high (or too low), or they may exhibit too wide a range of high and low. The financial manager must be aware of these possibilities and be able to make allowances for them. Problems may also be caused by different managers having different (and inconsistent) views, and the criteria used for assessing performance can produce further distortions of attitudes and objectives. Good management procedures based on an understanding of these problems can avoid their worst effects. The second part of the chapter focuses on the market in which the firm operates. This is discussed in the context of a small case study (Marvin Enterprises). Firms have to compete continually with each other, and they can never assume that the market will stay as it is for any length of time. Your company can *only* expect a positive NPV from a given project if it has some relative advantage in undertaking it compared with other companies. Remember, too, that new developments (of your own or of other companies) may affect the values of your existing assets.

WHAT TO LOOK FOR IN CHAPTER 11

This chapter is quite short, and it introduces hardly any new terms. Nevertheless it is one of the most important chapters in the book. The biggest practical difficulty in applying the NPV criterion is in establishing reliable cash-flow forecasts. Although the text cannot provide firm rules to cover specific situations, it does illustrate the most important dangers and difficulties in forecasting cash flows, and it provides advice on how best to combat them. Try to take from the chapter an understanding of what is necessary to get unbiased forecasts that are based on consistent assumptions. Look out too for the key idea that you can only *expect* a positive NPV if you have some kind of relative advantage.

Inconsistencies between forecasts (or attitudes) can take many forms. They usually arise from some failure of communication (such as, for instance, when the production manager's cost estimates are based on different assumptions about inflation from the marketing manager's forecasts of sales revenues). Obviously the larger the corporation the more likely these problems are to arise. Notice that there can be damaging effects even before projects begin to be evaluated, because of the process by which new projects are initiated. Establishing a framework which explicitly communicates basic economic forecasts and assumptions is an essential task of senior management. The objective is to reduce the scope for individual inconsistencies.

Bias is far more intractable: it is difficult to detect and even more difficult to eliminate. We often talk about overoptimism and exaggeration in financial forecasts. The two diagrams below illustrate exactly what we mean.

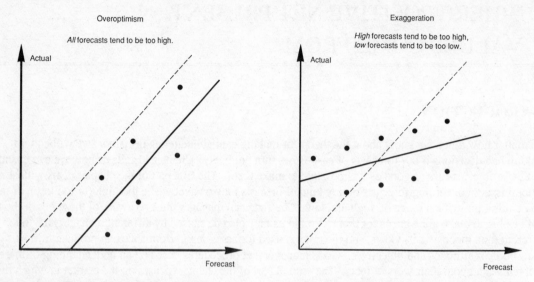

Of course, you can also get both kinds of bias occurring at once. If you are able to monitor a manager's forecasts over a long enough period, you may be able to make allowances for any personal biases of these kinds: but be careful that your actions don't result in a change of your manager's behavior. Second, remember that when managers are rewarded for being optimistic, they will be optimistic: people tend to tell you what they think you want to hear, and it is all too easy to create situations in which you are bound to get biased forecasts.

Forecasting errors can never be eliminated entirely. When you estimate a positive NPV, there is always a chance that it is simply your estimate that is wrong. How can you tell if your positive NPV is a forecasting error or if it represents a genuinely attractive project? The text suggests two useful approaches. *First*, if you can't be sure about future cash flows, as far as possible try to avoid having to discount them to get a present value: while this is correct in theory, in practice it can lead to large (random) errors which could be avoided. Instead, then, look at market values (when you can) to see the market's opinion of what various assets are worth in use. Then, if you can use your assets more efficiently than your competitors can, adjust their market value by an amount that reflects the value of your extra efficiency. *Second*, look for situations where your company has relative advantages. Even if your competitors keep on investing until their new projects have zero NPVs, you will still be able to earn what are called *economic rents*--that is, profits in excess of your opportunity cost of capital.

Marvin Enterprises is an extended and useful illustration of the nature of firms' economic behavior. Although this section is starred, there is really nothing very frightening about it, and it is well worth taking the time to work through it in detail. Don't be put off by the rather unreal and futuristic framework of the case. Certainly, the story is a piece of science fiction, and in some ways it shouldn't be taken too literally. At the same time, the problems it confronts are very real and have many parallels in today's world.

The main argument of the case runs as follows. The price of a product depends on the total amount of it that is produced. Producers compete with each other and will expand their capacity until new investment has a zero net present value. From this it follows that any single producer can only expect to find positive NPV projects if he or she has some kind of relative advantage over the competition. Such advantages certainly exist: a company may have built up a good reputation for its brand name in the market-place. You can see that these advantages are hard-won and must be protected tenaciously.

The Marvin Enterprises example is about a company that has developed a new technology, but there are other firms hot on its heels and its relative advantage is expected to last for only 5 years. After 5 years, new investment will come in and drive the price of the product (gargle blasters) down to its equilibrium level. The company will therefore earn abnormally high profits (economic rents) only over the first 5 years.

The case raises two other important issues. The first is the effect of Marvin Enterprise's new investment on its existing business. Its proposed expansion is sufficiently large to affect the price of the product it is selling. Marvin must worry about the loss of revenue on its existing operations and include this in its calculation of the NPV of the new project. In more extreme situations this could lead to the company's wishing to suppress its new technology completely.

Second, the less efficient producers play an extremely important role. As the capacity of the industry is increased, the price of the product falls and it becomes increasingly difficult for these producers to stay in business. If the price falls far enough, some producers may withdraw from the market, and other *marginal* producers may be on the point of doing so. In this situation the price of the product will be at the point where it just pays the least efficient remaining producer to stay in business. The size of the economic rent obtained by a more efficient producer will simply reflect the difference between their costs (including the opportunity cost of the capital employed).

Look out too for the misleading argument that a fully depreciated plant is cheaper to run than an otherwise identical undepreciated one. This argument is often made, but it is falsely based on interpreting accounting income as if it were cash flow. Remember, it is only cash flows that matter, and not accounting numbers. Since in this example there are no taxes, there is absolutely no difference between cash flows of a depreciated plant and an undepreciated one. If we were talking about two plants that had received different amounts of tax depreciation, that would be another matter -- and problem 5 gives an example of that.

So much for the concepts behind Marvin Enterprises. The worked example gives you a further opportunity to check that you understand how to work out the numbers.

WORKED EXAMPLE

PROBLEM: NEW TECHNOLOGY AND ECONOMIC RENTS
The Red Robbo Rubber Company is considering a new investment in a fully automated tire plant. Its existing plant produces 1 million tires a year. It cost $80 million 5 years ago and it could be scrapped for $30 million at any time. The production costs per tire of the old and new plants can be broken down as follows:

	OLD PLANT	NEW PLANT
Raw materials and energy	$15	$17
Labor	$10	$ 3
Other direct costs	$ 5	$ 5
Total direct costs	$30	$25

The new plant would be able to produce 500,000 tires a year, and it would cost $35 million. The current price of tires is $38 each. Red Robbo's new investment is not expected to affect this, but the price may fall when other companies complete their modernization programs in 2 years' time. If Red Robbo's cost of capital is 10 percent and there are no corporate taxes:

1. What is the NPV of the new plant?

2. When will the old plant be scrapped, and what is its value today?

3. The costs of raw materials and energy suddenly double. The price of tires changes to $50. What are the answers to (1) and (2) now?

Solution

1. The capital outlay required on the new plant is $70 per annual tire capacity. The break-even price to give a zero NPV is therefore (10 percent x $70) + $25 (direct costs) = $32. This is the price that we should expect to see in 2 years' time. With the price now at $38, Red Robbo can expect economic rents of $6 per tire per year for 2 years. The NPV of the new plant is therefore

$$500,000 \times (\$6/1.1 + \$6/1.1^2) = \$5,206,612$$

2. The old plant should be scrapped when it can no longer earn the opportunity cost of its salvage value, i.e., 10 percent x $30 million, or $3 on each tire produced. It will be scrapped when the price falls below $33, i.e., in 2 years' time. Meanwhile it will produce cash flows of $8 million for 2 years. Its value today is therefore

$$\$8,000,000/1.1 + \$8,000,000 + \$30,000,000/(1.1)^2 = \$38,677,686$$

3. The change in energy and materials costs modifies the direct costs to $45 and $42 for the old and new plants, respectively. This increases the break-even price on the new plant to $49, just $1 below the current price of $50. The economic rent is now only $1 per tire produced (for 2 years); so the NPV of the new plant is

$$500,000 \times (\$1/1.1 + \$1/1.1^2) = \$867,769$$

The old plant will now be scrapped only if the price of tires falls below $45 + $3 = $48. It is now sensible for manufacturers to build only sufficient new plants to push the price down to $49. The old plant is no longer expected to be scrapped but will earn $5 per tire for 2 years, and $4 per tire after that. In year 2 it will be worth 4/0.1 = $40 million; so *today* it is worth

$$\$5,000,000/1.1 + \$5,000,000 + \$40,000,000/1.1^2 = \$41,735,537$$

SUMMARY

Biases and Errors: Good investment decisions require good cash-flow forecasts. Watch out for the problems caused by inconsistencies, bias, and forecasting errors.

Inconsistencies can arise when:

1. Different managers expect different behavior of the economy: many companies establish a set of macroeconomic assumptions (e.g., figures for inflation, interest rates, GNP) to form the basis of all project analyses.

2. Different managers (or different divisions of a company) have different attitudes to risk.

3. Performance criteria affect managers' risk attitudes: a good reward system should have some tolerance for mistakes and be able to discriminate between good decisions and lucky ones.

There are two kinds of *bias*:

1. Optimism/pessimism: when forecasts on average are too high/low.

2. Exaggeration/understatement: when the expected differences between projects are over- or understated. This is a problem because of the way projects are selected based on our forecasts.

The net present value rule assumes *unbiased* forecasts. To control bias use these three guides:

1. Avoid such game situations in which managers are encouraged to produce either a "rosy picture" or forecasts which they can subsequently meet.

2. Make adjustments if you know something about the forecaster's track record.

3. Use ad hoc rules when necessary: imposing divisional budgets can limit the effect of overoptimism, and using payback may help if forecasters exaggerate their ability to make accurate long-term forecasts.

Forecasting errors can never be eliminated. An investment may look good *either* because it is good, *or* because you have made a forecasting error.

Unbiased cash-flow forecasts may give unbiased but exaggerated estimates of NPV. This would make our estimates tend to be over-optimistic for the projects we accept.

Market Values: In order to reduce the chance of forecasting errors swamping the genuine information, look first at *market values* to find the best available valuation of commonly known information. Information that is not generally known can be analyzed separately and added to (or subtracted from) the market value. For example, a department store should try to avoid forecasting real estate. On the other hand it should consider what evidence there is that the real estate is best suited to its department store rather than to some other use. A gold mine can look to the current gold price for the present value of future sales of gold.

Economic Rents: Look for *economic rents*, by which we mean profits in excess of the cost of capital. Remember the following three points:

1. When an industry is in a long-run *competitive* equilibrium, all assets just earn their opportunity cost of capital, their NPVs are zero, and economic rents are zero.

2. Firms may earn temporary (or permanent) economic rents if there is temporary disequilibrium, or if they have some degree of monopoly or market power.

3. Don't accept that a project has a positive NPV unless you understand why your firm has a special advantage in doing it.

The *Marvin Enterprises* case illustrates the following salient points:

1. Anticipated and prolonged economic rents are uncommon.

2. High economic rents usually attract competitors; try to estimate the timing and extent of new entry.

3. Identify your firm's comparative advantages and try to capitalize on them.

4. Successive generations of technology will tend to reduce the value of earlier generation assets. A growth industry has no mercy on laggards.

5. The NPV of a project may be reduced by the impact it has on the firm's existing business. This can provide an incentive to slow down the speed of innovation.

6. A marginal producer is one who will quit if the price goes any lower, i.e., for whom price *equals* manufacturing cost plus opportunity cost of not selling out. The economic rent to a more efficient producer is simply the *difference* between its costs and those of a marginal producer.

7. A higher salvage value increased economic rents. The book value of the old plant was irrelevant.

LIST OF TERMS

Bias
Economic rents
Marginal producer

EXERCISES

Fill-in Questions

1. A _____ is a producer who will cease production if there is any fall in the price at which the product is sold.
2. Profits which are in excess of the competitive equilibrium level are called _____.
3. Forecasts which tend on average to be too high are said to have an upward _____.

Problems

1. Which of the following are true and which are false:
   a. A monopoly can obtain permanent economic rents unless it is regulated in some way.
   b. The average forecasting error for the cash flow of a project is zero.
   c. New capacity decisions must take account of the effect on sunk costs, such as investments in existing plants.
   d. No firm can earn economic rents if it has to buy inputs at a price that reflects their value to the firm.
   e. Marginal producers have assets with zero market value.
   f. Fully depreciated assets always have a present value of zero.
   g. Stock prices reflect the value of growth opportunities only after the firm has announced its plans to invest in new capacity.

2. Kingsley Solomon is considering opening a second gold mine. This mine will cost $25 million to develop and it will produce 20,000 ounces of refined gold a year for 7 years at a cost of $250 an ounce. The current gold price is $400 an ounce, and the opportunity cost of funds is 10 percent. (a) What is the NPV, if he evaluates the mine assuming the gold price will grow at 5 percent per year? (b) What is the NPV, if he assumes that the gold price is expected to grow at the cost of funds?

3. Universal Comminicators, Inc., makes intergalactic message capsules that sell at $6 million each and cost $4 million each to manufacture. Their existing plant produces 2000 capsules per year, which represents a significant part of the total market. They are considering investing in a new plant that will increase their capacity by 500 additional units. When the increased volume of production hits the market, the market price of message capsules is expected to fall to $5.5 million. Universal is currently negotiating contracts for the construction of its new plant, which will reduce production costs to $3 million. The cost of capital for this project is 10 percent.

a. What is the maximum price that Universal should be prepared to pay for its new plant, assuming that it can expect to retain a monopoly of the more efficient production technology indefinitely?

b. What would the plant be worth to another company that did not already produce message capsules?

4. The manufacture and sale of Brand X is highly competitive. The industry is composed of three firms with the following capacities and manufacturing costs:

FIRM	SALES (MILLION UNITS)	UNIT COST ($)
A	8	8
B	6	9
C	4	10
Total	18	

The demand curve for Brand X is given by the following equation:

Price (in dollars) = $24 – 0.5 x$ (quantity in millions).

The industry opportunity cost of capital is 10 percent, and new plant costs $70 per unit of capacity. All the plants have indefinitely long lives but could be scrapped at salvage values of $30 per unit of capacity. Firm C discovers a way of reducing unit manufacturing costs to $7, keeping capital costs unchanged. It manages to secure monopoly rights to the technique for an extremely long period, and decides to challenge Firm A's market leadership by immediately adding 5 million units of the new capacity.

a. What is the present value of Firm C's existing plant after the new capacity is added?

b. What is the maximum addition to capacity before it is worthwhile to scrap Firm C's original plant?

c. What is the NPV of Firm C's new investment project?

d. Can Firm C make *any* profitable investment without first disposing of its old plant?

5. Companies Y and Z have identical plants which can each manufacture 100,000 "giggle chips" a year, at a unit cost of $6. These plants could be scrapped at any time with a scrap value of $1.5 million. Company Y's plant has been fully depreciated for tax purposes, whereas Company Z's plant has been depreciated only to a book value of $1 million, and will give rise to annual $500,000 depreciation allowances for the next 2 years. Since both companies pay tax at 50 percent, Company Y would realize only a net of $750,000 from scrapping its plant immediately, while Company Z would realize $1.25 million net. At what prices for "giggle chips" will each company find it economical to cease production immediately and scrap its plant? (Assume the opportunity cost of capital is 10 percent.)

*6. The market for shipping crude oil can be represented in terms of a number of types of tanker serving a number of different routes. One very simplified representation is given below. It shows, in millions, the available tonnage of each class of tanker, the total tonnage required on each route, and the operating costs of each tanker on each route.

TANKER TYPE	TONNAGE	ANNUAL OPERATING COSTS (PER TON)		
		ROUTE 1	ROUTE 2	ROUTE 3
VLCC	500	$30	$34	Too large
MLCC	400	35	37	$38
Other	300	40	40	40
Tonnage required		300	500	250

All tankers are available for charter in a competitive market, and the price mechanism will allocate them to routes so as to minimize the total costs of transporting crude. All tankers have a useful life of 15 years and can be sold for scrap at any time for $150 per ton. Assume the cost of capital is 10 percent.

a. What type or types of tanker will be used on each route?

b. What will be the annual rental (per ton) for chartering each type of tanker?

c. What will be the market price (per ton) for purchasing each type of tanker?

d. What could happen to the usage and the prices of each type of tanker if the tonnage of VLCCs increased to 700?

e. What would happen if (with no increase in the tonnage of VLCCs) an environmental lobby succeeded in banning VLCCs from 50 percent of the required tonnage of route 1?

Essay Questions

1. Describe the different kinds of biases in forecasts that can affect capital budgeting decisions. Give some guidelines for minimizing their effects.

2. Do you think that corporate management should make their own forecasts of the economy as a whole? Give your reasons.

3. Explain clearly why a company may have an economic incentive to suppress an improvement in technology.

4. Explain clearly what is meant by the statement "the level of economic rents is determined by the costs of the marginal producer."

5. In the Marvin Enterprises example, users of the earlier and more expensive technologies were prepared to continue to produce even at prices that gave negative profits after depreciation. Explain what factors determine their willingness to do so.

6. Describe an industry which has experienced the type of situation and decisions described in Marvin Enterprises. What are the most important similarities and differences between your example and the imaginary gargle blaster industry?

*7. Discuss whether a company can still have an incentive to suppress an improvement in technology if all its shareholders hold the market portfolio.

ANSWERS TO EXCERCISES

Fill-in Questions

1. marginal producer
2. economic rents
3. bias

Problems

1. (a) T; (b) F; (c) T; (d) T; (e) F; (f) F; (g) F

2. (a) For each ounce of gold mined per year the present value of the gross revenue stream is:

$$400 \times \text{(annuity factor: } t = 7, r = 4.76\%) = \$2,334.65$$

So, NPV = -25,000,000 + 20,000(2,334.65 - 250 x 4.868) = -$2,649,000

(b) NPV = -25,000 + 20,000(7 x 400 - 250 x 4.868) = $6,658,000

3. a. Universal will gain net revenues of $2.5 million on each of its 500 new units a year, and it will lose $500,000 on each of its existing 2000 units of output. This gives an incremental cash flow of

$$(500 \times \$2,500,000) - (2000 \times \$500,000) = \$250,000,000$$

At a 10 percent discount rate the present value is $2.5 billion, and this is the maximum price Universal should be prepared to pay.

   b. Another company would not stand to lose revenues on the existing plant. The new plant would be worth $12.5 billion to such a company.

4. a. The extra capacity will drive the price down to $12.50, but it is best to scrap C's old plant at any price below $13. The existing plant is therefore worth only its salvage value of $120 million.

   b. 4 million units.

   c. Assuming the equilibrium price is $13, the NPV of Firm C's project is given as

$$
\begin{aligned}
\text{NPV} &= [5,000,000 \times (\$6/0.1 - \$70)] - [4,000,000 \times (\$5/0.1 - \$30)] \\
&= -\$50,000,000 - \$80,000,000 \\
&= -\$130,000,000
\end{aligned}
$$

If Firm C scraps all its old plant and the price goes to $14.50, the NPV is still negative (-$55 million).

   d. It is not possible. When the price is $15, each unit of investment has a NPV of -$70 + $8/0.1 = $10, but unless the old investment has been scrapped, we also reduce the present value of the old plant by

$$4 \times \$0.5/0.1 = \$20$$

5. The incremental cash flows from Company Y's decision to maintain production are as follows:

	YEAR 0	YEAR 1
Net revenues after tax		$0.5 \times (P - 6) \times 0.1$
Proceeds on disposal	-0.75	0.75

where P is the unit price in dollars, and the cash flows are expressed in units of millions of dollars. These cash flows will have a positive NPV if the price is greater than $7.50.

Similarly, the incremental cash flows from Company Z's decision to maintain production are:

	YEAR 0	YEAR 1
Net revenues after tax		$0.5 \times (P - 6) \times 0.1$
Depreciation tax shield		0.25
Proceeds on disposal	-1.25	1.00

These cash flows will have a positive NPV if the price is greater than $8.50.

6. a. We can figure out from the structure of operating costs that the total costs of transporting crude are minimized when the demands of each route are satisfied as follows:

   Route 1: 300 VLCC
   Route 2: 200 VLCC, 300 MLCC
   Route 3: 100 MLCC, 150 other

   b. Since 150 "other" tankers are in use and the remaining 100 are idle, this category of tanker represents a marginal producer and its rent must equal the opportunity cost of salvage. Since the cost of capital is 10 percent and the salvage value is $150 per ton, the rental must be $15 per ton.

   MLCCs and "other" tankers are both used on route 3, but the MLCCs are cheaper to operate by $2 per ton. They can therefore command a $2 higher rental of $17 per ton.

   VLCCs and MLCCs are both used on route 2, with a $3 cost advantage to the VLCCs. This gives them a $3 rental advantage, and the VLCC rental is $20 per ton.

   c. Capitalizing the rentals of $20, $17, and $15, we find that the market prices of the VLCC, MLCC, and "other" tankers are $200, $170, and $150.

   d. Route 2: 400 VLCC, 100 MLCC; route 3: 250 MLCC. All "other" would be scrapped, MLCC would drop to salvage value of $150 per ton, and VLCC to $180 per ton.

   e. Compared with (a), 150 route 1 VLCCs would switch with 150 route 2 MLCCs. No change in tanker prices. Price for shipping oil on route 1 increases by $5 per ton.

CHAPTER 12
ORGANIZING CAPITAL EXPENDITURE AND
EVALUATING PERFORMANCE AFTERWARDS

INTRODUCTION

Chapter 12 describes how firms usually organize the investment process and subsequent performance measurement. Besides telling us what firms actually do, it also points out a number of weaknesses and shortcomings associated with the methods in common use. There are often four stages to the process of capital budgeting and expenditure:

1. Preparation of the capital budget: the list of investment projects planned each year.
2. Project authorization: to give authority to go ahead.
3. Procedures for the control of projects under construction.
4. Postaudits: to check on the progress of recent investments.

WHAT TO LOOK FOR IN CHAPTER 12

The various sections of Chapter 12 do not correspond exactly to the four stages of the capital budgeting process described above. You may find it helpful to see in advance just how this chapter is laid out:

Section 12-1 describes the first two stages in capital budgeting: the capital budget and project authorization. These comprise the decision-making part of the process.

Section 12-2 discusses a number of problems that can arise in the decision-making part of the capital budgeting process, and suggests some solutions to them.

Section 12-3 describes the third and fourth stages in capital budgeting: the control of projects under construction and the measurement of performance afterwards. These represent the control part of the process.

Section 12-4 consists of a long numerical example which illustrates the pitfalls in using ROI to measure performance.

Section 12-5 is a short section which makes two suggestions for avoiding the biases that can mess up performance measures based on ROI.

Notice that three different elements are involved in this chapter. First, there are descriptions of the procedures that companies most commonly use. Look out for the use of techniques that are theoretically inappropriate (such as payback and book rate of return), and for the reasons why it can still make sense for companies to continue to use them. Second, there are descriptions of problems that can occur within the usual types of system. These can arise in a number of different ways. The worst problems originate either because the originator of a project has a commitment to see a pet idea approved, or else because of the limitations of a particular technique (such as ROI). Finally, the chapter suggests some solutions to the problems that it raises.

The Capital Budgeting Process: You will probably find that the descriptive nature of this chapter makes it fairly easy going. Don't let this fool you! Watch out for the complexity of the capital budgeting process. Much of this complexity arises because we are dealing with a management problem. Senior management has neither sufficient time nor the necessary information to undertake a detailed analysis of every project. It is simply not its job to do so. Instead it must delegate, and the problem is how far to delegate and in what way to do so. If it is thoughtless in the way it delegates these responsibilities, many wrong decisions may be made.

All sorts of problems can occur. Many of them originate from the difficulty of maintaining accurate communication both up and down the ladder of authority. These problems can be made worse by the way managers are judged. You can hardly expect managers to make decisions solely on the basis of NPV if you then judge them on ROI. Communication is also affected by commitment. Almost any manager is likely to exaggerate the advantages of a pet scheme when trying to sell the idea to the boss and to the boss's boss. Maintaining control over the capital budgeting process poses other problems. If there is a way to beat the system, your managers will probably find it, unless the formal system is similar to the informal way in which people think about and communicate decisions. For example, there is no point in having elaborate controls on capital expenditures if managers can evade them by leasing the same equipment instead of purchasing it. These management problems are both complicated and difficult. Don't expect to find a foolproof system that neatly wraps them all up. Do expect to get an understanding of how problems can arise, and of the sorts of action that can be taken to reduce them.

Evaluating Performance: You will probably find that the hardest sections of the chapter are those concerned with the problems of evaluating performance (Sections 12-3, 12-4, and 12-5). After a short description of the kinds of procedures companies use for controlling expenditures and implementing postaudits, the rest of the chapter deals with the difficulties of evaluating operating performance. Look out for the two basic types of approach:

1. Compare actual performance with projected performance.
2. Compare actual performance against some absolute standard of profitability.

The first approach is fairly self-explanatory. The second approach contains a number of pitfalls that are examined in some detail. The standard way of measuring the profitability of operating performance is to calculate the accounting rate of return (that is, accounting profit expressed as a percentage of the book value of the assets employed). Unfortunately this figure is usually different from the true rate of return that we would calculate (in terms of economic income) on the basis of market values or present values. *Economic income* is simply the cash flow minus any reduction in present value. The reduction in present value is often called *economic depreciation* (remember that we also reduce book value by book depreciation). Economic income is therefore cash flow minus economic depreciation, and to see what rate of return we have earned we must divide this by the present value at the beginning of the period:

$$\text{True return} = \frac{\text{cash flow} - \text{economic depreciation}}{\text{initial present value}}$$

Notice how similar this is to ROI. Book income is essentially cash flow minus book depreciation. We may therefore write

$$\text{Book ROI} = \frac{\text{cash flow} - \text{book depreciation}}{\text{initial book value}}$$

It is now quite easy to see how ROI can give a distorted picture of the true return. Any differences between book values and present values or between book depreciation and economic depreciation will make ROI different from the true return. Often in the early years of a project's life, its economic depreciation is less than its book depreciation, so that ROI *understates* profitability, as economic depreciation may then be less than book depreciation, and the book value may also be less than the present value of the project. You may find the worked example helpful in clarifying your understanding of the differences between economic depreciation and book depreciation.

The chapter suggests that some of the biases in using ROI as a performance measure can be reduced by calculating it with economic depreciation instead of book depreciation. While of course this is true, it is worth pointing out that with this suggestion we have come back almost full circle to the first approach of comparing actual with projected to evaluate performance. The expected schedule of economic depreciation depends on the original estimates of future cash flows. If these cash-flow forecasts were to come true exactly, each year the true return would be exactly equal to the expected return that we used as the discount rate. The extent to which the realized return differs from this measures how far the actual cash flow differs from its forecast.

WORKED EXAMPLE

PROBLEM: ECONOMIC INCOME VERSUS BOOK INCOME
The Multicash Corporation is still considering a $500,000 new investment that will produce cash flows of $140,000 each year for 5 years. (We used this as our worked example in Chapter 5.) The required rate of return for this project is 10 percent. Calculate its expected economic depreciation and economic income in each year. How do these figures compare with straight-line depreciation and the corresponding accounting income?

SOLUTION
The easiest way to work this example is to set it out in the form of a table such as the one that follows:

ITEM ROW	YEAR (FIGURES IN $1000s)	0	1	2	3	4	5
1	Cash flow		140	140	140	140	140
2	PV at end of year	530.7	443.8	348.2	243.0	127.3	0
3	Economic depreciation		86.9	95.6	105.2	115.7	127.3
4	Economic income		53.1	44.4	34.8	24.3	12.7

The table was calculated as follows. First, we set out the five annual cash flows of $140,000 in the first row. Second, we discount them back a year at a time to get the PV at the end of each year. These are given in row 2, which is calculated working backwards from the last year, using the "bottom-up" calculator method we described in Chapter 3. The first number to be calculated here was for year 4 as $140/1.1 = 127.3. The next number was for year 3 as ($140 + $127.3)/1.1 = $243.0, and so on. Third, we calculate the economic depreciation for each year as the reduction in PV. Thus year 5 is $127.3 – 0 = $127.3, year 4 is $243.0 – $127.3 = $115.7, etc. Finally, the economic depreciation is subtracted from the cash flow each year to give economic income.

In this example economic depreciation increases each year, and economic income decreases each year. In contrast, straight-line book depreciation would give a depreciation figure of $100,000 each year, making accounting income a constant $40,000 every year. This understates true income in years 1 and 2 and overstates it in the remaining years. It may also be noted that the use of accelerated depreciation (such as the sum-of-the-year's-digits method) would increase this distortion. If the cash flow increased year by year, this would also increase the distortion.

SUMMARY

Capital Budgeting and Project Authorizations: The *capital budget* is a list of planned investment projects with their required outlays. It is usually prepared annually for review by senior management.

Project proposals usually come from the *bottom up*, being initiated at plant manager level and submitted upward for approval. Strategic planning may initiate proposals on a top-down basis.

The budget may contain estimates of likely expenditure for the next 5 years.

Project authorization is usually reserved for senior management. For example, one survey found division heads in companies with capital budgets averaging $130 million per year were on average given a ceiling of only $136,000 on individual projects.

A formal *appropriation request* must usually be prepared for each project after it has been approved in the annual budget. Most firms use checklists to make sure that all relevant costs and alternatives are considered.

Some firms distinguish among four types of projects:

1. Safety or pollution-control outlays required by law or company policy.
2. Maintenance or cost reduction.
3. Capacity expansion in existing business.
4. New products or ventures.

Decision Criteria: To evaluate investment projects, most companies use a combination of such different *decision criteria* as payback, ROI, and IRR. Many companies apply capital budgeting techniques incorrectly by treating, for example, depreciation as a cash flow.

In the process intuitive judgment may be as important as formal appraisal. Moreover, simple methods like payback make it easy to *communicate* an idea of project profitability. And, of course, we can't expect managers to concentrate on NPV if we judge their performance on book return.

Organizational Problems: Some organizational problems stem from *commitment of sponsors* and *evasion of controls*. Appropriation requests may reflect their sponsor's eagerness to obtain approval. Senior management cannot evaluate individual projects, but they can use *corporate staff* to check the assumptions and to ensure that the authorization request draws attention to all likely contingent expenditures. Management can also impose expenditure limits on individual plants and divisions: this uses capital rationing as a way of *decentralizing* decisions.

Managers permitted to approve projects up to a certain value may sometimes evade this control by breaking a project down into a number of smaller requests. A similar problem may arise with leased assets.

Partial solutions to these problems include:

1. Use of corporate staff (see above).
2. Planning: capital investments have to make sense in terms of the broader budgeting and planning cycle of operating budgets for plants and divisions, and planned marketing, research, etc.
3. Strategic choices: Capital investment should reflect a combination of "bottom-up" and "top-down" processes.
4. Decentralization: decentralization may be dictated by a lack of information at the top. It can work only if plant and division managers are rewarded for doing the right things.

Control of Projects in Progress: *Control of projects in progress* is necessary and takes the following steps:

1. Authorization: specifies how much money may be spent and when.
2. Accounting procedures: record expenditures as they occur.
3. Overruns: supplemental appropriation request required, but 10 percent overrun may be permitted without authorization.
4. Completion: formal notice of completion transfers accumulated costs to permanent accounts, and eliminates any hidden kitty.

Postaudits of capital expenditure are usually undertaken a year after construction is completed. This is usually too soon to provide a clear assessment of the project's success. Postaudits can provide useful insights into the next round of capital budgeting. It may be impossible to measure the incremental cash flows generated by a project. (Your records don't tell you what cash flows you would have had without the project.)

Evaluation of Operating Performance: Performance can be measured in two ways:

1. Actual versus predicted. Compare actual operating earnings with what you predicted.
2. Actual profitability versus an absolute standard of profitability. The accounting rate of return is usually used for this. It is full of pitfalls.

The accounting rate of return is equal to the true "economic" rate of return only when book depreciation is the same as economic depreciation (i.e., the reduction in the present value of the project). In general these are different; so book profitability does not measure true profitability. We have

$$\text{Economic income} = \text{cash flow} + \text{change in present value}$$
$$= \text{cash flow} - \text{economic depreciation}$$

(Remember *reduction* in present value represents economic depreciation.)

$$\text{Book income} = \text{cash flow} - \text{book depreciation}$$

$$\text{Book ROI} = \frac{\text{cash flow} - \text{book depreciation}}{\text{initial present value}}$$

Some important problems were illustrated by the Nodhead Stores example. For example, discounted cash flow and book earnings gave conflicting signals. Even in the long run the errors do not wash out because:

1. Book measures often understate the profitability of new projects and overstate the profitability of old ones.
2. Errors still occur when a company is in a "steady state" with a constant mix of old and new projects.
3. Errors occur because of inflation.
4. Book measures can be further confused by "creative accounting."

What can we do about these biases? Since the biases all stem from not using economic depreciation, why not switch to economic depreciation? In other words, specify a depreciation pattern that matches expected economic depreciation and use this as the basis of performance measurement.

Much of the pressure for good book earnings comes from top management. This can affect attitudes and decisions down the line. Financial managers should not emphasize book earnings at the expense of more fundamental characteristics of the firm.

LIST OF TERMS

Appropriation request	Postaudit
Capital budget	Project authorization
Economic depreciation	Return on investment
Economic income	

EXERCISES

Fill-in Questions

1. The first step in the investment process is the preparation of the annual list of planned investment projects called the _____.
2. Most companies stipulate that a formal _____ must be prepared before funds are granted for undertaking a project already listed in the budget.
3. The _____ approving expenditure on large investment projects is usually reserved for senior management.
4. Once they have begun to operate, most projects are subjected to an investigation, called a _____, to check on their progress.
5. Cash flows plus any change in present value measures _____.
6. Each year the book value of an asset is reduced by the amount of its _____.
7. The amount by which the present value of an asset falls over a period is called its _____.
8. Many firms use _____ to measure performance. This may be calculated as cash flow minus book depreciation divided by the initial book value of the assets.

Problems

1. Which of these statements are true and which are false?
   a. Postaudits are usually undertaken a year after project completion.
   b. ROI usually overstates the profitability of new projects and understates the profitability of old ones.
   c. The effect of inflation is to make ROI decrease through time.
   d. Most new capital investment projects are initiated from the "top down."
   e. Incremental cash flows cannot usually be calculated from accounting records.
   f. Safety or environmental outlays required by law do not usually pass through the formal capital budgeting process.

2. The ABC Company projects the following after-tax cash flows from its investment of $500,000:

	YEAR							
	0	1	2	3	4	5	6	7
Cash flow ($1000s)	-500	95	105	110	120	135	150	173

   a. If ABC's cost of capital is 15 percent, what is the expected economic income from this project each year?
   b. ABC's accounts are based on depreciating the investment straight-line over 7 years to its estimated salvage value of $45,000. What is the project's book income in each year?
   c. What is the true return on the project each year, and what is its ROI each year?

3. A project is expected to provide the following cash flows:

C_0	C_1	C_2	C_3
-168	60	75	90

   a. Show that the IRR is 15 percent.
   b. Find the accounting rate of return for each year under straight-line depreciation.
   c. Calculate the weighted average of accounting returns, where the weights are the beginning of period book values discounted at the IRR.

4. An asset costs $370,000, and it is expected to produce a cash inflow of $90,000 in each of the following 6 years. The cost of capital is 12 percent.
   a. Calculate each year's income after depreciating the asset using straight-line depreciation.
   b. Calculate each year's income after depreciating the asset using economic depreciation.
   c. Is economic depreciation accelerated or decelerated?
   d. What cash flows would be necessary to make economic depreciation straight-line and provide the same present value?

5. An asset costs $600,000 and is expected to produce after-tax cash flows of $160,000 in each of the following 6 years. The cost of capital is 12 percent and the tax rate is 50 percent. Calculate the NPV, IRR, payback period, and average return on book value for the project.

Essay Questions

1. Describe briefly the various stages in a capital budgeting system, from the origination of the idea for an investment project through to its postaudit.

2. ROI is often used to measure operating performance. What are the pitfalls associated with this technique and how can they be avoided?

3. Describe some of the problems involved in managing and controlling the capital budgeting process so that profitable new projects are suggested and later approved. What measures can be taken to minimize the effects of these problems?

4. "The only people qualified to make judgments about the likely outcomes of most of our new projects are the very managers who are involved in their implementation. This makes proper control quite impossible." Discuss.

5. Describe the differences between economic income and book income. Some people take the view that accountants should not even try to measure economic income. Why not, and what is your view?

ANSWERS TO EXERCISES

Fill-in Questions

1. capital budget
2. appropriation request
3. project authorization
4. postaudit
5. economic income
6. depreciation
7. economic depreciation
8. return on investment

Problems

1. (a) T;   (b) F;   (c) F;   (d) F;   (e) T;   (f) F

2. a. We must discount the cash flows to get the present value each year. Economic depreciation is given by the reduction in present value each year, and this must be subtracted from the cash flow to give the economic income. The worksheet is set out as in the following table (in $1000s).

				YEAR				
	0	1	2	3	4	5	6	7
Present value	500	480	447	404	345	261	150	0
Cash flow		95	105	110	120	135	150	173
Economic depreciation		20	33	43	59	84	111	150
Economic income		75	72	67	61	51	39	23

b. The book income is the cash flow minus book depreciation (in $1000s).

				YEAR				
	0	1	2	3	4	5	6	7
Book value	500	435	370	305	240	175	110	0
Cash flow		95	105	110	120	135	150	173
Depreciation		65	65	65	65	65	65	110*
Book income		30	40	45	55	70	85	63

*Includes write-off of salvage value on realization.

c.

TRUE RETURN, %	15	15	15	15	15	15	15
ROI	6	9	12	18	29	49	57

3. a. Discounting at 15 percent gives NPV = 0.06, at 15.1 percent NPV = -0.24, so IRR is 15.02 percent.

b.

		YEAR	
	1	2	3
Cash flow	60	75	90
Depreciation	56	56	56
Income	4	19	34
Initial book value	168	112	56
Accounting return, %	2.38	16.96	60.71

c.

YEAR	DISCOUNTED BOOK VALUE	WEIGHT (= DBV/TOTAL)	RATE OF RETURN	RETURN x WEIGHT
1	$168.00	.5459	2.38	1.30
2	97.39	.3165	16.96	5.37
3	42.34	.1376	60.71	8.35
Totals	$307.74	1.0000		15.02

The weighted average of 15.02 equals the IRR as noted in Brealey and Myers, footnote 6.

4. a. Straight-line depreciation is $370,000/6 = $61,667 per year, and income is $28,333.

b.

			YEAR				
	0	1	2	3	4	5	6
Cash flow		90	90	90	90	90	90
Present value	370	324	273	216	152	80	0
Economic depreciation		46	51	57	64	72	80
Economic income		44	39	33	26	18	10

c. Economic depreciation is decelerated.

d. The present values must reduce by $61,667 each year. Each year the cash flow must be the depreciation of $61,667 plus 12 percent of the initial present value. This gives:

YEAR	INITIAL PV	CASH FLOW
0	370,000	
1	308,333	106,067
2	246,667	98,667
3	185,000	91,267
4	123,333	83,867
5	61,667	76,467
6	---------	69,067

5. The annual cash flows (in $1000s) are as follows:

	YEAR 0	YEARS 1-6
Cash flow	-600	160

We can use the 6-year, 12 percent annuity factor to calculate the net present value:

$$\begin{aligned} NPV &= -\$600,000 + (\$160,000 \times 4.111) \\ &= \$57,760 \end{aligned}$$

IRR: At 15 percent the NPV is $5440. At 16 percent the NPV is -$10,400. Interpolating, the IRR is 15 percent + [$5440/($5440 + $10,400)] = 15.3 percent.

Payback: The cash flow of $160,000 per year pays back the investment of $600,000 in $600,000/$160,000 = 3.75 years.

Average return on book: Annual depreciation = $100,000; so book income = $60,000 each year. Average investment = $300,000; so ROI = 20 percent.

CHAPTER 13
CORPORATE FINANCING AND THE
SIX LESSONS OF MARKET EFFICIENCY

INTRODUCTION

This chapter marks the beginning of a whole new section of the book. Chapters 2 to 12 were about how companies should make capital investment decisions: the decisions on spending money. The next 12 chapters are about how companies should think about their financing decisions: the decisions on raising money.

Chapters 13 to 15 are particularly important. They provide a comprehensive introduction to the problems of financing. Chapter 13 sets us on the road with some cautions to bear in mind along the way. When we considered capital investment decisions, there was a good chance that our company had some kind of relative advantage in meeting the needs of its markets in a profitable way. These relative advantages enable a company to find investments it can make with positive net present values. However, when it comes to financing decisions, the company is much less likely to have a relative advantage as a participant in the financial markets. Financial markets are highly competitive, and firms should usually assume that the securities they issue will be fairly priced and that issuing them has a net present value of zero. Chapter 13 spells out a number of implications for financing decisions that follow from the competitive nature of financial markets.

Looking ahead to the later chapters, Chapter 14 describes the principal families of securities and explains how they are used by corporations to raise money, while Chapter 15 describes the processes that are involved in issuing those securities. Chapters 16 to 19 are concerned with the questions of what dividends a company should pay, how much debt it should have, and how the interactions between investment and financing decisions should be handled. Last of all, Chapters 20 to 26 include more detail about how various forms of debt can be valued, so that they won't be issued at a negative net present value.

WHAT TO LOOK FOR IN CHAPTER 13

The main point of this chapter is that there is no easy way to make money. We have already encountered this idea in earlier chapters, especially Chapters 3 and 11. Chapter 13 describes the competitive nature of financial markets and draws out a number of implications for financial managers.

One essential distinction is the difference between the markets for physical assets and for financial assets. Back in Chapter 11 we saw that a company may expect to find positive net present value investments if it has some kind of superior resource compared with its rivals. For example, it may be able to design a better product, produce it more efficiently, or sell it more effectively. Differences of these kinds among firms mean that similar assets can have different values to different firms and will give postive net present values to the more efficient firms. In principle, the same argument applies when we consider purely financial markets--the markets for companies' stocks and bonds. If a company were consistently better than its competitors at dealing in the financial markets, it would be able to make money from its financing operations. It would obtain net present values by selling (or issuing) securities at high prices and buying (or retiring) them at low ones--which, of course, is a recipe for making money in any market. However, here comes the rub. While it's hard enough to maintain the kinds of relative advantages necessary to obtain positive net present values in the markets for the company's products, it is infinitely harder to do so in financial markets.

The reasons for this are not hard to see. If we want to compete in the market for making and selling washing machines, we need a factory, skilled engineers and managers, and a work force and sales force. On the other hand, if we want to compete in the financial market, all we need is some money, a copy of the *Wall Street Journal*, and a telephone; this makes financial markets very competitive.

Investors who think that our company's stock looks cheap will buy it, while those who think it looks expensive will sell it. Of course, an investor can buy a share only if some other investor is willing to sell it. The stock price therefore always adjusts until the same number of shares are demanded for purchases as are offered for sale. The market price represents a kind of consensus as to what the stock is worth. As a result we shall be able to make money consistently from our financial market operations only if we have consistently better information than the rest of the markets as to what various securities are worth. However, information is widely disseminated in financial markets--through company reports, the financial press, and broker's circulars. Investors can also collect their own data and form their own judgments. This means that it is very unlikely that our company will be able to maintain a sufficient monopoly of information to earn economic rents form its financing operations. Companies should generally assume that their securities will be fairly priced.

Definitions of Efficient Markets: The previous section described what an efficient capital market is like. We usually define a efficient market as one in which the prices of all securities fully reflect all available information and no investor can expect more or less than a fair rate of return from purchasing any security. Economists sometimes like to spell out the conditions that will lead to a market of this kind. We can *expect* a market to be efficient if there are a large number of participants, all of whom have free access to all information that is available and who can trade without incurring significant transaction costs. While securities markets don't *exactly* meet these conditions, they very nearly do. There is a large number of investors, information is widely available, and transaction costs are low.

Look out for the three different forms of the efficient market theory. Of course, in one sense a market either is efficient or it isn't, but we often distinguish among different levels of efficiency on the basis of what categories of information are efficiently impounded in prices. Thus if past prices cannot be used to make superior profits, we can conclude that security prices reflect all the information contained in the record of past prices. This type of market efficiency is called *weak form* efficiency. The other two forms are the *semistrong* form, when consistently superior profits cannot be made on the basis of published information, and the *strong* form, when prices reflect all the information that can be obtained by even the most painstaking analysis.

Finally look out for the various sorts of implications that follow from market efficiency--the six lessons of market efficiency. Some of the lessons are bad news for financial managers. You can't expect to earn economic rents by "clever" financing. For example, repurchasing bonds or splitting stock is unlikely to do much to change the value of your company, and manipulating reported earnings by the choice of accounting method is unlikely to have much effect either. Finally, if markets are efficient, you won't be able to find companies to acquire at bargain prices, and neither will investors pay a premium for your company to diversify on their behalf: they are perfectly able to construct diversified portfolios for themselves.

On the other hand, not all the lessons are bad news. If markets are efficient, the financial manager can expect to be able to issue shares at a fair price at any time, and the high elasticity of demand for shares means that even very large issues may be made with a good deal of confidence. Further, since the prices of securities reflect investors' expectations about the future, we can use these prices to find out how investors expect interest rates or earnings to change in the future. Last of all, remember that efficient capital markets do *not* mean that financial managers can let financing take care of itself: there is still a great deal of work for the financial manager to do!

WORKED EXAMPLE

PROBLEM: RELEVANCE OF MARKET EFFICIENCY TO FINANCING DECISIONS
The board of the Eyeball Glazing Corporation is trying to decide on an issue of new shares. The company already has 4 million shares outstanding, and it is authorized to issue up to a further 1 million shares. What proportion of the company will have to be sold in order to raise $8 million if shares can be sold (1) at $32 each, (2) at only $20 each? (3) If the shares are really worth $32 but can be issued only at $20, what loss would existing shareholders suffer if they did not subscribe to such an issue? (4) What is the relevance of market efficiency to the board's decision?

SOLUTION
1. To raise $8 million at $32 a share requires selling $8,000,000/32 = 250,000 shares. The company will then have 4.25 million shares issued, and 0.25 million/4.25 million = 5.88 percent of the company will have to be sold to new shareholders.

2. Similarly, at a price of $20 a share, 400,000 shares must be issued, and this will represent 9.09 percent of the issued capital of the company.

3. Suppose that the company raises $8 million by selling 400,000 shares. If the original 4 million shares were worth $32 each (or $128 million in total), the company is now worth $136 million, which is divided among its 4.4 million shares. Each share will be worth $30.91 ($136,000,000/4,400,000 shares); so the original shareholders have a 3.41 percent loss form the previous value of $32. This drop seriously understates the true significance of their loss, for their total shareholdings are now worth only $123.64 million (4,000,000 shares x $30.91), $4.36 million below the previous figure. They have paid $12.36 million for $8 million worth of cash.

4. If the market is efficient, the situation described in 3 above cannot arise. The board can expect to issue new shares at very close to their true value and should therefore not be reluctant to issue new shares.

SUMMARY

About Financing Decisions: So far we have learned how companies decide to spend money on capital investment projects. Now we will learn how they raise the money to finance their investments. The financing choices include the following:

- What proportion of earnings should be retained and what proportion paid out in dividends?
- Should money be raised by borrowing or by issuing stock?
- Should borrowings be short-term or long-term?
- Should an issue of debt be made convertible into the stock of the company?

In many circumstance we can take the firm's investments as given and then determine what the best financing strategy is. The two kinds of decisions are independent of each other and can be dealt with separately. Sometimes decisions about capital structure depend on project choice (or vice versa), and then the financing and investment decisions have to considered jointly.

A financing decision has an NPV (which measures how attractive it is) just as an investment decision does. For example, if we can borrow $100,000 for 10 years at 3 percent interest (making 10 annual interest payments of $3000 before repaying the $100,000 principal), where we would normally have to pay 10 percent, then this loan has an

$$NPV \;=\; +\$100{,}000 \;-\; \left[\sum_{t=1}^{10} \frac{\$3000}{(1.1)^t} \right] \;-\; \frac{\$100{,}000}{1.1^{10}} \;=\; \$43{,}012$$

Financing decisions differ from investment decisions in that they are easier to reverse and are more likely to have a zero NPV. If a company is to get a positive NPV from selling a security, it must persuade the buyer to accept a negative NPV--not an easy thing to do. If capital markets are *efficient*, the purchase or sale of a security at the current market price is a zero NPV transaction.

What Is an Efficient Market? Economist say that a security market is *efficient* when information is widely and cheaply available and all relevant information is always reflected in security prices. This *implies* that the purchase (or sale) of any security has a zero NPV.

The theory of efficient markets developed from statistical studies of the movements of stock prices. Such studies show that stock prices do *not* follow predictable cycles. Instead, the successive price changes of a stock appear to be independent of each other: today's price change will not help us to predict tomorrow's price change. This *random walk* of stock prices was first discovered by Maurice Kendall in 1953.

At first economists were surprised at this randomness (that is, unpredictability) of stock price movements. However, it turns out that they should not have been surprised. We should expect this kind of price behavior in a security market that is efficient. In an efficient market prices reflect all relevant information, and price changes are caused by new information. If this new information could be predicted ahead of time, it wouldn't be new information, and the prices would already have adjusted to it. In other words, in an efficient market stock prices already reflect all that is predictable. Changes in stock prices are caused by new information that could not have been predicted.

The investment analysis carried out by investors helps to make price changes random. For example, if investors can forecast that a stock which sells at $50 today will go up to $60 next month, they will *immediately* rush to buy it until they have pushed the price up to the point where the stock offers a normal rate of return. There are two types of investment analysis: *Fundamental analysis* uses information about a company's business and profitability to appraise the value of its stock. *Technical analysis* simply uses the past price record to look for predictable patterns in the price series.

We sometimes distinguish among three forms of market efficiency. The *weak* form of efficiency means that prices reflect at least all the information contained in the record of past prices--this implies that it is important to make consistently superior returns by just using technical analysis. The *semistrong* form of efficiency means that prices reflect all published information, such as published accounting reports or published forecasts of earnings or dividends. Finally, the *strong* form of efficiency means that prices reflect all information that can be acquired by even the most painstaking fundamental analysis of the company and economy, including gathering information that is not publicly disseminated.

Empirical studies provide support for the weak and semistrong forms. They indicate that price changes seem to be random. Public announcements of many specific items of news are rapidly and accurately impounded in the price of the stock. The usual methodology for assessing market reaction to information is to calculate abnormal returns by adjusting for market movements, and to average these across similar events. Studies of the performance of professionally managed portfolios conclude that no group of institutions has been able to outperform the market consistently, after taking account of differences in risk. However, there are puzzles and inefficiencies in the semistrong and strong forms. The stocks of small companies have consistently performed better than their risks would seem to require. There are also some puzzling returns concentrated (on average) in the first week of January. There is some evidence against strong form efficiency. For example there are studies which show superior returns to New York Stock Exchange specialists and to company managers trading in their own stock.

Finally, there are three common misconceptions about the efficient-market hypothesis. To avoid them, remember that an efficient market *does not*:

- Imply perfect forecasting ability
- Mean that portfolio managers are incompetent (because of their inability to achieve superior returns)
- Mean that the market is irrational (because price changes are random)

The Six Lessons of Market Efficiency

1. *Markets have no memory*, and the history of the stock price is no guide as to whether it is overpriced or underpriced. Financial managers sometimes appear to ignore this. They tend to issue stock when their stock price is historically high and are reluctant to issue stock after a fall in price.

2. *Trust market prices*. There is no way for most investors to find bargains consistently that are underpriced. This should be borne in mind when considering the management of the firm's pension funds, its decision to acquire another company, or its decision to repurchase its own securities. The Northwestern Bell decision to repurchase its bonds at a price of $1160 in 1977 (following a fall in interest rates) *did* reduce future interest charges but nevertheless had a negative NPV. The company would apparently have done better to wait until 1979, when it could have exercised its valuable option to call the bonds at the lower price of $1085.70.

3. *There are no financial illusions*. Investors are concerned with the firm's cash flows and the portion of those cash flows to which they are entitled. It is unlikely that a firm can increase its market value by merely cosmetic changes such as stock splits or by manipulating the earnings reported to shareholders.

4. *The do-it-yourself alternative*. Investors will not pay others for what they can easily do themselves. What advantage is there to a company in pursuing a diversification policy when its shareholders can (and should) hold diversified portfolios of stocks themselves? What advantages is there to a company borrowing to provide financial leverage for its shareholders when they are free to borrow on their own accounts? This last question is examined in more detail in Chapters 17 and 18.

5. *Seen one stock, seen them all*. Investors don't buy a stock for its unique qualities; they buy it because it offers the prospect of a fair return for its risk. This means that a very slight increase in the expected return from one particular stock should be sufficient to induce a lot of investors to switch to it. Economists describe this situation by saying that stocks are almost perfect substitutes for each other, and the demand for any given company's stock is very elastic. This has the following important implication: contrary to popular belief, you can sell large blocks of stock at close to the market price as long as you can convince other investors that you have no private information. Myron Scholes' study of secondary offerings confirmed that large offerings had only a very small depressing effect on the price.

6. *Reading the entrails*. Security prices reflect what investors expect to happen in the future. They can therefore be used as a guide to what people expect. The return offered by a company's bonds, and the variability of its common stock are good indicators of the probability of its going bankrupt. The Dow Jones average is a leading indicator of the level of economic activity. Finally, the difference between long-term and short-term interest rates tells something about what investors expect to happen to the short-term rate in the future (Chapter 23 gives more details of this).

LIST OF TERMS

Call provision
Efficient market
Elasticity of demand
Fundamental analysis
Maturity
Random walk

Semistrong form efficiency
Stock dividend
Stock split
Strong form efficiency
Technical analysis
Weak form efficiency

EXERCISES

Fill-in Questions

1. A securities market is said to be _____, if the securities in it are fairly priced and reflect all known information.
2. The prices of securities appear to follow a _____ in which each successive price change is independent of all previous price changes.
3. Investment analysis to determine the worth of a company's shares by studying the company's business and trying to uncover information about its profitability is called _____.
4. Investment analysis based on studying the record of past prices is called _____.
5. If prices reflect all the information contained in the history of past prices the market is _____.
6. If prices reflect all published information, the market satisfies the conditions for _____.
7. In the _____ of efficiency prices reflect all information that investors can obtain from any sources.
8. The _____ for any article measures the percentage change in the quantity demanded for each percentage change in its price.
9. The _____ of a bond is when its original face value will be repaid.
10. A _____ on an issue of bonds provides the company with an option to repurchase its bonds at specified prices on specified dates.
11. A company makes a _____ when it increases the number of outstanding shares by subdividing the stock that is already outstanding.
12. A _____ occurs when a company issues more shares of stock as dividends to its shareholders.

Problems

1. The Catalytic Cracking Corporation is about to split its stock on a 4-for-1 basis. Before the split its share price is $76. What would you expect it to be afterwards?

2. High Potential Electronics Corporation believes that its stock is overvalued by the market. Its shares are selling at $80, although management believes they are worth only $60. There are currently 1.2 million shares outstanding, and the company plans to raise $7.5 million by issuing a further 100,000 shares at $75 each. The existing shareholders can sell their rights to subscribe to this issue for $461,500. If they do so and all the new shares are taken up by new investors, how much will the original shareholders have benefited (a) if the shares were worth only $60 before, and (b) if they were worth $80?

3. A company is eligible for a subsidized 5-year loan of $1 million at 8 percent interest where the usual market rate is 12 percent. The loan is to be repaid in five equal annual payments (of interest plus principal). What is the net present value of this loan?

4. Today I can buy an 11-percent coupon, 10-year bond at face value. I believe that in a year's time interest rates will have come down so that this bond (which will then be a 9-year bond) will be yielding only 8 percent. (a) If I am correct, what return will I have earned on my investment? (b) What implications does this have for forecasting interest rates in terms of (i) its usefulness and (ii) its difficulty? Assume interest is paid annually.

5. The highly respected economic forecasting department of a major United States bank announces that their latest forecast predicts a significant upturn in economic activity and corporate profits starting in 2 years and lasting for 3 or 4 years. What effect on share prices do you expect this to have: (a) immediately; (b) in 2 years; and (c) in 6 years?

6. Identify for which two of the following items demand is least elastic with respect to price, and for which two it is most elastic: (a) steak, (b) tobacco, (c) a financial security, (d) gasoline, (e) tuxedos, (f) shortening.

7. Company A has a market value of $40 million. Company B has a market value of $20 million. A proposed merger between them seems likely to reduce the standard deviation of their equity returns from 40 percent individually to 35 percent combined. What would you expect the market value of the combined company to be after the merger?

8. Which of the following is most likely to result in an increase in the value of the company's shares: (a) It announces that its long-awaited contract with the federal government has now been finalized, and production will begin as soon as a satisfactory specification can be agreed upon. (b) As a result of a change in its depreciation policy the earnings figure in its newly released annual report is almost double the figure for the previous year. (c) It announces a 50 percent increase in its dividend. (d) Its main competitor announces a price cut.

9. A random number generator provides me with the following sequence of random numbers: 18, -10, 12. Which of the following series most resembles the prices of a security on three successive dates in the future, where its price today is $50:
   (a) 50 x 1.18, 50 x 1.18 x 0.90, 50 x 1.18 x 0.90 x 1.12
   (b) 50 x 1.18, 50 x 0.90, 50 x 1.12; (c) Other: specify.

Essay Questions

1. Explain what is meant by an "efficient securities market", and describe the three forms of efficiency that are commonly distinguished.

2. Describe the most important implications of efficient financial markets for the corporate financial manager.

3. "This idea of market efficiency just doesn't make any sense to me at all. Why, I know of a dozen or more fortunes that have been made or lost on the stock exchange." Explain carefully why those two sentences are not incompatible.

4. "We can't afford to accept that the market might be efficient. If we accepted that, we'd have nothing to say to the investors who come to us for advice." Discuss.

5. "Even if the market is efficient, there's no need to lose money unnecessarily. I can still reduce my losses by making sure I always buy after a fall in price rather than after a rise in price." Discuss.

ANSWERS TO EXERCISES

Fill-in Questions

1. efficient
2. random walk
3. fundamental analysis
4. technical analysis
5. weak form efficient
6. semistrong form efficiency
7. strong form
8. elasticity of demand
9. maturity
10. call provision
11. stock split
12. stock dividend

Problems

1. $19.

2. (a) Before the issue of shareholdings were worth $72 million. Afterward, the shareholders have $461,500 in cash plus a 12/13[1,200,000 shares/(1,200,000 shares + 100,000 shares)] claim on $72 million plus $7.5 million. This gives them a total value of $73,846,115; so they have benefited by $1,846,115. (b) Before the issue the shareholdings were worth $96 million. Afterward, the value to the original shareholders is

   $461,500 + (12/13) x ($96,000,000 + $7,500,000)

   This is still $96 million; so there is no benefit (or loss) to the original shareholders.

3. To give the loan an 8 percent interest rate the annual payments must be $1,000,000/3.993 = $250,438 (3.993 is the 5-year annuity factor at 8 percent). Discounting those payments at 12 percent produces a PV of $902,829 ($250,438 x 3.605); so the NPV of the loan is $97,171.

4. (a) The price of the bond will be $1187.17[($110 x 6.247) + ($1000 x 0.5000)] at the end of a year, and in addition I will have $110 cash. This gives a total return of 29.72 percent. (b) (i) If I *could* forecast interest rates accurately, I could make a lot of money, but (ii) this makes forecasting extremely competitive and *very* difficult.

5. (a) A slight increase in share prices if this represents good news. (b) and (c) no effect

6. Least elastic: (b) tobacco, (d) gasoline. Most elastic: (c) a financial security, (f) shortening

7. $60 million. (The market price already represents market-related risk as measured by beta.)

8. (c)

9. (a)

CHAPTER 14
AN OVERVIEW OF CORPORATE FINANCING

INTRODUCTION

As you might expect from its title, Chapter 14 provides the kind of introduction to corporate financing that you just can't afford to miss. The first part of the chapter describes the four main families of securities that companies can issue: common stock, debt, preferred stock, and options of various kinds (such as warrants and convertible bonds.) The emphasis is on explaining the wide variety of methods that companies can use to raise money and on explaining the different terms that are used to describe them. The remainder of the chapter describes how securities are actually used by corporations. It examines the relative importance of various sources of finance for corporations in the United States and comments on some patterns in financing behavior.

WHAT TO LOOK FOR IN CHAPTER 14

Chapter 14 could change your life! After you have read this chapter, you may find that you begin to talk a strange new language using phrases like "shares that are issued but not outstanding" and "convertible subordinated debentures."

That is what this chapter is about. It doesn't contain any difficult new ideas but it does contain a large number of new terms that you have to be able to use if you want to speak the language of financing. In learning these new terms, you may want to devote more time than usual to our list of the main new terms and to the corresponding set of fill-in questions.

New Terms: Here is a brief guide to where the majority of new terms arise. First, a number of terms arise in connection with common stock. There are terms to describe how much stock a company has been authorized to issue, to describe how much stock it has and hasn't issued, and stock that has been issued which has subsequently been repurchased by the company. There are also terms for describing the arrangement by which shareholders vote for their board of directors, and sometimes we even have to distinguish between classes of common stock that have different rights to vote and receive dividends.

Second, a lot of new terms are needed to describe the enormous variety of debt that can be issued. The most common differences between debt issues concern their maturity, the kinds of provisions that are made for their retirement, their position in the pecking order of financial claims on the firm (their seniority), and whether they are secured. Secured debt has a direct claim on assets of the firm in the event of a default. Debt issues can also pay either a fixed rate of interest or a floating rate and may be denominated in currencies other than United States dollars.

Preferred stock introduces only a few new terms, but more are introduced by the different kinds of options that companies can issue. In particular we have warrants, which are simply a firm's securities that give the holder the right to purchase a set number of shares of common stock, at a set price, on or before a set date in the future. We also have convertible bonds which are bonds that give their holder a similar right to exchange them for a fixed number of shares at a future date or dates.

Types of securities and tax: Look out, too, for differences in the tax treatment of different securities. Notice that while interest payments on debt are paid out of pretax income, dividends on both common and preferred stock are paid out of after-tax income. On the other hand, companies that hold securities pay corporate income tax on the whole of their interest income from bonds, but pay tax on only 20 percent of the dividends they receive from common or preferred stock. Can you guess what this means for those who issue preferred stock and hold it? If you can't guess, Section 14-3 will tell you.

Sections 14-1 through 14-5 should give you a pretty good idea of the variety of different securities that a company can issue. Remember too that companies don't have to confine themselves to issuing the same kinds of securities that have already been issued by other companies. They are perfectly free to create entirely new securities; so if your company thinks that investors would like to buy a floating-rate Deutschemark bond that is convertible into its (dollar) common stock, there is no reason not to issue one.

Patterns of financing: Section 14-6 is about companies' requirements for external funds and how the different kinds of securities are used in practice. We shouldn't be surprised that a large proportion of firms' capital requirements come from internally generated cash. Remember that cash flow includes depreciation and if none of this were reinvested there would be a rapid decline in the country's stock of capital investment. Equally, internally generated cash is not sufficient to meet companies' expenditure requirements, and additional funds are raised by debt issues and issues of stock. The funds are supplied by pension funds an other financial intermediaries such as mutual funds, as well as by individual investors.

While, as we saw in the last chapter, we cannot predict future changes in the levels of stock prices, we can observe systematic and predictable patterns in firms' financing behavior. The amount of external money that companies require (their financial deficit) is linked to the general level of economic activity. This deficit is lowest when the economy is pulling out of a recession. At this stage of the business cycle companies have spare capacity and increases in sales have a big effect on their cash position, since inventories are reduced and major new investments are unlikely to be undertaken. The deficit is usually largest when economic activity begins to turn down, and investment that is already committed continues to be made. We may also observe patterns in the way companies choose between debt or equity financing. There is a pronounced tendency for companies to make equity issues when the stock market is historically high. Notice that neither of the patterns described conflicts with the efficient markets idea -- there is no way that anyone can make superior profits from knowing about these regularities in the volumes of money raised.

SUMMARY

The first five sections of our summary describe the main types of securities that firms can issue. The final section is about how firms tend to use these securities.

Common Stock: A company is allowed to issue shares up to the amount specified by its *authorized share capital*, which can only be increased with the permission of the shareholders. *Outstanding* shares are those held by investors. Shares that have been issued but subsequently repurchased by the company (and held in its treasury) are called *treasury shares*. They are said to be *issued but not outstanding*. All issued shares are entered in the company's accounts at their *par* (or *stated*) *value*. Because some states do not allow companies to sell shares below par value, par value is generally set at a low figure which has no economic significance.

The common stockholders are the owners of the company and have a general preemptive right to anything of value that the company may wish to distribute. Their control over the company's affairs is manifested by their right to vote on appointments to the board of directors and on some other issues. Voting may be on a majority basis or on a cumulative basis. Cumulative voting makes it more likely for minority groups to obtain representation on the board. Under this system shareholders may, if they wish, allot all their votes to one candidate. For example, if six directors are to be elected, a shareholder can allocate all six votes from each share to a single candidate and does not have to choose six candidates to vote for. Finally, a few companies separate classes of stock (for example, class A and class B) which are distinguished by having different rights to vote.

Corporate Debt: There is a great variety of ways in which companies can borrow money. The common feature is that the company promises to make regular interest payments and to repay the principal amount according to an agreed schedule. The company's liability is limited; so lenders can only look to the earnings and assets of the company for their payment. Lenders cannot look beyond those assets to the shareholders for repayment. Any debt can be classified along the following six dimensions:

- *Maturity:* The length of time before the debt is due to be completely repaid. Long-term debt which does not mature for more than a year is called *funded* debt. Short-term debt due in less than a year is called *unfunded*.
- *Provision for repayment:* Long-term loans may be repaid in a single "bullet" payment on their maturity date, or they may be repaid steadily over a period of time. A *sinking fund* is often used to retire publicly traded bonds gradually. The borrower may also have a *call* provision which provides the right to repay all or part of the debt issue before maturity at some specified premium above its face value.
- *Seniority:* Debt may be junior or senior. If the company goes bankrupt, its junior (or *subordinated*) debt is not eligible to receive payment until all senior debt has been paid in full.
- *Security:* Debt which (in the event of default) has first claim on specified assets is said to be *secured* on those assets. A mortgage is an example of this, while long-term bonds which are unsecured are called debentures.
- *Fixed rate or floating rate:* The interest rate may be fixed for the whole term of the loan when it is issued, or it may be determined from time to time during the term according to an agreed formula such as "1 percent above prime."
- *Country and currency:* While most borrowing by United States corporations is done in the United States and in United States dollars, firms may also borrow in foreign countries or in foreign currencies.

Preferred Stock: Every company has common stock. Most companies have debt. Relatively few have preferred stock, which has some of the characteristics of common stock and some of debt. Legally, preferred stock is part of the ownership of the company, but (like debt) it promises a fixed dividend every year. This dividend is payable at the discretion of the directors, with the provision that no dividends may be paid on the common stock until the preferred dividend has been paid. There is no final repayment date, but many issues provide for the periodic retirement of stock. Preferred stock rarely confers full voting privileges. In seniority it is senior to the company's common stock but junior to everything else.

A Note on Taxation: Interest payments on debt are regarded as a business expense and come out of pretax income. We can therefore think of debt as receiving a subsidy from the government. Dividends (whether on common stock or on preferred stock) are regarded as a distribution of income to the owners of the firm. Accordingly, they come out of after-tax income. Interest received is part of a company's income and is taxable. However, to reduce the incidence of double taxation, companies have to pay tax on only 20 percent of their dividend income. As a result most preferred stock is held by corporations (favorable treatment of dividend income), and most is issued by regulated utility companies (who would be made to lower their rates if they used subsidized debt instead).

Dilution: Because underpricing does not affect the value of the company, the only sense in which dilution can have any meaning is if the proceeds of the issue are to be used to finance poor investment projects. However, any share price fall which this may give rise to on the issue announcement is due solely to the poor investment decision and has nothing to do with the financing decision. Always try to avoid confusing the effects of the investment and financing decisions.

Warrants and Convertibles

- *Warrants:* These give their owner the right (known as a *call option*) to purchase one share of common stock at a specified price on or before a specified future date.
- *Convertible bonds:* These are bonds issued by the company that can be exchanged for (or *converted* into) a specified number of shares on specific future dates if the holder wishes.

The innovation of derivative instruments. The last decade has seen rapid growth in the use of

- *Traded Options:* the right to buy or sell an asset at a fixed price in the future (or not).
- *Futures and Forwards:* the obligation to buy (or sell) an asset at a fixed price in the future.
- *Swaps:* an exchange of obligations to service different debts.

Patterns of Corporate Financing: The figures for 1986 show the following percentage uses and sources of funds in nonfinancial corporations:

USES		SOURCES	
Capital expenditure	77%	Cash flow from operations	79%
Increase in inventories	1%	Net issues of:	
Increase in receivables	2%	Stock	-18%
Increase in liquid assets	11%	Long-term debt	23%
Other	10%	Short-term debt	15%
		Increase in payables	0%
		Total external funds	21%
Total uses	100%	Total sources	100%

The most important source of funds is clearly cash flows retained from operations (79 percent in 1986). We should not be surprised at this high predominance of internally generated funds, because the cash flow from operations includes depreciation provisions. There is still a substantial requirement for external funds. This requirement is sometimes called the *financial deficit*. It is usually largest when economic activity begins to turn down and smallest when the economy is pulling out of a recession.

The volume of new issues of stock varies substantially from year to year. The net repurchases of the 1984-6 period are unprecedented. Companies tend to issue more equity when stock prices are at historically high levels. Similarly, the volume of long-term debt issued is (inversely) related to the level of interest rates. Over the last 30 years companies' balance sheets show a marked increase in the proportion of debt to total assets (34 percent in 1954 to 56 percent in 1986). However, at least part of the reason for this is that progressive inflation has increased the market values of assets relative to their book values. Finally, the 1982 decreases in inventories, receivables, and payables are a little unusual.

LIST OF TERMS

Authorized share capital

Call

Convertible bond

Cumulative voting

Debenture

Dilution

Eurobond

Eurodollar

Floating rate

Forward

Funded debt

Future

Lease

Majority voting

Outstanding shares

Par value

Preferred stock

Prime rate

Proxy contest

Secured

Senior

Sinking fund

Subordinated

Swap

Traded Option

Treasury shares

Warrant

EXERCISES

Fill-in Questions

1. The maximum number of shares that a company can issue is known as its _____.
2. Shares that have already been issued and are held by investors are called _____.
3. _____ are shares that have been repurchased by the company.
4. The _____ of a security is the value at which it is entered in the company's books.
5. _____ is the name for the voting system under which each director is voted on separately.
6. The voting system under which a stockholder may cast all his or her votes for one candidate is known as _____.
7. A _____ arises when the firm's existing management and directors compete with outsiders for the votes of the shareholders in order to control the corporation.
8. _____ debt is debt that matures after more than 1 year.
9. To repay its long-term loans in an orderly fashion over an extended period of time, a company may pay each year a sum of cash into a _____ which is then used to repurchase the bonds.
10. In the event of bankruptcy, _____ debt must be repaid before subordinated debt receives any payment.
11. _____ debt represents a junior claim which, in the event of default, is paid only after all senior creditors are satisfied.
12. In the event of default _____ debt has first claim on specified assets.
13. A _____ is a long-term bond that is unsecured.
14. The interest on a _____ loan varies with the short-term interest rate.
15. Banks will lend to their most favored customers at the _____ rate.
16. A _____ is a dollar that has been deposited with a bank outside the United States.
17. A _____ is an issue of debt that is sold simultaneously in several countries.
18. A long-term rental agreement, known as a _____, can provide an alternative to borrowing.
19. _____ stock is an equity security which offers a fixed dividend that must be paid before any dividend can be paid on the common stock.
20. A _____ option provides the right to purchase an asset at a specified price on or before a specified exercise date.

21. A _____ is a long-term security issued by a company which gives the holder the right to purchase one share of common stock at a set price on or before a set date.

22. A bond that may be converted into the company's common stock at the discretion of the holder is called a _____.

23. A _____ gives the holder the right to buy (or sometimes to sell) an asset at a fixed price up to a specified date.

24. A _____ is like a _____ contract but is generally traded on an organized exchange. Both contracts give an obligation to buy (or sell) at a fixed price at some future date.

25. An arrangement by which two companies lend to each other on different terms (e.g., in different currencies) is called a _____.

26. When new shares are issued, each existing share is entitled to a smaller proportion of the income and assets of the firm than formerly. This phenomenon is called _____.

Problems

1. The authorized share capital of Shady Enterprises is 400,000 shares. The equity is currently shown in the company's accounts as follows:

Common stock ($0.25 par value)	$60,000
Additional paid-in capital	200,000
Retained earnings	20,000
Common equity	$280,000
Treasury stock (15,000 shares)	10,000
Net common equity	270,000

   a. How many shares are issued?
   b. How many are outstanding?
   c. How many more shares can be issued without the approval of the shareholders?
   d. What is the share price, if it is twice its book value?

2. Shady Enterprises of problem 1 issues a further 80,000 shares at an issue price of $0.90 a share. How will the equity be shown in the company's books after the issue?

3. There are nine directors to be elected and I own a round lot of 100 shares. What is the maximum number of votes I can cast for my favorite candidate under (a) majority voting, and (b) cumulative voting?

4. The shareholders of Shady Enterprises need to elect five directors. There are 305,000 shares outstanding. How many shares do you need to own to ensure that you can elect at least one director (a) under majority voting and (b) under cumulative voting?

5. The Shifty Transportation Company has the following income for the year:

Taxable income from operations	$253,000
Interest income	42,000
Dividends from preferred stock	20,000
Dividends from common stock	10,000
Total income	$325,000

It has paid interest charges amounting to $59,000 and dividends on its preferred and common stock of $35,000 and $50,000. If it pays tax at 34 percent, what is its tax bill for the year?

6. The Shifty Transportation Company of the last problem had the following income and payments in the previous year:

Income from:

Operations	$224,000
Interest	32,000
Preferred dividends	40,000
Common dividends	40,000
	$336,000

Payments:

Interest	$44,000
Preferred dividends	$35,000
Common dividends	$45,000

How much tax should it have paid?

7. Which of the following are true and which are false?
   a. The financial deficit is usually largest when the economy is pulling out of a recession.
   b. Firms tend to issue more equity when stock prices are historically high.
   c. If a bond is secured, the company makes regular payment of cash into a sinking fund.
   d. The firm's capital expenditure requirements are usually more than covered by internally generated cash.

Essay Questions

1. Explain how issued share capital is shown in a company's accounts, and describe what rights and privileges shareholders enjoy.

2. Describe the variety of different types of debt that a company can issue.

3. What is preferred stock, who issues it, who buys it, and why?

4. Describe the main sources and uses of companies' funds, What is meant by the financial deficit and how is it affected by the behavior of the economy?

5. "It's only when a company goes to the market to raise new equity that it's forced to earn the cost of capital on its funds." Discuss.

6. "If the firm has good projects and needs equity capital to finance them, then dilution should not bar it from going to the market." Discuss.

ANSWERS TO EXERCISES

Fill-in Questions

1. authorized share capital
2. outstanding shares
3. treasury shares
4. par value
5. majority voting
6. cumulative voting
7. proxy contest

8. funded
9. sinking fund
10. senior
11. subordinated
12. secured
13. debenture
14. floating-rate
15. prime rate
16. eurodollar
17. eurobond
18. lease
19. preferred
20. call
21. warrant
22. convertible bond
23. traded option
24. future, forward
25. swap
26. dilution

Problems

1. (a) 240,000; (b) 225,000; (c) 160,000; (d) 2 x ($270,000/225,000) = $2.40

2.
Common stock ($0.25 par value)	$80,000
Additional paid-in capital	252,000
Retained earnings	20,000
Common equity	$352,000
Treasury stock	10,000
Net common equity	$342,000

3. (a) 100; (b) 900
4. (a) More than half the outstanding shares are needed, that is 152,501 shares.
   (b) As long as your candidate gets at least a fifth of the total votes cast, she is bound to be elected. To ensure this, you need only 61,000 shares. Even this is more than you really need. One more than a sixth, that is, 50,834, is sufficient.

5. Shifty's taxable income is calculated as follows:

Income from operations	$253,000
Interest income	42,000
20 percent of dividends	6,000
	$301,000
Less interest expense	59,000
	242,000

Its tax bill is 34 percent of $242,000, which is $82,280.

6. Taxable income is given by:

Income from operations	$224,000
Interest income	32,000
20 percent of dividends	16,000
	$272,000
Less interest expense	44,000
Taxable income	$228,000

Tax is 34 percent of $228,000, which is $77,520.

7. (a) F; (b) T; (c) F; (d) F

CHAPTER 15
HOW CORPORATIONS ISSUE SECURITIES

INTRODUCTION

This chapter outlines how companies raise new long-term funds in the capital market. It not only covers a wealth of institutional material, but it also guides managers through the many decisions they face when embarking on any long-term funding exercise. Since in recent years United States companies have funded well over a third of their operations through external financing, more than two-thirds of which has taken the form of long-term security issues, it is clear that this chapter deals with a very important topic in corporate finance. It is important, therefore, that you should have a good understanding of this area and be conversant with the language and procedures involved.

WHAT TO LOOK FOR IN CHAPTER 15

This chapter is structured around the two major methods used to acquire capital:

1. *Public issues*, where the securities issued will be traded on the securities markets. There are two types: *general cash offers*, which are issues sold to investors at large, and (less common) *privileged subscription or rights issues*, which are offered to existing stockholders.

2. *Private placements*, where the securities issued are not traded on the securities markets.

This chapter contains both descriptions of the different issue methods and procedures in use and prescriptions for how they should be used by financial managers. The descriptive material is straightforward, but you will meet a lot of new terms -- more even than in the last chapter. Although most of those terms mean much what you might expect them to mean, you may find it worthwhile to make sure you are reasonably familiar with the various issue procedures and the terms used to describe them before you start to worry too much about the implications for financial managers.

Managers concerned with raising money need to decide:

- What issue method to use
- How large issues should be and how often to make them
- What the selling price should be
- Whether they should buy insurance (called underwriting) against an issue's failing
- How the market will react to the issue

These are interesting and important questions. On the whole, they are easy to understand, but where they are not, we will try to help you. The chapter will be easier to follow if you remember some of the lessons of market efficiency developed in Chapter 13. It's fair to point out, however, that you don't need to be a fully converted believer in market efficiency to accept the validity of the following points.

Financing Decisions and Stockholder Wealth: Financing decisions seldom affect total security holders' wealth. Furthermore, it is reasonable to assume that most financing decisions have a net present value of zero. This is because a positive NPV financing decision is one where the money raised exceeds the value of the liability created. In the highly competitive capital market, it is very unlikely that any firm could consistently fool investors in this way.

Financing Decisions and the Distribution of Wealth: Financing decisions can, however, affect the distribution of wealth between security holders. If new securities are underpriced, new holders will obtain a bargain at the expense of existing holders. This is not a problem, however, in the case of rights issues where existing holders are given rights to subscribe in proportion to the size of their holdings. The worked example should help you to handle the kind of calculations that arise in connection with rights issues.

The Importance of Market Prices: When deciding on the issue price for new securities, the best guide to what a company can hope to obtain is the price of closely comparable securities which are already traded.

There Are No Financial Illusions: It is the effect of financing decisions on stockholders' wealth that matters, and it is difficult to imagine that stockholders will believe one share at $20 is worth more than two shares at $10. Bear this in mind when you read about rights issues.

It Is Helpful to Separate Investment and Financing Decisions: If the market believes the investment projects for which the issue proceeds are destined will provide inadequate returns, the stock price will fall. However, this is the result of a poor investment decision and has nothing to do with the financing operation or the issue method employed. Keep this in mind when you read the section entitled A Word on Dilution.

With these points in mind, you should now read the chapter. On a first reading, you could easily skip the sections on Competitive Bidding and Pricing General Cash Offers in Other Countries.

WORKED EXAMPLE

PROBLEM: RIGHTS ISSUE ARITHMETIC

Pobble Footwear Corporation is making a rights issue to raise $10 million. Just before the issue Pobble's stock price was $42 and the terms of the issue are 1 for 5 at a subscription price of $33. Calculate (1) the expected price of the stock ex rights, and (2) the value of one right. (3) Mrs. Cobble owns 405 Pobble shares. How many rights will she have to sell to maintain the same ($17,010) investment in the company? (4) Show that in general the value of a right is given by the formula (rights-on price – issue price)/($N + 1$) when the terms of the issue are 1 for N.

SOLUTION

1. After the issue is completed, all shares will be ex rights. For every 5 shares worth $42 x 5 before the issue, there will correspond 6 shares worth $42 x 5 + $33 (= $243) after the issue. Each share will therefore be worth $243/6; so the ex-rights price is $40.50.

2. The value of one right is the difference between the rights-on price (the share price before the issue) and the ex-rights price. This is $1.50.

3. If Mrs. Cobble were to sell all her rights at $1.50 each, the total value of her holding would fall by 405 x $1.50 = $607.50. To make this up, she must subscribe to $607.50/$40.50 = 15 new shares (since after the issue each share will be worth $40.50). For each new share she will need 5 rights. She should therefore sell 405 – (15 x 5) = 330 rights, which will realize $495.

4. Proceeding in the same way as in the answer to part 1, we note that to every N shares at the rights-on price is added an additional share subscribed to at the offer price. This gives the basic equation

$$N \text{ x (rights-on price)} + \text{issue price} = (N + 1) \text{ ex-rights price}$$

Alternatively, this can be written as

$$[(N + 1) \times \text{rights-on price}] - (\text{rights-on price} - \text{issue price}) = (N + 1) \times \text{ex-rights price}$$

from which it follows immediately that since the value of a right is the difference between the right-on and ex-rights prices:

$$\text{Value of a right} = \text{rights-on price} - \text{ex-rights price} = (\text{rights-on price} - \text{issue price})/(N + 1)$$

In part 2 above, we could have used this formula to give value of right = ($42 – $33)/(5 + 1) = $1.50.

SUMMARY

This summary covers all the material in the chapter but structures it in a rather different way. It deals first with venture capital, next with the descriptive sections on issue procedures and then finally on to the prescriptive content by looking at the questions facing managers who are making new issues. In this way, material from different parts of the chapter is brought together on a topic-by-topic basis. For revision purposes, we think you will find this the most useful approach.

Venture Capital

Equity investment in young private companies is usually called venture capital. It may be provided by specialist partnerships, investment institutions or by wealthy individuals. First-stage financing, if successful, will lead to second-stage financing, and possibly further stages before the company is ready to go public with an initial public offering.

Descriptive Information: Issue Procedures

1. **Public issues:** The first formal step is approval of the issue by the board and also by stockholders if an increase in authorized capital is necessary.

   A registration statement is then prepared for submission to the Securities and Exchange Commission (SEC). This statement presents information about the proposed financing, the firm's history, existing business, and plans for the future.

   The statement, once accepted, is effective 20 days later. During this period, the company is prohibited from selling securities. Since February 1982 large companies have been allowed to file a single *shelf registration* statement covering financing plans for up to 2 years into the future. This provides prior approval to issue a stated amount of securities over this period, and without being tied to particular underwriters. The company is then able to issue securities gradually to the market, and it can take those decisions at short notice.

   After registration, the final prospectus is issued giving the issue price, which is fixed at this stage. From this point the procedures differ, depending on the type of offer:

   a. **General Cash Offer:** The marketing of a general cash offer is handled by the underwriters, who also provide advice and usually *underwrite* or guarantee the issue's subscription. Their remuneration is the spread between the issue price and the price at which they buy the securities from the company.

Large issues are usually handled by a syndicate of underwriters. The latter cannot sell securities below the issue price, although they may be allowed to "support" the market. If the issue cannot be sold, the syndicate will be broken.

b. **Privileged Subscription or Rights Issue:** This is unusual in the U.S., but very common elsewhere. Existing stockholders receive one right for every share they hold. These rights can be either sold or exercised.

At the end of the subscription period (roughly 3 weeks later), the holders of the rights will exercise them if the offer price is below the stock price. Otherwise the issue will fail unless it has been underwritten.

Rights issues can be underwritten for a fee.

2. **Private Placements:** Private placements involve no registration, and in general there will be no more than 12 buyers. Securities issued in this way are very illiquid and are held for long-term investment rather than resale.

Bond issues account for the bulk of private placements. A third are negotiated directly with the lender, while for larger issues, an investment banker will act as agent.

Prescriptive Information: Problems Facing the Manager

1. **Choice of Issue Method:**
   a. *Stock Issues*
      Public issues account for the vast majority of all stock issues. These will be by either
         General cash offer, which is the most popular method for seasoned companies and the only method for companies "going public," or by a
         Rights issue, which, although less common, is cheaper and fairer, involving no loss to existing holders
      Private placements of "letter stock" are normally limited to small, closely held companies.

   b. **Bond Issues**
      Public issues tend to be used by the larger companies and account for about 75 percent of bond issues.
      Private placements are suitable for small- to medium-sized companies, particularly if risky or if they require specialized, flexible loans. Issue costs are lower, but coupons are about 0.5 percent higher because of illiquidity.

2. **Issue Size, Frequency, and Costs:** Flotation costs, such as the costs of registration, printing, mailing, and underwriters' fees, can be a significant consideration for a company in deciding how often to make issues and how much to raise each time.

The high fixed-cost component can make a policy of frequent small issues very expensive. Because of the economies of scale from larger issues, it makes sense for companies to "bunch" issues, using short-term funds until a large issue is justified. Furthermore, companies should issue more than is dictated by their current needs in order to avoid frequent subsequent issues. This problem is most severe for small companies. Large companies can more easily arrange to make large issues, and they also benefit from shelf registration.

3. **Issue Pricing:**
   a. *Consequences of Incorrect Pricing* Pricing is important since, if an issue is *overpriced*, it will fail unless it has been underwritten and if it is *underpriced*, buyers will gain at the existing holders' expense.

Underpricing, however, is irrelevant for rights issues, since the offer is made to existing holders in proportion to their current stockholding.

b. *Some Pricing Guidelines* The golden rule is to use existing market prices as guidelines wherever possible.

For *seasoned stock issues* this is simple, since the issuer's stock price is already known. Furthermore, it is always possible to make a rights issue, where the degree of underpricing is irrelevant.

Pricing is far more difficult for *unseasoned stock issues*, since a rights issue cannot be made and since the stock is as yet untraded. The price is usually set by a combination of explicit valuations (see Chapter 4) and an examination of the prices of comparable stocks.

In pricing *bond issues*, guidelines can be obtained from recent issues by other companies, and from past issues by the issuing company.

4. **Underwriting:** Underwriting is just like insurance. The underwriters guarantee the issue's success, promising full subscription at the issue price in return for a fee. It is worthwhile as long as the value of the guarantee is worth at least as much as the fee paid.

The value of the guarantee depends on the risk of the issue failing. We will learn how to value guarantees of this sort when we study options in Chapters 20–21.

Underwriter's remuneration is usually 20 to 30 percent of the spread. In the case of rights issues, they are paid a fixed standby fee plus a take-up fee for any shares for which they have to subscribe.

If underwriting appears expensive, there is a simple remedy in the case of rights issues, since the issue price can be set low enough to minimize the chance of failure. For other issues, more reasonable quotations may possibly be obtained by shopping around or by competitive bidding. The latter seems to reduce spreads, but it is unclear whether it leads to any real net benefits.

5. **Effect on the Stock Price:**
a. *Underpricing* If new securities are issued at a price below their market price, it will lead to a fall in the price of their stock. In the case of a rights issue this is of no consequence, as stockholders receive a corresponding benefit from their rights to subscribe. The extent of underpricing does not affect the total value of the company, and this makes it possible to derive the value of a right as the amount by which the stock price will fall:

Value of one right = (rights-on price – issue price)/($N + 1$)

In the case of a general cash offer, the total value of the company is again unchanged but the fall in stock price represents a transfer of wealth from the existing stockholders to the purchasers of the new (and cheap) securities. Underpricing is not usually a serious consideration with seasoned issues.

b. *Price Pressure* The widely held belief that an increase in the supply of stock at the time of a new issue will depress the price appears to be largely a myth.

LIST OF TERMS

All-or-none	Registration statement
Best efforts	Rights issue
Competitive bidding	Seasoned stock issue
General cash offer	Secondary offering
Letter stock	Shelf registration
Negotiated underwriting	Spread
Preemptive rights	Tombstone
Primary offering	Transfer agent
Private placement	Underpricing
Privileged subscription	Underwriting
Prospectus	Unseasoned issue
Red herring	Venture capital
Registrar	

EXERCISES

Fill-in Questions

1. Equity investment in young private companies is generally known as _____.
2. The first issue of a security by a company is known as an _____.
3. A sale of shares is called a _____ when new shares are sold to raise additional cash for the company.
4. A sale of shares is called a _____ when it is to enable existing shareholders to reduce their holdings.
5. An issue of securities that is offered to investors as a whole is called a _____.
6. An issue of securities that is offered to current stockholders is usually called a _____.
7. Rights issues are also known as _____ issues.
8. For most public issues a _____ must be submitted to the Securities and Exchange Commission.
9. Information about an issue is provided in its _____, which must be sent to all purchasers and to all those who are offered securities through the mail.
10. The preliminary prospectus is called a _____.
11. A _____ is an advertisement which lists the underwriters to an issue of securities.
12. A financial institution is usually appointed as _____ to record the issue and ownership of the company's securities.
13. A _____ may be appointed to look after the transfer of newly issued securities.
14. The sale of a public issue is normally handled by an _____, who provides financial and procedural advice and usually buys the security for less than the offering price and accepts the risk of not being able to resell it.
15. The underwriter's _____ is the difference between the price at which the underwriter buys an issue from a company and the price at which it is offered to the public.
16. Occasionally the underwriter does not guarantee the sale of an entire issue but handles the issue on a _____ basis, promising only to sell as much of the issue as possible.
17. _____ underwriting is where the entire issue is canceled if the underwriter is unable to resell it all at the offer price.
18. _____ occurs in a general cash offer when securities are sold at an offer price which is below their market price.
19. Public utility holding companies are required to choose their underwriters by _____.

20. Most firms use _____ underwriting and don't require underwriters to bid formally against each other.
21. Stock for which there is an existing market goes by the spicy name of _____ stock.
22. The _____ right of common stockholders (to anything of value distributed by the firm) includes the right to subscribe to new offerings.
23. The _____ provides an alternative to making a public offering.
24. Privately placed common stock cannot easily be resold. It is often called _____ because the SEC requires a letter from the purchaser stating that the stock is not intended for resale.
25. _____ allows large companies to obtain prior approval for their financing plans for up to 2 years into the future.

Problems

1. Continuous Funding decides to issue the stock via a general cash offer. The board believes it can raise the $15 million the company requires by issuing shares at $20. Currently, the company is capitalized by 9 million shares at $20.
   Ignoring the underwriter's spread, calculate the following:
   a. The number of new shares that Continuous Funding will have to offer
   b. The expected price of the shares after the issue
   c. The loss per share to existing holders
   d. The percentage reduction in value of an existing stockholder's investment in the company
   e. The net present value of purchasing 100 shares via the general cash offer.

2. The Continuous Funding Corporation is also considering the alternative of a privileged subscription stock issue to raise $15 million. The terms of the issue are 1 for 9 at $15, and the corporation's current stock price is $20. Calculate the following:
   a. The market value of the corporation's equity prior to the issue
   b. The percentage increase in market value due to the issue
   c. The expected price of one right
   d. The expected price of the stock ex rights
   e. The number of rights that a stockholder who owned 975 shares would have to sell in order to take up her remaining rights and thus maintain a $19,500 investment in the company.

3. United Fasteners is issuing a 20-year bond to raise $10 million. The corporation can either
   a. Issue the bond publicly, in which case it will be sold at par and will carry a 9 percent coupon. The underwriter's spread would be 1/2 percent, and there are no other issue costs.
   b. Issue the bond through a private placement, in which case it will be sold at par and carry a 9 1/8 percent coupon. The total cost of the private placement will be $20,000.

   Which option should United Fasteners choose?

Essay Questions

1. Discuss the relative merits of a public issue versus a private placement for a company wishing to raise new debt finance. What factors should be taken into account in pricing the bond issue?

2. Compare and contrast the role of the investment banker (or underwriter) in (a) general cash offers of either stock or bonds, (b) privileged subscription issues of stock, (c) private placements of bonds.

3. What factors affect the choice between the general cash offer and the privileged subscription method for stock issues by seasoned companies?

ANSWERS TO EXERCISES

Fill-in Questions

1. venture capital
2. unseasoned issue
3. primary offering
4. secondary offering
5. general cash offer
6. rights issue
7. privileged subscription
8. registration statement
9. prospectus
10. red herring
11. tombstone
12. registrar
13. transfer agent
14. underwriter
15. spread
16. best efforts
17. all-or-none
18. underpricing
19. competitive bidding
20. negotiated
21. seasoned
22. preemptive
23. private placement
24. letter stock
25. shelf registration

Problems

1. a. Number of new shares = $15,000,000/$18 = 833,333 shares
   b. Value of company after issue = $180,000,000 + $15,000,000 = $195,000,000
      Share price after issue $195,000,000/9,833,333 = $19.83
   c. Loss per share to existing holders = $20 − $19.83 = $0.17
   d. Percentage reduction in value = ($0.17/$20) x 100 percent = 0.85 percent
   e. NPV purchasing shares via offer = $19.83 − $18 = $1.83

   The underpricing in the general cash offer ($18 rather than $20) results in a wealth transfer from existing to new holders. The latter gain $1.83 per share purchased, while existing holders lose $0.17 per share held, or 0.85 percent of their original holding.

2. a. Number of new shares issued = $15,000,000/$15 = 1,000,000.
      Number of shares before issue = 1,000,000 x 9 = 9,000,000 (issue is 1 for 9)
      Value of equity before issue = 9,000,000 x $20 = $180,000,000
   b. Increase in value = $15 m/$180 m x 100 percent = 8.33%
   c. Value of right = (rights-on price − issue price)/(N + 1) = ($20 − $15)/10 = $0.50
   d. Ex-rights price = (rights-on price − value of right) = $20 − $0.5 = $19.5
   e. Investment before issue = 975 x $20 = $19,500

To maintain $19,500 investment after issue, must hold $19,500/$19.5 = 1000 shares. To obtain 25 new shares, must exercise (25 x 9) = 225 rights

Thus number of rights sold = 975 – 225 = 750

(*Note*: Proceeds of sale = 750 x $0.50 = $375 covers cost of exercising 225 rights = 25 x $15 = $375).

3. a. Cost of public issue = $10,000,000 x 1/2 percent = $50,000
    b. Cost of private placement = $20,000 + additional interest cost

Additional interest = $10,000,000 x 1/8 percent = $12,500 per year for 20 years

If we discount these interest payments at 9 percent, i.e., the market rate for identical cash flows which are traded in the capital market, we obtain

Total cost of private placement = $20,000 + ($12,500 x 9.129) = $134,113

That is, shareholders will be better off if United Fasteners makes a *public* issue.

CHAPTER 16
THE DIVIDEND CONTROVERSY

INTRODUCTION

This chapter focuses on how dividend policy is established as well as whether and to what extent dividend policy affects the value of a firm. You should know that this is an unresolved issue. You should make it a point to understand the controversial elements which surround dividend policy. After all, financial managers cannot make intelligent decisions if they do not understand dividend policy.

WHAT TO LOOK FOR IN CHAPTER 16

This chapter emphasizes the financial manager's choices of obtaining equity capital: either by retaining earnings or by paying them out and issuing new shares. The issues are: which policy affects the firm's value, how, and to what extent? The question is analyzed under the assumption that the firm's capital budgeting and borrowing decisions are given.

Terminology: To familiarize yourself with the landscape of dividend policy, you should know such nuts-and-bolts concepts as record dates, with-dividend transactions, ex-dividend transactions, legal limitations on the payment of dividends, the various forms in which dividends are paid--regular cash dividends, extra dividends, and stock dividends--and the repurchase of shares.

Established Dividend Policies: Knowing how companies decide on dividend policy is important. Lintner's early, still relevant work indicates that most financial mangers zero in on a target payout ratio, which is the ratio of dividends to earnings per share. Moreover, evidence tends to confirm Lintner's contention that current dividends depend in part on current earnings and in part on the dividends for previous years, with more distant years being given less weight than more current years.

Information Content of Dividends: Cash dividend policies may signal important information to shareholders, because they may indicate management's assessment of future sustainable earnings: dividend increases are viewed as presaging increased earnings and *vice versa*.

Controversy about Dividend Policy: The essence of the dividend controversy centers on the extent to which dividend policy affects the value of the enterprise. Know the three main views in this controversy. The conservative view says that increased dividend payouts increase firm value; the middling view says that is irrelevant; and the third says that it reduces value. The dividend irrelevancy argument is Miller and Modigliani's (MM's); they argue convincingly that in a world of perfect capital markets dividend policy has no influence on value.

MM's position flies in the face of the traditional view which says the high payout ratios tend to increase the value of the firm. One of the cornerstones of this position is that cash dividends today are valued more highly than cash dividends in the future, because future cash dividends are more risky.

The third, radical left position in the dividend controversy focuses primarily on the tax effects which influence the preference for cash dividends. Their view: When dividends are taxed more heavily than capital gains, pay the lowest cash dividend possible. The Tax Reform Act of 1986 keeps the leftists' concept intact, even though both capital gains and dividends are taxed essentially at the same rates.

If criticisms are to be placed at the feet of the MM position, they must rest on market imperfections or inefficiencies. For example, does a special clientele prefer high-payout stocks? It seems so. Or, do cash dividend policies transmit important information to investors? This also seems to be the case.

Where does this leave the financial manager? Back to those who hold the middling position that dividend policy does not affect the value of the firm, that's where.

WORKED EXAMPLES

PROBLEM 1: TERMINOLOGY
In the fourth quarter of 1987 Washington Water paid a cash dividend of $0.62. Match each of the following dates:

(A) Friday, November 6	(a) record date
(B) Tuesday, November 17	(b) announcement date
(C) Friday, November 20	(c) ex-dividend date
(D) Tuesday, December 16	(d) payment date

SOLUTION
To answer problems such as these, you must know the meaning of the terms in the right-hand list. The first date of the *left-hand side* is the announcement date, the day on which the cash dividend is publicly announced. The next date, Tuesday, November 17, is the date on which the stock is traded without the cash dividend; it is the ex-dividend date and comes 4 business days *before the record date*, which is Friday, November 20, the third date and the date on which the list of shareholders eligible to receive the cash dividends is made. The last date, Tuesday, December 15, is the payment date.

PROBLEM 2: DIVIDEND YIELD
Assuming for the moment that Washington Water pays $0.62 per quarter throughout 1987, calculate the stock's dividend yield based on its December 31 market price of $23.375

SOLUTION
The formula for calculating dividend yields is

$$
\begin{aligned}
\text{Dividend yield} \ &= \text{yearly cash dividends} \div \text{current market price per share} \\
&= (4 \times \$0.62) \div 23.375 \\
&= \$2.48 \div \$23.375 \\
&= 0.1061 = 10.61 \text{ percent}
\end{aligned}
$$

PROBLEM 3: DIVIDEND PAYOUT
If Washington Water's 1987 earnings per share were $2.67 and per share cash dividends were $2.48, what was the company's estimated dividend payout?

SOLUTION

$$
\begin{aligned}
\text{Payout ratio} \ &= \text{estimated cash dividends per share} \div \text{estimated earnings per share} \\
&= \$2.48 \div \$2.67 \\
&= 0.9288 = 92.9 \text{ percent}
\end{aligned}
$$

PROBLEM 4: STOCK DIVIDEND
If Washington Water declared a stock dividend of 15 percent, its market price was $24, and nothing else changed, what would you expect the price of the shares to be after the new stock is distributed?

SOLUTION

There are several ways to approach this answer, but all must emphasize that the stock dividend, by itself, has no expected effect on the value of the shares. We conclude, then, that the aggregate value of the shares after the stock dividend must equal the aggregate value of the shares before it. Say you own 100 shares of Washington Water. The value of your holding is $2400 (100 shares x $24 per share). After the stock dividend you have 115 shares [100 original shares + (15 percent of 100)], the total value of which is still $2400. The value per share of the new set of shares is $20.87 (2400 ÷ 115 shares). Alternatively,

(100% + percentage stock dividend) x (price per share after stock dividend) = (price per share before stock dividend)

$$(100\% + 15\%)(x) = 24$$
$$115\%x = 24$$
$$x = 24 \div 1.15$$
$$= 20.87$$

PROBLEM 5: STOCK REPURCHASE

What-Not, Inc.'s financial numbers, as the financial community likes to call them, are as follows:

Net income	$5 million
Earnings per share	$1
Number of shares outstanding	5 million
Price-earnings ratio	10

The management plans to repurchase 20 percent of the company's outstanding shares at the going market price. What effect does the stock repurchase have on the above numbers? What effect does it have on the value of the firm? Explain.

SOLUTION

The stock repurchase is similar to the reverse of a stock split, *except* cash is needed to buy up the stock. Let's proceed to determine what happens to the numbers. First, the company has to have $10 million in cash in order to repurchase 1 million shares at $10 each. In order to do this it will have to sell a fifth of its assets. If it sells typical assets, its net income will subsequently shrink to $4 million. Second, the number of shares outstanding decreases to 4 million. Third, earnings per share remains at $1 ($4 million ÷ 4 million shares). And fourth, because the price-earnings ratio stays the same, the value of the shares also stays at $10 each. Look at it this way. Prior to the repurchase, the value per share was $10, 5 million shares were outstanding, and the firm's value was $50 million. After the repurchase, the value of the shares remains at $10 each, which, when multiplied by the 4 million then outstanding, results in a total value of $40 million. The size of the firm has contracted with no gain or loss to its shareholders.

SUMMARY

Dividend Mechanics

1. Paid by the board of directors

2. Some are paid quarterly and regularly; some are paid when extra cash is available; and some are paid in additional shares of stock.

3. Sometimes, especially recently, firms buy back their stock.

4. Some dates:
   a. Announcement: The date on which the dividend is announced.
   b. Ex-dividend: The date on which the stock trades without the cash dividend attached, which is 4 business days before the record date.
   c. Record: The date on which the record of shareholders to receive the dividends is made up.
   d. Payment: The date on which checks are sent to shareholders of record.
   e. With-dividend: Denotes that shares are selling with the cash dividend attached.

What do Companies Do?

1. Set long-run target dividend payout ratios, *á la* Lintner's empirical work.

2. Besides following current earnings, dividends also telegraph important information about the prospects for future earnings.

3. Cater to clienteles, which once established, reduce the incentive for other firms to change their dividend policies.

The Controversy: Dividend Irrelevance I (MM)

1. Three views exist regarding the impact of dividends on the value of the firm.

2. Middle-of-the-roaders: believe they have no effect, a position formulated by Miller-Modigliani (MM).

3. MM's argument begins with these assumptions:
   a. No taxes, transactions costs, or other market imperfections.
   b. A fixed investment capital budgeting program.
   c. A financing policy in which borrowing is set.
   d. Remaining needed funds come from retained earnings, and extra cash is paid as dividends.
   e. Efficient capital markets.

4. Conclusion: dividend policy is irrelevant.

5. See the figure below: a wealth transfer takes place but the value at the end of the day is the same.

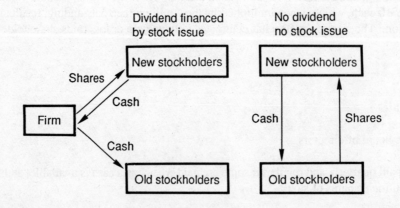

Two ways of raising cash for the firm's original shareholders. In each case the cash received is offset by a decline in the value of the old stockholders' claim on the firm. If the firm pays a dividend, each share is worth less because more shares have to be issued against the firm's assets. If the old stockholders sell some of their shares, each share is worth the same but the old stockholders have fewer shares.

    a. If dividends are increased, the firm must issue more shares (because investments and borrowing are fixed).
    b. No one will buy the shares at less than their true value.
    c. The total market value of the firm is unchanged, and the sale of new shares transfers wealth between new and old shareholders.
    d. The new purchasers receive shares at a price less than that on the old shares and it is less by the amount of the extra cash.

6. In efficient capital markets shareholders who need cash either sell shares or receive cash dividends and incur an equal drop in value of shares.

7. Thus, dividend policy is irrelevant and depends on the firm's investment and financing decisions.

8. Share repurchases are the reverse of the above process: dividend reductions are accompanied by an equivalent reduction in shares, and total wealth of shareholders is unaffected.

The Rightists: The High Payout View

1. Traditionalists favor liberal dividends because they believe increased dividends today make shareholders better off.

    a. A dividend in hand is worth more than a capital gain in the bush.
    b. Dividends received today are certain; tomorrow's capital gains are risky.
    c. If investment and financing policies are set, a firm's total cash flows are unaffected, the risk of all shareholders is the same, and dividend policy is still irrelevant.

2. Even though clienteles exist for high payouts and dividends signal important messages about a firm's profitability, this does not imply that one target dividend is better than another.

3. The empirical evidence supporting the traditional view is skimpy and flawed.

Taxes and the Radical Left

1. Leftists say that when dividends are taxed more heavily than capital gains, an incentive exists to retain rather than pay out, because the overall tax bill is less and that makes shareholders better off.

2. Empirical studies: investors in high marginal tax brackets appear to prefer low-payout stocks, and vice versa.

Dividend Irrelevance: One More Time

1. Back to the middle-of-the-roaders.

2. If low payouts increase share prices, financial managers would have such policies. They do not.

3. The "supply effect": no one firm believes it can increase its share price by adjusting its dividend policies because all clienteles are presently being taken care of by all other existing firms.

4. The uncertainty effect: deters shareholders from preferring low-payout stocks.

5. High-dividend stocks may be preferred by those investors who are able to defer taxes on them.

6. Where do Brealey and Myers stand?

7. Where are you?

8. More importantly, why?

LIST OF TERMS

Dividend policy	**Record date**
Ex-dividend	**Regular cash dividend**
Extra dividend	**Retaining earnings**
Greenmail	**Stock dividend**
Legal capital	**Target payout ratio**
Par value	**With dividend**
Payout ratio	

EXERCISES

Fill-in Questions

1. Dividend policy is concerned with the trade-off between _____ and paying out cash and _____.

2. The _____ is the date on which the list of registered shareholders who are to receive cash dividends is made.

3. Shares bought and sold before the _____ are said to be transacted _____, whereas those bought and sold after the _____ are said to be transacted _____.

4. A firm's _____ consists of the par value of all its outstanding shares.

5. _____ are cash dividends which a company usually expects to be able to maintain in the future; _____ are cash dividends paid irregularly and are not necessarily expected to be maintained in the future.

6. _____ are similar to stock splits in that neither makes shareholders better off.

7. The percentage ratio of cash dividends to earnings is called the _____.

Problems

1. On June 27, 1983, Standard Products Company announced a stock spilt of 3-for-1 and an increase in quarterly cash dividends from 20 cents a share before the stock split to 30 cents a share after the stock split. At the time of the announcement, the stock closed on the American Stock Exchange at $70.25 a share. (a) What would you expect the price of the stock to be after the split, assuming nothing else changes? (b) The amount of the quarterly dividend? (c) Could the adjustments in per share price and cash dividends have been accomplished by a stock dividend? (d) If so, what size would the stock dividend have had to be to accomplish this goal?

2. On Friday, August 12, 1988, Sink, Inc. announced a quarterly dividend of 12.5 cents and a stock dividend of 10 percent payable on Monday, September 12, 1988, to shareholders of record on Friday, August 26, 1988. (a) If the August 12 market price of $16.50 remains the same, at what price would you expect the stock to sell after the cash and stock dividends? (b) When would you expect the stock to go ex-dividend? (c) Assuming that the quarterly cash dividend of 12.5 cents per share will continue after the stock dividend, what is the effective percentage increase in the cash dividend? What is the expected annual dividend yield using your estimate of the ex-dividend price and the 12.5-cent quarterly cash dividend? (d) If expected annual earnings per share are $3, what is the annual expected dividend payout?

Essay Questions

1. Explain the mechanics of paying dividends.

2. "I've heard it said a million times that dividends are paid out of surplus. Yet just the other day I heard this financial expert say that dividends can only be paid out of cash. What I would like to know is which of these is correct." Formulate an answer for this bewildered person.

3. Why would a firm repurchase its common shares? (That is, what economic or financial significance is attached to share repurchases?)

4. "This dividend controversy stuff really bothers me. First off, I'm not even sure what the controversy is about. Second, *everybody* knows that dividend policy is really important. Finally, as investors, let's face it, it's the after-tax return that really counts!" Formulate a one-page response to this statement.

5. How can it be said that cash dividends are financially equivalent to stock issues, once investment and financing policies are fixed? Explain fully.

6. "Ya know what? The Tax Reform Act of 1986 really took the thunder away form the radical left's dividend position, cuz cash dividends and capital gains are taxed at the same marginal rate. If I were the financial manager of a firm, I'd wouldn't pay any dividends." Compose a one-page analysis of this position.

ANSWERS TO EXERCISES

Fill-in Questions

1. retaining earnings, issuing new shares
2. record date
3. record date; with dividend; record date; ex-dividend
4. legal capital
5. regular cash dividends; extra dividends
6. stock dividends
7. payout ratio

150

Problems

1. (a) $70.25 x 1/3 = $23.42 or 23 3/8 to the nearest eighth of a point; (b) $0.30 x 1/3 = $0.10; (c) Yes; (d) 200 percent, so that two additional shares are outstanding for every one old share

2. (a) ($16.5 – $0.125)/1.1 = $14.89; (b) Tuesday, August 23, 1988; (c) 10 percent; ($0.125 x 4)/$14.89 = 3.36 percent; (d) $0.50/$3 = 16.7 percent

CHAPTER 17
DOES DEBT POLICY MATTER?

INTRODUCTION

This chapter emphasizes Modigliani and Miller's (MM) argument that debt policy does not matter, the conditions under which their case is made, and the counterargument put forth by the more traditional view. MM argue from two fundamental propositions. Proposition I states that regardless of the way in which a firm's total cash flows are split between debt and equity, the total value of the firm remains unchanged. If Proposition I holds, debt policy does not matter, and financing and investing decisions are separable.

Proposition II states that the expected rate of return on and risk of common stocks of a firm that has debt increases in proportion to the ratio of debt to equity. Proposition II's major implication is that the weighted cost of capital to the firm remains unchanged as the capital structure mix changes. This is another way of saying that the value of the firm does not change as debt policy changes.

WHAT TO LOOK FOR IN CHAPTER 17

This chapter sets forth the famous Modigliani-Miller (MM) propositions concerning the capital structure of business firms. Their first argument, Proposition I, says that the style by which a firm is financed, its mix between debt and equity, does not affect the value of the firm. Proposition II follows from the first, namely, that the rate of return required by equity shareholders increases as debt increases so that both the weighted average cost of capital and the value of the firm remain constant.

Perfect Markets Assumption: The MM argument rests on the assumptions of perfect capital markets and the absence of taxes. In this world all investors, regardless of their feelings toward risk and expected returns, agree that the value of an unlevered firm is equal to the value of a levered firm, provided the two firms are alike in operating characteristics.

Magnification Effects of Financial Leverage: Financial leverage tends to magnify returns and risk to common shareholders. Because of the magnification effects resulting from going into debt, MM's Proposition II emerges: the expected rate of return on common shares of a financially levered firm increases proportionally to the debt-equity ratio, as measured by market values.

The Traditional Position: The traditional view argues that the cost of capital will tend to decrease initially as debt is added to the capital structure but that it will increase only after a market-determined intolerable threshold level of risk is passed. At that point the cost of equity and the cost of debt increase significantly.

Some Possible Flaws in the MM Position: Although Chapter 18 explores these notions in greater detail, violations in MM's propositions are to be found in the lack of perfect capital markets. Also, unsatisfied clienteles may likewise violate the MM position. AT&T's efforts to sell the equivalent of a savings bond, the emergence of money market mutual funds, and floating rate notes are examples of catering to special needs of special clienteles.

WORKED EXAMPLES

PROBLEM 1: PERFECT MARKETS, NO TAXES

What Not, Inc. operates in perfect capital markets with no corporate or personal taxes. Calculate its expected return on assets, given the following information: 40 percent debt-financed, 10 percent expected return on debt, 60 percent equity-financed, and 15 percent expected return on equity.

SOLUTION

$$r_A = [D/(D+E) \times r_D] + [E/(D+E) \times r_E]$$
$$= (0.40 \times 0.10) + (0.60 \times 0.15)$$
$$= 0.04 + 0.09$$
$$= 0.13 = 13 \text{ percent}$$

PROBLEM 2: SELLING DEBT TO RETIRE EQUITY

Macbeth Spot Removers' expected operating income is $2000 and the market value of all its all-equity-financed securities is $12,000. Assuming that it operates in perfect capital markets with no corporate or personal taxes, what happens to the rate of return on equity capital when it decides to sell $4800 of debt and retire an equal amount of equity? The return debtholders expect is 9 percent.

SOLUTION

The return on assets is

$$r_A = \text{expected operating income/market value of all securities}$$
$$= \$2000/\$12,000$$
$$= 0.1667 = 16.67 \text{ percent}$$

In an all-equity-financed firm the return on equity r_E is equal to the return on assets; so

$$r_E = r_A = 16.67 \text{ percent}$$

After the borrowing, the return on equity will change but the return on assets will remain the same, because the value of the firm does not change--the expected operating income does not change and the value of the outstanding securities does not change. The return on equity is calculated thus:

$$r_E = r_A + (D/E)(r_A - r_D)$$
$$= 0.1667 + (\$4800/\$7200)(0.1667 - 0.09)$$
$$= 0.1667 + 0.667(0.0767)$$
$$= 0.1667 + 0.0512$$
$$= 0.2179 = 21.79 \text{ percent}$$

PROBLEM 3: CHANGING DEBT-EQUITY RATIOS AND BETA

Given the information in Problem 2 and assuming the beta of the firm is 1.2 before the debt financing, what is the beta of the equity after the financing? Assume the beta of the debt is 0.5. What would the beta of the equity be if the debt-equity ratio were 30, 50 60, and 70 percent?

SOLUTION

The answer before the debt financing is straightforward: the beta of the equity is the same as the beta of the firm, because no other securities are outstanding. After the financing, the beta of the equity changes as follows:

$$
\begin{aligned}
\beta_E &= \beta_A + D/E \ (\beta_A - \beta_D) \\
&= 1.2 + 0.667(1.2 - 0.5) \\
&= 1.2 + 0.667(0.7) \\
&= 1.2 + 0.467 \\
&= 1.667
\end{aligned}
$$

For the other debt proportions, β_E is

D/E'%	β_E
30	1.41
50	1.55
60	1.62
70	1.69

PROBLEM 4: EQUITY BETAS WHEN DEBT BETAS CHANGE

Using the data in Problems 2 and 3, what are the betas of the equity if the beta of the debt is zero, that is, risk-free? What would they be if the beta of the debt were equal to the beta of the firm before debt financing? Compare these results with those of Problem 3.

SOLUTION

	β_E		
D/E'%	$\beta_D = 0$	$\beta_D = 1.2$	$\beta_D = 0.5$
30	1.56	1.2	1.41
40	1.68	1.2	1.48
50	1.80	1.2	1.55
60	1.92	1.2	1.62
70	2.04	1.2	1.69

Although the data are contrived, several interesting relations emerge. First, if the beta of the debt is equal to the beta of the firm when it is all-equity-financed, for all practical purposes the company has issued another dose of equity and not debt. Consequently, the beta of the equity does not change.

If the company were able to issue debt at the zero beta level, the risk-free rate, the betas of the equity would tend to increase substantially over the all-equity scheme of financing. In almost all instances, the beta of corporate debt is greater than zero but less than the beta of the all-equity-financed firm.

PROBLEM 5: DEBT, EARNINGS PER SHARE, AND RISK

"The way I see it," says the financial manager of Milk 'Em Dry, Inc. (MED, Inc.), "if I buy half of the 10,000 outstanding common shares with the proceeds from the sale of debt, I can increase earnings per share. After all, I can borrow at 10 percent and I am currently earning 20 percent on my all-equity-financed firm. I estimate the risk of borrowed money at 0.4 and the beta of my equity before borrowing is 1.2. The price-earnings ratio of the common shares is 5 on operating income of $25,000, and I expect to continue to generate that amount of operating income after the debt financing. Seems to me this will be a good deal for shareholders. And that's the way I am supposed to behave, isn't it, on behalf of the shareholders? In fact, it seems dumb not to go into debt." Formulate the answer for this financial manager, assuming operation in perfect capital markets with no corporate or personal taxes.

SOLUTION

Begin by placing a value on the firm before the debt financing. The operating earnings are capitalized at 20 percent; so the value of the firm when it is all-equity-financed is $125,000 ($25,000 ÷ .20). The value per share is $12.50; earnings per share are $2.50 ($25,000 ÷ 10,000 shares), with the price earnings ration being 5.0 times ($12.50/$20).

Next, determine the earnings per share after the debt financing. The financial manager must sell $62,500 of debt at the going market rate of 10 percent in order to repurchase an equivalent amount of equity. Remember, because the operating income remains unchanged, the firm's total value remains unchanged at $125,000. The equity earnings change, however, as follows:

Operating income	$25,000
Interest	6,250
Equity earnings	$18,750

With 5000 shares now outstanding, earnings per share increase to $3.75 ($18,750 ÷ 5000 shares). Now here's the trap in this thought process. *If* the price-earnings ratio remains unchanged at 5, the shares have a market price of $18.75 (5 x $3.75). But going into debt entails additional risk to shareholders. How much more risk? Work it out in terms of the betas before and after the debt financing.

The formula:

$$\beta_E = \beta_A + D/E\,(\beta_A - \beta_D)$$

Before	After
$\beta = 1.2 + 0.0\,(1.2 - 0)$	$\beta = 1.2 + 1.0\,(1.2 - 0.4)$
$= 1.2$	$= 1.2 + 0.8 = 2.0$

And we all know that with increased risk comes increased expected (required?) returns. What is the return now required by equity-holders? Look at it this way. If the return on assets stays the same, as it does, the required return on equity is affected by the riskiness of the debt financing. In formula format, the result is

$$r_E = r_A + D/E\,(r_A - r_D)$$
$$= 0.20 + 1.0(0.20 - 0.10)$$
$$= 0.20 + 0.10 = 30 \text{ percent}$$

So the answer to the financial manager is: "Whereas it is true that earnings per share increase, so does the risk. Hence the rate at which the increased earnings are evaluated is increased as well, and proportionally at that, thereby mitigating the hoped-for results of increased share prices." The new price-earnings ratio is the reciprocal of the earnings yield. The earnings yield is 30 percent ($3.25 ÷ $12.50), the reciprocal of which is 3.333. When the price-earnings ratio of 3.333 is multiplied by the new earnings per share of $3.75, we obtain a market price per share of common of $12.50, which is where we were at the beginning.

These phenomena are depicted below. Because the relations are linear, the implied risk-free rate is 5 percent, as represented by the dashed line extending down from the 10 percent, beta = 0.4 portion of the graph.

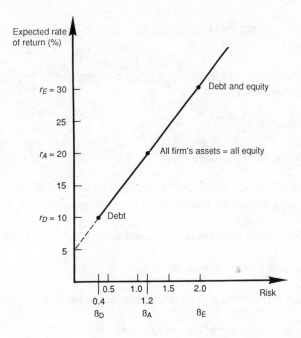

SUMMARY

The Permutations

1. If you own 100 percent of an all-equity financed firm, you are entitled to all the operating cash flow; you share with no one.

2. If you own a part of an all-equity financed firm, you are entitled to only a part of the operating cash flow; you share with the other owners.

3. If you own all the debt and all the equity of a debt- and equity-financed firm, you are entitled to all of the cash flow; you share with no one.

4. If you own all a firm's equity but none of its debt, you are entitled to that portion of total cash flow that is available after all other claims are met; you share with others.

5. If you own all the debt of a 100 percent debt-financed firm, you are entitled to all the operating cash flow (if any); you share with no one; you own the firm.

The Issue

Whether going into debt affects the value of the firm and its shares.

MM's Replication Argument

1. Two companies with identical assets: NoDebt is all-equity-financed; SomeDebt is financed by a mixture of debt and equity.

2. The outcomes from holding equity in NoDebt can be replicated by buying both debt and equity in Some Debt.

3. The outcomes from holding equity in SomeDebt may be replicated by buying equity in NoDebt and borrowing on personal account.

4. The outcomes are the same.

5. Personal loans create similar debt-equity mixes.

6. Modigliani-Miller (of dividend irrelevancy fame): splitting the total income stream between debt- and equityholders cannot change the total value of its securities and hence the firm.

7. Just so much cash flow comes from the business, and sharing it does not increase the firm's value.

Proposition I: Firm Value and Capital Structure

1. MM: capital structure is irrelevant as long as the firm's investment decisions are given.

2. Proposition I: value is independent of capital structure.

3. Proposition I is equivalent to a law of conservation of value, which says that the firm's assets are not affected by the income stream being split between debt and equity claims.

4. Ms. Macbeth's fallacious argument: because expected EPS increases with leverage, so too should the value of the firm.
   a. EPS increase, but share price does not.
   b. Equity risk and required return increase as well, as explained by Proposition II.

Proposition II: The Expected Return on Equity

1. Expected (required) returns on equities increase, thereby adjusting the higher earnings to the old market price.

2. Starting with the notion that expected returns on assets are not affected by borrowing--the return on real assets stays the same--the expected return on real assets is;

$$r_A = [D/(D+E) \times r_D] + [E/(D+E) \times r_E]$$

3. Rearranging, the expected return on equity is:

$$r_E = r_A + (D/E)(r_A - r_D)$$

4. MM's Proposition II: The expected return on equity of a leveraged firm increases proportionately to the increase in the debt-equity ratio (D/E).

5. As the required return on equity increases, the market value of shares decreases.

6. The rate of increase in required equity returns depends on the spread between the return on assets and the expected return on debt.

Effect on Leverage on Beta: The Risk-Return Trade-off

1. Beta of the firm's assets:

$$\beta_A = [D/(D+E) \text{ x } \beta_D] + [E/(D+E) \text{ x } \beta_E]$$

2. Rearrange to obtain the beta of the equity of a leveraged firm.

$$\beta_E = \beta_A = D/E (\beta_A - \beta_D)$$

3. This is an alternative explanation of why equity investors require higher returns as debt increases.

4. Proposition II is consistent with CAPM.

The Traditional View

1. Rests on the weighted average cost of capital--the expected return on the portfolio of all of the company's securities.

$$r_A = (D/V \text{ x } r_D) + (E/V \text{ x } r_E)$$

2. r_A is often used in capital budgeting when the project being evaluated does not differ from the firm's business risk.

3. Holds that the expected return on equity does not increase as a firm borrows more.
   a. Means that the weighted average cost of capital declines at first as the debt-equity ratio increases and then rises.
   b. Means that an optimal D/E ratio exists, that is, where the cost of capital is lowest.

4. Watch it: Minimizing the weighted average cost of capital may not maximize shareholder value.

Can MM's Propositions Be Violated?

1. MM's Achilles heel: perfect markets assumption.

2. Financial manager's task: to find market imperfections and structure a package of securities that exploits them.

LIST OF TERMS

Capital structure	**Proposition I**
Earnings-price ratio	**Proposition II**
Financial leverage	**Return on assets**
Gearing	**Value additivity**
Law of conservation of value	**Weighted-average cost of capital**

EXERCISES

Fill-in Questions

1. A firm's mix of debt and equity is called its _____.
2. _____ states that the value of the firm is not changed by the mix of debt and equity.
3. A firm that borrows is said to engage in _____.
4. The _____ states that the value of an asset is preserved regardless of the nature of the claim on it.
5. The _____ is equal to the return on debt multiplied by the ratio of debt to the market value of the firm plus the return on equity multiplied by the ratio of _____ to the market value of the firm.
6. _____ states that the expected return on the common stock of a financially leveraged firm increases in proportion to the debt ratio.
7. _____ is another term for financial leverage.
8. The price-earnings ratio is the reciprocal of the _____.

Problems

1. What is the expected return on assets for a firm that is 60 percent debt-financed and pays an expected return on debt of 9 percent and has required return on equity of 20 percent? Assume the firm operates in perfect capital markets with no corporate or personal income taxes. Show all calculations.

2. Your firm's expected operating income is $5000 and the market value of its outstanding securities is $25,000, when it is *all-equity-financed*. If the firm operates in perfect capital markets with no corporate or personal taxes, what will happen to its return on equity after it sells enough debt to repurchase half of the outstanding equity? Assume that bondholders require a 10 percent return on their money. An 8 percent return. A 12 percent return.

3. Using the data in Problem 2 above, a beta for the firm of 1.5, and a beta for the debt of 0.6, what is the beta of the equity after the financing?

4. The financial manager of Ballpoint, Inc., estimates that she will increase the earnings per share of her presently all-equity-financed firm if she borrows at the going market rate of 8 percent. She estimates the debt's beta to be 0.3 and the beta of the all-equity firm is 0.8. A return of 12.5 percent is expected on the all-equity firm, the price-earnings ratio of 8 is expected to persist, expected operating income is $300,000 and 100,000 shares are outstanding. She plans to replace 40 percent of her equity with debt. She feels the argument is so compelling that she is chomping at the bit to borrow money. "After all," she argues, "the price of debt is not going to get any cheaper. So now is the time to get the value of the shareholders up." If she operates in perfect capital markets in which there are also no corporate and personal income taxes, what reasonable evaluation should you make of her financing scheme? Show all calculations you may make.

Essay Questions

1. What is Modigliani and Miller's (MM) Proposition I, and what implication does this have for financial managers?

2. "The way I see it, financial leverage tends to magnify the potential returns to equity shareholders. I know, it also tends to magnify losses. But any rational shareholder has gotta like firms that engage in financial leverage more than those that don't. And, to make my long story short, that has to reduce the cost of capital to the firm because shareholders will prefer to pay more for equal amounts of earnings in firms that have debt outstanding as compared to those that don't. And, finally!, that means the value of the firm will increase. Doesn't it?" Articulate your evaluation of this statement.

3. "I guess what bothers me the most about Modigliani and Miller's position is that they hang their hat on perfect capital markets in a way that really ticks me off. 'Cause *everybody* knows that capital markets ain't perfect. How come Modigliani (I can't even pronounce the guy's name) and Miller can't figure that out?" Give a detailed response to that statement.

4. How may individual investors augment or undo the debt policy of firms in which they wish to invest? Explain fully. Also explain why this concept is important to the Modigliani-Miller position regarding debt policy.

5. What is Modigliani and Miller's Proposition II? What implications does that have for financial managers who must deal with these knotty problems day in and day out?

6. Demonstrate how the beta of a firm is dependent on the beta of the capital structure components.

ANSWERS TO EXERCISES

Fill-in Questions

1. capital structure
2. Proposition I
3. financial leverage
4. law of conservation of value
5. return on assets; value; equity
6. Proposition II
7. gearing
8. earnings yield

Problems

1. $(0.6 \times 0.09) + (0.4 \times 0.2) = 13.4$ percent

2. $r_A = r_E$ \$5000/\$25,000 = 20 percent; when $r_D = 10$ percent, $r_E = r_A + D/E(r_A - r_D) = 0.20 + 0.5$ $(0.20 - 0.10) = 25$ percent; when $r_D = 8$ percent and 12 percent, $r_E = 26$ percent and 24 percent, respectively.

3. $\beta_E = \beta_A + D/E(\beta_A - \beta_D) = 1.5 + 0.5(1.5 - 0.6) = 1.95$

4. Take this one in stages. The analysis is the same as that for Problem 5 of the Worked Examples.

   Stage 1: all-equity firm:

   Value = \$300,000 ÷ 12.5 percent = \$2,400,000
   Value per share: \$2,400,000 ÷ 100,000 shares = \$24
   Earnings per share: \$300,000 ÷ 100,000 = \$3

Stage 2: effect of debt financing on earnings per share:

Amount of required debt: 0.4 ($2,400,000) =	$960,000
Operating income	$300,000
Interest (0.8 x $960,000)	76,800
Equity earnings	$223,200

Earnings per share: $223,200 ÷ 60,000 = $3.72

Stage 3: beta of equity:

Before-debt financing: 0.8; after: β_E = $\beta_A + D/E\ (\beta_A - \beta_D)$
= $0.8 + 0.4/0.6(0.8 - 0.3)$
= 1.133

Stage 4: return on equity, after debt financing:

$$r_E = r_A + (D/E)(r_A - r_D)$$
$$= 0.125 + (0.4/0.6)(0.125 - 0.08)$$
$$= 15.5 \text{ percent} = \text{earnings yield}$$

Stage 5: market price of equity after debt financing:

Price/earnings ratio =	1/earnings yield = 1/0.155 = 6.452
Market price per share =	price-earnings ratio x earnings per share
=	6.452 x $3.72 = $24

Value of equity =	market price per share x number of shares
=	$24 x 60,000 = $1,440,000

Stage 6: value of firm after debt financing:

Value of debt	$ 960,000
Value of equity	1,440,000
Value of firm	$2,400,000

Stage 7: Value of firm before debt financing = $2,400,000.

Stage 8: You have just demonstrated MM's Proposition.

CHAPTER 18
HOW MUCH SHOULD A FIRM BORROW?

INTRODUCTION

The point of this chapter is to combine some practical and relevant issues with the MM analysis of Chapter 17. Capital markets work well, but corporate and personal income taxes, the probability of bankruptcy and other forms of financial distress, and differing goals of creditors and shareholders complicate debt-policy decisions. Debt policy matters.

WHAT TO LOOK FOR IN CHAPTER 18

This chapter's major point is that *debt policy does matter*, once taxes, the probability of bankruptcy, financial distress, and potential conflicts of interest among the firm's security holders are included.

Corporate Taxes: Corporate taxes combined with the tax-deductibility of interest are compelling reasons why debt policy counts. Interest on debt is deductible before corporate taxes are paid and that creates a *tax shield* which enhances the after-tax value of the firm. Tax shields are valuable assets, their value being the present value of reduced taxes. MM corrected Proposition I to include tax shields. It continues to be flawed, however, because it leads to the conclusion that all firms should be 100 percent debt-financed.

Corporate and Personal Taxes: Miller corrected this view by including *both* corporate and personal income taxes. The object: to minimize the present value of all after-tax taxes. That analysis recognizes that cash dividends may be taxed differently from capital gains, especially inasmuch as capital gains may be deferred. Interest income is taxed at the personal level and equity income is taxed at the corporate level.

Miller's Capital Structure View: Merton Miller's view (pre-1986 Tax Reform Act) of capital structure effects on firm value when investors have different tax rates states that as companies borrow more and more, investors can be persuaded to hold corporate debt, rather than common stock, only by offering bondholders high returns than they can obtain from holding common stock. Miller's model indicates that there is an optimal debt-equity ratio for all corporations but not for any single corporation. Miller's model holds up only if the effective tax rate on equity income is substantially lower than that on interest income. The Tax Reform Act of 1986 brought the two taxation rates closer, and a modification of Miller's model is needed, the upshot of which is that the present value of the tax shield is uncertain, making financial managers chary about issuing the model's optimal amount of debt. Moreover, different companies face different tax rates, which militates against the model's predicted debt-equity ratio. After the Tax Reform Act of 1986 Miller's model, but not the conceptual analytical basis, becomes less plausible because interest income, dividends, and non-deferred capital gains are taxed at the same personal rates.

Costs of Financial Distress: The non-trivial costs of financial distress also impinge on debt policy. Because promises made to creditors may be broken, or honored only with substantial difficulty, a firm is not able to borrow as much as it may choose. Consequently, the prospective cost of financial distress influences negatively the value of the firm. Such costs include the cost of bankruptcy as well as such indirect costs of time and effort to resolve a financially distressed condition.

Stockholders and Financial Distress: Whenever financial distress arises, there are a variety of games in which stockholders may engage in order to minimize their risk exposure, such as risk shifting, refusing to contribute equity capital, taking cash out of the enterprise, and making decisions which defer the day of reckoning. All may be very costly to creditors. To forestall the possibility of such maneuvers, restrictive provisions are often incorporated into bond contracts, the most typical being dividend limitations, limitation on additional borrowing, restrictions on selling assets, specific accounting procedures, and constraints on operating and investment decisions.

Explaining Financing Choices: The *tradeoff theory* of capital structure argues that a firm's debt-equity decision is really one of trading off interest tax shields against the cost of financial distress, and partially helps to explain why companies have different debt-equity ratios. The *pecking order theory* says that financial managers have a preferred, ordered set of financing options, and they go down that list in order of preference, the first being internal funds, then targeted but sticky cash dividends, and then external financing, the safest first, usually debt, and equity last.

Choosing the Firm's Debt-Equity Ratio: Debt may not be a good alternative to equity financing. Factors to consider are the total tax liability to shareholders; a firm's business risk; the types of assets that produce operating income; and the need for financial slack.

WORKED EXAMPLES

PROBLEM 1: TAX SHIELD
Demonstrate how interest paid on debt is a tax shield.

SOLUTION
To make this demonstration, take two firms alike in all respects except that one firm is 100 percent financed by common stock and the other is 50 percent equity-financed and 50 percent debt-financed at 9 percent a year. The balance sheets of the two firms are as follows:

ALL EQUITY				EQUITY AND DEBT		
Assets	$10,000	Equity	$10,000	Assets	$10,000	Debt 9% $5,000
						Equity 5,000
Total	$10,000	Total	$10,000	Total	$10,000	Total $10,000

Their income statements are as follows:

	ALL EQUITY	EQUITY AND DEBT
Earnings before interest and taxes	$1500	$1500
Interest expenses		450
Pretax income	1500	1050
Tax at 34 percent	510	357
Net income to stockholders	$ 950	$ 693
Total income to both bondholders and stockholders	$0 + 990 = 990	$450 + 693 = 1143
Interest tax shield (0.34 x interest)	$0	(0.34) x (450) = 153

PROBLEM 2: PRESENT VALUE OF TAX SHIELD

What is the present value of the tax shield as calculated in Problem 1.

SOLUTION

Again, assume that the risk of the investment in the tax shield requires a rate of return equal to that paid on the debt, namely, 9 percent. If the financing is considered permanent, the problem is one of solving for the present value of a perpetuity.

$$\text{Present value of tax shield} = \$153/0.09 = \$1700$$

Because the total amount of the debt is $5000, the present value of the tax shield is the amount of the total debt which the government underwrites when it allows interest to be deducted as an expense. The difference between the total debt and the federal subsidy, $3300 ($5000 – $1700), is the amount the company underwrites. Also note that the present value of the tax shield is independent of the return on the debt. The cash difference between taxes paid, $153 ($510 – $357), makes going into debt a profitable investment, and worth $1700, although not as profitable as under the old tax laws. Restated

$$
\begin{aligned}
\text{Present value of tax shield} \quad &= \quad \frac{\text{corporate tax rate x expected interest payment}}{\text{expected return on debt}} \\[2ex]
&= \quad \frac{T_c(r_D D)}{r_D} \\[2ex]
&= \quad T_c D \\[2ex]
&= \quad 0.34 \times (0.09 \times \$5000)/0.09 \\[2ex]
&= \quad 0.34 \times \$5000 \\[2ex]
&= \quad 1700
\end{aligned}
$$

PROBLEM 3: INTEREST TAX SHIELDS AND SHAREHOLDER VALUE

Demonstrate how interest tax shields under the new tax laws contribute to the value of William Wrigley Jr. Company's shareholders. Note that, Wrigley has no long-term debt.

SOLUTION

Table 18-1a
SIMPLIFIED BALANCE SHEETS FOR WILLIAM WRIGLEY JR. COMPANY, 1987 (IN MILLIONS).

BOOK VALUES				MARKET VALUES			
Net working capital	$155	$0	Long-term debt	Net working capital	$ 155	$0	Long-term debt
Long-term assets	165	0	Other long-term liabilities	Long-term assets	1071	0	Other long-term liabilities
		320	Equity			1226	Equity
Total assets	$320	$320	Total liabilities and equity	Total assets	$1226	$1226	Total liabilities and equity

Table 18-1b
BALANCE SHEETS FOR WILLIAM WRIGLY, JR. COMPANY WITH $160 MILLION OF LONG-TERM DEBT SUBSTITUTED FOR STOCKHOLDERS' EQUITY (IN MILLIONS).

BOOK VALUES				MARKET VALUES			
Net working capital	$155	$160	Long-term debt	Net working capital	$155	$160	Long-term debt
Long-term assets	165	0	Other long-term liabilities	Long-term assets	1125	0	Other long-term liabilities
		160	Equity			1120	Equity
Total assets	$320	$320	Total liabilities and equity	Total assets	$1280	$1280	Total liabilities and equity

First, construct simplified book and market value balance sheets, such as those in Table 18-1a. The next step is to estimate the value of the firm if it were to borrow $160 million in permanent long-term debt, and use the proceeds to buy that much stock. Because of the tax shield effects, assuming a 34 percent tax rate, this financing scheme should increase the firm's value by T_cD, the corporate tax rate T_c times the amount of permanent long-term debt D. Inasmuch as the additional debt is $160 million, the market value of the firm should increase by .34 x $160,000,000 = $54,400,000. If the MM theory, corrected for taxes, holds, the value of the firm must increase by 54.4 million to 1280.4 million. The new balance sheets will be those in Table 18-1b. The value of the equity declines by $105.6 million, which is $(1 - T_c)(D)$. The question remains: Are the shareholders better off? If you, as the financial manager, purchased $160 million of stock and it dropped in value by only $105.6 million, the stockholders are ahead of the deal to the tune of

$54.4 million ($160 million – 105.6 million). To put it another way, the shareholders received $160 million in exchange for $105.6 million, not a bad deal by anybody's standards.

SUMMARY

Corporate Taxes:

1. Debt policy matters because of market imperfections, one of which is the tax deductibility of interest.

2. Interest: a tax shield enabling bondholders to escape taxation at the corporate level.

3. PV tax shield

$$= \frac{T_c(r_D D)}{r_D}$$

$$= T_c D$$

4. Interest tax shields contribute to the value of stockholders' equity.

MM and Taxes, and 100 Percent Debt:

1. Merck & Co. example: develops MM's Corrected Proposition I:
   Value of firm = value if all-equity financed + PV tax shield

2. Implies the extreme absurdity of 100 percent debt.

Be Sure to Include Both Corporate and Personal Taxes:

1. If all personal taxes are equal, they do not reduce the tax advantage of corporate borrowing.

2. Dividends, interest and realized capital gains are now taxed identically.

3. If interest and dividends are taxed at the same personal rate, no reduction in the tax advantage to corporate borrowing exists.

4. If personal taxes on bond interest exceed those on equity income, the advantage of corporate borrowing is reduced.

5. Objective: to minimize the present value of the total tax bill, personal and corporate; or: maximize after-tax income.

6. Corporate debt policy is irrelevant if:

$$1 - T_p = (1 - T_{pE}) \times (1 - T_c)$$

Merton Miller's "Debt and Taxes":

1. Focuses on capital market equilibrium when investors have different tax rates. Considered debt policy before 1986 Tax Reform Act.

2. With taxes on debt but not on equity, only corporate tax rates apply and a strong incentive exists to borrow.

3. As borrowing begins, investors have to be induced to hold corporate debt instead of stocks.
   a. Tax-exempt investors are tapped first, leaving personal taxes unchanged and saving on corporate taxes.
   b. As more is borrowed, investors have to be persuaded to migrate from stocks to bonds; higher bond returns are offered in order to offset the loss on personal taxes.
   c. Migrations stop when, at the margin, corporate tax savings equal personal tax losses.

Implications of Miller's Model:

1. It predicts what the aggregate equilibrium debt-equity ratio will be.

2. For any single firm capital structure is irrelevant.

3. If corporate taxes increase, migration toward debt begins and higher debt-equity ratios result.

4. If personal taxes increase, migration to equities begins and lower debt equity ratios result.

5. If both corporate and personal tax rates increase by the same amount, debt-equity ratios remain the same.

Comments and Questions:

1. Tax-exempt funds should invest only in bonds.

2. Highly taxed individuals should invest only in stocks.

3. Either is difficult to reconcile with reality.
   a. No observable and obvious clienteles exist.
   b. There is evidence that the effective personal tax rate on equities cannot be zero. This implies an unrealistically small clientele for equities.
   c. The yield on tax-exempt municipal bonds has historically been about 78 percent of that on taxable issues. This implies that there is some tax advantage to borrowing.

A Compromise:

1. The issue: centers on the tax position of the marginal lender.
   a. MM assume that it is zero.
   b. Miller says investors are subject to different tax rates and must be induced to take on more and more debt.

2. If companies are unsure that the corporate tax shield will be used to full advantage, the total amount of debt issued will be less than in Miller's model.

3. Because companies cannot be sure of benefitting from the corporate tax shield, they will not be prepared to pay such a high rate on debt.

4. Because companies have different expected tax rates, tax shields are worth more to some firms than to others.

5. The Brealey and Myers view: a moderate tax advantage to corporate borrowing exists for companies that are reasonably sure they can use the corporate tax shelter.

Financial Distress Costs:

1. The prospect of financial distress concerns investors and has a negative impact on the present value of the firm.

2. The majority holds that as more is borrowed the risk and cost of financial distress increase, affecting the firm's value.

   Value of firm = value if all-equity financed + PV tax shield - PV costs of - financial distress

3. Bankruptcy costs arise when shareholders exercise their right to default and creditors take over.

4. Present value of court and legal fees reduces the total payoff to shareholders and creditors.

5. Evidence suggests that bankruptcy costs are large absolutely but are nominal relative to firm value.

6. Indirect costs arise from the difficulties of running a bankrupt firm.
   a. Market price adjustments when a firm enters bankruptcy (e.g., Texaco) is a significant cost to investors.
   b. Nonbankrupt, financially troubled firms may create conflicts of interest between creditors and shareholders.
   c. To avoid game-playing, debt documents contain restrictive covenants.

7. Financial distress costs vary with asset types.

Explaining Financing Choices:

1. The debt-equity mix is a tradeoff between tax shields and the costs of financial distress.

2. The Tradeoff Theory suggests that firms may have different target debt ratios.
   a. The facts of everyday financial life more or less confirm the tradeoff theory.
   b. Some of the most profitable companies--those that would tend to benefit the most from tax shields--borrow the least.

3. The Pecking Order Theory says that a preferred, ordered set of financing is at work among financial managers.

Choosing the Firm's Debt-Equity Ratio:

1. No simple answers.

2. Use four-dimensional matrix: (1) taxes, (2) risk, (3) asset type, and (4) financial slack.

3. Plan ahead with *pro forma* financial statements.

LIST OF TERMS

Bankruptcy
Bankruptcy costs
Capital gains
Cost of financial distress
Default
Distress
Financial distress
Financial slack
Leveraged buyouts

Pecking order
Present value of tax shield
Pro forma balance sheet
Pro forma income statement
Tax-deductible
Tax shield
Tradeoff theory
Value of all-equity firm

EXERCISES

Fill-in Questions

1. The main advantage to corporate debt is that the interest is a _____ expense whereas cash dividends are not.
2. If a company has permanent long-term debt carrying an interest rate of 9 percent and is in the 40 percent tax bracket, the tax shield amounts to _____ for every $1000 of debt.
3. The present value of a permanent tax shield of $46 is _____ when the effective long-run rate is 9 percent.
4. The new MM Proposition I says that firm's value is equal to _____ + _____.
5. If investors are willing to lend at a before-tax return of 9 percent, they must be willing to lend at an after-tax return of _____, if they are in a 28 percent marginal income tax bracket.
6. In Merton Miller's "Debt and Taxes" scheme of the financial world, migrations between stocks and bonds continue to take place up to the point where _____ tax losses are just equal to _____ tax savings.
7. Once we add the cost of _____ to the analysis of a firm's value, we find that the value of the firm is equal to the value of an all-equity firm if the present value of the tax shield is equal to the present value of _____.
8. _____ is an operating problem and not a financial problem.
9. The expected cost of bankruptcy is equal to the probability of bankruptcy times the cost of bankruptcy as a _____ of the firm's current _____ value.
10. In a financially distressed firm stockholders (gain, lose) _____ when the business risk is increased.
11. In a financially distressed firm, a project whose net present value is $200 will add (exactly, less than, more than) _____ $200 to the value of shareholders.
12. The bondholders of a financially distressed firm have (more, less) _____ to gain from investments which increase firm value, the greater the probability of default.
13. Acquisitions of public companies by private investors, financed with large fractions of debt capital, are called _____.
14. Firm's should strive to maximize the (after-, before-tax) _____ income of shareholders.
15. If $(1 - Tp)$ is greater than $[(1 - TpE) \times (1 - Tc)]$, corporate borrowing is (better, worse) _____ than personal borrowing.
16. Bankruptcy is a (financing, operating) _____ decision, not a (financing, operating) _____ decision.
17. Firms that have ample positive NPV projects may rely on _____ to finance them.
18. It pays companies to issue more debt as long as the corporate tax shield (exceeds, is less than) _____ the personal tax cost to the marginal lender.
19. The _____ of capital structure says that target debt ratios vary from firm to firm.

20. Firms whose assets are risky and mostly intangible tend to borrow (less, more) _____ than firms whose assets are tangible and relatively safe.

21. A defined ranking of financing preferences is called the _____ theory of capital structure.

Problems

1. Compute the present value of interest tax shields resulting from each of the following debt issues. Consider only corporate taxes, the marginal rate of which is 34 percent. Show all calculations.
   a. A $1000, 1-year loan at 9 percent.
   b. A 7-year loan of $1000 at 9 percent. Assume principal is repaid at maturity.
   c. A $1000 perpetuity at 8 percent.

2. Consider the following book and market value balance sheets of PaperWeight, Inc.:

BOOK VALUE				MARKET VALUE			
Net working capital	$40	Debt	$ 70	Net working capital	$ 40	Debt	$ 70
Long-term assets	70	Equity	40	Long-term assets	110	Equity	80
	$110		$110		$150		$150

Answer the following questions in light of these assumptions:

(1) The MM theory holds except for taxes. (2) No growth. (3) The debt is permanent. (4) 34 percent corporate tax rate. (5) The interest rate on debt is 8 percent.

   a. How can the market value of the firm be greater than its book value?
   b. Demonstrate the extent to which the stockholders would be better off if the company were to sell additional debt at 8 percent, using the proceeds to purchase $40 of stock.
   c. Demonstrate the effects of replacing $40 of permanent 8 percent debt with equity.

3. Compute the total corporate and personal taxes paid on debt and equity income for each of the following cases. In which cases does the tax advantage lie, with a levered or unlevered firm? For convenience assume a corporate income tax rate of 34 percent; realized capital gains and all cash dividends are taxed as ordinary income; the interest rate on debt is 10 percent; earnings before interest and taxes are $1000; the levered firm borrows $1000 and, where the condition calls for it, all earnings for shareholders are paid to them.

CASE	BONDHOLDERS' TAX BRACKET	STOCKHOLDERS' TAX BRACKET	FORM OF EQUITY INCOME
1	0	0	All dividends
2	0.15	0.15	All dividends
3	0.15	0.15	All unrealized capital gains
4	0.15	0.15	All realized capital gains
5	0.28	0.28	All dividends
6	0.28	0.28	All unrealized capital gains
7	0.28	0.28	All realized capital gains

What implications do the differences you observe have for making financial decisions of the firm? For individual investors?

4. PaperWeight, Inc. has fallen onto hard times and is bankrupt; its market value balance sheet is as follows:

Net working capital	$500	Bonds	$650
Long-term assets	200	Equity	50
	$700		$700

You are brought in to evaluate each of the following possible actions the financial manager is contemplating. Present an objective evaluation of each action. Assume each action is independent of all other actions.

a. The company pays a cash dividend of $75.

b. The company sells its long-term assets for $100, collects $450 from its net working capital, closes its doors, and invests the cash of $550 in U.S. Treasury bills at the going rate of 8 percent.

c. The company is confronted with an investment opportunity which has a net present value of $200 but decides not to undertake it.

d. The company is confronted with an investment project whose net present value is $200 and sells new equity to undertake it.

e. The company is confronted with an investment opportunity whose net present value is $200 and borrows $200 to undertake it.

f. The lenders agree to extend the due date of its debt from 1 year to 2 years. From 1 year to 5 years.

g. The lenders agree to extend the due date of its debt from 1 year to 2 years, provided the lenders control all working capital and investment decisions, as well as prohibiting the issuance of any further debt.

5. You are the financial manager of Dun & Bradstreet Corporation. You are asked to demonstrate how interest tax shields may contribute to the value of the stockholders' equity. Create the numbers needed to support the case for adding debt to a presently debt-free corporation. The book and market value balance sheets are presented in Table 18-2a. Because of your high credit rating (what else!!!) assume that debt can be issued at a rate equal to that of Aaa companies, that is, 9 percent, and that the corporation's income tax rate is 34 percent.

Essay Questions

1. Explain why tax shields are valuable assets.

2. What is MM's Proposition I, as corrected? Why was the correction necessary?

3. "This much I know, as more and more debt is taken on the chances of bankruptcy increase. It only stands the test of reason that the value of a firm which has 'too much' debt is likely to be less than a firm that has 'just the right amount' of debt." Evaluate this statement.

4. How can it be said that: "It may not be in the stockholders' self-interest to contribute fresh equity capital even if that means forgoing positive net present value investment opportunities"?

ANSWERS TO EXERCISES

Fill-in Questions

1. tax-deductible
2. $36
3. $511.11
4. The value of an all-equity firm; the present value of the tax shield
5. 6.48 percent
6. personal; corporate
7. financial distress; the cost of financial distress
8. bankruptcy
9. proportion; market
10. gain
11. less than
12. more
13. leveraged buyouts
14. after
15. better
16. operating, financing
17. Financial Slack
18. exceeds
19. tradeoff theory
20. more
21. pecking order

Problems

1. a. Interest tax shield: 0.34($1000 x 0.09) = $30.6; present value of tax shield = $30.6/1.09 = $28.07.
   b. Present value of tax shield = $30.6 x 5.033 = $154.01; (c) [.34($1000 x .08)]/0.08 = $340

2. a. Book values are based largely on historical costs, whereas market values are based on expected productivity.
   b. $T_cD = 0.34$ x $40 = $13.60, the amount by which total assets increase. The decline in equity is $(1 - T_c)D = \$26.40$. In sum,

Amount received by shareholders	$40.00
Decline in shareholder value	<u>26.40</u>

Net gain to shareholders $13.60

Market value balance sheet after the debt issue:

Net working capital	$ 40.00	Debt	$110.00
Long-term assets	123.60	Equity	53.60
	$163.60		$163.60

c. Assets now decline by $13.60 and equity increases by $26.40. In sum,

Increase in shareholder value	$26.40
Amount paid by shareholders	40.00
Net loss to shareholders	$13.60

Market value balance sheet after the equity issue:

Net working capital	$ 40.00	Debt	$ 30.00
Long-term assets	96.40	Equity	106.40
	$136.40		$136.40

3. Take case 4.

	Tax Rate	Levered Firm	Unlevered Firm
Earnings before interest and taxes		1000	1000
Interest		100	0
Earnings before taxes		900	1000
Taxes on the firm	34%	306	340
Net available to shareholders		594	660
Tax on bondholders	28%	28	0
Tax on shareholders	28%	166	185
Total taxes paid		500	525

All Cases

Case	Levered Firm	Unlevered Firm
1	306	340
2	410	439
3	410	439
4	321	340
5	334	340
6	500	525
7	500	525

4. a. Bond value falls, stockholders gain.
   b. Bondholders will get $550; stockholders will get nothing.
   c. Everyone loses.
   d. Bondholders gain because the debt ratio improves; stockholders also gain.
   e. Bondholders could gain or lose, depending on the risk of the project.
   f. Bondholders lose in both instances.
   g. Bondholders may win in this case.

TABLE 18-2a
SIMPLIFIED BALANCE SHEETS FOR D&B, 1987 (IN MILLIONS).

BOOK VALUES				MARKET VALUES			
Net working capital	$526	$0	Long-term debt	Net working capital	$526	$0	Long-term debt
Long-term assets	1134	0	Other long-term liabilities	Long-term assets	6922	0	Other long-term liabilities
		1660	Equity			7448	Equity
Total assets	$1660	$1660	Total liabilities and equity	Total assets	$7448	$7448	Total liabilities and equity

TABLE 18-2b
BALANCE SHEETS FOR D&B WITH $1 BILLION OF LONG-TERM DEBT SUBSTITUTED FOR STOCKHOLDERS' EQUITY (IN MILLIONS).

BOOK VALUES				MARKET VALUES			
Net working capital	$526	$1000	Long-term debt	Net working capital	$526	$1000	Long-term debt
Long-term assets	1134	0	Other long-term liabilities	Long-term assets	7262	0	Other long-term liabilities
		600	Equity			6788	Equity
Total assets	$1660	$1660	Total liabilities and equity	Total assets	$7788	$7788	Total liabilities and equity

(1) Construct simplified book and market value balance sheets, such as those in Table 18-2a. (2) Estimate the value of the firm if it were to borrow $1 billion in permanent long-term debt and use the proceeds to buy that much stock. (3) Because of the tax-shield this financing scheme should increase the firm's value by T_cD, the corporate tax rate T_c times the amount of permanent long-term debt D. Inasmuch as the additional debt is $1 billion, the market value of the firm should increase by 0.34 x $1,000,000,000 = $340,000,000. (4) The value of the firm must increase by $340 million to $7,788 billion. (5) The new balance sheets will be those in Table 18-2b. The value of the equity declines by $660 million $(1 – T_c)(D)$. (6) The shareholders are better off because the financial manager purchased $1 billion of stock and it dropped in value by only $660 million, the stockholders are ahead on the deal to the tune of $340 million ($1 billion – $660 million).

CHAPTER 19
INTERACTIONS OF INVESTMENT AND FINANCING DECISIONS

INTRODUCTION

This chapter takes us off in a new direction, because we drop the assumption that investment and financing decisions are separable and independent of each other. This important shift in emphasis forces us to search for a method of valuing the firm which includes the interplay between investment and financing decisions. It also tells us how to determine the discount rate on a risk-free asset.

WHAT TO LOOK FOR IN CHAPTER 19

To this point you lived primarily in the idealized Modigliani-Miller financial world in which (1) investment decisions were separated from financing decisions, (2) financing decisions were irrelevant to the value of the firm, and (3) an all-equity-financed firm was assumed. The emphasis is now shifted to include the influence of financing decisions on the value of the firm. Retained is the value-additivity assumption. As you proceed remember that the analyses begin with a base case all-equity financed firm and then evaluates the side effects of financing the project.

Adjusted Present Value Is Preferred: To trace the impact of financing decisions on the value of the firm, several approaches are taken, including adjusted net present value, the Modigliani-Miller formula, and the weighted-average cost of capital formula, and discount safe, nominal cash flows.

How APV Works: The adjusted-present-value (APV) rule is applied by first determining the present value of a project assuming that it is an all-equity-financed mini-firm. The resulting base-case net present value is thereafter adjusted for the influence of financing decisions. Issue costs, for example, are evaluated; their present value tends to reduce the base-case net present value, and APV decreases.

Debt Capacity and APV: Additions to the firm's debt capacity tend to add to the project's adjusted net present value. Debt capacity depends on the firm's target debt-equity ratio and expands as new investment projects are undertaken, even though the target is maintained. Expansion of debt capacity is valuable because it generates the interest tax shield of which we made quite a to-do in Chapter 18. The present value of the tax shield is added to the base-case net present value so that the adjusted net present value increases. The true value of the tax shield is invariably less than that implied by the corporate marginal tax rate.

Adjusted-Discount-Rate Approaches: The adjusted-discount-rate approach to the valuation of investment opportunities is an alternative to adjusted present values. The discount rate is adjusted upward or downward to accommodate the specific riskiness of the investment.

Adjusted Discount Rates: Three ways by which to adjust discount rates are the Modigliani-Miller (MM) formula, the Miles and Ezzell formula, and the weighted-average cost of capital. The MM formula accounts for the opportunity cost of capital for the firm under an all-equity condition but adjusts for the tax shield arising from debt financing. The MM formula may be adjusted for the opportunity costs of the specific project being evaluated. The MM formula is deficient because it requires perpetual cash flows and permanent debt financing. The MM formula is still useful because it produces results which are "close enough." Miles and Ezzell have given us an equation which overcomes some of MM's difficulties by allowing adjustments in debt. Both formulas are useful for their analytical insights.

Weighted-Average Cost of Capital: The weighted-average cost of capital approach to adjusting discount rates says the proper discount rate used to evaluate projects is the market-value weighted cost of capital. This approach assumes that all projects possess the same risk as the firm. Consequently, the weighted-average cost of capital may not be used to evaluate investment projects whose risk is different from the entire firm.

Discounting Safe, Nominal Cash Flows: The correct discount rate to use to evaluate safe, nominal cash flows is the after-tax, unsubsidized borrowing rate. The cash flows may be viewed as the amount of money needed to service an equivalent amount of debt; the project may be viewed as being equivalent to a loan, the cash flows of which are needed to repay the loan's interest and principal. Two commonplace equivalent loans are depreciation and payouts that are fixed by contract. The procedure of treating cash flows as debt equivalent loans is consistent with adjusted discount rate approaches.

WORKED EXAMPLES

PROBLEM 1: THE BASE CASE ALL-EQUITY FIRM

What-Not, Inc. is considering an investment project which will generate a level after-tax cash flow of $500,000 a year in the next 5 years. Returns on comparable-risk investment opportunities are 14 percent. The investment requires a cash outlay of $1.5 million. Compute the net present value of this project.

SOLUTION

This straightforward capital budgeting problem requires you to find the present value of the $500,000 a year for each of 5 years, using the discount rate of 14 percent. The cash outlay is then deducted from the present value of that stream of cash to obtain NPV. The calculations are

$$\text{NPV} = -\$1,500,000 + \sum_{t=1}^{5} \frac{\$500,000}{(1.14)^t}$$

$$= -\$1,500,000 + (\$500,000)(3.433)$$
$$= -\$1,500,000 + \$1,716,500$$
$$= \$216,500$$

PROBLEM 2: ISSUES COSTS

Because What-Not, Inc. does not have the cash available to undertake the project, it is investigating the possibility of selling stock. The financial manager discovered that for issues of that size, the effective cost to the firm would be 16 percent of the gross proceeds to the company. How much must the company raise in order to net $1.5 million and what impact does the cost of issuing common stock have on the project's NPV?

SOLUTION

This is a problem of determining the adjusted present value (APV) of the investment, taking into account the costs incurred when external financing is needed. To find the amount of money that must be raised so that the company obtains the needed $1.5 million, simply set up the problem this way: the company will receive only 84 percent of the amount raised; $1.5 million is 84 percent of what unknown (x) amount to be raised? Algebraically it is set up thus:

$$\$1,500,000 = 0.84x$$

Solving for x by dividing both sides of the equation by 0.84, the result is $1,785,714. To obtain the needed $1.5 million, the company must raise $1,785,714 because that amount, when adjusted for the cost of selling the issue, results in the desired amount, that is, [$1,785,714 – ($1,785,714 x 0.16)] = $1,500,000. Or equivalently $1,785,714 x 0.84 = $1,500,000. So the issue cost is $285,714 ($1,785,714 – $1,500,000). Because this is an additional cash outlay prompted by this project, it must be included in the analysis. The APV is

$$
\begin{aligned}
\text{APV} &= \text{base-case NPV} - \text{issue cost} \\
&= \$216,500 - \$285,714 \\
&= -\$69,214
\end{aligned}
$$

The issue cost makes the project unacceptable.

PROBLEM 3: ISSUE COSTS, DEBT CAPACITY AND TAX SHIELDS

Let's add another twist to What-Not, Inc.'s financing schemes. Say financial management is comfortable with a 65 percent target debt ratio. Say it borrows at the rate of 12 percent, pays the principal in equal yearly installments, and pays interest based on the unpaid balance. Debt issue costs are 5 percent of the gross proceeds and equity issue costs are those of problem 2. The tax on the corporation, bondholders, and shareholders is 30 percent. What does this do to APV?

SOLUTION

This extension of the basic problem requires you to incorporate the present value of the interest tax shield to make it complete. Let's go through it in steps.

Step 1. We already know the value of the base case is $216,500.

Step 2. Determine issue cost. To calculate the issue cost of debt, determine how much will be needed. It is $975,000 (0.65 x $1,500,000). Next determine how much should be raised to obtain that amount: It is $1,026,316 ($975,000/0.95). The issue cost is determined by taking the difference between the amount that must be raised and the amount that is actually used: It is $51,316 ($1,026,316 – $1,500,000). The issue costs of equity are similarly determined. The amount needed is $525,000 ($1.5 million x 35 percent). The amount to be raised is $625,000 ($525,000/0.84). The issue cost is $100,000 ($625,000 – $525,000).

Step 3. Determine the present value of the interest tax shield. Before you can do that, however, you must determine the annual installment payments, the annual interest payable in each year, the annual tax shelter, and the present value of the annual tax shelter. The annual installments are $205,263 [(0.65 x $1,500,000)/5 years] plus interest on the remaining balance. The table is as follows. (Because the debt is not subsidized, it is evaluated at the 12 percent borrowing rate.)

YEAR	DEBT OUTSTANDING AT START OF YEAR	INTEREST	INTEREST TAX SHIELD	PRESENT VALUE TAX SHIELD
1	$1,026,316	123,518	36,947	32,989
2	821,053	98,526	29,558	23,563
3	615,790	73,895	22,168	15,779
4	410,527	49,263	14,779	9,392
5	205,264	24,632	7,390	4,193
			Total	$85,916

Combine all the PVs to obtain APV

$$
\begin{aligned}
\text{APV} &= \text{base-case PV} - \text{PV of issue cost} + \text{PV of tax shield} \\
&= \$216,500 - (\$51,316 + \$100,000) + \$85,916 = \$151,000.
\end{aligned}
$$

Accept the project.

PROBLEM 4: DEBT CAPACITY AND TAX SHIELDS

You are asked to demonstrate the impact of using the proper marginal tax rate on the adjusted present value of a $3 million project which promises to generate before-tax cash flows of $1 million a year for the next 10 years. The firm's target debt ratio is 50 percent. What is the value of the project when the financial manager assumes the marginal tax rate is equal to the 34 percent corporate rate? When the financial manager assumes the firm's overall tax rate of 30 percent? For the sake of convenience assume the debt is paid off in equal yearly installments and that the firm borrows at the rate of 12 percent. Projects of comparable risk warrant a return of 15 percent.

SOLUTION

As may be seen from the table, the project's present value is about $2,918 million at the 34 percent rate. The 30 percent rate makes the NPV slightly positive.

YEAR	EARNINGS BEFORE TAXES AND INTEREST	OUTSTANDING DEBT	INTEREST	EARNINGS BEFORE TAXES	EARNINGS AFTER TAXES	PV OF AFTER-TAX EARNINGS	EARNINGS AFTER TAXES	PV OF AFTER-TAX EARNINGS
1	$1000	$1500	$180	$820	$541	$471	$574	$499
2	1000	1350	162	838	553	418	587	444
3	1000	1200	144	856	565	371	599	394
4	1000	1050	126	874	577	530	612	350
5	1000	900	108	892	589	293	624	310
6	1000	750	90	910	601	260	637	275
7	1000	600	72	928	612	230	650	244
8	1000	450	54	946	624	204	662	216
9	1000	300	36	964	636	181	675	192
10	1000	150	18	982	648	160	687	170
Present Value						2918		$3095

PROBLEM 5: PERPETUAL TAX SHIELDS, MINIMUM NPV, AND IRR

Let's take the case of Forever and Ever Company, which is considering an investment project that costs $2 million and is expected to generate savings of $295,000 a year, forever and ever, naturally. The business risk of this project warrants a rate of return of 15 percent.

In successive steps, your task as the financial manager is to calculate the net present value of the project, assuming no tax shields. Then calculate the project's NPV assuming tax shields which arise because additional 12 percent debt may be issued in amounts equal to 30 percent of the cost of the project. The overall tax rate is 30 percent. Finally, determine the minimum acceptable base-case NPV as well as the minimum internal rate of return.

SOLUTION

The solution to this problem is straightforward. The base-case NPV is

$$\text{Base-case NPV} = \text{cash outlay} + \text{present value of a perpetuity}$$
$$= -\$2,000,000 + (\$250,000/0.15)$$
$$= -\$2,000,000 + \$1,966,667$$
$$= -\$33,333$$

Obviously you must reject this project, for it takes away more value from the firm than it adds to it.

Now add the effects of the financing scheme. A total of $600,000 ($2 million x 30 percent) is borrowed at the 12 percent rate. The tax shield is

$$\text{Tax shield} = \text{debt x interest x tax rate}$$
$$= \$600,000 \times 0.12 \times 0.30$$
$$= \$21,600$$

This annual tax shield lasts, remember, forever and ever; so to find the present value of this perpetuity, divide it by the required rate of return of 12 percent, the resulting answer being $180,000. Now the project is acceptable, its APV being

$$\text{APV} = \text{base-case NPV} + \text{PV tax shield}$$
$$= -\$33,333 + \$180,000$$
$$= \$146,667$$

Finding the minimum acceptable level of income for the project alone, that is, *without the tax shield*, is another story. What you want to know is the annual income that is needed to make the project acceptable. To find the minimum level of income *net* of the of the tax effects (of -$180,000), set up the problem this way.

$$\text{Present value of tax shield} = \text{cash outlay} + \frac{\text{annual income}}{\text{required rate of return}}$$

$$-\$180,000 = -\$2,000,000 + \frac{\text{annual income}}{0.15}$$

Solving for annual income, we obtain

$$\text{Annual income} = (\$2,000,000 - \$180,000) \times 0.15$$
$$= \$273,000$$

This is the minimum annual income this project must generate in order to make it acceptable.

The minimum acceptable rate of return is

$$\$270,000/\$2,000,000 = 0.1365 = 13.65 \text{ percent}$$

PROBLEM 6: MM'S ADJUSTED COST OF CAPITAL

Use the MM formula to determine the adjusted cost of capital in problem 5.

SOLUTION

Their formula for projects is

$$r^* = r(1 - T^*L)$$

where r^* = adjusted cost of capital
r = opportunity cost of capital
T^* = net tax saving on a dollar of future interest payments
L = firm's target debt ratio

The target debt ratio from problem 5 is 0.3 and the completed equation is

$$r^* = 0.15[1 - (0.30)(0.3)]$$
$$= 0.1365 = 13.65 \text{ percent}$$

which is precisely the answer we obtained.

PROBLEM 7: MILES AND EZZELL'S ADJUSTED COST OF CAPITAL

"Cuz I don't wish to assume that I will always borrow the same dollar amount, as the MM formula implies, I will use the Miles and Ezzell formula instead. Betcha I get better answers."

SOLUTION

The Miles and Ezzell formula is

$$r^* = r - Lr_D T^* (1 + r/1 + r_D)$$

The calculated adjusted cost of capital is:

$$r^* = 0.15 - 0.3(0.12)(0.3)(1.15/1.12)$$
$$= 0.15 - 0.0111$$
$$= 0.1389 = 13.89 \text{ percent}$$

Whether the answer is "better" depends on how well the financing scheme conforms to the assumption of adjusting debt in order to maintain constant debt proportions. The 0.24 percent difference is really quite small.

PROBLEM 8: WEIGHTED-AVERAGE COST OF CAPITAL

You are engaged as a financial consultant to estimate the value of a privately held firm which earns $500 thousand a year. You are to assume that the cash flows will continue indefinitely at that level. Because you estimate the risk of the private firm to be about that of the public ones comparable in business risk, the weighted average cost of capital seems like a suitable approach. (You use average data of firms publicly held.) The firm's marginal tax rate is 34 percent. The weighted average bond yield of the comparable companies is 12.2 percent. The risk of the comparable companies approximated a portfolio beta of 1.2. With U.S. Treasury Bills yielding 8 percent and adding the historical risk premium of 10 percent to that, your estimated average cost of equity is 1.2 x 18 percent = 22 percent. The desired debt ratio is 40 percent.

SOLUTION

The formula for the weighted average cost of capital is

$$r^* = r_D(1 - T_c)D/V + r_E E/V$$

where r^* = the adjusted cost of capital
r_D = the firm's current borrowing rate
T_c = the marginal *corporate* income tax
r_E = the expected rate of return on the firm's stock (a function of the firm's business risk and its debt ratio)
D, E = the market values of currently outstanding debt and equity
$V = D + E$ = the total market value of the firm

The weighted average cost of capital for the firm is, therefore:

$$r^* = 0.122(1 - 0.34)\,0.4 + 0.22(0.6)$$
$$= 0.032208 + 0.132$$
$$= 0.1643 = 16.43 \text{ percent}$$

The value of the firm is slightly more than $3.0 million ($500,000/0.1643).

PROBLEM 9: DISCOUNTING SAFE, NOMINAL CASH FLOWS

Your city faces a chronic unemployment problem and makes its largest employer an offer it says it cannot refuse. Here it is. It implores the employer to abandon its previously announced plant closure and offers to finance the plant's needed $10 million modernization by lending the company the money at 5 percent (the going rate is 12 percent). The modernized facility will generate $500 thousand a year for the next five years. A good deal? The firm's marginal tax rate is 30 percent ($T_c = 0.30$.) Show all calculations.

SOLUTION

The after-tax unsubsidized borrowing rate is 8.4 percent [$0.12(1 - 0.30)$]. This is the rate at which to evaluate the cash flows. The following table contains the arithmetic. In effect, the modernization costs are cut by about $1.4 million.

Table 19-1

Discounting Safe, Nominal Cash Flows

Period	0	1	2	3	4	5
Cash Flow (in thousands)	10,000	-500	-500	-500	-500	-500
Tax shield		150	150	150	150	150
After-tax cash flow	10,000	-350	-350	-350	-350	-350
Marginal tax rate	30%					
Borrowing rates						
Before tax	12.00%					
After tax	8.40%					
Factor	0.922509					
Present value of outlay	10,000	-323	-298	-275	-253	-234
Net present value of inflows	8,617					
Difference	1,383					

PROBLEM 10: SAFE, NOMINAL CASH FLOWS AS EQUIVALENT LOANS

You have an investment project that is expected to produce $200 thousand in one year and it is to be financed at a subsidized 5 percent rate. Demonstrate how this is an equivalent loan in that amount. The before-tax opportunity cost of borrowing is 12 percent. The marginal tax rate of 30 percent.

SOLUTION

To see this point one must assume the point of view of both the borrower and lender. The after-tax rate is the appropriate rate to use in both cases because it is only the after-tax dollars that count (are spendable) by either party to the transaction. The after-tax rate is 8.4 percent [12(1 – 0.30)]. The cash flow at the end of one year is $210 thousand, the tax shield is $3 thousand ($200 x 0.05 x 0.30), and the after-tax cash flow is $207 thousand. The equivalent loan is the amount of cash that could be borrowed through regular channels in order to set aside $207 thousand to pay off the borrowing. To borrow through regular channels you need a total cash flow at the end of one year of $224 thousand [$200,000 + (0.12 x $200,000)], or 12 percent more than the amount borrowed. But there is an interest tax shield of 3.6 percent (0.30 x 12%). So the net difference is 8.4 percent (12% – 3.6%). This means that 108.4 percent of the amount borrowed is needed to repay that amount plus after-tax interest. That comes to $216.8 thousand. The difference between that amount and the after-tax cashflows of the subsidized loan is the net present value of the loan. It is $9,800 ($216,800 – $207,000).

SUMMARY

Review: Evaluating Capital Investments Using the Following Steps:

1. Forecast the project's incremental after-tax cash flow.

2. Assess the project's risk.

3. Estimate the opportunity cost of capital.

4. Calculate NPV using the discounted cash-flow formula.

Adjusted Net Present Value Rule

When investment and financing decisions interact or cannot be separated: adjust for the NPV of the financing decisions, resulting in adjusted net present value, ANPV or APV.

1. Assume the project is an all-equity financed mini-firm; this is the base-case.

2. Determine the NPV of the project, without financing side effects.

3. Adjust for financing side effects.
    a. Issue costs take away from the project's NPV.
    b. Depreciation adds to NPV. Discount the savings at the interest rate the firm would have to pay on an unsubsidized loan.
    c. Additions to the firm's debt capacity add to a project's NPV, because of the debt's interest tax shield.

    $$APV \ = \ \text{base-case NPV} + \text{PV tax shield}$$

    d. The effective tax shield on interest is probably less than the firm's tax rate (Miller's - Chapter 18 - argument).

Adjusted Discount Rates

1. APV works well, but the adjusted cost of capital may be used in its place.

2. The steps:
    a. Determine the minimum acceptable income from the project.
    b. Calculate the minimum acceptable IRR.
    c. If rates of return exceed IRR, accept, and vice versa.
    d. IRR
        (1) Minimum acceptable rate of return.
        (2) Reflects the project's business risk.
        (3) Reflects the project's contribution to the firm's debt capacity.
    e. The rule:

Accept projects which have a positive NPV at the adjusted cost of capital r^*.

    f. The adjusted cost of capital
        (1) Hurdle rate of return.
        (2) Opportunity cost of capital.
        (3) Required return expected from capital markets on comparable-risk investments.
    g. A universally correct method for calculating r^* does not exist.

MM's Formula

1. $r^* = r(1 - T \times L)$

2. T^*: net tax saving attached to a dollar of future interest payments.

3. Works for projects that generate level and perpetual cash flows and support permanent debt.

4. Works reasonably well for other projects.

Uncertain Future Debt Levels

The Miles and Ezzell formula:

$$r^* = r - Lr_D T^* (1 + r/1 + r_D)$$

1. Works for firms that maintain a constant debt proportion.

2. Is exact for any cash flow pattern or project life.

On the Usefulness of Adjusted-Cost-of-Capital Formulas

1. The two adjusted cost of capital formulas differ in their assumptions about the amount of debt the firm can or will issue against the project.
    a. MM assume it is fixed.
    b. Miles and Ezzell assume it varies over the project's future value.
    c. Both formulas assume that financing affects firm value only through interest tax shields-but there are other financing side effects.

2. Brealey and Myers' third law: Good investment decisions do more for you than good financing decisions.

The Weighted-Average Cost of Capital

The formula:

$$r^* = r_D (1 - T_c) D/V + r_E (E/V)$$

1. All the variables refer to the firm as a whole.

2. Gives the proper discount rate only when the project replicates the present firm's condition.

3. Miles and Ezzell tell us the formula works for any cash-flow pattern, if the firm adjusts its borrowing to maintain a constant D/V.

4. Used in practice, but often incorrectly.
    a. Works only for projects that are carbon copies of the firm as a whole.
    b. The immediate source of funds is not necessarily connected with the hurdle rate.
    c. Extreme financial leverage is not implied by the formula.

Discounting Safe Nominal Cash Flows

1. You commit to making the stipulated dollar cash flows.

2. The correct discount rate to use is the after-tax unsubsidized borrowing rate.

3. As a general rule such cash flows may be evaluated as if they were equivalent loans. That is:
   Equivalent loan = present value of the cash flows needed to service the debt.

LIST OF TERMS

Adjusted cost of capital   Financing decisions

Adjusted discount rate   PV of financing decisions

Adjusted net present value   Subsidized financing

Base-case NPV   Target debt ratios

Business risk   Value additivity

Corporate debt capacity   Weighted-average cost of capital

EXERCISES

Fill-in Questions

1. The adjusted net present value is equal to _____ plus the present value of
   _____.

2. If the net present value of a base-case investment is $100,000 and equity is issued to finance it at a cost of $125,000, the project may be (accepted, rejected) _____.

3. Corporate borrowing power is (increased, decreased) _____ when an investment is made in tangible assets which are highly related to the firm's fortunes.

4. The opportunity cost of capital depends on the _____ of the investment project to be undertaken.

5. Using the adjusted cost of capital approach to investment analysis, the lowest return a firm is willing to accept from projects of comparable risk occurs when the internal rate of return is such that the adjusted present value is _____.

6. If the minimum acceptable internal rate of return is 9 percent, a project which has a 10 percent rate of return will produce a (positive, negative) _____ adjusted present value.

7. The MM formula for calculating the adjusted cost of capital applies to projects which are equal in riskiness to the firm as well as to projects which have their own unique risk characteristics, whereas the weighted-average cost of capital formula applies only to the (former, latter) _____.

8. The Modigliani-Miller formula is correct only for projects whose cash flows and debt are
   _____.

Problems

1. If-Not, Inc. is evaluating a $1 million investment project which is expected to generate level, after-tax cash flows of $300,000 a year in each of the next 6 years. Rates of return obtainable on investments of comparable risk are 12 percent. Compute the net present value of this project.

2. If-Not, Inc. will finance the project in problem 1 entirely by the sale of stock. The cost of floating the stock is 12 percent of the gross proceeds. How much must the company raise and what impact do the flotation costs have on the net present value of the project?

3. Say the management of If-Not, Inc.'s target debt ratio is 40 percent. To finance the $1 million in problem 1 the six-year loan will carry a 10 percent rate and be repaid in equal annual installments, with the annual interest payable on the unpaid balance. Issue costs are 2 and 12 percent respectively of the net proceeds of the debt and equity. Using a marginal tax rate of 34 percent, trace the impact of this additional twist on the project's net present value.

4. The Perpetual Motion Company is evaluating a $6 million plant expansion which it estimates will generate $750,000 in after-tax cash, year in and year out, perpetually. The return obtainable on investments of comparable risk is 13 percent. (a) Calculate the net present value of the project, assuming no tax shields. (b) Calculate the project's net present value, assuming tax shields produced by the issuance of 9 percent debt in amounts equal to 40 percent of the project's cost. The company's marginal tax rate is 34 percent. (c) Determine the minimum acceptable base-case NPV. (d) Determine the minimum acceptable internal rate of return.

5. Use the MM and Miles and Ezzell formulas to determine the adjusted cost of capital in problem 5.

6. Using the data in problem 4, calculate the weighted average cost of capital. Further assume that U.S. Treasury Bills yield 7 percent; the risk premium for all stocks is 10 percent; and the company's beta is 0.90. Show all calculations.

7. Your company is considering a relocation of its outdated plant. The state offers to loan your firm the $15 million it needs to update the facilities if it agrees to stay at least five years. The loan rate is 5 percent, whereas your market rate for borrowing is 12 percent. You expect that the modernized facility will generate $600 thousand a year for the next five years. A good deal? Show why or why not? The firm's marginal tax rate is 34 percent.

8. If you have an investment project that is expected to provided $400 thousand at the end of one year and it is financed at a subsidized 5 percent rate, demonstrate how this is an equivalent loan in that amount. The before-tax opportunity cost of borrowing is 12 percent. The marginal tax rate of 34 percent.

Essay Questions

1. What are issue costs and what bearing do they have on adjusted present value? Demonstrate as well as explain your answer.

2. Contrast the weighted-average-cost-of-capital formulation with Modigliani and Miller's and Miles and Ezzell's formulas. Wherein are they similar? Dissimilar? Explain fully.

ANSWERS TO EXERCISES

Fill-in Questions

1. base-case net present value; net present value of financing decisions (caused by project acceptance)
2. accepted; rejected
3. decreased
4. business risk
5. zero
6. positive
7. latter
8. permanent

Problems

Some of the answers below were determined with a hand-held calculator or microcomputer. If you use the tables in the Appendix of the text, your answers will be slightly different.

1.

$$NPV = -\$1,000,000 + \$300,000(4.111)$$
$$= -\$1,000,000 + \$1,233,420$$
$$= \$233,300$$

2. Proceeds needed: $\$1,000,000/(1 - 0.12) = \$1,136,364$
   Issue cost: $\$1,136,364 - \$1,000,000 = \$136,364$

$$APV = \text{base-case NPV} - \text{issue cost}$$
$$= \$233,300 - \$136,364 = \$96,936$$

3. a.

$$\text{Amount of debt needed} = (\$1,000,000 \times \text{Debt Ratio})/(1 - \text{issue costs})$$
$$= (\$1,000,000 \times 0.4)/(1 - 0.02)$$
$$= \$408,163$$

$$\text{Debt issue cost} = \$408,163 - \$400,000 = \$8,163$$

Annual Principal Payment: $\$408,163 \div 6 \text{ years} = \$68,027$

   b.

$$\text{Amount of common stock needed} = \$1,000,000(1 - \text{debt ratio})$$
$$= \$1,000,000(1 - 0.4)$$
$$= \$600,000$$
$$= \$600,000/(1 - \text{issue costs})$$
$$= \$600,000/0.88$$
$$= \$681,818$$

$$\text{Equity issue cost} = \$681,818 - \$600,000 = \$81,818$$

   c. PV of interest tax shield

YEAR	DEBT OUTSTANDING AT BEGINNING OF YEAR	INTEREST	INTEREST TAX SHIELD	PV OF TAX SHIELD
1	408,163	40,816	13,878	$12,616
2	340,136	34,014	11,565	9,558
3	272,109	27,211	9,252	6,951
4	204,082	20,408	6,939	4,739
5	136,055	13,606	4,626	2,872
6	68,028	6,803	2,313	1,306
				$36,736

   d.

$$APV = \text{base-case NPV} - \text{PV of issue cost} + \text{PV of tax shield}$$
$$= \$233,420 - \$8,163 - \$81,818 + \$36,736$$
$$= \$180,175$$

4. a.

$$\text{Base-case NPV} = -\$6,000,000 + \$750,000/0.13$$
$$= -\$6,000,000 + \$5,769,231$$
$$= -\$230,769$$

b. Amount borrowed: $\$6,000,000 \times 0.4 = \$2,400,000$

Tax shield $= \$2,400,000 \times 0.09 \times 0.34 = \$73,440$

$$\text{APV} = \text{base-case NPV} + \text{PV of tax shield}$$
$$= -\$230,769 + (\$73,440/0.09)$$
$$= -\$230,769 + \$810,000$$
$$= \$585,231$$

c. Base-case NPV = cash outlay + (annual income/required rate of return)

Annual income $=$ (cash outlay – minimum base case NPV) x required return
$$= (\$6,000,000 - \$816,000) \times 0.13$$
$$= \$173,920$$

d. Minimum return = $\$673,920/\$6,000,000 = 11.23$ percent

5.

$$r^* = r(1 - T \times L)$$
$$= 0.13[1 - (0.34)(0.4)] = 11.23\%$$

$$r^* = r - Lr_D T^*(1 + r/1 + r_D)$$
$$= 0.13 - (0.34)(0.09)(0.4)(1.13/1.09) = 11.73$$

6.

$$r^* = r_D(1 - T_c)\, D/V + r_E\, E/V$$
$$r^* = 13\% \,(1 - 0.34)(0.40) + (16\%)(0.60)$$
$$= 3.43 + 9.60 = 13.03\%$$

Expected equity return $=$ U.S. Treasury bill rate + (beta times the risk premium)
$$= 7\% + (0.09 \times 10\%) = 16\%$$

7.

Table 19-2

Discounting Safe, Nominal Cash Flows						
Period	0	1	2	3	4	5
Cash Flow (in thousands)	15,000	-600	-600	-600	-600	-600
Tax shield		204	204	204	204	204
After-tax cash flow	15,000	-396	-396	-396	-396	-396
Marginal tax rate	34%					
Borrowing rates						
Before tax	12.00%					
After tax	7.92%					
Factor	0.926612					
Present value of outlay	15,000	-367	-340	-315	-292	-271
Net present value of inflows	13,416					
Difference	1,584					

8. After-tax rate: 7.92 percent [12(1 – .34)]. Cash flow at the end of one year: $210 thousand. Tax shield: $3 thousand ($200 x .05 x .3). After-tax cash flow: $207 thousand. The equivalent loan is the amount of cash that could be borrowed through regular channels in order to set aside $207 thousand to pay off the borrowing. To borrow through regular channels you need a total cash flow at the end of one year of $224 thousand [$200,000 + (.12 x $200,000)], or 12 percent more than the amount borrowed. Interest tax shield = 3.6 percent (0.30 x 12%). Difference = 8.4 percent (12% – 3.6%). Needed 108.4 percent more to repay that amount plus after-tax interest, that is, $216.8 thousand. Net present value of the loan = $9,800 ($216,800 – $207,000).

CHAPTER 20
CORPORATE LIABILITIES AND THE VALUATION OF OPTIONS

INTRODUCTION

This chapter focuses on the valuation of options. When making financial decisions, financial managers are faced with many options. Knowing the nature of options and how to evaluate them helps financial managers make better decisions. The value of options depends on the exercise price, the expiration date of the option, the price of the assets, the variability in the rate of return, and the return on the risk-free asset.

WHAT TO LOOK FOR IN CHAPTER 20

As you traverse the landscape of this chapter, keep in mind that whenever a firm borrows it creates an option. Moreover, many investment decisions contain options.

What They Are: A call option gives its owner the right to buy an asset at a specified exercise, or striking, price during a specified time period; a put option gives its owner the right to sell an asset at a specified striking price during a specified time period. Although this chapter focuses primarily on options on stocks, the ideas may be extended to all assets and liabilities.

The difference between European and American calls lies in the timing at which they may be exercised, the latter being exercisable anytime before the option's expiration date and the former being exercisable only on the expiration date.

Option Combinations: Calls, puts, and shares may be held in combination. By being able to hold calls, puts, and shares, and to borrow and lend, combining any three creates the fourth. The process of creating one from the three others is called an option conversion. This leads to the conclusion that whenever a firm borrows, the lender in effect acquires the company and shareholders obtain the option to buy it back by paying off the debt.

The Black-Scholes Model: The Black-Scholes formula says that the present value of the call option depends on the exercise price of the option, the time remaining to the exercise date, the price of the stock now, the per period variance in the rate of return on the stock, and the risk-free rate of interest.

WORKED EXAMPLES

PROBLEM 1: VALUE OF CALL OPTION
Find the value of a call option, given that the present value of the exercise price is $10, the value of the put is $15, and the share price is $25.

SOLUTION

To find the answer to this exercise, use the formula

$$\text{Value of call} + \text{present value of exercise price} = \text{value of put} + \text{share price} \tag{1}$$

Rearranging,

$$\begin{aligned}\text{Value of call} &= \text{value of put} + \text{share price} - \text{present value of exercise price} \tag{1a}\\ &= \$15 + \$25 - \$10 \\ &= \$30\end{aligned}$$

PROBLEM 2: PRESENT VALUE OF EXERCISE PRICE

Find the implied present value of the exercise price of a 13-week call, given that the value of the call option is $19, the value or the put option is $5, and the market price is $30.

SOLUTION

Rearranging equation (1) to solve for the present value of the exercise price, we have

$$\begin{aligned}\text{Present value of exercise price} &= \text{value of put} + \text{share price} - \text{value of call} \tag{1b}\\ &= \$5 + \$30 - \$19 \\ &= \$16\end{aligned}$$

PROBLEM 3: TO BUY A CALL OR A PUT?

If the present value of the exercise price on a call option is $23, the call option is selling for $5, the put option is selling for $10, and the market price of the stock is $20, should a call or a put on the stock be purchased, if you wish to take a position in the issue?

SOLUTION

Using equation (1b) as the starting point, determine the implied present value of the exercise price and compare that with the actual present value. The implied present value of the exercise price is

$$\begin{aligned}\text{Present value of exercise price} &= \$10 + \$20 - \$5 \\ &= \$25\end{aligned}$$

Because the actual present value ($23) is less than its implied present value ($25), one would expect either the call option to be bid up, the put option bid down, or the share price to decline. To what price? To prices which equilibrate the value on both sides of the equation. Assuming that the give in the system will be in the call option, the value of the call will have to increase to $7, the $5 present call option value plus $2 for the difference between the implied present value of the exercise price and the actual present value.

PROBLEM 4: AN ACQUISITION OPTION

Private, Inc., a privately held company, has embarked on an acquisition strategy and has an opportunity to buy several other privately held companies. Before it completes its evaluations, however, it wants an option to buy one company in the next 6 months. How much is the option worth to Private, Inc., given that the estimated standard deviation of the firm to be acquired is 0.60, the value of each share is $50, and the estimated equivalent to an exercise price is $70? Assume the interest rate is 10 percent.

192

SOLUTION
Using the steps outlined in the chapter and then the tables in the Appendix to the book:

1. Standard deviation x $\sqrt{time}$ = 0.60 x $\sqrt{0.5}$ = 0.42

2. Present value of exercise price = $70/(1.10)^{0.5}$
    $$= \$70/(1.0488)$$
    $$= \$66.74$$

3. Asset value ÷ present value of exercise price = $50/$66.74
    $$= 0.75$$

From the table in the Appendix, the estimated value of the call option is about 9.5 percent of the asset value, or $4.75 a share.

PROBLEM 5: A PUT OPTION FOR THE ACQUIRED FIRM
Assume for the moment that the firm to be acquired views the conditions set forth in problem 4 as a put option. How much is it worth?

SOLUTION
Using the Appendix Table 7, the value of the put is about 40.69 percent of the exercise price, or $20.34.

SUMMARY

Why Study Options

1. All corporate securities are options.

2. Many capital investments contain option features that may be valued.

3. Whenever a firm borrows it creates an option.
    a. When debt obligations exceed firm value, an unexercised call option is created.
    b. Common stock of a levered firm is a call option on the firm's assets.

4. When the firm borrows, the lender acquires the company and the shareholders have the option to buy it back.

5. Whatever we learn about traded call options applies to corporate liabilities.

Calls, Puts, and Shares

1. Call option: right to buy stock at a specified exercise or striking price

2. Put option: right to sell stock at a specified exercise price.

3. European option: exercisable only on one particular day

4. American option: exercisable anytime before maturity

Selling Calls, Puts, and Shares

1. A buyer obtains the option from the seller who "writes" the option.

2. The seller's loss is the buyer's gain and vice versa.

Holding Calls, Puts, and Shares in Combination

1. A portfolio of both the share and an option to sell (put) the shares provides a fundamental relationship for European options

    Value of a call + present value of exercise price = value of put + share price

    from which we have

    Value of call – value of put = share price – present value of exercise price,

    and

    Value of put = value of call – value of share + present value of exercise price

    all of which leads to the following

    a. Buying a call and investing the present value of the exercise price in a safe asset is identical in payoff to buying a put and buying the share.
    b. Buying a call and selling a put is identical in payoff to buying a share and borrowing the present value of the exercise price.
    c. Buying a put is identical in payoff to buying a call, selling a share, and investing the present value of the exercise price.

2. Option conversions: when calls, puts, shares, and borrowing or lending are present one of them may be created from the other three.

Bondholders Own the Firm but Shareholders Have a Call Option to Buy It Back

1. When a firm borrows, lenders acquire the firm and shareholders have a call option to buy it back.

2. Circular File stockholders have a put option when they borrow because of the presence of limited liability. They have the option to default.
    a. bond value = asset value – value of call
    b. bond value = present value of promised payments to bondholders – value of put
    c. stock value = value of call
       firm value = asset value
    d. Bondholders have (1) bought a safe asset and (2) given the shareholders the option to sell them the firm's assets.
    e. The risky bonds are equal to a safe bond less the value of the shareholders' option to default.
    f. The value of the option to default depends on the likelihood of default, which is great in the Circular File case.
    g. Owning the stock is equivalent to a call option of the firm's assets.

It is also equivalent to:
(1) owning the firm's assets
(2) borrowing the present value of debt with a mandatory repayment obligation, and
(3) buying a put on the firm's assets with exercise price equal to the present value of obligatory debt.

h. Spotting the Options
(1) Options do not always stand up and say "here I am."
(2) When in doubt, draw a position diagram.
(3) Remember that you are dealing with contingent payoffs – payoffs that are contingent on the value of some other asset.
(4) The general theorem: Any set of contingent payoffs can be valued as a mixture of simple options on that asset.

Characteristics that Determine Option Values

1. The value of an option increases as stock price increases, if the exercise price is held constant.

2. When the stock is worthless the option is worthless.

3. When the stock price becomes large, the option price approaches the stock price less the present value of the exercise price.

4. The value of an option increases with the rate of interest and the time to maturity (the product of r_f and t).

5. The probability of large stock price changes during the remaining life of an option depends on:
a. The variability of the stock price per period.
b. The number of periods until the option expires.

6. The value of an option increases with both the variability of the share and the time to expiration (that is, σ^2_t). All of which is summarized in Table 20-1.

TABLE 20-1
WHAT THE PRICE OF A CALL OPTION DEPENDS ON

1. If the following variables *increase,*	the changes in the *call option prices are:*
Stock price (P)	Positive
Exercise price (ES)	Negative
Interest rate (r_f)	Positive
Time to expiration (t)	Positive
Volatility of stock price (s)	Positive

2. Other properties:

a. *Upper bound.* The option price is always less than the stock price.
b. *Lower bound.* The option price never falls below the payoff to immediate exercise ($P - EX$ or zero, whichever is larger).
c. If the stock is worthless, the option is worthless.
d. As the stock price becomes very large, the option price approaches the stock price less the present value of the exercise price.

An Option-Valuation Model

1. Fischer Black and Myron Scholes

2. Why discounted cash flow won't work for options
   a. A forecast of cash flow is doable but difficult.
   b. Finding the opportunity cost of capital is impossible because an option's risk changes every time its price changes.
   c. Options are always riskier than the underlying stock because they have higher betas and higher standard deviations of return.
   d. An in-the-money option is safer than one out of the money.
   e. A stock price increase raises option prices and reduces risk, and vice versa, each time stock prices change.

Constructing Option Equivalents from Common Stocks and Borrowing

1. **The Problem:** Options are difficult to evaluate using standard discounted cash flow methods

2. **The Answer:** Create an option equivalent by combining common stock and borrowing
   a. The net cost of buying the option equivalent must equal the value of the option.

3. Wombat Corporation illustrates that the payoffs from the levered investment in stock is identical to the payoffs from two call options, so that

   Value of 2 calls = value of share – value of bank loan

4. To value the option, borrow money and buy stock in such a way that the payoff from the call option is replicated.
   a. The **hedge ratio** (option delta): the number of shares needed to replicate one call.

5. **Another Answer:** Pretend investors are risk-neutral so that their expected return from owning the stock equals the interest rate; estimate the expected future value of the option; and discount it at the interest rate.

6. To account for the necessary continuous adjustment for leverage effects, use the Black-Scholes formula:

   Present value of call option $= PN(d_1) - EXe^{-r_f t}N(d_2)$

   where $d_1 = \dfrac{\log(P/EX) + r_f t + \sigma^2 t/2}{\sigma\sqrt{t}}$

   $d_2 = \dfrac{\log(P/EX) + r_f t - \sigma^2 t/2}{\sigma\sqrt{t}}$

   $N(d)$ = cumulative normal probability density function
   EX = exercise price of option
   t = time to exercise date
   P = price of stock now
   σ^2 = variance per period of (continuously compounded) rate of return of return on the stock
   r_f = (continuously compounded) risk-free rate of interest

7. The formula's story: Neither one's willingness to bear risk nor the expected return on the stock affects the option's value. An option's value increases with the level of the stock price relative to the exercise price (P/EX), the time to expiration times the interest rate (r_ft), and the time to expiration times the stock's variability ($\sigma^2 t$).

Using the Black-Scholes Formula

Four steps:
1. Multiply the standard deviation (σ) of the proportionate changes in the asset's value by the square root of time (t) to expiration.

2. Calculate the ratio of the asset's value to the present value of the option's exercise price.

3. Using Appendix Table 6 of the text, find the values you calculated in steps 1 and 2.

4. Use Appendix Table 7 in the text to find the option delta (hedge ratio).

LIST OF TERMS

American call	**Option conversions**
Black-Scholes	**Option-pricing model**
Bondholders	**Present value of exercise price**
Call option	**Put option**
Chicago Board Options Exchange	**Striking or exercise price**
European Call	**Warrants**

EXERCISES

Fill-in Questions

1. The second largest security market in terms of dollar value is the _____.
2. A _____ gives its owner the right to buy stock at a specified price; a _____ gives it owner the right to sell stock at a specified price; the specified price is called the _____.
3. _____ call options may be exercised only on the expiration day, whereas _____ call options may be exercised on or before the expiration day.
4. For European options the value of a call option plus _____ equals the _____ plus the share price.
5. _____ allow call options to be transformed into put options, and vice versa, thereby eliminating the need for the presence of calls, puts, shares, and borrowing and lending.
6. When a firm borrows, (shareholders, creditors) _____ acquire the company and (shareholders, creditors) _____ obtain an option to buy it back.
7. The value of limited liability lies in the option to default and is the value of a (put, call) _____ option on the firm's assets with an exercise price equal to the promised payment to (creditors, owners) _____.
8. If the following variables decrease, the changes in the call option prices are (positive, negative):
   Stock price   _____
   Exercise price   _____
   Interest rate   _____
   Time to expiration   _____
   Stock price volatility _____

Problems

1. Find the value of a call option, given that the present value of the exercise price is $6, the value of the put is $5, and the share price is $16.

2. Find the implied present value of the exercise price of a 26-week call, given the value of the call option is $12, the value of the put option is $12, and the market price is $55.

3. If the present value of the exercise price of a call option is $20, the call option is selling for $5, the put option is selling for $7, and the market price of the stock is $22, should a put on the stock be purchased? Why or why not?

4. Private, Inc., a privately held company, has an opportunity to buy several other privately held companies. One deal in particular intrigues the company but it needs more time to evaluate it. It wants an option to buy the company within the next year. How much is the option worth to Private, Inc., given that the estimated standard deviation of the firm to be acquires is 0.70, the value of each share is $40, and the estimated equivalent to an exercise price is $60? Assume the required rate of return is 10 percent.

5. Assume that the firm to be acquired views the conditions set forth in problem 4 as a put option. How much is it worth to the firm?

Essay Questions

1. Explain why financial managers should be interested in options, as they are traded on the Chicago Board Options Exchange, and the means by which to place a value on such options.

2. "As soon as we sold some bonds, I felt as though we gave away the firm. That is, now it seems as though bondholders own the firm, not the stockholders, and stockholders have a claim on the firm. When I took corporate finance courses many years ago, I was taught that bondholders have a claim on the firm and shareholders own it. I no longer believe that is true." In what sense is this statement correct?

3. List and explain the key elements which determine the value of options.

ANSWERS TO EXERCISES

Fill-in Questions

1. Chicago Board Options Exchange
2. call option; put option; exercise or striking price
3. European; American
4. present value of exercise price; value of put option
5. option conversions
6. creditors; shareholders
7. put; creditors
8. negative; positive; negative; negative; negative

Problems

1. Value of call = value of put + share price – PV of exercise price
   = $5 + $16 – $6 = $15

2. PV exercise price = value of put + share price – value of call
   = $12 + $55 – $12 = $55

3. Put-call parity implies that the put should be worth: $20 – $22 + $5 = $3. Therefore don't buy it for $7 as it can be constructed $4 more cheaply.

4. (1) 0.70 x 1 = 0.70; (2) $60/1.10 = $54.54; (3) $40 $54.54 = 0.73; the call option is about 16 percent of the asset value, or $6.40 a share.

5. $20.94.

CHAPTER 21
APPLICATIONS OF OPTION PRICING THEORY

INTRODUCTION

This chapter applies and extends the ideas concerning options introduced in the previous chapter. The essence of an option is that it gives us the right to buy (call option) or sell (put option) something at a fixed price in the future. Note that the price is fixed and that we don't have to buy or sell unless we want to. This chapter demonstrates how elements of both call options and put options can be found in many capital budgeting decisions. If we ignore the managers' scope for reacting to changing conditions in the future, we will be liable to bias our capital budgeting appraisals and make poor decisions. It turns out, however, that options are often too complicated for us to use the Black-Scholes formula given in the previous chapter. Luckily, there is an alternative, and the chapter describes it; it is the Binomial Method. The Binomial Method is also used extensively for evaluating financial options.

WHAT TO LOOK FOR IN CHAPTER 21

Limitations of Discounted Cash Flow: The discounted cash flow method of evaluating capital investment projects tends to ignore the fact that managers are paid to manage! It views a project as something unchangeable, which is either accepted or rejected, but which once started is never changed. This is unsatisfactory, because one of the main functions of management is to react to changing circumstances. Managers make timing decisions as to when to make investments to enter particular markets. When an initial investment succeeds, we look to the managers to bring forward expansion plans or follow-on investment in a related product. Similarly, when an investment fails, we expect the managers to take actions to limit losses. Until recently, it has only been possible to consider these aspects of capital investment decisions in an informal, qualitative way. Option pricing theory enables us to be much more precise about how the potential for such future decisions affects the value of a new investment. The value of future management actions is important, and will often make all the difference between whether an investment has a negative NPV or a positive one. Look in this chapter for two main components: how to identify option elements in capital budgeting situations, and the Binomial Method which provides a technique for completing the calculations in situations which are too complicated for the Black-Scholes method to work.

Identifying Option Elements: The key here is in understanding what an option is, and what it is not. People sometimes talk rather loosely about "having the option to buy this or that in the future." However, simply being free to buy shares, in the future, at the future market price is *not* an option. Neither is it an option, if I have agreed in advance to buy at a fixed price. It is only an option if I am free to buy at a fixed price and also free not to. This is a call option. The same remarks apply to put options, as giving the right to sell (or not) at a fixed price.

In identifying option elements we look, therefore, for future payments that may (or may not) occur at a manager's discretion, and which are relatively fixed in magnitude. These will correspond to the exercise price. When undertaking capital investments, the required cash outlay is often relatively certain compared to the stream of cash flows that we expect. Think of the outlay as an exercise price that buys the value of the stream of cash flows. Look for this type of option in two contexts:

1. The manager's decision regarding the best time to make a particular capital investment. This is an option problem of when to exercise an (American) call option.

2. Some worthwhile projects may be hard to justify on a conventional NPV basis. The NPV comes out negative, but the investment is attractive because without it the company will be unable to enter other potentially profitable markets later on. Here, the original project provides an option to make further fixed investment in the future (but without any commitment to do so). The value of this option must be added to the original NPV.

Some investments produce risky cash flows but involve the use of assets which are relatively safe. For example, if I buy a car to start a taxi service, I can always sell it again if I don't get enough fares to make it profitable. The price at which I can sell the car is like an exercise price. This time my option is to give up the value of the taxi business and take the value of the car instead. It is a put option, to sell the business for the value of the car, and we call it the abandonment put. If we ignore this option in evaluating a proposed investment we may seriously undervalue it. It gives us the value of flexibility. In many practical situations managers will select the technology which has "intangible" flexibility advantages, even though it may look inferior in conventional DCF terms. They are implicitly recognizing the value of the abandonment put option.

The Binomial Method: The Binomial Method is an extension of a valuation approach introduced in the last chapter. There, an example of option valuation was given where the price of the underlying stock (in Wombat Corporation) would either rise or fall by known amounts over a single period (of a year). Because there were only two possible values for the stock price, we were able to replicate the outcomes on the call option by cleverly buying stock, partly financed with borrowing. Whether the stock goes up or down, the future value of the stock held, less the amount of borrowing to be repaid, will equal the payoff on the call option. The value of the option was therefore given by the cost of setting up the initial position: the initial cost of the stock purchased, less the present value of the amount borrowed.

Being able to solve this type of problem with one period to go means that we can solve more difficult problems with any number of periods remaining! (The previous chapter mentioned this briefly.) All we have to do is to draw an extended diagram to show what can happen to the stock over several time periods. The diagram will show the stock price either going up or down by a fixed percentage in each period. We can easily work out option values one period before the end, using the method just described. But, this now enables us to work out the values in the period before that. Proceeding in this manner we gradually fill in options on the entire diagram until we finally obtain the value of the option today. This valuation approach is called the Binomial Method because the stock return takes one of two values each period, and follows a Binomial statistical distribution.

In carrying out the procedure we may rely entirely on the idea of replicating option payoffs at each stage. Alternatively, we may invoke the risk neutral trick described in the last chapter. If we pretend that the probabilities of each outcome are such that the expected return on the risky asset is the risk-free rate, the future outcomes (from any asset, and especially the option) are evaluated by taking expected values and discounting at the risk-free rate.

The Binomial Method is important because it enables us to deal with options that may be exercised early and other complicated situations. We advise you to read the material describing the method slowly and carefully, and to look particularly at our second Worked Example.

WORKED EXAMPLES

PROBLEM 1: SPOTTING OPTIONS

Technology Unlimited is considering investing in a computer aided manufacturing plant that will make a new range of components for the car industry. The plant will cost $100 million and is expected to produce cash flows of $25 million a year for seven years. It is possible to defer the investment for up to 3 years. The required rate of return is 20 percent. The plant is usable for manufacturing other products, and its resale value is projected to decline straight line from $60 million initially, to zero when it is seven years old. Making the initial investment will provide the company with the expertise that will enable it to make an investment of $200 million in five years time, which prospectively will generate seven years of cash flows at $50 million a year.

You are required (a) to calculate the conventional NPV of the investment, and (b) to identify the three options involved in this situation in terms of the type of option, its length, its exercise price and the underlying asset. (For simplicity you may prefer to ignore the interactions among these various options.)

SOLUTION

a. The conventional calculation is

NPV = $25 million x Annuity factor – $100 million
    = $25 million x 3.605 – $100 million
    = $90.125 million – $100 million
    = -$9.875 million

(Note that the follow-on investment will not be projected to add to this).

The investment will be rejected unless the option elements are regarded as sufficiently important to swing the balance (whether quantified or not)

b. The three options present are:

Description	Type	Length years	Exercise price	Underlying Asset
Timing of investment	American call	3	$100 million	PV of $25 million CF + other options
Follow-on-investment	European call	5	$200 million	PV of $50 million CF (+ abandonment option)
Abandonment option	American put	7	Stated resale values	PV of remaining $25 million + follow-on option

Set out in this way, the formulation looks deceptively simple. It certainly isn't and the numerical solution would involve the Binomial Method or some other advanced method of calculation.

PROBLEM 2: THE BINOMIAL METHOD

The share price of Molly Millar is initially $100. Each year it will either go up by exactly 40 percent or down by exactly 10 percent The risk free rate is 10 percent per year. Use the Binomial Method to calculate the value of two-year European and American put options on Molly Millar with an exercise price of $120.

SOLUTION

The possible share prices and the final put option values are given below:

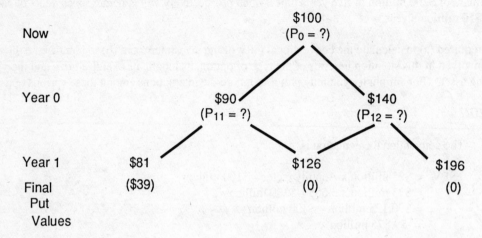

Risk Neutral Probabilities

If we use the "risk neutral" trick, the probability of going up each period is given by

$$p = \frac{r-d}{u-d} = \frac{.10 - (-.10)}{.40 - (-.10)} = 0.4$$

(Alternatively, we could calculate this from

$$\$140p + \$90(1-p) = \$100 \times 1.1$$

The general relation is derived in Problem 5 of this chapter).

Year 1 Values

We now take expected values and discount at the risk free rate of 10 percent:

$$P_{11} = \frac{0.6 \times \$39}{1.1} = \$21.27.$$

For the American put

P_{11} is the maximum of $21.27 and $120 - $90, so it is worth $30.

$$P_{12} = 0$$

Year 0 Values

Repeating the process we have

European put, $P_o = 0.6 \times \$21.27/1.1 = \$11.60$

American put, $P_o = 0.6 \times \$30/1.1 = \$16.36$

Replication Method

As an alternative approach we could find the replicating portfolio period by period. For example, in year one when the stock price is $90, the stock promised $126 or $81 and the difference between these outcomes is $45. We require a difference of -$39 so we must go short (that is, sell) by $39/$45 = 0.8667 shares of stock, receiving cash of 0.8667 x $90 = $78. To get 0 if our short position increases by 40 percent to $109.20, we must lend $109.26/1.1 = $99.27. The net cost is $99.27 – $78 = $21.27, the same value for the European option as before. We prefer the "risk-neutral/trick," as it is much simpler.

SUMMARY

Three Examples of Real Options

1. *Timing of Capital Investment* is essentially the decision of when to exercise a call option. By waiting, you will get more information about how good the market is. On the other hand, you will lose the benefits of the earlier cash flows. Within the call option, the exercise price is the (relatively) fixed amount of required investment. The option provides the opportunity to buy the uncertain present value of the project's future cash flows. This is analogous to the stock price in an option on stock. The cash flows are analogous to dividends paid by a stock, and the option can be exercised on a number of dates (American option rather than a European one).

2. *Follow-on Investment Opportunities* are options to make follow-on investments (e.g., a Mark II product) which would not be available if the original Mark I investment had not been undertaken. Besides its own cash flows, the original investment provides a call option to make a subsequent investment (exercise price) to receive the present value of the cash flows from a later product (the underlying asset).

3. *The Abandonment (Put) Option:* If a risky business venture fails, it may still be possible to sell the assets used in the venture at some reasonably certain abandonment value. This is a put option, inasmuch as it enables us to sell a risky asset (the present value of the venture) at a fixed price (the asset's abandonment value). If other things are equal, we prefer projects for which the abandonment put is valuable. The more risky the venture, the more important it is for the assets to be flexible and have high value in alternative uses.

The Binomial Method For Valuing Options

Many of the option problems that arise in practice (for both real and financial options) cannot be solved using the Black-Scholes formula. For example, it won't give us the value of an American put option, or of an American call option on an asset that pays dividends. In these situations (and in some others) we need the Binomial Method. It consists of the following steps:

1. Work out a binomial grid to show what might happen to the value of the underlying asset at each relevant date into the future.

2. Work out the value of the option wherever required on the grid. This is straight forward for the final date. At earlier dates we can use the "risk neutral trick":
   a. Calculate what the probabilities would have to be if investors were risk neutral and the required return on the asset were the risk-free rate. $[p_{rise} = (r - d)/(u - d)]$.
   b. Take expectations of future values.
   c. Discount at the risk-free rate.

   (Our second worked example provides an illustration of this technique).

   For a grid that is consistent with the Black-Scholes model we may choose

   upside change $= u = e^{\sigma\sqrt{h}} - 1$

   downside change $= d = e^{\sigma\sqrt{h}} - 1$, where h = the interval between grid dates as a fraction of a year.

Some Complicated Options

1. American Options:

An American put option is generally more valuable than the corresponding European put option. By exercising early we receive the exercise price at an earlier date when it is more valuable (just because of the time value of money). The Black-Scholes formula works for the European option but, because it ignores the possibility of early exercise, it does not work for American put options.

We can instead use the Binomial Method. Working backwards through the binary grid, we must check at each point whether the option is worth more exercised immediately or left open. In other words, at each point on the grid we simply fill in the greater of its expected value discounted from the next date, and its value if exercised immediately.

2. Options on Assets Paying Dividends:

Again, if we are dealing with European options we can use the Black-Scholes formula (this time after subtracting the present value of dividends from the asset value).

If we are dealing with an American call option on a stock that will pay one dividend prior to expiration, we will want to either exercise immediately before the dividend or else immediately before the expiration date. The value of the option is approximately the maximum of the two European options corresponding to exercising at these dates. This approximate value is called the "pseudo-Black-Scholes" value.

The pseudo-Black-Scholes value corresponds to choosing in advance which exercise date will be used.

The whole point of an American option is that we are free to exercise at any time, and so it is worth more than this. The Binomial Method is usable to find out exactly how much more it is worth. At each grid point, on the date immediately prior to the dividend, we have to check whether the option is more valuable if it is exercised immediately, or if it is left open. In other words, we fill in the maximum of the immediate exercise value (capturing the dividend) and the value of the option on the asset net of the dividend.

This approach also enables us to value currency options. In an option to buy pounds sterling for a fixed number of dollars, the opportunity cost of the sterling interest rate acts exactly like a dividend which is foregone by the holder of the option. It provides an incentive for early exercise and again impels us to use the Binomial Method.

*Hedging and Volatility

Option values depend on the variability of the assets concerned, and can be viewed as a way of trading in variability. Providing we make good forecasts of the variability, we are able to calculate the delta to form a hedged portfolio. If variability is mis-estimated over the life of the option, the delta will also be incorrect and a risky position will result. Transactions costs often dictate in practice that it is best to adjust a hedge portfolio only when the option delta has changed by some minimum amount.

Insurance Against Risk

Options provide insurance to buy currency at no worse than a given rate, or to insure the future value of a stock portfolio.

LIST OF TERMS

Abandonment option	**Hedging**
American	**Pseudo-Black-Scholes**
Binomial	**Put**
Call	**Real options**
Currency option	**Risk neutral**
Delta	**Stock index option**
European	**Volatility**
Hedge ratio	

EXERCISES

Fill-In Questions

1. Decisions concerning the timing of investments and the value of follow-on investments are examples of _____ options.
2. The timing decision is essentially one of choosing the best exercise date, so the option must be an _____ option rather than a _____ one.
3. The option to get out of a risky venture and dispose of the assets employed is called the _____ option. Because it is an option to sell it is a _____ option.
4. All of the above are _____ options rather than financial ones.
5. These options are evaluated numerically using the _____ method.
6. The replicating portfolio does not depend on the probabilities of asset movements. We may pretend that these give all assets the same expected return. This is sometimes called the "_____" trick.
7. The Black-Scholes formula can be used to obtain an approximate value for an American call on an asset that pays a dividend. This is called its _____ value.
8. An option to buy sterling at a fixed exchange rate is a _____ option.
9. An option on an index of traded shares is called a _____ option.
10. Both of the above two options can be used for _____ particular kinds of risks.

11. The number of shares needed to replicate one call option is called its _____ (or _____ for short).

12. Hedging between an option and the underlying asset will usually only work if the asset's _____ has been correctly forecast.

Multiple Choice

1. Indicate which of the following options can be valued using the Black-Scholes formula, and which can not:

	Call Options		Put Options	
	European	American	European	American
No dividend				
Dividend prior to option expiry				

Problems

1. A forestry company is faced with the decision of when to incur the fixed costs of felling and replanting.
   a. Describe the nature of the problem in the language of options.
   b. How does the problem differ from that of when to exploit an oil well concession?

2. I own an office building worth $1 million from which I operate a financial consulting company. The cash flows fluctuate roughly in line with the stock market index.
   a. Describe the situation in the language of options.
   b. How could I hedge the value of my capital?

3. I own a one-year option to sell five acres of land in Lake County for $1 million. It is currently worth $1.1 million, and I get a 5 percent yield from renting it a year at a time. The interest rate is 10 percent and the annual standard deviation of returns on land is 10 percent. Use the Black-Scholes model to calculate how much this put is worth.

4. The share price of Sward, Inc. is $200. Every six months it will give a return of either 35 percent or minus 5 percent. The risk-free rate is 5 percent per 6-month period. A six-month call option has an exercise price of $250.
   a. What is the option delta?
   b. What is the composition of the replicating portfolio?
   c. What is the value of the option?

5. An asset follows a process which gives either a return, u, or a return, d, each period. Show that for the expected return on the stock to be, r, the probability of the return, u, occurring must be given by

$$p = \frac{r-d}{u-d}$$

6. Use the "risk neutral" trick and the formula of problem 5 to value the option described in problem 4.

7. Sward, Inc. of problem 4 will pay a dividend in six months time equal to 10 percent of its (*cum* dividend) price at that date. Use the binomial method to evaluate a one-year call option on Sward with a $200 exercise price,
   a. for a European option, and
   b. for an American option.

8. In problem 4 you were asked to find the portfolio that will replicate the outcomes on a six-month call option on Sward, Inc., assuming returns of either 35 percent or minus 5 percent. What replication errors will be committed if the returns are instead
   a. 30 or 0 percent (volatility over-estimated),
   b. 40 or minus 10 percent (volatility under-estimated)?

9. How much would the option of a follow-on investment add to the project considered by Technology Unlimited (in our Worked Example 1), if the value of the discounted cash flows evolve with a standard deviation of 30 percent, and the risk-free rate is 8 percent? Assume that the required return on the follow-on investment is 16 percent.

10. An investment of $6.2 million in machining equipment has a -$0.2 million NPV calculated in the conventional way. Its value evolves giving total returns of 40 percent or minus 10 percent each year, and it generates cash flows of 1/3, 1/2, and all of its value in years 1, 2 and 3. The risk-free rate is 10 percent. The equipment can be sold for 3.5 million in year 1 or for 2.5 million in year 2. Calculate a revised NPV to take account of the abandonment option.

Essay Questions

1. What are the main difficulties in applying option theory to capital budgeting situations?

2. A friend has a computer program which uses the binomial method to value European options. Explain how to modify it to value American options.

3. Describe the binomial method for evaluating options, and explain its advantages and disadvantages as compared to Black-Scholes.

4. What are the advantages and disadvantages of hedging foreign currency exposure by buying put options which have alternatively either a high exercise price, or a low one?

*5. "You tell me that American options are much harder to value than European ones. Then why the heck are exchange traded options generally American?" Discuss.

ANSWERS TO EXERCISES

Fill-in Questions

1. call
2. American, European
3. Abandonment, put
4. real
5. binomial
6. risk neutral
7. pseudo-Black-Scholes
8. currency option
9. stock index option
10. hedging

11. hedge ratio, delta
12. volatility

Multiple Choice

1. Black-Scholes works for all except the American puts, and the American call on an asset paying a dividend. (Pseudo-Black-Scholes will give an approximate value for the latter).

Problems

1.
    a. The problem is to value a sequence of American call options. (The follow-on investments matter too).
    b. The oil well problem is simpler, for there are no follow-on investments.

2.
    a. The opportunity to sell the building provides me with an abandonment put option.
    b. Writing call options on the market index would enable me to hedge.

3. The present value of the exercise price is $1/1.1 = \$0.9091$ million.
The current asset value must be adjusted downwards for the rental yield, which will reduce its capital appreciation.

Adjusted asset value = $1.1/1.05 = \$1.0476$ million.

$$\frac{\text{Adjusted asset value}}{\text{PV (Exercise price)}} = \frac{1.0476}{0.9091} = 1.1524$$

Standard deviation x time = 0.10

Interpolating from Appendix Table 6, a call option would be worth $0.136 \times 1.0476 = \$0.1421$ million.

The put is worth $0.9091 + 0.1421 - 1.0476 = \$0.0036$ million.

4.

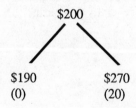

$200

$190 $270
(0)   (20)

    a. Delta = 20/80 = 0.25
    b. 0.25 shares at $200: $50.00
       less borrow 47.5/1.05:   -$45.24
                          $4.76

    c. Option value is $4.76

5. The expected return, r, is simply given by

$$r = p u + (1 - p) d.$$

Solving for p we have,

$$r = p (u - d) + d,$$

so $p = \dfrac{r - d}{u - d}$ as required.

6.

$$p = \frac{.05 + .05}{.35 + .05} = 0.25$$

Call value = 0.25 x 20/1.05 = $4.76 as before.

7. The European option, (E), worth $17.76.
   The American option, (A), is worth $21.92

   The full binomial diagram is given below:

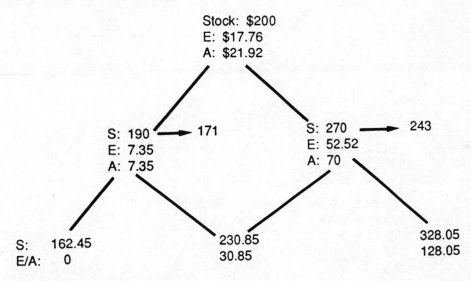

Stock: $200
E: $17.76
A: $21.92

S: 190 → 171
E: 7.35
A: 7.35

S: 270 → 243
E: 52.52
A: 70

S: 162.45
E/A: 0

230.85
30.85

328.05
128.05

8. The replicating portfolio was 0.25 shares plus a future liability of $47.5. Instead of outcomes of $0 or $20 the portfolio will give

   a. $2.5 or $17.5
   b. –$2.5 or $22.5

   Replication errors are

   a. $2.5 or $7.5
   b. –$2.5 or –$7.5

9. Standard deviation x $\sqrt{\text{time}}$ = 0.30 x $\sqrt{3}$ = 0.52

$$\frac{\text{Asset value}}{\text{PV(Exercise Price)}} = \frac{180.253(1.16)^3}{200/(1.08)^3} = 0.73$$

$$\underline{\text{Call value}} \quad = \quad 10.0 \text{ (from Appendix Table 6).}$$
$$\text{Asset value}$$

Call value = $11.5 million, which makes the project NPV = $0.6 million (at least).

10. Using the binomial method with the "risk neutral" trick:

$$p = \frac{.1 + .1}{.4 + .1} = 0.4$$

The diagram shows the underlying present values at each date split into an xd amount plus a cash distribution. Beneath this is given the values where they are protected by the abandonment put. The investment is now worth $6.26 million instead of $6 million, giving a positive NPV of $0.06 million.

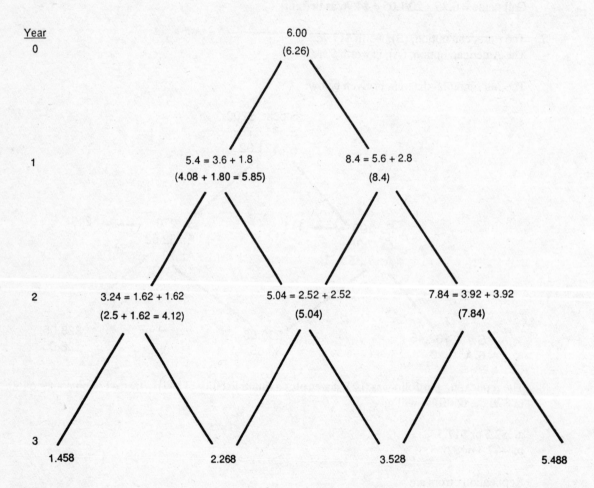

Year		
0	6.00 (6.26)	
1	5.4 = 3.6 + 1.8 (4.08 + 1.80 = 5.85)	8.4 = 5.6 + 2.8 (8.4)
2	3.24 = 1.62 + 1.62 (2.5 + 1.62 = 4.12)	5.04 = 2.52 + 2.52 (5.04) 7.84 = 3.92 + 3.92 (7.84)
3	1.458 2.268	3.528 5.488

CHAPTER 22
WARRANTS AND CONVERTIBLES

INTRODUCTION

As compared with convertible securities, warrants are typically of shorter duration, are detachable from the securities from which they are issued, and carry an exercise price which requires a cash payment when used. The Black-Scholes option-valuation formula may be used to place a value on warrants, but care must be taken to allow for the effects of dividends and changes in the number of shares outstanding.

The owner of a convertible bond gives it up when exercising the option to acquire common stock. The value of a convertible bond depends on its value as a bond standing apart from the conversion feature as well as the value of the conversion feature itself. Forced conversion may result when the value of convertible securities exceeds the call price. The financial manager's rule for calling convertible securities is: Call them when, and only when, the value of the convertible security reaches the call price.

WHAT TO LOOK FOR IN CHAPTER 22

Warrants and convertible securities are studied in this chapter. Warrants are an option to buy common stock for cash. Convertible securities give their owners the right to exchange the securities for stock.

Warrants: Warrants are usually detachable, meaning that they may be exercised apart from the security with which they were offered. Warrant holders are not entitled to vote nor do they receive cash dividends. Their interest in the company is usually protected against stock splits and stock dividends. Often the exercise price is stepped up over the life of the warrant. Usually the life of a warrant is shorter than the conversion feature of a convertible bond. The Black-Scholes option-valuation formula may be used to place a value on a warrant. Cash dividends and potential dilution arising from the additional shares potentially outstanding, however, present difficulties in using the Black-Scholes model. Consequently, adjustments for dilution are required. The binomial method is used to avoid the cash dividend problem.

Convertible Bonds: Convertible bonds resemble warrants because they are options to acquire common stock. The warrant and conversion options differ in that warrants are exercised by the payment of cash to the issuing firm whereas holders of convertible securities exchange them for common stock on predetermined terms. The value of convertible bonds consists of the value of the bond as a bond, and the value of the conversion feature, itself being evaluated as an option. Thus, the price of convertible securities has two lower bounds: the value as a security standing apart from the conversion feature and the value of the conversion feature itself. The conversion option is evaluated just as warrants are, making certain to adjust for cash dividends and potential dilution. The bonds are evaluated just as any other bond would be.

Forced Conversion: Holders of convertible securities may be forced to convert by calling the bonds in. Even though the appropriate decision rule is to call the bond when its value reaches the call price, the evidence indicates that the rule is not consistently followed by financial managers.

Differences between Warrants and Convertibles: You should know the major differences between warrants and convertibles. They are set forth in the Summary.

Reasons for Using Warrants and Convertibles: Historically, the two main, but superficial reasons for issuing warrants and convertible securities were that they were a rather cheap source of debt and they were often regarded as a deferred sale of stock at an attractive price. Both reasons are difficult to defend. Circumstances arise, however, under which it makes eminently great sense to issue either convertible securities or warrants, as, for example, when it is unusually costly to assess the risk of debt or when investors are worried that management may not act in the bondholder's interests.

WORKED EXAMPLES

PROBLEM 1: WARRANTS

Table 22-1 contains information about Leisure Products, Inc.'s recently issued subordinated debenture bonds with detachable warrants.

1. Calculate the cost of the warrants.
2. Calculate the call option value without the dilution effects.
3. Calculate the call option value with the dilution effects. (Assume the alternative firm's standard deviation of stock price changes is 53%.)

Table 22-1 Sometime Leisure Products, Inc.

Item	Value
Amount of loan	$50,000,000
Debt value without warrants	$47,000,000
Number of shares outstanding	9,000,000
Current stock price	$32.00
Value of firm before the debt issue	$288,000,000
Existing loans	$30,000,000
Number of warrants issued per share outstanding	0.10
Total number of warrants issued	900,000
Exercise price of warrants	$40.25
Time to expiration of warrants	6
Annual standard deviation of stock price changes	0.51
Rate of interest	10.00%

SOLUTION

Cost of warrants = total amount of loan – value of loan without warrants
= $50 million – $47 million = $3 million
= $30.00 per warrant

$\sigma\sqrt{t}$ (for use with Appendix Table 6 of text) = $0.51 \sqrt{6}$ = 1.25

Share price ÷ PV (EX) (*for use with Appendix Table 6 of text*)

$$= \{ \{\$32 \div [\$40.25 \div [(1.1)^6]\}\} = 1.41$$

From Appendix Table 6, with $\sigma\sqrt{t}$ = 1.25 and [share price ÷ PV(EX)] = 1.41: 55.65% = 0.5565

Value of call option value = share price x value from Appendix Table 6
= $32.00 x 0.5564 = $17.80

Dilution factor $= 1 \div (1 + q)$

Current equity value (v) = original firm's total assets – value of loans
= \$338 million – \$70 million
= \$268 million

Current share price of alternative firm = $V \div N$
= \$268 million ÷ 9 million shares
= \$29.78 per share

$\sigma\sqrt{t}$ (for use with Appendix Table 6 of text) = 0.53 $\sqrt{6}$ = 1.30

Share price ÷ PV (EX) (*for use with Appendix Table 6 of text*)

$= \{\{\$29.78 \div [\$40.25 \div (1.1)^6]\}\} = 1.31$

From Appendix Table 6, with $\sigma\sqrt{t}$ = 1.30 and share price ÷ PV(EX) = 1.31: ≈ 53.21% ≈ 0.5321

Value of call on alternative firm = (C/P) x (V/N)
= 0.5321 x \$29.78 = \$15.85

Warrant value of original firm with dilution = $[\{1 \div (1 + q)\}]$ x value of call on alternative firm
= (1 ÷ 1.1) x \$15.85
= \$14.41

PROBLEM 2: MECHANICS OF CONVERTIBLES

Flying Colors Airlines issued a 5.5 percent convertible bond which matures 25 years from now. The conversion price is \$36 and the bonds are callable at 106.25. The market price of the common stock is \$42 per share.

1. What is the conversion ratio of the bonds?

2. If the conversion ratio were 33.33, what would be the conversion price?

3. At the current market price for common shares, what is the minimum price at which you would expect the bond to sell? Explain your answer.

4. If bonds of comparable risk to those of Flying Colors were selling to return 10 percent, at what price would you expect the bond to be selling if it did not have the conversion feature? Assume interest is payable annually.

5. Based on your answer in 4, what part of the bond's total value is ascribable to the value of the bond alone and what part is ascribable to the conversion feature? Explain fully.

6. Should the financial manager call the bonds? Why or why not?

SOLUTION

1.

Conversion ratio = face value of convertible security
conversion price
= \$1000/\$36
= 27.78 shares

2. Using the formula for the conversion ratio in 1 immediately above, the setup is:

$$33.33 = \$1000/\text{conversion price}$$
$$\text{Conversion price} = \$1000/33.33$$
$$= \$30$$

3. Conversion value of the conversion convertible

$$\text{security} = \text{conversion ratio x market price of common shares}$$
$$= 27.78 \text{ shares x } \$42 \text{ per share}$$
$$= \$1166.76 = 116.68$$

In other words, one convertible bond may be exchanged for $1166.76 worth of common stock and must be worth at least this value.

4. Using present-value tables, we obtain the PV of $55 a year for 25 years and the present value of $1000 to be received at the end of the twenty-fifth year.

9.077 x $55 =	$499.24
0.092 x $1000 =	92.00
	$591.24

5.

Conversion value of bond	$1166.76
Value of bond alone	591.24
Value of conversion feature	$ 575.53

6. Yes, because the price of the bond exceeds the call price.

SUMMARY

What Is a Warrant?

1. An option to buy another asset, usually stock, at a specified price during a specified time period

2. Often issued with bonds

3. Often detachable

4. Valuing warrants
   a. Similar to American calls
   b. Actual value prior to expiration exceeds theoretical value, which is the lower limit of value
   c. Value depends on

$$(\sigma^2 t) \text{ and } (r_f t)$$

5. Two complications: exercise price may change; warrant holders not entitled to cash dividends

6. Adjusting for dilution
   a. Dilution lowers price of shares and warrants
   b. Cost of warrants = total amount of loan – value of loan without warrants
   c. $\sigma \times \sqrt{t}$ (for use with Appendix Table 6 of text)

    d.   Share price ÷ PV(EX)

    e.   Call option value ÷ share price = C ÷ P = factor from Appendix Table A

    f.   Solve for call option value in: call option value x share price = C x P

    g.   Share price after exercise = (V + NqEX) ÷ (N + Nq)

    h.   Dilution factor = 1 ÷ (1 + q)

    i.   Current equity value = V = Original firm's total assets – value of loans

    j.   Current share price of Alternative firm = V ÷ N

    k.   Value of call on alternative firm = (C/P) x (V/N)

    l.   Warrant value of original firm = [(1 + (1 + q)] x value of call on alternative firm

What Is a Convertible Bond?

1.   A bond convertible into common stock at the option of the holder at a specified price for a specified time period.

    a.   Conversion price: the price at which the bond is convertible.

    b.   Conversion ratio: the number of shares received in exchange for each bond.

    c.   Usually protected against stock splits and stock dividends.

2.   Valuing convertible bonds.

    a.   Price depends on the value of the bond portion and the value of the convertible (option) portion.

    b.   Bond portion: Present value of coupon payments and face value.

       (1) Establishes a floor.

       (2) Low firm value and low bond values go together, and vice versa.

    c.   Conversion value: price of bond if bondholders converted immediately.

$$\text{Conversion value} = \text{conversion ratio} \times \text{market price per share}$$

    d.   Two lower bounds:

       (1) Bond value

       (2) Conversion value: will never sell below it

3.   Dividends and dilution revisited

    a.   Value of convertible = value of bond + value of conversion option

    b.   Missed cash dividends and dilution may materially affect value.

4.   Forcing conversion

    a.   Firm value does not change when bonds are converted; but how total asset value is distributed does.

    b.   To maximize shareholders' welfare, minimize convertible bondholders' position.

    c.   The rule: Call the bond, when, and only when, its value reaches the call price.

    d.   Convertibles are usually called after they are worth much more than the call price.

The Difference between Warrants and Convertibles

1.   Warrants are usually issued privately; convertibles are usually issued publicly.

2.   Warrants are usually detachable and exercisable alone; when a convertible bond is exercised both the bond and the option are given up.

3.   Warrants may be issued alone; convertible securities always consist of the security and the conversion option.

4.   Warrants are exercised for cash; convertible securities are not.

5. The cash receipts from exercised warrants may be taxable; there are no unusual tax features with convertible securities.

Why Do Companies Issue Warrants and Convertibles?

1. Two alleged motives: cheap stock or deferred sale of common stock.

2. No evidence to suggest either holds.
   a. Cheap only if marketplace fails to value properly the difference between straight bond price and bond with convertible option.
   b. A sale of stock is more easily accomplished by a direct sale.

3. Reasons are complex.

4. Tend to be issued by small, more speculative firms and are unsecured and subordinated.
   a. Difficult to estimate required return.
   b. Use convertibles or warrants when it is unusually costly to assess risk or when investors are worried that management may not act in bondholders' interest.

LIST OF TERMS

Bond value	**Detachable warrant**
Call premium	**Dilution**
Call price	**Exercise price**
Conversion price	**Nondetachable warrants**
Conversion ratio	**Overhanging convertibles**
Conversion value	**Warrant**
Convertible bond	

EXERCISES

Fill-in Questions

1. A _____ gives its owner the right to (buy, exchange) _____ for cash, whereas a convertible security gives its owner the right to (buy, exchange) _____ a the bond for stock.

2. The price at which common stocks may be purchased with warrants is called the _____.

3. A warrant which is sold originally with bonds but which may be resold apart from the bonds is called a _____ warrant.

4. If the Whozits Corporation has a number of $1000 convertible bonds outstanding, each of which is convertible into 40 shares of common stock, the (conversion rate, conversion price) _____ is _____ dollars and the (conversion ratio, conversion price) _____ is _____ shares.

5. The value of a convertible bond depends on both its _____ and its _____.

6. The value of a convertible bond depends on both its value as a bond as if it (were, were not) _____ converted and its _____ as if the bond were converted.

Problems

1. Table 22-2 contains information about What-Not, Inc.'s recently issued debenture bonds with detachable warrants.
    1. Calculate the cost of the warrants.
    2. Calculate the call option value without the dilution effects.
    3. Calculate the call option value with the dilution effects. (Assume the alternative firm's standard deviation of stock price changes is 45%.)

Table 22-2 What-Not, Inc.

Item	Value
Amount of loan	$15,000,000
Debt value without warrants	$13,000,000
Number of shares outstanding	2,000,000
Current stock price	$28.00
Value of firm before the debt issue	$56,000,000
Existing loans	$10,000,000
Number of warrants issued per share outstanding	0.15
Total number of warrants issued	300,000
Exercise price of warrants	$29.25
Time to expiration of warrants	4
Annual standard deviation of stock price changes	0.40
Rate of interest	11.80%

2. How-Not, Inc., issued an 8 percent convertible subordinated debenture bond 9 years ago at a price of 99.95. The bonds mature in 20 years and contain a sinking fund which begins next year and which requires annual cash payments equal to 5 percent of the outstanding face amount of bonds. The conversion price at the time of issuance was $35 and is stepped up as follows: $40 five years after issuance, $45 ten years after issuance, and $50 thereafter. The bonds are presently callable at 105, and the common stock's current price is $55 a share.
    a. What is the bond's present conversion ratio?
    b. What is the conversion ratio in each of the other periods?
    c. At the current market price for common shares, at what price would you expect the bond to sell? Explain fully.
    d. If the market price of the common shares declined to $25 a share, and comparable bonds were selling to return 8 percent, what is the lowest price at which you would expect How-Not's bonds to sell?
    e. If the market price of the common shares were $50 and comparable bonds were selling to return 11 percent, at what price would you expect the bonds to be selling, if they did not contain the conversion feature? Assume interest is payable annually.
    f. Based on your answer in e, what part of the bond's minimum value is ascribable to the value of the bond alone and what part is ascribable to the conversion feature? Explain fully.
    g. Is it financially smart to call the bonds in, given the conditions in e above?

3. Use the data from problem 1 to answer the following questions.
    a. What is the current market value of old equity, new equity, and exercise price?
    b. How much will the warrant holders' share of the new equity be worth before they exercise?
    c. By how much must the old equity increase before the warrant holders are likely to exercise at a profit?

Essay Questions

1. How should one adjust for dilution in valuing warrants?

2. Compare the major characteristics of a convertible bond with a bond possessing a detachable warrant.

3. It has been well stated that convertible bonds have a floor or lower limit to their price. What is this floor and how is it determined? Is there more than one floor? Is there also an upper bound? If so, what is it and how is it determined?

4. "The way I see it, financial managers should call in outstanding convertible bonds when their value reaches the call price. Yet, empirical evidence suggests that many financial managers don't do this. And I would like to know how come." Explain.

5. Under what conditions do convertible securities and warrants make sense? Are they a lower cost of capital source? Do they defer the sale of common stock?

ANSWERS TO EXERCISES

Fill-in Questions

1. warrant; buy; exchange
2. exercise price
3. detachable
4. conversion price; 25; conversion ratio; 40
5. bond value; conversion value
6. were not; conversion value.

Problems

1. Cost of warrants = $15 – $13
$$= \$2 \text{ million} = \$6.67 \text{ per warrant}$$

$$\sigma \sqrt{t} = 0.40 \sqrt{4} = 0.80$$

Share price ÷ PV(EX) = {{$28.00 + [$29.25 ÷ (1.118)^4]}} = 1.50

From Appendix Table 6: 45.61% = 0.4561

Value of call option value = $28.00 x 0.4561 = $12.77

Dilution factor = 1 ÷ (1 + q)

Current equity value (V) = $56 – $25 = $31

Current share price of alternative firm: $31 ÷ 2 = $15.50 per share

$$\sigma \sqrt{t} = 0.45 \sqrt{4} = 0.90$$

Share price ÷ PV(EX) = {{$15.50 + [$29.25 ÷ (1.118)^4]}} = 0.94

From Appendix Table 6: 32.73% = 0.3173

Value of call on alternative firm = 0.3273 x $15.50 = $5.07

Warrant value of original firm with dilution = (1 + 1.118) x $5.07 = $4.54

2. a.   Conversion ratio = face value/conversion price
$$= 1000/40$$
$$= 25$$

    b.   1000/35 = 28.57
1000/40 = 25.00
1000/45 = 22.22
1000/50 = 20.00

    c. $55 x 25 = $1375
    d. $1000
    e.   (7.963 x $80) + (0.079 x $1000) = $761.04
    f.   ($50 x 25) – $761.04 = $488.96
    g.   Yes

3. a.   Old equity = common stock + warrants
$$= (\$2,500,000 \text{ x } 40) + (\$250,000 \text{ x } 25)$$
$$= \$106,250,000$$

       New equity = old equity + exercise money
$$= \$106,250,000 + (\$250,000 \text{ x } 15)$$
$$= \$110,000,000$$

    b.   0.0909 (new equity) = 0.0909 (old equity + exercise money)
$$= 0.0909 \text{ x } \$110,000,000$$
$$= \$10,000,000$$

    c.   Only when
0.0909 x old equity > 0.9091 x exercise money
Point of indifference
0.0909 x $106,250,000 = 0.9091 x $6,250,000
$9,658,125 > $5,681,875
Not at all because, it exceeds exercise money

CHAPTER 23
VALUING RISKY DEBT

INTRODUCTION

The most important things to be learned from this chapter are: a term structure of interest rates exists; nominal rates of return must be adjusted for inflation; and wise financial managers must comprehend the nature of bond pricing in order to understand capital markets, however efficient they may be. Intelligent financial decisions are made only when the financial manager is conversant with the many nuances of the bond markets and the way in which bonds are valued, regardless of whether a public offering of bonds is made, but especially if bonds are offered privately.

WHAT TO LOOK FOR IN CHAPTER 23

The chapter begins with Irving Fisher's classical theory of interest. He postulated that real rates of return are determined by the equilibration of the supply of and demand for capital. He also postulated that real rates of return on bonds must include an adjustment for anticipated inflation. This insight has carried over to the present in that nominal, money, or stipulated rates of interest clearly must be adjusted for prospective rates of inflation. Even after the fact, nominal rates of returns on bonds, or the returns on any other asset for that matter, must be adjusted for inflation. The commonplace method used by financial managers to adjust nominal rates of return is to subtract from that rate the rate of inflation.

Nominal Rate and Inflation: Picking up on Fisher's idea, Professor Fama found that nominal interest rates appear to be unbiased forecasters of changes in the inflation rate. He also found that changes in inflation expectations are the principal cause of changes in nominal interest rates. This is important to financial managers who are considering offering bonds and must negotiate the offering terms.

Spot Rates and the Term Structure: The spot rate is the rate of interest obtainable on a bond at the present, or spot, time period. The series of spot rates of different maturities results in a term structure of interest rates; typically, the term structure is upward sloping, with long-term rates higher than short-term ones.

Yield to Maturity: As much as the investment community uses yield to maturity to evaluate bonds, it suffers from all the infirmities of the internal rate of return concept, which it is. The yield to maturity assumes that the same rate is used to discount all payments to bondholders; that is, each spot rate is equal. The evidence suggests that spot rates are not all equal.

Explaining the Term Structure: The three primary explanations of the upward-sloping term structure of interest rates are the expectations hypothesis, the liquidity preference theory, and the inflation premium theory. The expectations hypothesis says that the investor's expectations that future spot rates will be higher than the current spot rates explain an upward-sloping term structure. The liquidity preference theory says that a liquidity premium, which is the difference between forward rates and expected future spot rates, is required because of the uncertainty regarding the reinvestment rate when bonds mature. The inflation premium argument says that the typically upward-sloping term structure is attributable to the risk associated with uncertainty about the inflation rate. None of these explanations is totally satisfactory, although the expectations hypothesis is the least satisfactory of all.

Default Risk: When the value of bonds and the term structure of interest rates are determined, default risk must also be considered. The threat of default on bonds, similar in all respects except their expected ability to pay interest and principal, is another reason different rates of return exist. Bonds are evaluated by financial services whose ratings are reasonably good predictors.

Debt as Options: When option pricing is extended to debt analysis, corporate bonds become the equivalent to lending money with no chance of default while giving stockholders a put option on the firm's assets. Thus the value of a bond consists of the value of risk-free debt less the value of the put option.

Guaranteed Debt: Government loan guarantees are valuable because they lift the onus of default from the borrower. A loan guarantee is valued as a put option on the firm's assets. The value of the loan without the guarantee is equal to the value assuming no chance whatsoever of a default less the value of the put.

WORKED EXAMPLES

PROBLEM 1: FINDING THE REAL RATE
Find the real rate of interest given that the nominal rate is 10 percent and the inflation rate is 8 percent.

SOLUTION
The solution is obtained by using the formula

$$1 + r_{money} = (1 + r_{real})(1 + i) \tag{1}$$

$$\text{where } r_{money} = \text{nominal or money rate of interest}$$

$$r_{real} = \text{real rate of interest}$$

$$i = \text{inflation rate}$$

Substituting in the equation, we obtain

$$1 + 0.10 = (1 + r_{real})(1 + 0.08)$$

We then solve for r_{real}.

$$1 + r_{real} = (1 + r_{money}) \div (1 + i)$$

$$= (1 + 0.10) \div (1 + 0.08)$$

$$= (1.10) \div (1.08)$$

$$= 1.0185$$

$$r_{real} = 0.0185 = 1.85 \text{ percent}$$

PROBLEM 2: ESTIMATING THE INFLATION RATE
If the money rate of interest is 12 percent and the real rate is expected to be 2 percent, what is the assumed inflation rate?

SOLUTION

The answer is obtained from equation (1) by solving for i.

$$1 + i = (1 + r_{money}) \div (1 + r_{real})$$

$$= (1 + 0.12) \div (1 + 0.02)$$

$$= 1.12 \div 1.02$$

$$= 1.0980$$

$$i = 0.0980 = 9.80 \text{ percent}$$

PROBLEM 3: FINDING THE NOMINAL RATE

If the real rate of interest is expected to be 3 percent and the inflation rate is expected to be 8 percent, what nominal interest rate would you expect?

SOLUTION

Once again use equation (1) and solve for the money or nominal rate of interest.

$$1 + r_{money} = (1 + r_{real})(1 + i)$$

$$= (1 + 0.03)(1 + 0.08)$$

$$= (1.03)(1.08)$$

$$= 1.1124$$

$$r_{money} = 0.1124 = 11.24 \text{ percent}$$

PROBLEM 4: THE INFLATION RATE

In December 1987 the annualized nominal rate of interest on 90 day U.S. Treasury notes was about 5.7 percent. Assuming that the real rate on such bills continues at its historical average of about 0.3 percent, what is the forecasted inflation rate for the year ahead?

SOLUTION

One way to solve this problem is to subtract the real interest rate from the nominal rate to obtain the estimated 1-year inflation rate.

Forecasted inflation rate = nominal interest rate – real interest rate
                                = 5.7 percent – 0.3 percent
                                = 5.4 percent

PROBLEM 5: YIELD TO MATURITY

Calculate the yield to maturity on a 10-year bond carrying a coupon rate of 8 percent. Assume that the interest is payable annually and the bond is selling at 87.

SOLUTION

The setup for the solution of this problem is similar to every other internal-rate-of-return problem, for that is what solving for the yield of maturity is, an internal rate-of-return problem. Using the present value of an annuity formula allows you to find the present value of the 10 equal interest payments. You also have to calculate the present value of the maturity value of $1000. Doing this by hand requires a hunt-and-peck method, unless your hand-held calculator contains this routine, because the object is to find the present value that sums to the present market price of $870. Many hand-held financial calculators and the major micro-computer spreadsheets solve for internal rates of return. For fun (?), let's do this one by hand.

Taking some arbitrary interest rate, such as 10 percent, is a good place to start. (We know that the yield to maturity must be higher than the coupon rate, for the price of the bond is selling below its face value. Were it selling at its face value, the yield to maturity would be 8 percent. And, remember, interest rates and bond prices fluctuate inversely so that when prices go down, yields increase.) Using that 10 percent rate we find

$$\text{PV of interest} = \$80 \times 6.145 = \$491.60$$

$$\text{PV of principal} = \$1000 \times 0.386 = \$386.00$$

the sum of which is $877.60, which is so very close to the market value of 87 that further calculations are not worthwhile. (The actual yield to maturity is 10.13 percent.)

PROBLEM 6: YIELD TO MATURITY AND SPOT RATES

It is 1990 and you notice that the yield to maturity of your company's two bonds, 5s of '94 and 9s of '94, are selling at 87.44 and 100.71, which results in yields to maturity of 8.87 and 8.78 percent. You are a recently hired finance major and are asked to explain this phenomenon. "After all," says the financial manager, "the bonds are of the same quality and come due at exactly the same time. Consequently, they should have the same yield to maturity, shouldn't they?" What reasonable answer will you give?

SOLUTION

The answer lies in estimating the spot rates for each of the remaining years and taking the present value of the payments to be received. This is done in Table 23-1, where a set of assumed spot rates are presented.

Although this assumption is not necessary to the analysis, it should be clear that the yield to maturity does not tell the entire story about the period-by-period spot rates on the bonds. And it is the spot rates that count, not yield to maturity.

TABLE 23-1 PRESENT VALUE OF TWO COMPARABLE RISK BONDS WITH DIFFERENT COUPON RATES

PERIOD	INTEREST RATE, r_t	C_t	5s of '94 PV AT r_t	C_t	9s of '94 PV AT r_t
$t = 1$	0.06	$50	$47.17	$90	84.91
2	0.07	50	43.67	90	78.61
3	0.08	50	39.69	90	71.44
4	0.09	1050	743.85	1090	772.18
		Totals	$874.38		$1007.14

PROBLEM 7: SPOT RATES

Given that there are two bonds, alike in all respects except coupon rates, calculate the estimated spot rate in the fifteenth year of two 15-year bonds, one of which has a coupon rate of 5 percent and a price of 60 and the other which has a coupon rate of 10 percent and a price of 100. Assume interest is payable annually.

SOLUTION

To solve this problem, begin by finding the present value of the cash flow, using 10 percent as the discount rate for each. Calling the first bond 1 and the second 2,

$$PV_1 = \frac{\$100}{1 + r_1} + \frac{\$100}{(1 + r_2)^2} + \ldots + \frac{\$1100}{(1 + r_{15})^{15}}$$

$$= \$1000$$

$$PV_2 = \frac{\$50}{1 + r_1} + \frac{\$50}{(1 + r_2)^2} + \ldots + \frac{\$1050}{(1 + r_{15})^{15}}$$

$$= \$600$$

Next compare two investment strategies, one which purchases one 10 percent bond at 100, the other which purchases two 5 percent bonds at 60 (for a total of 2 x $600 = $1200). Each strategy generates $100 a year in income, although in the fifteenth year the first produces $1100 in cash whereas the second produces $2100 (2 x $1050). Strategy 2 generates an advantage in cash flows over strategy 1 only in the fifteenth year, and a disadvantage at the beginning of the first year because an additional $200 is required to undertake the investment. The problem is one of comparing the value of the advantages with the disadvantages; that is, compare the present value of $1000 to be received 15 years from now with the present value of the additional present cash outlay of $200. This procedure determines the fifteenth year's spot rate and is set up in this way:

$$PV = \frac{\$1000}{(1 + r_{15})^{15}}$$

$$= \$200$$

or

$$\$200 = \frac{\$1000}{(1 + r_{15})^{15}}$$

This is how to solve for r_{15}:

$$
\begin{aligned}
(1 + r_{15})^{15} \, (\$200) &= \$1000 \\
&= \$1000 \div \$200 \\
&= 5.00
\end{aligned}
$$

We may solve this directly in several ways. First, use a table of future values of $1, by going across the 15-year column until you find a value close to 5.00. Chances are the exact value will not be found, so that interpolation between two adjacent values is required. It turns out that the interest rate required to get $200 to grow to $1000 at the end of 15 years is between 11.0 and 11.5 percent, which is close enough for our purposes.

A second solution involves logarithms. Because most hand-held calculators now have logarithmic functions, this is convenient. The solution follows this setup:

1. Take the natural logarithms of both sides of:

$$(1 + r_{15})^{15} = 5.00$$

$$15 \ln (1 + r_{15}) = 1.6094$$

2. Divide by 15:

$$\ln (1 + r_{15}) = 0.1073$$

3. Take the antilog of both sides:

$$1 + r_{15} = 1.1133$$

4. Subtract 1 and multiply by 100:

$$r_{15} = 0.1133$$
$$= (0.1133)(100) = 11.33 \text{ percent}$$

The third way in which to solve this problem is to use a hand-held calculator's present value ÷ future value routine and solve for the interest rate in percent. As expected, the answer is 11.33 percent.

PROBLEM 8: SPOT RATES

Determine the better financial strategy when confronted with a 2-year spot rate of 9 percent, a 1-year spot rate of 8 percent, and an expected spot rate on 1-year bonds 1 year from now of 10 percent. Assume you do not need your money for 2 years and are not bothered by risk.

SOLUTION

To find the answer to this, you want to know the expected return of each strategy. The setup is:

$$\$1000(1 + r_1)[1 + E(_1r_2)] \text{ compared with } \$1000(1 + r_2)^2$$

where r_1 = 1-year spot rate
$E(_1r_2)$ = expected spot rate on 1-year bonds 1 year from now
r_2 = 2-year spot rate

Substituting the values above, we obtain

$\$1000(1 + 0.08)(1 + 0.10)$	compared with	$(\$1000(1 + 0.09)^2$
$\$1000(1.08)(1.10)$	compared with	$\$1000(1.09)^2$
$\$1000(1.188)$	compared with	$\$1000(1.1881)$
$\$1188$	compared with	$\$1188.10$

For all practical purposes there is no difference between the two outcomes; therefore, you would be indifferent about this investment.

If you wish to lock in the final outcome of $1188, say, because of your queasiness about the expected 1-year spot rate, choose the 9 percent 2-year spot rate. You should also note that the implied forward rate is

$$(1 + r_2)^2 = (1 + r_1)(1 + f_2)$$

where f_2 is the implied forward rate. Substituting the above values, we obtain

$$
\begin{aligned}
(1 + 0.09)^2 &= (1 + 0.08)(1 + f_2) \\
(1.09)^2 &= (1.08)(1 + f_2) \\
1.1881 &= 1.08(1 + f_2) \\
1 + f_2 &= 1.1881 \div 1.08 \\
&= 1.1001 \\
f_2 = 0.1001 &= 10.01
\end{aligned}
$$

As expected, the implicit forward rate is almost exactly equal to the expected future spot rate, again indicating a condition of relative indifference.

PROBLEM 9: TERM STRUCTURE

As you proceed to explain to the nonfinancial managers in your organization the nature of the term structure of interest rates, the following question is posed: "Say I want to invest for only 1 year. Am I better off buying a 2-year bond and selling it at the end of the year, or buying a 1-year bond and cashing it in at the end of the year?" Say the quoted 2-year spot rate on Treasury issues is 8.98 percent, whereas the quoted spot rate on a 1-year Treasury bill is 9.42 percent. What response would you give?

SOLUTION

The answer begins with a determination of the present value of the 2-year bond at the end of the 1-year period.

$$
\begin{aligned}
\text{PV of 2-year bond at year 1} &= [\$1000(1 + r_2)^2] \div (1 + {_1}r_2) \\
&= [\$1000(1 + r_1)(1 + f_2)] \div (1 + {_1}r_2)
\end{aligned}
$$

Because we have too many unknown variables to solve this equation, we must make an assumption about one of them, typically ${_1}r_2$. We can determine the implied forward rate, however:

$$
\begin{aligned}
(1 + r_2)^2 &= (1 + r_1)(1 + f_2) \\
(1 + 0.898)^2 &= (1 + 0.0942)(1 + f_2) \\
1.1877 &= (1.0942)(1 + f_2) \\
1 + f_2 &= 1.1877 \div 1.0942 \\
&= 1.0854 \\
f_2 &= 0.0854 = 8.54 \text{ percent}
\end{aligned}
$$

We only benefit from purchasing the 2-year bond if next year's 1-year rate ${_1}r_2$ is less than this value of f_2. Say you expect ${_1}r_2$ to be 9.2 percent, the present value of the 2-year bond 1 year from now is

$$
\begin{aligned}
\text{PV} &= \$1000(1 + r_2)^2 \div 1 + {_1}r_2 \\
&= \$1000(1 + 0.898)^2 \div 1 + 0.092 \\
&= \$1000(1.187664) \div 1.092 \\
&= \$1187.66 \div 1.092 \\
&= \$1087.60
\end{aligned}
$$

Alternatively, compare the payoff from buying the 1-year bond which generates a 9.42 percent return for certain with the payoff from investing in a 2-year bond and selling it at the end of the first year. That means we must forecast the expected future spot rate $E({_1}r_2)$. Say we think it will most likely be the 9.2 assumed above. The solution then is

CERTAIN PAYOFF		EXPECTED PAYOFF
$\$1000(1 + r_1)$	compared with	$[\$1000(1 + r_2)^2] \div [1 + E(_1r_2)]$
$\$1000(1 + 0.0942)$	compared with	$[\$1000(1 + 0.0898)^2] \div (1 + 0.092)$
$\$1000(1.0942)$	compared with	$[\$1000(1.0898)^2] \div (1.092)$
$\$1094.20$	compared with	$(\$1187.66) \div (1.092)$
$\$1094.20$	compared with	$\$1087.60$

The certain payoff should be taken; invest in the 1-year bond.

SUMMARY

The Classical Theory of Interest: Real Interest Rates

1. Without inflation, the real interest rate is the price at which the supply of and demand for real capital is equilibrated.

2. Supply depends on savings.

3. Demand depends on firms' investment opportunities.

4. The point: real interest rates depend on real economic phenomena.

Inflation and Interest Rates

1. Real rate = nominal rate – inflation rate

2. A change in the expected inflation rate will cause the same change in the nominal interest rate.

3. The relation between money and real rates: $1 + r_{money} = (1 + r_{real})(1 + i)$

4. Critics of Fisher's theory:
   a. Some say the real rate is not changed by changes in the inflation rate.
   b. Data do not exist to prove the matter.
   c. Actual inflation and real ex-post interest rates may be traced
      (1) Real historical rates have been close to zero.
      (2) Fisher's theory states that changes in anticipated inflation produce corresponding changes in the rate of interest.
      (3) Studies indicate that inflation expectations have been the principal causes of nominal interest rate changes.
         (a) Real rate is an anticipated rate
         (b) Real interest rate = *expected* real rate of return from U.S. Treasury bills
                        = nominal rate of return on Treasury Bills – *expected* rate of inflation
         (c) The real interest rate itself varies over time and is subject to its own risk.

Term Structure and Yields to Maturity

1. The term structure is a series of spot rates, $r_1, r_2, r_3, \ldots$, for however long we wish to estimate the structure.

2. Yield to maturity:
   a. an internal rate of return.
   b. Need bond price, coupon, and maturity to solve for y.
   c. Bond tables, financial calculators, and microcomputers are used.
   d. Unambiguous and easy to calculate.
   e. A quick summary measure.

3. Problems with yield to maturity:
   a. Assumes that yield to maturity does not change.
   b. Assumes a constant reinvestment rate of return.
   c. Yield to maturity does not determine price; it is vice versa.

*Measuring the term structure

1. Estimate the spot rates on each of a series of mini bonds.

2. Need a complete series of matching bonds, which is only approximated in practice.

Explaining the Term Structure

1. The term structure is usually upward-sloping.

2. Ms. Long wants to invest $1000 for 2 years and has two options.
   a. Buy a 1-year bond at rate r_1 and reinvest proceeds in a second 1-year bond at the then prevailing spot rate, $_1r_2$. Requires an estimate of next year's spot.
   b. Buy a 2-year bond at the 2-year spot rate
      (1) The 1-year spot rate and forward rate in the second year are built into the 2-year spot rate.
      (2) The forward rate is implicit in the spot rate.

3. Mr. Short wants to invest $1000 for 1 year and has two options.
   a. Buy a 1-year bond at the spot rate.
   b. Buy a 2-year bond and cash it in at the end of 1 year.

4. Some yield curve theories
   a. Expectations hypothesis
      (1) An upward-sloping term structure exists because investors expect future spot rates to be higher than current spot rates; and vice versa for a downward-sloping term structure.
      (2) Ignores risk.
      (3) Implicitly assumes future inflation rates are known.
   b. Liquidity preference theory
      (1) Incorporates risk.
      (2) A difference exists between forward rates and expected future spot rates and is called a liquidity premium.
      (3) The premium causes the upward-sloping curve.
      (4) Implicitly assumes future inflation rates are known.
   c. Introducing inflation
      (1) Assume that only uncertain inflation causes uncertain interest rates.
      (2) No truly risk-free asset exists because of uncertain future inflation rates.
      (3) Inflation introduces another risk into the analysis of the term structure.
   d. Comparison of theories
      (1) Not many adhere to strict expectations theory, although Fama's study indicates that long-term rates reflect, partly, investor's expectations about future short-term rates.
      (2) Liquidity preference theory supposes that risk comes only from uncertainty in real rates.
      (3) Inflation premium theory assumes that risk comes only from changes in inflation.

Allowing for the Risk of Default

1. Bonds have market-related risks and firm-specific default risks.

2. Bond ratings reflect the probability of default, and a close relation exists between bond ratings and promised yields.

3. Bond ratings are reasonably good guides to default risk.

*Option Pricing and Risky Debt

1. Holding a corporate bond is equivalent to lending money with no chance of default while giving stockholders a put option on the firm's assets.

    Bond value = bond value with no chance of default – value of put

2. The value of put equals the value of limited liability--of stockholder's right to walk away from the firm's debt in exchange for handing over the firm's assets to creditors.

3. Determining the value of a bond comes in two parts.
    (a) First calculate the value of the bonds, assuming no default.
    (b) Next calculate the value of the put written on the firm's assets, with maturity of the put equaling the maturity of the debt, and the exercise price equaling the interest and principal payments promised to the bondholders.

4. Owning a corporate bond is equivalent to owning the firm's assets *and* giving a call option on the assets to the firm's shareholders.

    Bond value = asset value – value of call on assets

*Valuing Government Loan Guarantees: Lockheed Example

1. Loan guarantees ensured that both the firm and lenders will get money.

2. One looks to the government if a firm cannot deliver on the debt promises.

3. Government absorbs all the risk.

4. The present value of a loan guarantee is the amount lenders are willing to pay to relieve themselves of all default risk on an equivalent unguaranteed loan. It is the difference between the present values of the loan with and without the guarantee.

5. Valued as a put on the firm's assets:

    Value of guarantee = value of guarantee loan – loan value without the guarantee

6. With the guarantee we have:

    Value of ordinary loan = value assuming no chance of default – value of put

LIST OF TERMS

Expectations hypothesis

Forward rate

Inflation premium

Liquidity preference theory

Liquidity premium

Money rate of interest

Nominal interest rate

Real interest rate

Spot rate

Term structure of interest rates

Yield to maturity

EXERCISES

Fill-in Questions

1. _____ include a premium for anticipated inflation.
2. The nominal rate of interest must equal the _____ plus the _____.
3. If the money (nominal) rate of interest is 10 percent and the anticipated inflation rate is 10 percent, the real rate of interest is _____.
4. Under Fisher's scheme of interest rates, if the forecasted inflation rate is 5 percent and the real interest rate is 0.3 percent, the nominal interest rate is _____.
5. The real rate of interest is equal to the _____ minus the _____.
6. Any interest rate which is fixed today is called the _____.
7. The term structure of interest rates consists of a series of _____ on bonds of comparable risk.
8. A bond's internal rate of return is called _____.
9. Ordinarily the term structure of interest rates presents a condition in which the _____ rates are higher than the _____ rates and therefore the term structure slopes upward.
10. The _____ rate in the second year of a 2-year bond is the rate implied by the 2-year spot rate.
11. Ignoring risk considerations, a person who desires a 2-year investment should purchase 1-year bonds in each of the 2 years if the _____ exceeds the forward rate.
12. Ignoring risk considerations, if you wish to make a 1-year investment but are considering a 2-year bond to be sold at the end of that 1 year, the 2-year bond should be purchased if the forward rate is (less than, greater than, equal to) _____ the future spot rate.
13. Ignoring risk considerations--on the one hand, if the forward rate of a 2-year bond exceeds the expected spot rate, you should be (willing, unwilling) _____ to hold 2-year bonds, whereas if the forward rate were less than the expected future spot rate, you should be (willing, unwilling) _____ to hold 2-year bonds.
14. The _____ of the term structure of interest rates says the only reason for an upward-sloping term structure is that investors expect future spot rates to be higher than current spot rates.
15. The difference between forward rates and expected future spot rates is called _____.
16. The _____ theory of term structure of interest rates takes into account risk, whereas the _____ explanation does not.
17. The _____ theory of the term structure of interest rates assumes that the risk from holding bonds comes only from uncertainty about expected inflation rates.
18. The history of bond ratings indicates that they are (good, poor) _____ indicators of overall quality.
19. When one assumes that bonds create options, the bond value is equal to the value of the bond assuming no chance of default minus _____.
20. A loan guarantee may be valued as a _____ on the firm's assets.

Problems

1. Find the real interest rate, given that the nominal rate is 9 percent and the inflation rate is 5 percent.

2. If the money rate of interest is 9.3 percent and the real rate is expected to be 5 percent, what is the assumed inflation rate? How realistic is it to assume that the real rate will be 5 percent?

3. If the nominal annualized rate of interest on 90 day Treasury bills is 8.2 percent, what is the likely estimate of the inflation rate for the year ahead?

4. Calculate the yield to maturity on a 15-year bond carrying a coupon rate of 9 percent. Assume that the interest is payable annually and the bond is selling at 92.

5. As the financial manager of Ink, Inc., you estimate the following spot interest rates on Treasury securities:

YEAR	SPOT INTEREST RATE, %
1	$r_1 = 4.00$
2	$r_2 = 5.00$
3	$r_3 = 5.60$
4	$r_4 = 7.20$
5	$r_5 = 6.50$

   Your company's bonds have an 11 percent coupon rate, interest is payable annually, and mature in exactly 5 years.
   a. What is the present value of the bonds?
   b. Calculate the present values of the following Treasury issues: (1) 5 percent, 3-year bond; (2) 8 percent, 3-year bond; (3) 6 percent, 5-year bond.
   c. Determine the yield to maturity of each of the bonds.
   d. What differences between the yields to maturity do you observe and how might you explain them to the board of directors, who also happen to have noticed the differences?

6. Ink, Inc.'s board of directors are hard at it trying to learn more about the bond markets. They ask you to explain how to estimate tenth-year spot rates, given that there are two 10-year bonds, alike in all respects except one carries a 6 percent coupon and the other carries a 12 percent coupon. The price of the 6 percent bond is 74; that of the 12 percent bond is 111. How would you make your presentation?

7. Ink, Inc.'s board of directors simply cannot get enough of which of two financial strategies is better: a 2-year investment horizon, with a 2-year spot rate of 8 percent, a 1-year spot rate of 9 percent, and the expected 1-year spot rate 1 year from now of 7 percent. Give them the analysis they seek.

8. Ink, Inc.'s directors are really warming up to the term structure of interest notions, enlightened as they are by your sterling presentations, and now they wish to know which investment strategy should be followed, given the following conditions: they desire to invest for 1 year; the 1-year spot rate is 6 percent; the 2-year spot rate is 7.5 percent; and the expected spot rate 1 year from now is 9 percent. Go to it!

232

Essay Questions

1. Differentiate between real rates of interest and nominal rates of interest.

2. How are nominal rates of interest adjusted for the effects of inflation? Explain fully, using whatever equations you feel are necessary.

3. First explain the concept of yield to maturity and then evaluate its usefulness.

4. "The book says that yields to maturity do not determine bond prices; rather it is just the other way around. What I want to know is: How come?" Present an explanation for this comment.

5. Why are there bond ratings and what influence do you think they have on the value of bonds?

6. How do you think bond-rating agencies determine the ratings they place on bonds?

ANSWERS TO EXERCISES

Fill-in Questions

1. nominal interest rates
2. real rate; inflation premium
3. zero
4. 5.3 percent
5. nominal rate on Treasury bills; expected inflation rate
6. spot rate
7. spot rates
8. yield to maturity
9. long; short
10. forward
11. expected future spot rate
12. greater than
13. willing; unwilling
14. expectations hypothesis
15. liquidity premium
16. liquidity preference; expectations hypothesis
17. inflation premium
18. good
19. value of a put
20. put option

Problems

1. $1 + r_{real} = (1 + r_n) \div (1 + i)$
$= (1.09) \div (1.05)$
$= 3.81$ percent

2. $1 + i = (1 + r_n) \div (1 + r_{real})$
$= (1.093) \div (1.05) = 4.10$ percent

Not very, because it is well above the long-term rate.

3. $1 + r_n = (1 + r_{real})(1 + i)$
   $= (1.02)(1.07) = 9.14$ percent

4. $i = r_n - r_{real}$
   $= 8.2$ percent $- 0.3$ percent $= 7.9$ percent

5. 10.00 percent

6. a.

PERIOD	INTEREST RATE	CASH FLOW	PRESENT VALUE
1	4.00	110	105.77
2	5.00	110	99.77
3	5.60	110	93.41
4	7.20	110	83.29
5	6.50	1110	802.87
			1188.82

b.

PERIOD	INTEREST RATE	CASH FLOW	PRESENT VALUE
1	4.00	50	48.08
2	5.00	50	45.35
3	5.60	1050	891.66
			985.08
1	4.00	80	76.92
2	5.00	80	72.56
3	5.60	1080	917.13
			1066.62
1	4.00	60	57.69
2	5.00	60	54.42
3	5.60	60	50.95
4	7.20	60	45.43
5	6.50	1060	773.67
			982.17

c. Using the prices above:

A	5.75%
B	5.50
C	6.43

7. The price of the 6 percent bond is $740. Buying two 6 percent bonds requires $1480, or $370 more than the 12 percent bond. The estimated spot rate is 10.45 percent.

8. $1000(1 + .09)(1.07) = $1166.30 compared with $1166.40[$1000 x $(1.08)^2$]. They should be indifferent.

9. Implied forward rate is
$$(1 + r_1)^2 = (1 + r_1)(1 + f_2)$$
$$(1.075)^2 = (1.06)(1 + f_2)$$
$$f_2 = 9.02 \text{ percent} = {}_1r_2$$
They should be indifferent.

CHAPTER 24
THE MANY DIFFERENT KINDS OF DEBT

INTRODUCTION

We know that some argue that debt does not increase the value of the firm and others say it does. Regardless of which position you take, as a budding financial manager you cannot escape the realities of the various types of debt available for your use and the rationale for the various provisions contained in debt contracts. These topics are the sum and substance of this chapter.

WHAT TO LOOK FOR IN CHAPTER 24

Debt is differentiated among straight bonds, private debt, and project financing. All are promissory notes, although each has characteristics peculiar to it. The bond contract contains the specific terms, called covenants, to which borrowers and lenders agree. Bonds contain such features as being fully registered, unsecured, subordinated, mortgage, collateral trust, a variety of repayment provisions, and restrictive provisions. Debt is either sold publicly or placed privately, the latter being less costly to issue, containing nonstandard features, and imposing more restrictive terms on the borrower.

Domestic Bonds, Foreign Bonds, and Eurobonds: U.S. firms may borrow either domestically or in foreign bond markets. The international market for long-term debt is called the eurobond market. Among some of the nuances that concern financial managers is the currency in which the principal or interest will be paid and local securities markets regulation (or lack thereof).

The Bond Contract: All bonds are IOU's. U.S. publicly issued bonds are covered by bond indentures, which are included in the registration statement and whose main provisions are contained in the prospectuses.

Bond prices are quoted as a percentage of their face value. Sometimes they are sold at a discount from their face value. Most often interest payments are fixed for the life of the bond, although recently more and more floating-rate notes have been issued. Bonds may or may not be registered.

Security and Seniority: The significance of the legal security and seniority of bonds depends largely on the extent to which assets and earnings are available to meet the legal obligations of semiannual interest payments as well as the repayment of principal when due. Debenture bonds are general creditors of the company and have no legal security other than the general bill-paying ability of the company. Secured debt, by contrast, has a specific claim on specific assets: Mortgage bonds have a claim on a specific physical asset; collateral trust bonds have a claim on other securities; and equipment obligations have an ultimate claim on the specific equipment bought with the sale proceeds. The repayment of the principal claims of some debtholders may be subordinated to that of other debtholders.

Repayment Provisions: Sinking funds require issuers to repay some or all of the principal amount of the debt before maturity. Payment may be in cash or an equal face value amount of bonds.

Call Provision: For most industrial firms, but not for public utility companies, repayment provisions are commonplace. Perforce, the call provision which allows the corporation to call in (retire) its bonds before they mature is a valuable option because when it is invoked under the proper conditions--when the market price equals the call--it tends to minimize the value of the bonds, which is equivalent to saying that it tends to maximize the value of the firm's stock.

Restrictive Covenants: Because the company has the valuable option to default on its bonds, restrictive bond provisions are the order of the day. Maintaining an adequate ratio of assets to debt, minimum working capital requirements, ensuring that all subsequent debt will be subordinated to existing debt, incorporating a negative pledge clause, restricting the amount of cash dividends paid, and requiring a minimum level of net worth are typical restrictive provisions, all of which are intended to enhance the security of bondholders.

Innovations in the Bond Market: Many recent bond market innovations seem to be so much puffery, appealing to specific clienteles with specific needs, and usually short-lived. Some arise because of quirks in "the system," the issuance of zero coupon bonds being a case in point. When the innovation survives, it is usually because of economies of scale, widened investor choices, and changes that accommodate changing perceptions of investor risk. The process is known as securitization.

Project Finance: Project finance, discussed in Appendix B, are loans that finance particular projects through a parent company or one of its major subsidiaries. Project loans rely on the project itself for repayment of principal and payment of interest. Because that may not be sufficient security for lenders, tangible property, production payments, completion guarantees, and recourse to stockholders are commonly incorporated into the lending agreement.

Two benefits of project finance are: the parent company may be insulated from the adverse results of the project and the loans are not shown on the balance sheet.

WORKED EXAMPLES

PROBLEM 1: BOND PRICE
If Whozits Company's 8 percent debenture mature in 10 years and the yield on comparable-risk bonds is 6 percent, at what price would you expect the bonds to be selling?

SOLUTION
The object here is to determine the present value of the bond, the formula for which is

$$PV = \sum_{t=1}^{n} \frac{C_t}{(1+r)^t}$$

where PV = present value
C_t = per period cash flow
r = required rate of return on assets of this risk level
t = number of periods over which the cash flows will be forthcoming

Inasmuch as interest is paid semiannually, the interest cash flow per period is $40 ($80/2), the semiannual interest rate r is 3 percent (6% divided by 2), and the total number of periods t over which the cash flows will be forthcoming is 20 (2 x 10 years). The completed formula is

$$PV = \sum_{t=1}^{20} \frac{\$40}{(1+0.06/2)^t} + \frac{\$1000}{(1+0.06/2)^{20}}$$

$$PV = \sum_{t=1}^{20} \frac{\$40}{(1+0.03)^t} + \frac{\$1000}{(1+0.03)^{20}}$$

$$PV = \sum_{t=1}^{20} \frac{\$40}{(1.03)^t} + \frac{\$1000}{(1.03)^{20}}$$

Next use the present-value tables. The first term on the right-hand side of the equation is the present value of an annuity of $40 for 20 periods at 3 percent. The second term is the present value of a lump sum of $1000 to be received at the end of the twentieth period. The arithmetic of the matter looks like this:

$$
\begin{aligned}
PV &= (\$40)(14.88) + \$1000(0.554) \\
&= \$595.20 + \$554.00 \\
&= \$1149.20
\end{aligned}
$$

PROBLEM 2: THE CALL DECISION
If the bonds in problem 1 are callable at 106, what should the financial manager do?

SOLUTION
The financial manager should call the bond because the present value of the bond ($1149.20) is greater than the present value of the call price ($1060.00). If needed, a new issue of bonds may be sold at the going rate of 6 percent, thereby lowering the firm's cost of capital, reducing the drain on cash, and improving its interest coverage ratio, all to the benefit of the shareholders.

PROBLEM 3: BOND PRICES AND CALL PROVISIONS
If the call provision of problem 2 exists, what is the maximum price you would expect the bond to achieve when bonds of comparable risk are selling to yield 6 percent?

SOLUTION
The bond will sell for no more than the call price, which is $1060 a bond. The difference between the present value of the bond without the call provision and $1060 is the value of the call provision (option), or $89.20.

PROBLEM 4: PROTECTION PROVISIONS
Whozits Company's bonds have a provision which stipulates that senior debt will never fall below a ratio of senior debt to total assets of 40 percent. Say the company is at the limit of that ratio and it wishes to issue still another $5 million in senior debt. How much additional equity capital must it raise to comply with this restrictive provision?

SOLUTION
Begin by setting up the problem as a proportion, which it is. The required ratio of 40 percent senior debt implies that equity must be 60 percent. So the ratio of senior debt to equity is 40 percent to 60 percent, or two thirds. If they desire to issue $5 million of new debt, the amount of new equity required x will be determined thus:

$$
\begin{aligned}
0.40/0.60 &= \$5 \text{ million}/x \\
0.4x &= 0.6(\$5 \text{ million}) \qquad \text{(cross-multiplying)} \\
&= \$3 \text{ million} \\
x &= \$7.5 \text{ million}
\end{aligned}
$$

SUMMARY

Introduction

1. Each financial manager chooses the type of debt and its covenants that are best for him or her.

2. Some major distinctions between debt sold to the public and privately placed debt are:
   a. The former's contract is more complex.
   b. The former's characteristics and formats are more standardized.
   c. Restrictive covenants of publicly sold debt are less severe than privately placed debt.

Domestic Bonds, Foreign Bonds and Eurobonds

1. May borrow either in domestic or foreign markets.

2. Eurobond market is for foreign bonds.

3. Have to consider the currency in which the principal or interest is to be paid.

4. Local securities laws may be a consideration.

The Bond Contract

1. Contract terms are found in the indenture or trust deed, a copy of which is in the registration statement and a condensed version of which is in the prospectus.

2. Bond terms
   a. Accrued interest
   b. Underwriting fee = offering price – price to underwriters
   c. Semiannual interest payments (Eurobonds pay annually): a hurdle to test ability to pay
   d. Interest is usually fixed for the life of the issue, although floating rate debt is used too
   e. Registered; bearer

Security and Seniority

1. Unsecured debt: Debentures; general creditors with no claim on specific assets.

2. Secured debt
   a. Mortgage debt: a claim on specific assets, usually tangible
   b. Collateral debt: a claim on other securities
   c. Equipment obligations: a claim, through a third party, on specific equipment.

3. Subordinated debt: debt whose claim on assets is subordinate to other specified claims.

Repayment Provisions

1. Sinking fund: periodic allocation of cash or bonds to be used to retire part or all of the debt before maturity
   a. Mandatory, optional, or both.
   b. Another test of firm solvency, unless the firm is allowed to purchase them in the open market.

2. Call provision: the company's option to retire debt before it is due
    a. Invariably callable at a premium.
    b. Frequently noncallable in the first 10 years of existence.
    c. Available options
        (1) When interest rates decline, bond prices tend to rise, and it may be attractive to call.
        (2) Call when the value of equity will be enhanced, i.e., by minimizing the value of the debt.
        (3) Call when market price equals call price.

Restrictive Covenants

1. The corporation's option to default is a plus to the firm and a negative to bondholders.

2. Debtholders impose restrictions on debtors to protect their interests.

3. Restrict cash dividends.

4. Cross-default clause: default on one issue is an act of default on all issues.

5. Try to maintain the ratio of debt to market value.
    a. Limit further borrowing unless more assets are added.
    b. Limit cash dividends.
    c. No limit on subordinated debt, from senior debtholders' viewpoint.
    d. Subordinated debt may limit issuance of senior debt and contain a negative pledge clause.
    e. Because leasing is a form of debt, include leases as part of prohibited debt.

Innovations in the Bond Market

1. LYON: Callable, retractable, convertible, and zero coupon, all in one bundle (Whew!!!!).

2. Most innovations arise from inconsistencies in the tax code.

3. Lasting innovations are likely to result from economies of scale in financial markets and widened investor choices.

Project Finance

1. Tries to insulate the parent or related companies.

2. Ties debt servicing to the fortunes of the project being financed.

3. Most suitable for tangible assets.

LIST OF TERMS

Call provision	Indexed bonds
Collateral trust bonds	Mortgage bonds
Debenture bonds	Negative pledge clause
Equipment trust certificates	Private debt
Eurobonds	Project finance
Floating-rate bonds	Registered bonds
Income bonds	Sinking fund
Indenture	

EXERCISES

Fill-in Questions

1. Private placements are (easier, more difficult) _____ to flat than publicly issued contracts.
2. Private placements are more likely to possess (nonstandard, standard) _____ loan features.
3. The contract provisions of private placements are (more, less) _____ stringent than public issues, but they are (more, less) _____ difficult to renegotiate.
4. The document in a public issue of bonds which incorporates all the contract provisions between the borrower and lender, through an agreement with a trust company, is called an _____.
5. Bondholders whose names appear on the records of the company as being owners of the bonds and to whom bond interest and principal will be paid hold _____ bonds, whereas those who must clip coupons in order to collect their interest and turn in the bond for repayment of principal are called _____ bonds.
6. A bond which is unsecured and relies on the general credit of the corporation is called _____.
7. If an issue of bonds has a _____, then, if interest rates fall, the company may be able to retire them for less than their present value.
8. A provision which allows debenture bondholders to become mortgage bondholders, when mortgage bonds are issued after the debentures were sold is called _____.
9. Bonds whose rate of interest is contingent on the rate of interest paid on Treasury bills are called _____.
10. The international market for foreign bonds is called the _____ market.

Problems

1. If Whatsits Company's 6 percent debenture bonds mature in 8 years and the yield on comparable-risk bonds is 10 percent, at what price would you expect the Whatsits bonds to be selling, all else the same?

2. If Whatsits Company has 10 percent mortgage bonds maturing in 9 years, and comparable-risk bonds are selling to yield 8 percent, at what price would you expect the Whatsits bonds to be selling if they were noncallable? If they were callable at 105?

3. What is the value of the right to call a 10-year 10 percent coupon bond at a price of 106, when bonds of comparable risk yield 6 percent?

4. Whatsits Company's bond indenture contains a provision stipulating that the ratio of senior debt to total assets must be kept at 30 percent at all times. If the company is at the limit of that ratio, determine how much more additional equity capital it must raise in order to float an additional $40 million of bonds.

Essay Questions

1. Differentiate between a debenture bond, a subordinated bond, and a mortgage bond.

2. In what sense, if any, may subordinated debt be viewed as equity capital?

3. Why does a call provision have value to the financial manager?

4. Explain what a sinking fund is and how it is most likely to work.

5. Why is the option to default on a corporate bond valuable? Explain fully.

ANSWERS TO EXERCISES

Fill-in Questions

1. easier
2. nonstandard
3. more; less
4. indenture
5. fully registered; bearer
6. a debenture
7. call provision
8. a negative pledge clause
9. floating-rate bonds
10. Eurobond

Problems

1. $30 x 10.84 = $325.20
   $1000 x 0.458 =   458.00
                                      $783.20

2. $50 x 12.66 = $ 633.00
   $1000 x 0.494 = $ 494.00
   Value without the call = $1127.00
   If callable, = $1050.00

3. Bond Value less call price   = value of call provision

   $50 x 14.88 = $744.00
   $1000 x .554 =   554.00
   Value of Bond = $1298.00
   Call Price =   1060.00
   Value of Call provision = $238.00

4. $0.3/0.7 = \$40$ million$/x$; $93.3 million

CHAPTER 25
HEDGING FINANCIAL RISK

INTRODUCTION

Financial managers can diversity or hedge risks. Hedging offsets risks by trading assets or liabilities for other assets. This is accomplished with options, futures, and other financial instruments. One of the primary purposes of hedging is to control the individual risks of an enterprise and thereby control its total risk. Such hedging techniques are part and parcel of today's financial manager's tasks. The point of hedging is to minimize risks. The object is to find the number of units of an asset that is needed to offset changes in the value of an obligation. Those discussed in this chapter are the most prominent, such as standardized commodities, exchange rates, and interest rates.

WHAT TO LOOK FOR IN CHAPTER 25

Hedging is the focus of this chapter. As you study this chapter keep in mind that hedging is an important tool used by financial managers to offset, not eliminate, risks. The hedge is established by trading in options, futures, and other financial instruments. Because hedging mitigates the risk of individual assets, the firm's collective risk is also mitigated. Hedging tactics are important because they allow financial managers to concentrate their energies on matters whose risks are not easily hedged or diversified.

The Technique of Hedging: Hedging is not unlike diversifying a portfolio of securities. One looks for investments not closely correlated with each other in order to reduce risk. Ideally, a perfect hedge is one in which two assets are brought together that are perfectly negatively correlated: If the expected return on one declines, the return on the other will definitely increase, and the net position is unchanged. This is rarely the case in practice, so the object is to minimize the residual risk of the net position from buying one asset in order to offset it against a liability. Hedging only minimizes risk, it does not eliminate it, because market-related risk cannot be totally avoided.

The size of the investment in the asset depends on how the cash flows of the asset *and* the liability are correlated. Delta measures the sensitivity of an asset's value to changes in the value of the liability. It is also the hedge ratio, which tells the financial manager the number of units of an asset to buy in order to hedge the liability.

A zero-value hedge results when the net difference between the value of two less than perfectly hedged investments is placed in a bank deposit. Because the liability and the asset purchased to hedge that liability change constantly, a dynamic hedging strategy is needed to rebalance the hedge to the original position.

Duration and Volatility: Because the average time for the total cash flow to be realized from an asset, such as a bond, is less than its maturity date, the concept of duration is valuable. It measures the average time that the total cash flow from an asset is realized over the life of that asset. It is always less than the maturity of the asset. As interest rates change, the asset's volatility changes, and it is directly related to the asset's duration. Volatility in the context of duration is a useful summary measure of the impact of a change in interest rates on both the debt and the equity portions of the financial structure. When the duration of the asset and the duration of the liability associated therewith are equal, the two are said to be immunized against changes in interest rates.

When considering the duration of both an asset and a liability associated with it, the hedge ratio is needed-- in this instance it is the ratio of the durations of the liability and the asset. The immunization scheme assumes that there are across-the-board (parallel) changes in interest rates. As time passes and interest rates change, an immunized asset and liability cash flow stream must be rebalanced in order to maintain the hedge ratio.

Hedging with Futures: When a financial manager hedges with futures, he agrees to deliver a specified "commodity" at a specified price, location, and time. Futures contracts allow one to hedge the risk of a present commodity by buying (the long hedge) or selling (the short hedge) the contract for future delivery-- all this done against the present or spot price. Excess demand for or supply of futures contracts are absorbed by speculators. Futures contracts are important for the management of physical commodities, exchange rates, and interest rates. Futures contracts allow financial managers to fix today prices on commodities that will not be available until some time in the future. Each day future contracts are marked to market to determine profits or losses.

When financial futures are bought, one does not pay for the security immediately (one can earn interest on the purchase price) and any income that accrues on the futures contracts are not available to the purchaser. When dealing in commodity futures, payment is not made immediately for the entire contract and interest may be earned. In addition, there are no storage fees for the purchaser of the contract, for the commodity is bought to be delivered in the future. The convenience yield is foregone, however, when one buys commodity futures because the commodity is not available for immediate use.

Forward Contracts: A high degree of liquidity exists in futures markets, because futures contracts are standardized and mature on a limited number of specified dates each year. But what about financial managers who wish to customize futures contracts to suit their special needs or make deals that mature on dates other than those found on organized futures markets? The answer is to construct a forward contract which is the equivalent of a home-made futures contract. The forward rate agreement (FRA) is one mode of customizing futures contracts. Most forward contracts arise from dealings in foreign exchange currency markets. A financial manager may manufacture a forward loan by borrowing short term and lending long term. This may occur either in foreign exchange or in loans.

Swaps: Often financial managers who deal in international markets are better known in one country than another. Their firm may issue debt in the country in which it is well known, receive that currency, and then swap it for another country's currency. This is a currency swap. Swaps also exist on loans, where a fixed interest rate loan is exchanged for a floating rate loan, or a floating-rate loan is subsequently tied to different base rates.

WORKED EXAMPLES

PROBLEM 1

Say your local investment banker is recounting to you how she shorted $15 million of Wild Gyrations, Inc.'s stock and that she wants your help in determining how much of the Standard & Poor's 500 Index (S&P 500) she should buy in order to hedge the market-related risk to which she is exposed. The historical relation between the stock's change in price and the change in price of the market index is

(Monthly change in value of Wild Gyrations) = a + ∂ (Monthly changes in Market index)

= 0.05 + 1.25 (Monthly changes in Market index)

The index stands at 302

SOLUTION

To hedge the short sale she must set aside $18,750,000 (1.25 x $15,000,000). This minimizes her risk in this short position.

PROBLEM 2

Calculate the duration of 8 and 14 percent, five-year Treasury bonds whose yield is 7.85 percent.

Duration = $[PV(C_1)/V \times 1] + [PV(C_2)/V \times 2] + [PV(C_3)/V \times 3] + \ldots$

SOLUTION

	Rate	7.85%
	Coupon	8.00%

Year	C_t	PV(C_t) at 7.85%	Proportion of Total Value [PVC$_t$)/V]	Proportion of Value x Time
1	$80	74.18	0.0737	0.0737
2	$80	68.78	0.0684	0.1367
3	$80	63.77	0.0634	0.1902
4	$80	59.13	0.0588	0.2351
5	$1,080	740.16	0.7357	3.6787
Totals	$1,400	1,006.01	1.00	4.314

	Rate	7.85%
	Coupon	14.00%

Year	C_t	PV(C_t) at 7.85%	Proportion of Total Value [PV(C_t)/V]	Proportion of Value x Time
1	$140	129.81	0.1041	0.1041
2	$140	120.36	0.0966	0.1931
3	$140	111.60	0.0895	0.2686
4	$140	103.48	0.0830	0.3321
5	$1,140	781.28	0.6268	3.1338
Totals	$1,700	$1,246.53	1.00	4.032

PROBLEM 3

Trace the impact of a 0.5 percentage point increase and decrease in interest rates on the present value of each of the two bonds in problem 2. Then compute their volatilities.

SOLUTION

The yields are now 7.35% and 8.35%. The computations are as follows

| | Yield | 7.35% |
| | Coupon | 8.00% |

Year	C_t	PV(C_t) at 7.35%	Proportion of Total Value [PV(C_t)/V]	Proportion of Value x Time
1	$80	74.52	0.0726	0.0726
2	$80	69.42	0.0676	0.1353
3	$80	64.67	0.0630	0.1890
4	$80	60.24	0.0587	0.2348
5	$1,080	757.55	0.7381	3.6903
Totals	$1,400	1,026.40	1.00	4.322

| | Yield | 8.35% |
| | Coupon | 8.00% |

Year	C_t	PV(C_t) at 8.35%	Proportion of Total Value [PV(C_t)/V]	Proportion of Value x Time
1	$80	73.83	0.0749	0.0749
2	$80	68.14	0.0691	0.1382
3	$80	62.89	0.0638	0.1913
4	$80	58.05	0.0589	0.2354
5	$1,080	723.23	0.7334	3.6669
Totals	$1,400	986.15	1.00	4.307

| | Yield | 7.35% |
| | Coupon | 14.00% |

Year	C_t	PV(C_t) at 7.35%	Proportion of Total Value [PV(C_t)/V]	Proportion of Value x Time
1	$140	130.41	0.1027	0.1027
2	$140	121.49	0.0956	0.1913
3	$140	113.17	0.0891	0.2673
4	$140	105.42	0.0830	0.3320
5	$1,140	799.64	0.6296	3.1479
Totals	$1,700	1,270.13	1.00	4.041

	Yield	8.35%
	Coupon	14.00%

Year	C_t	PV(C_t) at 8.35%	Proportion of Total Value [PV/(C_t)/V]	Proportion of Value x Time
1	$140	129.21	0.1056	0.1056
2	$140	119.25	0.0975	0.1949
3	$140	110.06	0.0900	0.2699
4	$140	101.58	0.0830	0.3321
5	$1,140	763.41	0.6239	3.1197
Totals	$1,700	1,223.52	1.00	4.022

	8% Bonds		14% Bonds	
	New Price	Change	New Price	Change
Yield falls	1,026.40	2.03%	1,270.03	1.89
Yield rises	986.15	-1.97	1,223.52	-1.85
Difference	40.25	4.00	46.68	3.74

$$\text{Volatility} = \frac{\text{duration}}{1 + \text{yield}}$$

For the 8 percent bonds volatility is: $4.314 \div 1.0785 = 4.00$; for the 14 percent bonds, it is $4.032 \div 1.0785 = 3.74$

PROBLEM 4

If the volatility of an asset is 4.12 percent and the yield on bonds is 12 percent, find the asset's duration.

SOLUTION

$$\text{Volatility} = \frac{\text{duration}}{1 + \text{yield}}$$

$$4.12\% = \frac{\text{duration}}{(1 + .12)}$$

$$= \text{duration}/(1.12)$$

$$\text{duration} = \frac{4.12}{1.12} = 3.68 \text{ years}$$

PROBLEM 5

The expected cash flows from your company's $25 million investment are $5 million a year for the next 10 years. The required return on projects of this risk is 15 percent. You plan to finance the present value of the project with ten-year debt at the going rate for bonds of this risk of 12 percent. If the new investment and the debt are viewed as a package, does your company stand to lose if there is a change in interest rates?

SOLUTION

The present values and durations of the project, at 15 percent, and of the debt, at 12 percent, are in the following two tables.

Present value and duration of project

| | Rate | 15.00% |
| | Cash flow | 5.00 |

Year	C_t	PV(C_t) at 15.00%	Proportion of Total Value [PV(C_t)/V]	Proportion of Value x Time
1	5.00	4.35	0.1733	0.1733
2	5.00	3.78	0.1507	0.3013
3	5.00	3.29	0.1310	0.3930
4	5.00	2.86	0.1139	0.4557
5	5.00	2.49	0.0991	0.4953
6	5.00	2.16	0.0861	0.5169
7	5.00	1.88	0.0749	0.5243
8	5.00	1.63	0.0651	0.5211
9	5.00	1.42	0.0566	0.5098
10	5.00	1.24	0.0493	0.4925
Totals	50.00	25.09	1.00	4.383

Debt Analysis

$4.44 Annual payments

Principal	Interest	Total	Balance
25.09	3.01	28.11	23.67
23.67	2.84	26.50	22.06
22.06	2.65	24.71	20.27
20.27	2.43	22.71	18.27
18.27	2.19	20.46	16.02
16.02	1.92	17.94	13.50
13.50	1.62	15.12	10.68
10.68	1.28	11.96	7.52
7.52	0.90	8.42	3.98
3.98	0.48	4.46	0.02

248

Present value and duration of debt

| | Rate | 12.00% | | |
| | Cash flow | 4.44 | | |

Year	C_t	$PV(C_t)$ at 12.00%	Proportion of Total Value $[PV(C_t)/V]$	Proportion of Value x Time
1	4.44	3.96	0.1580	0.1580
2	4.44	3.54	0.1411	0.2822
3	4.44	3.16	0.1260	0.3779
4	4.44	2.82	0.1125	0.4499
5	4.44	2.52	0.1004	0.5021
6	4.44	2.25	0.0897	0.5380
7	4.44	2.01	0.0801	0.5604
8	4.44	1.79	0.0715	0.5718
9	4.44	1.60	0.0638	0.5744
10	4.44	1.43	0.0570	0.5698
Totals	44.40	25.09	1.00	4.585

Hedge ratio = Duration of project ÷ duration of debt
= 4.383 ÷ 4.585 = 0.956

PROBLEM 6

The S&P 500 stock index futures is trading at 314, and the spot S&P 500 index is at 300. The six-month Treasury Bill rate is 7.64 percent, and the average annual yield on stocks is 3 percent. Are these rates consistent?

SOLUTION

[Futures price ÷ $(1 + r_f)^t$] = spot price – PV(dividends or interest payments forgone)

Semi-annual T-Bill yield = $(1.0764)^{1/2}$ = 3.75%

Semi-annual dividend yield = 3% ÷ 2 = 1.75%

Completing the formula, we have:

Futures price = [314 ÷ (1.0375)] = 302.65 = 303
Expected spot price = Futures price – PV (dividends)
= 314 – [(314 x .0175) ÷ 1.0375]
= 314 – 5.30 = 308.7 = 309

The numbers are not consistent. One would expect this large discrepancy to be arbitraged away. To what point? We cannot say for certain, but the futures contract should be shorted and the spot contract should be bought long until, except for trading costs, there is no room left for arbitrage profits.

PROBLEM 7

Say MPG Motor Company is able to borrow at 8 percent for one year, using its automobile loans as collateral. The loans are made from MPG Acceptance Corporation, a wholly owned subsidiary. Say also it estimates that its overall return from car loans is 12 percent once the return on the loans, 6.9 percent, and economies realized from manufacturing costs are factored into the analysis. If the average automobile loan is 3 years in length, what forward interest rate is implied by this homemade forward contract?

SOLUTION

$$\text{Forward interest rate} = \frac{(1 + \text{3-year spot rate})^3}{1 + \text{1-year spot rate}} - 1$$
$$= [(1.12)^3 \div 1.08] - 1 = 30.09\%$$

Not bad, eh? A pretty compelling case to offer consumers low-interest rate loans.

PROBLEM 8

MPG Motor Company plans to build a parts plant in Germany. It finds it can get better financing terms in the United States than in any other country. It issues $15 million of 5-year, 10 percent notes in the U.S. capital markets. Simultaneously, it enters into another agreement with its bank, the details of which are: (1) to swap its dollar liabilities (the U.S. notes) into deutsche marks; (2) for the bank to pay MPG sufficient dollars to service the debt; and (3) MPG agrees to make annual payments in deutsche marks to the bank. Demonstrate the "numbers" of this currency sway if the exchange rate is 2.10 deutsche marks to the dollar.

SOLUTION

	Year 0		Years 1-4		Year 5	
	$	DM	$	DM	$	DM
Issue dollar notes	+15	0	-1.5	0	-16.5	0
Swap $s for DMs	-15	7.14	+1.5	-.71	+16.5	-7.85
Net cash flow	0	7.14	0	-.71	0	-7.85

MPG made a 10 percent loan a 9.94 percent loan by engaging in the swap: $[(7.85 \div 7.14) - 1] = 9.94\%$

SUMMARY

1. **Introduction**
   a. All risks are not created equal; some may be diversified; some may be hedged.
   b. Hedged risks occur in options and futures markets primarily.
   c. For hedges to exist standardized products or commodities are usually necessary.
   d. Unpredictable fluctuations in prices may be hedged.
   e. Most hedges are intended to reduce risk.
   f. Risk reduction of controllable risk allows financial managers to worry about the things that are worth worrying about.

2. **The Technique of Hedging**
   a. Diversification and hedging are closely related but not identical.
   b. Diversification attempts to isolate assets whose expected returns are not highly correlated, with the view to reducing the risk of the total portfolio.
   c. Hedging may do the same thing but often liabilities are *offset* by assets.
   d. The idea is still to try to find investments whose cash flows are negatively correlated.
      1) They are not likely to exist so that some residual risk exists despite the hedge.
      2) Conceptually well-diversified stock portfolios contain no residual risk.
      3) The object is to minimize the uncertainty of the net position.
      4) The size of the investment in asset A depends on how the values of A and B are related.

   $$(\text{Expected change in value of A}) = a + \partial \ (\text{change in value of B})$$

   f. Delta measures the sensitivity of A to changes in the value of B.
      1) It is called the hedge ratio.
      2) It is the number of units of B which should be purchased to hedge the liability of A.
   g. To establish a zero-value hedge set aside the difference between the change in value of the liability and the change in value of the asset in a bank deposit.
   h. Dynamic hedging is needed to rebalance the hedge ratio, because of changes in interest rates and market values.

3. **Duration and Volatility**
   a. Duration is the average time that is needed to recoup the total value of the bond.

   $$\text{Duration} = [PV(C_1)/V \times 1] + [PV(C_2)/V \times 2] + [PV(C_3)/V \times 3] + \ldots$$

   b. Volatility
      1) Measures the sensitivity of duration to changes in the interest rate.

   $$\begin{array}{ll} \text{Volatility} & = \dfrac{\text{duration}}{1 + \text{yield}} \\ (\text{percent}) & \end{array}$$

      2) summarizes the effective changes in interest rates on our debt.
   c. Duration concepts may be used for any asset or liability.
      1) The illustration in the text deals with leasing arrangements.
      2) The issue always at work is the impact of changes in interest rates.
      3) The illustration deals with the purchase of any asset and leasing it.
      4) The financing arrangement (going into debt) and the leasing arrangement ("selling" the assets) have different cash flow streams.
      5) Again we focus on the duration of the cash flow streams and the impact of changes in interest rates on both.
   d. Equalizing the durations of an asset and a liability creates a package that is immunized against changes in interest rates.
   e. When duration is used, the hedge ratio is measured by the ratio of the duration of the cash flow stream from the asset to the duration of the cash flow stream of the debt.
   f. Duration schemes assume that across-the-board (parallel) shifts in interest rates take place.
   g. As interest rates change and time passes, the hedge ratio of the immunized portfolio changes, because the duration of the asset's cash flow stream and the liability cash flow stream change.
      1) This calls for adjusting the duration of the outstanding debt; the asset's cash flow stream is fixed. This is a dynamic hedging strategy.
      2) An alternative to dynamic hedging is to devise debt issues whose cash flows exactly match the cash flows from the asset.
      3) Dynamic hedging strategies are not cost-free.

4. **Hedging with Futures**
    a. Futures contracts deal in commodities.
    b. Foreign currencies and stock indices may be viewed as commodities.
    c. Futures contracts specify a date, price, and commodity which is to be delivered.
    d. Futures contracts are obligations to deliver or take delivery of the commodity, whereas options are not.
    e. Selling futures contracts is a short hedge.
    f. Buying futures contracts is a long hedge.
    g. Speculators are essential to futures contracts markets because they take up the imbalances between futures contracts supply and futures contracts demand. Spot prices are prices for immediate delivery of the contracts. As the delivery date for futures contracts approaches, the contracts become more and more like spot contracts and the prices approach the spot price.
    h. Futures contracts are bought and sold on organized futures exchanges.
    i. Typical "commodities" traded in the financial futures market are interest rates and exchange rates.
    j. Margin is required to buy or sell a futures contract. Futures contracts are daily marked to market to determine profits and losses.
    k. Financial futures are orders for buying a security for later delivery.
    l. Financial futures differ from buying exactly the same item in the spot market in that the financial manager does not pay for the security at the time the order is placed (he can earn interest during the interim) and he does not receive dividends or interest during this period.

    $$[\text{Futures price} \div (1 + r_f)^t] = \text{spot price} - PV \text{ (dividends or interest payments forgone)}$$

    m. Foreign exchange futures are important to firms dealing in international markets

    $$\frac{\text{Futures price of Swiss francs}}{1 + r_\$} = \text{spot price} - PV(\text{forgone interest on Swiss francs})$$

    $$PV(\text{forgone interest}) = [(r_{sf} \times \text{spot price}) \div 1 + r_{sf}]$$

    n. Commodity futures are more complicated than financial futures.
        1) The buyer of a commodity future earns interest on the money which is the deferred payment.
        2) Buying commodity futures shifts the cost of storage to another party.
        3) Commodity futures contracts have no convenience yield.

5. **Forward Contracts**
    a. Futures contracts are standardized and mature on a limited number of dates each year.
    b. If financial managers wish to trade in future contracts which are non-standardized or which mature at dates other than those traded in the futures markets, they must enter the forward contract market.
        1) Forward contracts are tailor made futures contracts.
        2) A commonplace forward contract is the forward rate agreement (FRA) from a bank in which an interest rate today is locked in for a loan to be delivered from the bank at some future date.
    c. Most forward contracts occur in foreign exchange markets, primarily currency markets.
    d. Homemade forward contracts may be constructed by borrowing short term and lending long term, or vice versa, or by buying and selling foreign exchange.

    $$\text{Forward interest rate} = [(1 + 2\text{-year spot rate})^2 \div (1 + 1\text{-year spot rate})] - 1$$

    e. Any significant differentials between forward and futures markets will attract arbitrageurs and such discrepancies will be eliminated.

6. **Swaps**
    a. Swaps occur when a firm borrows in one currency and swaps it for another currency.
    b. A firm may have a more favorable negotiating posture in one country, borrow in that country but need to make delivery in another currency. A swap is then arranged.
    c. Swaps also occur with fixed-interest rate loans in exchange for floating-rate loans.

LIST OF TERMS

Arbitrageurs	Immunized
Convenience yield	Long hedge
Delta	Marked to market
Duration	Short hedge
Dynamic hedging	Spot price
Forward contract	Storage costs
Forward rate agreement (FRA)	Swap
Hedge	Volatility
Hedge ratio	Zero-value hedge

EXERCISES

Fill-in Questions

1. A _____ offsets risks by trading assets or liabilities for other assets.
2. _____ measures the sensitivity of an asset's value to changes in the value of the liability.
3. A _____ results when the net difference between the value of two less than perfectly hedges investments is placed in a bank deposit.
4. Because the liability and the asset purchased to hedge that liability change constantly, a _____ strategy is needed to rebalance the hedge to the original position.
5. _____ measures the average time that the total cash flow from an asset is realized over the life of that asset.
6. _____ measures the impact of a change in interest rates on both the debt and the equity portions on the financial structure.
7. When the duration of the asset and the duration of the liability associated therewith are equal, the two are said to be _____ against changes in interest rates.
8. In the context of duration, the _____ is measured by the ratio of the duration of the cash flow stream from the asset to the duration of the cash flow stream of the debt.
9. Selling futures contracts is a _____.
10. Buying futures contracts is a _____.
11. Today's price of a commodity is called the _____.
12. Buying commodity futures shifts _____ costs to another party.
13. Commodity futures contracts (do, do not) _____ have convenience costs.
14. Financial managers who wish to trade in future contracts which are non-standardized or which mature at dates other than those traded in the futures markets, must enter the _____ market.
15. A _____ is an agreement with a bank in which an interest rate today is locked in for a loan to be delivered from the bank at some future date.
16. If significant price differentials exist between forward and futures markets, _____ will buy and sell contracts so that such discrepancies will be eliminated.
17. Firms that issue debt in the country in which they are well known, receive that currency, and then exchange it for another country's currency are said to have engaged in a currency _____.

Problem

1. You are having lunch with the investment manager of Make-Me-a-Million & Co. He tells you how he shorted $20 million of Mildly Wild Gyrations, Inc.'s stock and that he wants your help in determining how much of the Standard & Poor's 500 Index (S&P 500) he should buy in order to hedge the market-related risk to which he is exposed. The index stands at 285.

    The historical relation between the stock's change in price and the change in price of the market index is

    (Monthly change in value of Wild Gyrations) = a + ∂ (Monthly changes in Market index)

    = 0.25 + 0.85 (Monthly changes in Market index)

2. Calculate the duration of 9 and 13 percent, five-year Treasury bonds whose yields are 8.00 percent.
3. Trace the impact of a 0.5 percentage point increase and decrease in interest rates on the present value of each of the two bonds in problem 2. Then compute their volatilities.
4. If the volatility of What Not, Inc.'s asset is 3.75 percent and the 8yield on its bonds is 11 percent, find the asset's duration.
5. The expected cash flows from If Not, Inc.'s $10 million investment are $2 million a year for the next 10 years. The required return on projects of this risk is 20 percent. The financial manager plans to finance the present value of the project with ten-year debt at the going rate for bonds of this risk of 10 percent. If the new investment and the debt are viewed as a package, does If Not stand to lose if there is a change in interest rates?
6. The six-month S&P 500 stock index futures is trading at 252.50 and the spot S&P Index is at 250.83. The six-month Treasury Bill rate is 6.65 percent, and the average annual yield on stocks is 3.5 percent. Are these data consistent?
7. Say MPG Motor Company is able to borrow at 10 percent for one year, using its automobile loans as collateral. The loans are made from MPG Acceptance Corporation, a wholly owned subsidiary. Say also it estimates that its overall return from car loans is 16 percent once the return on the loans, 6.9 percent, and economies realized from manufacturing costs are factored into the analysis. If the average automobile loan is 3 years in length, what forward interest rate is implied by this homemade forward contract?
8. MPG Motor Company plans to modernize its West German manufacturing facility. It finds it can get better financing terms than in any other country, if it issues $25 million of 6-year, 12 percent notes in the U.S. capital markets. Simultaneously, it enters into another agreement with its bank, the details of which are: (1) to swap its dollar liabilities (the U.S. notes) into deutsche marks; (2) for the bank to pay MPG sufficient dollars to service the debt; and (3) MPG agrees to make annual payments in deutsche marks to the bank. Demonstrate the "numbers" of this currency swap if the exchange rate is 1.85 deutsche marks to the dollar.

Essay Questions

1. Set forth the rationale for establishing a hedging tactic for the foreign currency division of a multinational firm.
2. Of what particular value is the concept of duration for financial managers? Is it helpful in managing the financial-risks of the firm? If so, how? If not, why not?
3. Put in words how financial managers may hedge with financial futures and use a typical example to demonstrate the concepts you raise.
4. Demonstrate how forward contracts may be constructed to suit a particular need you can think of.
5. Of what value are currency swaps to a financial manager? Under what conditions might he use them? Explain fully.

ANSWERS TO EXERCISES

Fill-in Questions

1. hedge
2. Delta
3. zero-value hedge
4. dynamic hedging
5. Duration
6. Volatility
7. immunized
8. hedge ratio
9. short hedge
10. long hedge
11. spot price
12. storage
13. do not
14. forward contract
15. forward rate agreement (FRA)
16. arbitrageurs
17. swap

Problems

1. To hedge the short sale she must set aside $17,000,000 (0.85 x $20,000,000).

2.

Yield	8.00%	
Coupon	9.00%	

Year	C_t	PV(C_t) at 8.00%	Proportion of Total Value[PV(C_t)/V]	Proportion of Value x Time
1	$90	83.33	0.0801	0.0801
2	$90	77.16	0.0742	0.1484
3	$90	71.44	0.0687	0.2061
4	$90	66.55	0.0636	0.2545
5	$1,090	741.84	0.7134	3.5668
Totals	$1,450	1,039.93	1.00	4.256

	Yield	8.00%			
	Coupon	13.00%			

Year	C_t	PV(C_t) at 8.00%	Proportion of Total Value [PV(C_t)/V]	Proportion of Value x Time
1	$130	120.37	0.1003	0.1003
2	$130	111.45	0.0929	0.1858
3	$130	103.20	0.0860	0.2581
4	$130	95.55	0.0797	0.3186
5	$1,130	769.06	0.6411	3.2054
Totals	$1,650	1,199.64	1.00	4.068

3. The yields are now 7.50% and 8.50%. The computations are as follows.

	Yield	7.50%			
	Coupon	9.00%			

Year	C_t	PV(C_t) at 7.50%	Proportion of Total Value [PV(C_t)/V]	Proportion of Value x Time
1	$90	83.72	0.0789	0.0789
2	$90	77.88	0.0734	0.1468
3	$90	72.45	0.0683	0.2049
4	$90	67.39	0.0635	0.2541
5	$1,450	759.25	0.7158	3.5790
Totals	$1,450	1,060.69	1.00	4.264

	Yield	8.50%			
	Coupon	9.00%			

Year	C_t	PV(C_t) at 8.50%	Proportion of Total Value [PV(C_t)/V]	Proportion of Value x Time
1	$90	82.95	0.0813	0.0813
2	$90	76.45	0.0750	0.1499
3	$90	70.46	0.0691	0.2073
4	$90	64.94	0.0637	0.2547
5	$1,090	724.90	0.7109	3.5545
Totals	$1,450	1,019.70	1.00	4.248

	Yield	7.50%	
	Coupon	13.00%	

Year	C_t	PV(C_t) at 7.50%	Proportion of Total Value [PV(C_t)/V]	Proportion of Value x Time
1	$130	120.93	0.0989	0.0989
2	$130	112.49	0.0920	0.1840
3	$130	104.64	0.0856	0.2568
4	$130	97.34	0.0796	0.3185
5	$1,130	787.11	0.6438	3.2192
Totals	$1,650	1,222.52	1.00	4.077

	Yield	8.50%	
	Coupon	13.00%	

Year	C_t	PV(C_t) at 8.50%	Proportion of Total Value [PV(C_t)/V]	Proportion of Value x Time
1	$130	119.82	0.1018	0.1018
2	$130	110.43	0.0938	0.1876
3	$130	101.78	0.0864	0.2593
4	$130	93.80	0.0797	0.3187
5	$1,130	751.50	0.6383	3.1916
Totals	$1,650	1,177.33	1.00	4.059

	9% Bonds		13% Bonds	
	New Price	Change	New Price	Change
Yield falls	1,060.69	2.00%	1,222.52	1.91
Yield rises	1,019.70	-1.95	1,177.33	-1.86
Difference	40.25	3.95	46.68	3.77

$$\text{Volatility} = \frac{\text{duration}}{1 + \text{yield}}$$

For the 9 percent bonds volatility is: $4.256 \div 1.075 = 3.96$; for the 13 percent bonds, it is $4.077 \div 1.075 = 3.79$. (Differences exist because of rounding.)

4.

$$
\begin{aligned}
\text{Volatility} &= \text{duration} \div (1 + \text{yield}) \\
3.75\% &= \text{duration} \div (1 + .11) \\
&= \text{duration} \div (1.11) \\
\text{duration} &= 3.75 \div 1.11 = 3.378 \text{ years.}
\end{aligned}
$$

5. The present values and durations of the project, at 20 percent, and of the debt, at 10 percent, are in the following two tables.

Present value and duration of project

Rate		20.00%		
Cash flow		$2.00 million a year		

Year	C_t	PV(C_t) at 20.00%	Proportion of Total Value [PV(C_t)/V]	Proportion of Value x Time
1	2.00	1.67	0.1988	0.1988
2	2.00	1.39	0.1656	0.3313
3	2.00	1.16	0.1380	0.4141
4	2.00	0.96	0.1150	0.4601
5	2.00	0.80	0.0959	0.4793
6	2.00	0.67	0.0799	0.4793
7	2.00	0.56	0.0666	0.4660
8	2.00	0.47	0.0555	0.4438
9	2.00	0.39	0.0462	0.4160
10	2.00	0.32	0.0385	0.3852
Totals	20.00	8.38	1.00	4.074

Debt Analysis

$1.36 Annual payments

Principal	Interest	Total	Balance
8.38	0.84	9.22	7.86
7.86	0.79	8.65	7.29
7.29	0.73	8.02	6.66
6.66	0.67	7.32	5.96
5.96	0.60	6.56	5.20
5.20	0.52	5.72	4.36
4.36	0.44	4.80	3.44
3.44	0.34	3.78	2.42
2.42	0.24	2.66	1.30
1.30	0.13	1.43	0.07

Present value and duration of debt

Rate   10.00%
Cash flow $1.36 million a year

Year	C_t	PV(C_t) at 10.00%	Proportion of Total Value [PV(C_t)/V]	Proportion of Value x Time
1	1.36	1.24	0.1480	0.1480
2	1.36	1.12	0.1345	0.2690
3	1.36	1.02	0.1223	0.3668
4	1.36	0.93	0.1112	0.4446
5	1.36	0.84	0.1011	0.5053
6	1.36	0.77	0.9019	0.5512
7	1.36	0.70	0.0835	0.5846
8	1.36	0.63	0.0759	0.6074
9	1.36	0.58	0.0690	0.6212
10	1.36	0.52	0.0627	0.6275
Totals	13.60	8.36	1.00	4.725

Hedge ratio = Duration of project ÷ duration of debt
             = 4.074 ÷ 4.725 = 0.862

6.

Semi-annual T-Bill yield = $(1.0665)^{1/2}$ = 3.27%

Semi-annual dividend yield = 3.5% ÷ 2 = 1.75%

Completing the formula, we have:

Futures price = [252.50 ÷ (1.0375)] = 244.50
Expected spot price = Futures price – PV (dividends)
             = 252.50 – [(252.50 x .0175) ÷ 1.0327]
             = 252.50 – 4.28 = 248.22

The numbers are consistent. After trading costs are considered, the differential that exists is next to zero. That is, no arbitrage profits exist.

7.

Forward interest rate = $[(1 + 3\text{-year spot rate})^3 ÷ (1 + 1\text{-year spot rate})] - 1$

= $[(1.16)^3 ÷ 1.10] - 1 = 41.9\%$

8.

	Year 0		Years 1-4		Year 5	
	$	DM	$	DM	$	DM
Issue dollar notes	+25	0	-3.0	0	-28.0	0
Swap $s for DMs	-25	13.51	+3.0	-1.35	+28.0	-14.85
Net cash flows	0	13.51	0	-1.35	0	-14.85

MPG made a 12 percent loan a 9.89 percent loan by engaging in the swap: $[(14.85 \div 13.51) - 1] =$ 9.89%

CHAPTER 26
LEASING

INTRODUCTION

Almost all this chapter's major points focus on financial leases, that is, leases that extend over almost all of an asset's estimated economic life and that are noncancellable by the lessee or cancellable only if the lessor is reimbursed for expected losses arising from foregone income. The list of important things to know is contained in the summary. A continuing comparison between leasing and borrowing is made as financing alternatives.

WHAT TO LOOK FOR IN CHAPTER 26

The central focus of this chapter is the valuation of a lease to determine whether and to what extent it tends to enhance the value of the firm. The decision rule which emerges is: A financial lease is superior to buying and borrowing if the financing provided by the lease exceeds the present value of the liability it creates. That's it.

Terms to Know: Before you embark on an analysis of leases, you must know a variety of terms: lessor; lessee; operating leases; financial leases; full-service leases; net leases; direct leases; leveraged leases, and as if that were not enough, the sale and lease-back arrangement, to mention some.

Some Background Ideas: Financial leases are studied in depth because they are a source of financing, they displace debt, and all other leases may be analyzed in exactly the same way. With financial leases the lessee (the user) assumes the risks and rewards of ownership.

On the path to determining how to analyze a lease, you discovered that sometimes it makes a difference who owns the assets: when the lease expires, the owner obtains its salvage value; when bankruptcy and reorganization occur, the lessee loses the asset's use whereas the lessor does not.
The Internal Revenue Service and the accounting profession must be given their due when structuring leases and reporting them to the investing public. Regardless of the reporting or recording method used, the value of the firm will not be materially affected if capital markets are efficient.

When Leasing Pays: Typically, leasing pays: when the asset is needed only for a short period; cancellation options are available; maintenance is more easily provided by a lessor; standardized and low administrative and transaction costs are better provided by the lessor; the alternative minimum tax is to be avoided; or lessors can make better use of the tax shields arising from depreciation and investment tax credits.

Evaluation: The evaluation of financial leases assumes the same format as the evaluation of any other asset: the direct cash flows are discounted at a tax-adjusted rate appropriate to the level of risk, which is typically assumed to be the firm's present borrowing rate. The present borrowing rate is used because the lease displaces debt in the company's financial structure but has no effect on the required amount of equity financing.

Financial leases may be evaluated in one of two ways, each of which gives the same answer: (1) the easy way is to discount the lease cash flows at the after-tax interest rate that the firm would pay on an equivalent loan; (2) the hard way is to construct a table that indicates the equivalent loan needed to purchase the equipment and service the debt.

Leasing is preferable to buying and borrowing when: (1) the financing generated by the lease exceeds the financing that could have been generated by an equivalent loan or (2) the lease's adjusted present value if positive.

WORKED EXAMPLES

PROBLEM 1: LEASE EVALUATION

What-Not, Inc. is evaluating the lease of a minicomputer which if purchased would cost $150,000. Its estimated useful life is 5 years, at the end of which time it will be obsolete. The annual lease payments are $35,000. The company is in the 34 percent marginal income tax bracket. Set up a statement of cash flow consequences of the lease contract.

SOLUTION

What you want to is determine, line-by-line, the cash flows in each of the years, as contained in Table 26-1. The upper portion of the table contains the data that pertain to the analysis. The bottom portion of the table contains information used to answer some of the following questions. Note that the depreciation schedule is contained in that portion of the table (from Table 6-5, page 102 in the text).

Table 26-1
Cash flow consequences of lease contract (Value of lease to lessee)

| | Year | | | | | |
	0	1	2	3	4	5
Cost of computer	150					
Lost depreciation tax shield	-10.20	-16.32	- 9.79	- 5.88	- 5.88	- 2.94
Lease payment	-35.00	-35.00	-35.00	-35.00	-35.00	-35.00
Tax shield of lease payment	11.90	11.90	11.90	11.90	11.90	11.90
Cash flow of lease	116.70	-39.42	-32.89	-28.98	-28.98	-26.04
NPV	-10.27					
Tax depreciation rate on cost	0.2000	0.3200	0.1920	0.1152	0.1152	0.0576
Required return	12.00%					
Marginal tax rate	34.00%					
After-tax discount rate	7.92%					
Discount factor	1.0000	1.0792	1.1647	1.2569	1.3565	1.4639
PV	116.70	-36.53	-28.24	-23.05	-21.36	-17.79
Cumulative present value	116.70	80.17	51.93	28.88	7.52	-10.27

PROBLEM 2: NPV OF LEASE

If What-Not, Inc.'s before-tax borrowing rate on long-term debt is 12 percent, estimate the net present value (NPV) at 12 percent of the lease arrangement in problem 1.

SOLUTION

Because leasing displaces debt and the riskiness of the cash flows from leasing approximate the riskiness of the cash flows that would have been incurred had the firm borrowed, the current borrowing rate appears to be the appropriate rate at which to evaluate the lease. But it must be adjusted for taxes. That is, the discount rate is the after-tax borrowing rate. Note from that bottom portion of Table 26-1 that it is 7.92 percent. The arithmetic is:

$$NPV = \$116,700 - \$39,420/1.0792 - \$32,892/(1.0792)^2 - \$28,975/(1.0792)^3 -$$
$$\$28,975/(1.0792)^4 - \$26,038/(1.0792)^5$$

$$= \$116,700 - \$36,527 - \$28,241 - \$23,052 - \$21,361 - \$17,787$$

$$= -\$10,268$$

PROBLEM 3: EQUIVALENT LOAN: THE HARD WAY

"Okay, okay, I know what they mean about debt displacing debt. But what I really don't understand is how this equivalent loan stuff works. It looks like it is very important on the one hand and a lot of mumble-jumble on the other hand." As the financial manager, it is your task to lead this poor babe out of the woods of ignorance. What is your response?

SOLUTION

Begin by setting up a table similar to Table 26-2. Before you get to that point, however, you must determine how much you will need at the outset. The table differs from that in the text in that the upper part begins with the last year and ends with the beginning one. This is done because to determine how much will be needed at the beginning, we have to work from the amount left at the end.
The setup for the fifth year goes like this. Because a cash flow of $26.04 will be available to pay principal and after tax interest on an equivalent amount of borrowed money, formulate the problem thus:

$$
\begin{aligned}
\text{Cash Flow} &= PMT + (PMT)(r)(1 - T) \\
&= PMT\{1 + [(r)(1 - T)]\} \\
&= PMT\{1 + [(0.12)(0.66)]\} \\
\$26.04 &= PMT(1.0792) \\
PMT &= \$24.13
\end{aligned}
$$

The principal payment allowed by the cash flow is $24,130, and the remainder of $1.91 ($26.04 – $24.13) is used to make after-tax interest payments. The before-tax interest payment is $2.90 thousand [$1.91/(1 – T)].
Deriving the values for the fourth and other years is slightly more complicated. We know that the amount of cash available for after-tax interest and principal payments is $28.98 thousand. So the setup is:

$$\$28.98 = PMT + \text{loan}(r)(1 - T)$$

where the amount of the loan equals the amount of the principal payment in the previous period (period 5) and the payment to be made in this period, that is,
$\text{Loan} = PMT_{t-1} + PMT$

Substituting the dollar values we have

$$
\begin{aligned}
\text{Cash Flow} &= \text{PMT} + (\text{PMT}_{t-1} + \text{PMT})(r)(1 - T) \\
\$28.98 &= \text{PMT} + (\$24.13 + \text{PMT})(0.12)(0.66) \\
&= \text{PMT} + (\$24.13 + \text{PMT})(0.0792) \\
&= \text{PMT} + \$1.91 + \text{PMT}\ 0.0792 \\
&= 1.91 + 1.0792\ \text{PMT} \\
\$27.07 &= 1.0792\ \text{PMT} \\
\text{PMT} &= \$25.08
\end{aligned}
$$

The payment of principal in the fourth period is $25.08 thousand. The total cash available is $28.98 thousand, so the after-tax interest paid is $3.90 thousand ($28.98 – $25.08); the before-tax interest is $5.90 thousand ($3.37/0.66). The remaining columns are set up in the same way as year 4.

The middle part of Table 26-3 contains results from using a microcomputer spreadsheet. All the formulas are set up in the interior of the table. Then the required return, tax rate, and cash flows are referenced. The initial amount borrowed, in this case $126.97, is derived from the upper portion of the table.

The data may be subjected to sensitivity analysis by changing the interest rates, for example, with a new estimate of the loan analysis. For example, if the required return were 10 percent, the equivalent loan is easily determined to be $131.2 thousand. At 16 percent the equivalent loan is $119.16. (The "Totals" column is for data checking.)

Table 26-2 Equivalent Loan Analysis

Required return	12.00%
Marginal tax rate	34.00%
After-tax discount rate	7.92%

(Reference items for spreadsheet analysis)

				Year			
	5	4	3	2	1	0	Totals
Cash flow	-26.04	-28.98	-28.98	-32.89	-39.42		-156.30
Interest							
Before taxes	- 2.90	- 5.90	-8.69	-11.71	-15.24		- 44.44
After taxes	- 1.91	- 3.90	- 5.74	- 7.73	-10.06		- 29.33
Principal repaid	-24.13	-25.08	-23.24	-25.16	-29.36	-126.97	
Total payments	-26.04	-28.98	-28.98	-32.89	-39.42		-156.30
Debt outstanding equivalent loan	-24.13	-25.08	-23.24	-25.16	-29.36	-126.97	

				Year			
	0	1	2	3	4	5	Totals
Amount borrowed at year end	126.97	87.55	54.66	25.68	-3.29	-29.33	
Interest paid	0.00	-15.24	-10.51	-6.56	-3.08	0.40	- 34.99
Interest tax shield	0.00	5.18	3.57	2.23	1.05	-0.13	11.90
Interest paid after tax	0.00	-10.06	-6.93	-4.33	-2.03	0.26	- 23.09
Principal repaid	0.00	-29.36	-25.96	-24.65	-26.94	-26.30	133.21
Net cash flow of equivalent loan	0.00	-39.42	-32.89	-28.98	-28.98	-26.04	-156.30

				Year			
	0	1	2	3	4	5	Totals
Cash flow of lease	116.70	-39.42	-32.89	-28.98	-28.98	-26.04	-39.60
Net cash flow of equivalent loan	126.97	-39.42	-32.89	-28.98	-28.98	-26.04	-29.33
Difference	-10.27	0.00	0.00	0.00	0.00	0.00	-10.27

PROBLEM 4: COMPARING LEASE AND EQUIVALENT LOAN

"Hey, that's the hard way. Why not use the easy way? You'd get the same answer wouldn't you?"

SOLUTION

The lowest portion of Table 26-2 contains the after-tax cash flows. Indeed, the sum of the lease cash flows when discounted at the after-tax rate equals the equivalent loan cash flows.

PROBLEM 5: WHEN LEASING PAYS
Another director wants to know the value of the lease to the lessor.

SOLUTION
The cash flows to the lessor are the same as those to the lessee except the signs are different. The setup is identical to problem 2, but with the signs reversed. The NPV to the computer manufacturer is $10.27 thousand.

PROBLEM 6: VALUE OF LEASE WHEN TAX RATES DIFFER
Assume the lessee's tax rate is zero. What value is the deal to her?

SOLUTION
Table 26-3 shows that the results are slightly worse.

Table 26-3
Cash flow consequences of lease contract

				Year		
	0	1	2	3	4	5
Cost of computer	150					
Lost depreciation tax shield	0.00	0.00	0.00	0.00	0.00	0.00
Lease payment	-35.00	-35.00	-35.00	-35.00	-35.00	-35.00
Tax shield of lease payment	0.00	0.00	0.00	0.00	0.00	0.00
Cash flow of lease	115.00	-35.00	-35.00	-35.00	-35.00	-35.00
NPV	-11.17					
Tax depreciation rate on cost	0.2000	0.3200	0.1920	0.1152	0.1152	0.0576
Required return	12.00%					
Marginal tax rate	0.00%					
After-tax discount rate	12.00%					
Discount factor	1.0000	1.1200	1.2544	1.4049	1.5735	1.7623
PV	115.00	-31.25	-27.90	-24.91	-22.24	-19.86
Cumulative present value	115.00	83.75	55.85	30.94	8.69	-11.17

SUMMARY

Some Fundamentals

1. Lessee: the user; lessor: legal owner.

2. Lessee promises to make a series of payments to lessor.

3. At end of lease period, equipment reverts to lessor.

4. Operating lease: short-term, cancellable at option of lessee.

5. Financial lease: noncancellable or cancellable with penalties; asset leased for most of useful life.

6. Source of financing, because lease displaces debt.

7. Full service lease: lessor maintains, insures, and pays taxes on equipment.

8. Sale and lease-back: firm sells and leases it back from buyer.

9. Leverage lease: financial lease; lessor borrows part of purchase price; uses the leased equipment as collateral.

10. Example: Graymore Bus Line's lease-or-buy bus decision. Work out the net cash flows from the leasing decisions, taking into account:
    a. Cost
    b. Lease payments
    c. Tax shield of the lease payments
    d. Lost depreciation tax shield

11. Who really owns the leased asset?
    a. Lawyers and accountants say: lessor.
    b. Financial economists say: user.

12. Leasing and the Internal Revenue Service. Be careful how the lease is structured so that the benefits to both parties are clear.

13. Leasing and the accountants.
    a. Off-balance-sheet financing of major leases is no longer allowed.
    b. Leases must be capitalized and their estimated present values carried as an asset and a liability.
    c. The issue of substance: Are financial analysts or the financial community in general fooled by accounting manipulations? Answer: not likely to be fooled if markets are highly, not perfectly, efficient.

Why Lease?

1. Some sensible reasons:
   a. Convenient.
   b. Cancellation options are valuable.
   c. Maintenance is provided.
   d. Standardization leads to low administration and transactions costs.
   e. Tax shields may be advantageous.
   f. Avoiding alternative minimum tax.

2. Some dubious reasons:
   a. Affects book income positively (can the marketplace for assets be fooled?)
   b. Avoid capital expenditure controls (for how long?)
   c. Preserves capital (a debt equivalent?)

Valuing Financial Leases

1. The first pass
   a. Direct cash flows are assumed safe and are discounted at the firm's long-term borrowing rate.
   b. Tax shields may be more risky and therefore should be evaluated at a higher rate.
   c. Using separate discount rates for each cash flow is technically correct but may be unduly complicated; use a single rate, the after-tax rate of interest paid if firm had borrowed instead of leased.
   d. Find NPV of the estimated cash flows. If positive, accept; if negative, reject.
   e. Financial leases displace debt (and must be accounted for).

2. Calculating the equivalent loan: making the buy or borrow decision
   a. Equivalent loan: a loan that exactly matches the lease liability at each point in time, i.e., commits the firm to exactly the same cash outflows as the lease would.
   b. Equivalent loan depends on the lease liability, i.e., on the present value of the cash outflows of the lease.

3. Calculating the value of the lease:
   a. Compare the financing by the lease with the financing provided by the equivalent loan.

   $$\text{Value of lease} = \text{cash flows from leasing} - \text{cash flows from equivalent loan}$$

   b. Calculated by discounting the lease cash flows at the after-tax interest rate the firm would pay on an equivalent loan.

4. The story so far
   a. he principle: A financial lease is superior to buying and borrowing if the financing provided by the lease exceeds the present value of the liability created by the lease.
   b. The formula:

   $$\text{Net value of lease} = \text{initial financing provided} + \text{the present value of cash flows attributable to the lease when discounted at the after-tax required rate of return.}$$

   c. When subsidies arise, the adjusted net present value should be determined.

   $$\text{APV} = \text{NPV of subsidy} + \text{NPV of lease}$$

   (1) Applies to net financial leases.
   (2) Owner-offered maintenance increases NPV.
   (3) Lost salvage value decreases NPV.
   (4) Maintenance and salvage value flows are less predictable and require higher discount rates.

5. When leasing pays
   a. If all else were the same, the value to the lessor and lessee would be equal, and no net advantage would be present.
   b. Both lessor and lessee may be ahead, however, if their tax rates are different.
      (1) The lessor's tax rate exceeds the lessee's.
      (2) Depreciation tax shields are received early in the lease period.
      (3) The lease period is long and the lease payments are concentrated toward the end of the period.
      (4) The interest rate is high; zero or very small interest rates take away the tax incentives.

268

LIST OF TERMS

Capital leases
Direct lease
Equivalent loan
Financial lease
Full-service lease
Lease
Lessee (user)

Lessor (owner)
Leveraged leases
Net lease
Off-balance-sheet financing
Operating lease
Sale and lease-back

EXERCISES

Fill-in Questions

1. The user of a leased asset is called the _____, whereas the owner of a leased asset is called the _____.
2. Leases which are short-term and cancellable during the contract period at the option of the _____ are called _____ leases.
3. Leases which are long-term or extend over the economic life of the asset and which cannot be canceled or can be canceled only if the _____ is reimbursed for losses are called _____ leases.
4. When the lessors promise to maintain and insure the leased assets and pay property taxes on it, they have taken out a _____ lease.
5. When the _____ agrees to maintain the leased asset, insure it, and pay property taxes due on it, the lease is known as a net lease.
6. When the lessee identifies the equipment to be used and arranges for the leasing company to buy it from the manufacturer, the signed contract is called a _____ lease.
7. When a firm sells an asset it owns and leases it back to the buyer, the arrangement is known as _____.
8. When lessors borrow part of the purchase price of a leased asset and they use the lease contract as security for the loan, the entire financing scheme is known as a _____ lease.
9. Generally accepted accounting standards no longer allow _____ financing; rather lease payments of _____ leases must be _____, which is to say that the present value of the lease payments must be estimated and shown as debt on the right-hand side of the balance sheet.
10. An _____ is one that exactly matches the lease liability, or to put it another way, one which commits the firm to exactly the same cash outlays as a lease would.

Problems

1. What-If, Inc. decided to lease additional computer equipment for the next 5 years. The deal requires annual lease payments of $75,000. Had the equipment been purchased, it would have cost $325,000. The company's marginal tax bracket is 30 percent, and its long-term borrowing rate is 12 percent. Calculate the net present value of the lease and its equivalent loan.

2. What-If, Inc.'s second alternative required annual lease payments of $50,000 in years 0-4, and $200,000 in year 5. Evaluate this proposal using the data from problem 1.

3. A third alternative faced What-If, Inc., which was the same in all respects as that contained in problem 1 except the year-by-year lease payments are now $200,000 in year 0, and $50,000 thereafter. Evaluate this proposal and compare it with those in problems 1 and 2. Assume all other conditions are the same.

Essay Questions

1. How can it be said that financial leases are a source of financing? Explain fully.

2. What is meant by off-balance-sheet financing?

3. In what sense may lease payments be viewed as the equivalent of interest payments?

4. Some people say that long-term lease obligations should be regarded as debt, even though they may not appear on the balance sheet. What rationale can you give for this point of view?

5. List and explain some of the reasons that make leasing dubious, and provide an explanation for each item.

6. Usually the direct cash flows from the lease are assumed to be safe and are discounted at roughly the same rate of interest obtainable on a secured bond issued by the lessee. Why?

ANSWERS TO EXERCISES

Fill-in Questions

1. lessee; lessor
2. lessee; operating
3. lessor; financial
4. full-service
5. lessee
6. direct
7. sale and lease-back
8. leveraged
9. off-balance-sheet; financial; capitalized
10. equivalent loan

Problems

1., 2., and 3. Tables 26-5 - 26-7 illustrate the analyses. Note that the classic and compelling arguments for considering the time value of money are highlighted. The first case, Table 26-5, is the benchmark against which to compare the other two cases. In the second case, the sweetner offered is deferral of a substantial portion of the lease payments and turns a "no-go" deal into an accept deal, while all the other terms of the deal remain the same. The equivalent dollar amount of the loans are not dramatically different; it's the timing of the lease payments, and, therefore, the net cash flows that drives the analysis. As one might expect, the third alternative, with a $200 lease payment up front, is the worst deal because it makes a "no-go" deal even worse. True the equivalent loan is less. Because....?

Table 26-5
Cash flow consequences of lease contract

	Year					
	0	1	2	3	4	5
Cost of computer	325.00					
Lost depreciation tax shield	-19.50	-31.20	-18.72	-11.23	-11.23	- 5.62
Lease payment	-75.00	-75.00	-75.00	-75.00	-75.00	-75.00
Tax shield of lease payment	25.50	25.50	25.50	25.50	25.50	25.50
Cash flow of lease	256.00	-80.70	-68.22	-60.73	-60.73	-55.12
NPV	- 4.99					
Tax depreciation rate on cost	0.2000	0.3200	0.1920	0.1152	0.1152	0.0576
Required return	12.00%					
Marginal tax rate	30.00%					
After-tax discount	8.40%					
Discount factor	1.0000	1.0840	1.1751	1.2738	1.3808	1.4967
PV	256.00	-74.45	-58.06	-47.68	-43.98	-36.82
Cumulative present value	256.00	181.55	123.50	75.85	31.83	- 4.99

Table 26-5 (continued) Equivalent Loan Analysis

Required return	12.00%
Marginal tax rate	30.00%
After-tax discount rate	8.40%

(Reference items for spreadsheet analysis)

	Year						
	5	4	3	2	1	0	Totals
Cash Flow	-55.12	-60.73	-60.73	-68.22	-80.70		-325.50
Interest							
Before taxes	-6.10	-12.35	-18.12	-24.27	-31.32		-92.16
After taxes	-4.27	- 8.65	-12.68	-16.99	-21.92		-64.51
Principal repaid	-50.85	-52.09	-48.05	-51.23	-58.78		-260.99
Total payments	-55.12	-60.73	-60.73	-68.22	-80.70		-325.50
Debt outstanding equivalent loan	-50.85	-52.09	-48.05	-51.23	-58.78		-260.99

	Year						
	0	1	2	3	4	5	Totals
Amount borrowed at year end	260.99	180.29	112.07	51.34	-9.39	-64.51	
Interest paid	0.00	-31.32	-21.63	-13.45	-6.16	1.13	- 71.44
Interest tax shield	0.00	9.40	6.49	4.03	1.85	-0.34	21.43
Interest paid after tax	0.00	-21.92	-15.14	-9.41	-4.31	0.79	-50.01
Principal repaid	0.00	-58.78	-53.08	-51.32	-56.42	-55.90	275.49
Net cash flow of equivalent loan	0.00	-80.70	-68.22	-60.73	-60.73	-55.12	-325.50

	Year						
	0	1	2	3	4	5	Totals
Cash flow of lease	256.00	-80.70	-68.22	-60.73	-60.73	-55.12	-69.50
Net cash flow of equivalent loan	260.99	-80.70	-68.22	-60.73	-60.73	-55.12	-64.51
Difference	-4.99	0.00	0.00	0.00	0.00	0.00	-4.99

Table 26-6
Cash flow consequences of lease contract (Value of lease to lessee)

	Year					
	0	1	2	3	4	5
Cost of computer	325.00					
Lost depreciation tax shield	-19.50	-31.20	-18.72	-11.23	-11.23	-5.62
Lease payment	-50.00	-50.00	-50.00	-50.00	-50.00	-200.00
Tax shield of lease payment	17.00	17.00	17.00	17.00	17.00	68.00
Cash flow of lease	272.50	-64.20	-51.72	-44.23	-44.23	-137.62
NPV	10.56					
Tax depreciation rate on cost	0.2000	0.3200	0.1920	0.1152	0.1152	0.0576
Required return	12.00%					
Marginal tax rate	30.00%					
After-tax discount rate	8.40%					
Discount factor	1.0000	1.0840	1.1751	1.2738	1.3808	1.4967
PV	272.50	-59.23	-44.01	-34.73	-32.03	-91.94
Cumulative present value	272.50	213.27	169.26	134.53	102.50	10.56

Table 26-6 (continued) Equivalent Loan Analysis

Required return	12.00%
Marginal tax rate	30.00%
After-tax discount rate	8.40%

(Reference items for spreadsheet analysis)

	Year						
	5	4	3	2	1	0	Totals
Cash Flow	-137.62	-44.23	-44.23	-51.72	-64.20	-342.00	
Interest							
Before taxes	-15.23	-18.95	-22.38	-26.37	-31.43	-114.37	
After taxes	-10.66	-13.27	-15.66	-18.46	-22.00	-80.06	
Principal repaid	-126.95	-30.97	-28.57	-33.26	-42.20	-261.94	
Total payments	-137.62	-44.23	-44.23	-51.72	-64.20	-342.00	
Debt outstanding equivalent loan	-126.95	-30.97	-28.57	-33.26	-42.20	-261.94	

	Year						
	0	1	2	3	4	5	Totals
Amount borrowed at year end	261.94	197.74	146.02	101.79	57.56	-80.06	
Interest paid	0.00	-31.43	-23.73	-17.52	-12.22	-6.91	-91.81
Interest tax shield	0.00	9.43	7.12	5.26	3.66	2.07	27.54
Interest paid after tax	0.00	-22.00	-16.61	-12.27	-8.55	-4.84	-64.27
Principal repaid	0.00	-42.20	-35.11	-31.97	-35.68	-132.78	277.73
Net cash flow of equivalent loan	0.00	-64.20	-51.72	-44.23	-44.23	-137.62	-342.00

	Year						
	0	1	2	3	4	5	Totals
Cash flow of lease	272.50	-64.20	-51.72	-44.23	-44.23	-137.62	-69.50
Net cash flow of equivalent lease	261.94	-64.20	-51.72	-44.23	-44.23	-137.62	-80.06
Difference	10.56	0.00	0.00	0.00	0.00	0.00	10.56

Table 26-7
Cash flow consequences of lease contract (Value of lease to lessee)

	Year					
	0	1	2	3	4	5
Cost of computer	325.00					
Lost depreciation tax shield	- 19.50	-31.20	-18.72	-11.23	-11.23	- 5.62
Lease payment	-200.00	-50.00	-50.00	-50.00	-50.00	-50.00
Tax shield of lease payment	68.00	17.00	17.00	17.00	17.00	17.00
Cash flow of lease	173.50	-64.20	-51.72	-44.23	-44.23	-38.62
NPV	- 22.30					
Tax depreciation rate on cost	0.2000	0.3200	0.1920	0.1152	0.1152	0.0576
Required return	12.00%					
Marginal tax rate	30.00%					
After-tax discount rate	8.40%					
Discount factor	1.000	1.0840	1.1751	1.2738	1.3808	1.4967
PV	173.50	-59.23	-44.01	-34.73	-32.03	-25.80
Cumulative present value	173.50	114.27	70.26	35.53	3.50	-22.30

Table 26-7 (continued) Equivalent Loan Analysis

Required return	12.00%
Marginal tax rate	30.00%
After-tax discount rate	8.40%

(Reference items for spreadsheet analysis)

	Year						
	5	4	3	2	1	0	Totals
Cash Flow	-38.62	-44.23	-44.23	-51.72	-64.20		-243.00
Interest							
Before taxes	- 4.27	- 8.84	-13.05	-17.77	-23.50		-67.43
After taxes	- 2.99	-6.19	-9.14	-12.44	-16.45		-47.20
Principal repaid	-35.62	-38.04	-35.10	-39.28	-47.75		-195.80
Total payments	-38.62	-44.23	-44.23	-51.72	-64.20		-243.00
Debt outstanding equivalent loan	-35.62	-38.04	-35.10	-39.28	-47.75		-195.80

	Year						
	0	1	2	3	4	5	Totals
Amount borrowed at year end	195.80	131.60	79.88	35.65	-8.58	-47.20	
Interest paid	0.00	-23.50	-15.79	-9.59	-4.28	1.03	-52.12
Interest tax shield	0.00	7.05	4.74	2.88	1.28	-0.31	15.64
Interest paid after tax	0.00	-16.45	-11.05	-6.71	-2.99	0.72	-36.48
Principal repaid	0.00	-47.75	-40.67	-37.52	-41.24	-39.34	206.52
Net cash flow of equivalent loan	0.00	-64.20	-51.72	-44.23	-44.23	-38.62	-243.00

	Year						
	0	1	2	3	4	5	Totals
Cash flow of lease	173.50	-64.20	-51.72	-44.23	-44.23	-38.62	-69.50
Net cash flow of equivalent lease	195.80	-64.20	-51.72	-44.23	-44.23	-38.62	-47.20
Difference	-22.30	0.00	0.00	0.00	0.00	0.00	-22.30

CHAPTER 27
ANALYZING FINANCIAL PERFORMANCE

INTRODUCTION

This chapter shows us how to use a firm's financial data to analyze past performance and assess its current financial condition. Understanding the past usually helps us understand the future. The use of financial ratios is demonstrated and the limitations are discussed.

WHAT TO LOOK FOR IN CHAPTER 27

"Financial ratios are no substitute for a crystal ball," says it all. Such convenient summaries as ratios are always to be viewed with healthy skepticism. Four major classes of ratios help you ask the right questions about a firm's financial performance.

Leverage Ratios: These ratios tell us about a firm's financial leverage. Book values are often used in place of market values. Several debt ratios are used. No generally satisfactory measure of earnings variability exists, although all financial analysts try to get a handle on it.

Liquidity Ratios: These ratios attempt to measure the short-run ability of the firm to meet its current liabilities. Reserve borrowing power may mean more than any of these ratios.

Profitability or Efficiency Ratios: More ambiguity exists in these ratios than in any others. One ratio alone is likely to be misleading; the entire set and trends are likely to provide more insights. Most of these ratios measure the activity of the firm and its efficiency, the linkage of which helps to analyze a firm's potential.

Market Value Ratios: These are often used to measure a firm's performance. Some analysts prefer them to other performance measures precisely because they use market data and because capital markets send information to a firm's management.

Benchmarks: Ratios without benchmarks don't go anywhere. Among the options are: year-by-year for the same firm, one firm to a set of comparable firms, one firm to firms classified in the same industry, and industry-to-industry and one firm. Be cautious. Also be careful about which ratios you select; all ratios may be created equal, but some ratios are likely to be more equal than others.

The Earnings Record: Wouldn't you know it, earnings seem to follow a random walk. So think about the difficulty of forecasting tomorrow's earnings based on past years' earnings, especially using simple linear regression techniques. Some studies show that over 40 percent of a firm's total variation in income is ascribable to the combined effects of variations in aggregate corporate income and industry income. Also, be aware that accounting numbers may be suspect because of the various methods of calculating them and the potential distortions caused by inflation.

Applications of Financial Analysis: Financial analysis is used to evaluate the creditworthiness of borrowers. Evidence suggests that failed firms tended to have identifiable financial characteristics peculiar to themselves several years before they actually failed. Credit analysis of bonds indicates that financial analysis predicts a large percentage of bond ratings. Financial ratios were used successfully to estimate a firm's market-related risk.

WORKED EXAMPLES

PROBLEM 1: FINANCIAL RATIOS
For 1988 make a thorough financial ratio analysis of Universal Paperclips, Inc. Use the data in Table 27-1.

Table 27-1
Universal Paperclips, Inc.

	1988	1987
Balance Sheet		
Cash & short-term securities	100	75
Receivables	350	300
Inventories	600	650
Other current assets	100	75
Total current assets	1150	1100
Plant and equipment	1100	850
Other long-term assets	150	100
Total assets	2400	2050
Current liabilities	550	450
Long-term debt and capital leases	375	425
Other long-term liabilities	225	175
Shareholder's equity	1250	1000
Total liabilities	2400	2050
Net working capital	600	650
Income Statement		
Net sales	3465	3119
Cost of goods sold	2252	2119
Other expenses	346	314
Other income	123	111
Earnings before interest and tax (EBIT)	990	797
Interest	85	80
Tax	308	244
Net income	597	473

Other Financial Information

Depreciation	77
Current cost of inventories	750
Current cost of plant and equipment	1925
Market value of equity	6675
Market value of equity plus other liabilities	7825
Average number of shares	100
Dividends per share	1.80
Earnings per share	5.97
Share price	66.75
Average equity per share	11.25
Current cost of all assets	3375

SOLUTION

1. Leverage ratios

   a.

   $$\text{Debt ratio} = (\$375 + \$225) \div (\$375 + \$225 + \$1250)$$
   $$= 32.4 \text{ percent}$$

   b.

   $$\text{Debt-equity ratio} = (\$375 + \$225) \div \$1250$$
   $$= 48.0 \text{ percent}$$

   c.

   $$\text{Times interest earned} = (\$990 + \$77) \div \$85$$
   $$= 12.6 \text{ times}$$

2. Liquidity ratios

   a.

   $$\text{Net working capital to total assets} = (\$1150 - \$550) \div \$2400$$
   $$= 25.0\%$$

   b. Current $= \$1150/\$550 = 2.09$

   c. Quick $= (\$100 + \$350) \div \$550 = 0.82$

   d. Cash $= \$100/\$550 = 0.18$

   e.

   $$\text{Interval measure} = (\$100 + \$350) \div [(\$2252 + \$346) \div 365]$$
   $$= 66.2 \text{ days}$$

3. Profitability or efficiency ratios

   a.

   $$\text{Sales to total assets} = \$3465 \div (\$2400 + \$2050) \div 2$$
   $$= 1.56$$

b.

$$\text{Sales to net working capital} = \$3465 + (\$600 + \$650) + 2$$
$$= 5.54$$

c.

$$\text{Net profit margin} = (\$990 - \$308) + \$3465$$
$$= 19.7 \text{ percent}$$

d.

$$\text{Inventory turnover} = \$2252 + (\$600 + \$650) + 2$$
$$= 3.6$$

e.

$$\text{Average collection period} = [(\$350 + \$300)] + [2 + (\$3465 + 365)]$$
$$= 34.2 \text{ days}$$

f.

$$\text{Return on total assets} = \$990 - \$308 + (\$2400 + \$2050) + 2$$
$$= 30.7 \text{ percent}$$

g.

$$\text{Return on equity} = \$597 + (\$1250 + \$1000) + 2$$
$$= 53.1 \text{ percent}$$

h. Payout = \$1.80/\$5.97 = 30.2 percent

   (1) Plowback = 1 − 0.302 = 69.8 percent

   (2) Growth in equity from plowback $= [(\$5.97 - \$1.80) + \$5.97 \times (\$5.97 + \$11.25)]$
$$= 37.1 \text{ percent}$$

4. Market value ratios

   a. Price-earnings = \$66.75 + \$5.97 = 11.2 times

   b. Dividend yield = \$1.80 + \$66.75 = 2.70%

   c. Market-to-book = \$66.75 + (\$1250 + 100) = 5.3 times

   d.
   Tobin's q $= [(\$2400 - \$1250) + (100 \times \$66.75)] + (\$750 + \$1925 + \$100 + \$350 + \$100 + \$150)$
$$= (\$1150 + \$6675) + \$3375$$
$$= \$7825 + \$3125 = 2.3$$

PROBLEM 2: FINANCIAL RATIOS

Table 27-2 contains financial data for Number Crunchers, Inc., manufacturer of the world-famous Swift-Calcs-NPV calculators. Calculate a complete set of financial ratios for the company and make a statement about the financial soundness of the firm.

Table 27-2
Number Crunchers, Inc.

	1988	1987
Balance Sheet		
Cash & short-term securities	125	75
Receivables	438	300
Inventories	750	650
Other current assets	125	75
Total current assets	1438	1100
Plant and equipment	1375	850
Other long-term assets	188	100
Total assets	3001	2050
Current liabilities	715	450
Long-term debt and capital leases	488	425
Other long-term liabilities	293	175
Shareholder's equity	1505	1000
Total liabilities	3001	2050
Net working capital	723	650
Income Statement		
Net sales	3985	3586
Cost of goods sold	2815	2590
Other expenses	484	436
Other income	111	84
Earnings before interest and tax (EBIT)	575	655
Interest	179	126
Tax	135	180
Net income	261	349

Other Financial Information

Depreciation	96
Current cost of inventories	938
Current cost of plant and equipment	2406
Market value of equity	2485
Market value of equity plus other liabilities	3981
Average number of shares	70
Dividends per share	1.80
Earnings per share	3.73
Share price	35.50
Average equity per share	12.53
Current cost of all assets	4220

SOLUTION

First calculate the ratios contained in the summary of this chapter of the *Study Guide*. The results are shown in Table 27-3. Also shown are data for the firm's past 5 years of operations and for the industry. The last two columns show deviations from the 5-year average and from the industry. Although hardly conclusive, these comparisons suggest that the company is doing okay, not much better on average, and not much worse.

Table 27-3
Number Crunchers, Inc.

	1988	Prior 5-year Average	Industry Average Average	Deviations from Firm Average	Industry
Leverage ratios					
Debt ratio	34.2%	37.6%	30.7%	3.4%	-3.5%
Debt-equity ratio	51.9%	57.0%	60.0%	5.1%	8.1%
Times interest earned	3.7	4.1	7.1	0.4	3.4
Liquidity ratios					
Net working capital to total assets	24.09%	0.22	0.3	-2.09%	5.91%
Current	2.01	2.25	2.35	0.24	0.34
Quick	0.79	0.83	1.01	0.04	0.22
Cash	0.17	0.17	0.24	0.00	0.07
Interval measure	62.30	54.8	110.10	-7.50	47.80
Profitability or efficiency ratios					
Sales to total assets	1.58	1.63	1.34	0.05	-0.24
Sales to net working capital	5.51	5.52	4.23	0.01	-1.28
Net profit margin	11.0%	11.5%	10.3%	0.5%	-0.7%
Inventory turnover	4.0	3.8	3.4	-0.2	-0.6
Average collection period	33.8	35.1	31.6	1.3	-2.2
Return on total assets	17.4%	19.9%	17.9%	2.5%	0.5%
Return on equity	20.8%	21.3%	19.2%	0.5%	-1.6%
Payout	48.3%	54.7%	52.4%	6.4%	4.1%
Plowback	51.7%	45.3%	47.6%	-6.4%	-4.1%
Growth in equity from plowback	15.4%	10.9%	11.3%	-4.5%	-4.1%
Market value ratios					
Price earnings	9.5	14.4	10.5	4.9	1.0
Dividend Yield	5.07%	3.01%	4.32%	-2.06%	-0.75%
Market to book	2.4	4.7	3.5	2.3	1.1
Tobin's q	0.94	1.02	1.50	0.08	0.56

SUMMARY

Financial Analysis

1. The use of financial data and ratios to analyze past performance and to assess current financial standing and to help plan for the future.
2. Financial ratios seldom provide answers. More often than not they provide the basis for asking questions.
3. No international standards exist for financial ratios.
4. Be selective in your use of financial ratios.

Financial Ratios

1. Leverage ratios: summarize financial leverage

    a. Debt ratio = (long-term debt + value of leases) ÷ (long-term debt + value of leases + equity)

    b. Debt-equity ratio = (long-term debt + value of leases) ÷ equity

    c. Times interest earned = (EBIT + depreciation) ÷ interest

2. Liquidity ratios: measure short-term financial position

    a. Net working capital to total assets = net working capital ÷ total assets

    b. Current = current assets ÷ current liabilities

    c. Quick = (cash + marketable securities + receivables) ÷ current liabilities

    d. Cash = (cash + marketable securities) ÷ current liabilities

    e. Interval measure = (cash + marketable securities + receivables) ÷ average daily expenditures from operations

3. Profitability or efficiency ratios

    a. Sales to total assets = sales ÷ average total assets

    b. Sales to net working capital = sales ÷ average net working capital

    c. Net profit margin = (EBIT – tax) ÷ sales

    d. Inventory turnover = cost of goods sold ÷ average inventory

    e. Average collection period = average receivables ÷ average daily sales

    f. Return on total assets = (EBIT – taxes) ÷ average total assets

    g. Return on equity = earnings available for common ÷ average equity

    h. Linkage among return on assets, sales-to-assets, and net profit margin

    Income ÷ Assets = (sales ÷ assets) x (income ÷ sales)

    i. Payout ratio = dividend per share ÷ earnings per share

    (1) Plowback = 1 – payout ratio = (earnings – dividends) ÷ earnings

    (2) Growth in equity from plowback = [(earnings – dividends)] ÷ earnings x (earnings ÷ equity)

4. Market value ratios

   a.

   $$\text{Price-earnings ratio} = \text{stock price} \div \text{earnings per share}$$
   $$= (\text{DIV}_1 \div \text{EPS}_1) \times (1 \div r - g)$$

   b.

   $$\text{Dividend yield} = \text{Dividend per share} \div \text{stock price}$$
   $$= \text{DIV}_1 \div P_0 = r - g$$

   c. Market-to-book = stock price $\div$ book value per share

   d. Tobin's q = market value of assets $\div$ estimated replacement cost

5. Benchmarks
   a. Year-to-year for the same firm
   b. Use a set of comparable firms

The Earnings Record

1. Look for systematic changes in income stemming from changes in aggregate corporate profits.
2. Earnings generally follow a random walk.
   a. Past growth may be estimate of future growth.
   b. Trend line analysis may not help.
*3. Meaning of accounting earnings:
   a. Economists' definition of income: cash flow plus change in value of firm.
   b. Accounting numbers may be biased and tend to focus on long-run average profitability.
   c. Accounting earnings are not likely to capture economic earnings.
   d. Must normalize earnings.
4. How inflation affects book returns:
   a. Increases nominal value of work-in-process and finished-goods inventory.
   b. May give rise to inventory profits.
   c. Book value of fixed assets may have little correspondence to replacement value.

Applications of Financial Analysis

1. Using financial ratios in credit analysis.
   a. Failed firms had financial ratios generally inferior to those of survivors.
   b. Financial weaknesses were observable as much as 5 years before failure.
2. Using financial ratios to estimate market risk.
   a. Accounting betas using changes in company earnings with respect to aggregate earnings.
   b. Accounting and market factors together tend to give better estimates of risk than either alone.
3. Financial ratios seem to be reasonably good predictors of bond ratings.

LIST OF TERMS

Average collection period

Current assets

Current liabilities

Current ratio

Debt ratio

Debt-equity ratio

Dividend yield

Inflation premium

Inventory profit

Leverage ratio

Net profit margin

Net working capital

Payout ratio

Price-earnings ratio

Quick ratio

Random walk

Return on equity (ROE)

Return on total assets (ROA)

Sales to assets ratio

Tobin's *q*

EXERCISES

Fill-in Questions

1. The difference between current assets and current liabilities is called _____.
2. _____ measure the firm's financial leverage.
3. Long-term debt and the value of leases are included in the (numerator, denominator) _____ of both the _____ ratio and the _____ ratio.
4. Times interest earned is a (liquidity, profitability, leverage) _____ ratio.
5. Assets which are either in cash or will be turned into cash in the near future are called _____.
6. Liabilities which are to be paid in the near future are called _____.
7. The _____ ratio is the same as the _____ ratio except inventories and "other current assets" are dropped from the numerator.
8. The extent to which a firm's assets are being turned over is captured by the _____ ratio.
9. _____ measures the percent of sales which finds its way into profits.
10. The speed with which customers pay their bills is measured by the _____.
11. One overall measure of financial performance is captured by the _____ ratio.
12. The _____ ratio is computed by relating earnings available to common to (average, ending, beginning) _____ equity.
13. Nuts, Inc.'s cash dividend per share was $2.40 and its earnings per share were $6.20, so its _____ ratio was 38.7 percent. Nuts, Inc.'s market price per share is $75.25, so its _____ ratio is 12.14 times and its _____ is 3.19 percent.
14. If Nuts, Inc.'s equities and liabilities have a market value of $175 million and a replacement cost of $160 million, its _____ is 1.09.
15. As with share prices, earnings seem to follow a _____; there is almost no relationship between a company's earnings growth in one period and the rest.
16. If finished goods that would have produced a profit of $1000 are sold at prices to reflect a 10 percent inflation rate, the incremental gain is called _____ and is $ _____.

Problems

1. For 1988 make a thorough financial ratio analysis of Terrific!, Inc. Use the data in Table 27-3.

Table 27-3

Terrific!, Inc.

	1988	1987
Balance Sheet		
Cash & short-term securities	150	135
Receivables	481	433
Inventories	863	776
Other current assets	113	101
Total current assets	1607	1445
Plant and equipment	1856	1671
Other long-term assets	375	338
Total assets	3838	3454
Current liabilities	715	644
Long-term debt and capital leases	975	878
Other long-term liabilities	229	206
Shareholder's equity	1919	1727
Total liabilities	3838	3455
Net working capital	892	801
Income Statement		
Net sales	5757	5181
Cost of goods sold	4030	3708
Other expenses	576	518
Other income	80	68
Earnings before interest and tax (EBIT)	1231	1024
Interest	230	207
Tax	340	278
Net income	661	539

Other Financial Information

Depreciation	130
Current cost of inventories	1035
Current cost of plant and equipment	4909
Market value of equity	8641
Market value of equity plus other liabilities	10,560
Average number of shares	155
Dividends per share	0.80
Earnings per share	4.26
Share price	55.75
Average equity per share	18.23
Current cost of all assets	7063

2. Table 27-4 contains financial data for Not-So-Hot, Inc., manufacturer of the Slow-Calc-Payback calculators. Calculate a complete set of financial ratios for the company and make a statement about the financial soundness of the firm.

Table 27-4
Not-So-Hot, Inc.

	1988	1987
Balance Sheet		
Cash & short-term securities	180	162
Receivables	529	476
Inventories	992	893
Other current assets	101	91
Total current assets	1802	1622
Plant and equipment	2506	2255
Other long-term assets	750	675
Total assets	5058	4552
Current liabilities	715	644
Long-term debt and capital leases	2195	1976
Other long-term liabilities	229	206
Shareholder's equity	1919	1727
Total liabilities	5058	4553
Net working capital	1087	978
Income Statement		
Net sales	6575	5918
Cost of goods sold	5918	5444
Other expenses	658	592
Other income	23	20
Earnings before interest and tax (EBIT)	23	-99
Interest	377	339
Tax	-120	-149
Net income	-234	-289

Other Financial Information

Depreciation	175
Current cost of inventories	1091
Current cost of plant and equipment	3907
Market value of equity	956
Market value of equity plus other liabilities	4095
Average number of shares	98
Dividends per share	2.40
Earnings per share	-2.39
Share price	9.75
Average equity per share	18.23
Current cost of all assets	6558

Essay Questions

1. To what purposes are leverage ratios put?
2. How might unused borrowing ability affect the interpretation of liquidity ratios that do not compare well with reasonable benchmarks?
3. "As near as I can judge, Brealey and Myers are less than excited with the profitability ratios. Yet I hear business types talking about ROA (you know, return on assets) and ROE (return on equity) as if some real magic were at work. How comes these guys don't care much for those ratios? And if they don't care much for them, how come we have to spend so much time computing them? That's what I want to know!" You are the instructor in the class. What do you say?
4. Explain the linkage between return on assets, the sales to total assets ratio, and the net profit margin ratio.
5. What connection is there among the payout ratio, plowback, return on equity and growth in equity? Explain fully.
6. What is the financial significance of the expression, $r - g$?
7. You are a newly hired financial analyst at an investment firm specializing in genetic engineering companies. Your first task is to review all the studies the firm produced and to recommend a system by which to compare individual companies. You are somewhat perplexed because the "industry" is not well-defined and most of the companies are new and small and do not have any earnings. What do you do? Do the ratios contained in the text help? Explain fully.
8. "Geez! These finance types have gotta be weird. First, they tell ya that stock prices follow a random walk. Now they tell ya that earnings also follow a random walk. Don't try to predict share prices on the one hand, and don't try to predict earnings on the other hand! Earnings determine the value of share prices. Share prices determine the value of the firm. Ya can't predict none of this stuff. So what does a financial manager do, lie down and die?" What response do you present to this ill-begotten notion? Do financial managers have any control over the financial destiny of their firms?

ANSWERS TO EXERCISES

Fill-in Questions

1. net working capital
2. leverage ratios
3. numerator; debt; debt-equity
4. leverage

5. current assets
6. current liabilities
7. quick; current
8. sales to assets
9. net profit margin
10. average collection period
11. return on total assets
12. return on equity; average
13. payout; price-earnings; dividend yield
14. Tobin's q
15. random walk
16. inventory profit; $100

Problems

Terrific!, Inc.

1. Leverage ratios

    a.

    $$\text{Debt ratio} = (\$975 + \$229) \div (\$975 + \$229 + \$1919)$$
    $$= 38.6 \text{ percent}$$

    b.

    $$\text{Debt-equity ratio} = (\$975 + \$229) \div \$1919$$
    $$= 62.7 \text{ percent}$$

    c.

    $$\text{Times interest earned} = (\$1231 + \$130) \div \$230$$
    $$= 5.9 \text{ times}$$

2. Liquidity ratios

    a.

    $$\text{Net working capital to total assets} = (\$1606 - \$715) \div \$3838$$
    $$= 0.23$$

    b. Current = $1606 \div $715 = 2.25

    c. Quick = ($150 + $481) \div $715 = 0.88

    d. Cash = $150 \div $715 = 0.21

    e.

    $$\text{Interval measure} = (\$150 + \$481) \div [(\$4030 + \$576) \div 365]$$
    $$= 50.0 \text{ days}$$

3. Profitability ratios

    a.

    $$\text{Sales to total assets} = \$5757 \div [(\$3838 + \$3454) \div 2]$$
    $$= 1.58$$

b.

    Sales to net working capital $= \$5757 + [(\$891 + \$802) + 2]$
                               $= 6.8$

c.

    Net profit margin $= (\$1231 - \$340) + \$5757$
                      $= 15.5$ percent

d.

    Inventory turnover $= \$4030 + [(\$863 + \$776) + 2]$
                      $= 4.9$ times

e.

    Average collection period $= [(\$481 + \$433) + 2] + (\$5757 + 365)$
                             $= 29.0$ days

f.

    Return on total assets $= (\$1231 - \$340) + [(\$3838 + \$3454) + 2]$
                          $= 24.4$ percent

g.

    Return on equity $= \$661 + [(\$1919 + \$1727) + 2]$
                     $= 36.3$ percent

h. Payout $= \$0.80 + \$4.26 = 18.8$ percent

    (1) Plowback $= 1 - 0.188 = 81.2$ percent

    (2) Implied growth from plowback $= (\$4.26 - \$0.80) + \$4.26 \times (\$4.26 + \$18.23) = 19.0$ percent

4. Market value ratios

    a. Price-earnings $= \$55.75 + \$ 4.26 = 13.1$ times

    b. Dividend yield $= \$ 0.80 + \$55.75 = 1.44$ percent

    c. Market-to-book $= \$ 55.75 + (\$1919 + 155) = 4.50$

    d. Tobin's q = [(market value of equity + current liabilities + long-term debt and capital leases + other long-debt)] + (cash + receivables + other current assets + other long-term assets + current cost of inventories + current cost of plant and equipment)

        $= (\$8,641 + \$715 + \$975 + \$229) + (\$150 + \$481 + \$113 + \$375 + \$1,035 + \$4,909)$
        $= \$10,560 + \$7,063 = 1.50$

Table 27-4
Not-So-Hot, Inc.

	1988	Prior 5-year Average	Industry Average Average	Deviations from Firm Average	Industry
Leverage ratios					
Debt ratio	55.8%	61.4%	54.6%	5.6%	-1.2%
Debt-equity ratio	126.3%	139.0%	123.7%	12.7%	-2.6%
Times interest earned	0.5	0.6	0.5	0.1	0.0
Liquidity ratios					
Net working capital to total assets	21.49%	0.22	0.3	0.51%	8.51%
Current	2.52	2.25	2.70	-0.27	0.18
Quick	0.99	0.99	1.19	0.00	0.20
Cash	0.25	0.25	0.30	0.00	0.05
Interval measure	39.4	44.1	52.9	4.7	13.5
Profitability or efficiency ratios					
Sales to total assets	1.37	1.63	1.96	0.26	0.59
Sales to net working capital	6.05	6.06	7.27	0.01	1.22
Net profit margin	2.2%	1.7%	156.0%	-0.5%	153.8%
Inventory turnover	6.3	3.8	3.4	-2.5	-2.9
Average collection period	27.9	25.1	22.3	-2.8	-5.6
Return on total assets	3.0%	19.9%	17.9%	16.9%	14.9%
Return on equity	-12.8%	21.3%	19.2%	34.1%	32.0%
Payout	-100.4%	82.5%	112.5%	182.9%	212.9%
Plowback	200.4%	17.5%	-12.5%	-182.9%	-212.9%
Growth in equity from plowback	-26.3%	3.8%	11.3%	30.1%	37.6%
Market value ratios					
Price earnings	-4.1	14.4	12.5	18.5	16.6
Dividend Yield	24.62%	3.01%	3.23%	-21.61%	-21.39%
Market to book	0.5	4.4	3.5	3.9	3.0
Tobin's q	0.62	0.70	0.63	0.08	0.01

Conclusion regarding the firm's financial condition: not so hot.

CHAPTER 28
APPROACHES TO FINANCIAL PLANNING

INTRODUCTION

The important thing to remember about financial planning is that it is both necessary and one of the most difficult tasks a financial manager faces. The two major purposes of financial planning are to avoid surprises and to anticipate the future.

WHAT TO LOOK FOR IN CHAPTER 28

Because it melds all investing and financing decisions, a financial plan is the confluence of each of the previous chapters in which a topic here and a topic there were studied. As each of these decisions percolates up the organization and is amalgamated into the financial planning process, the risk aversion of financial management is fitted to the riskiness of all investing and financing decisions. In other words, financial planning is not concerned with minimizing risks; financial planning is concerned with which risks to assume and which ones to shun.

A Complete Financial Plan: A complete financial plan usually includes pro forma financial statements, a statement of capital expenditures, overall business strategy, planned financing, a forecast of revenues and expenses, and an attempt to find the optimal financial plan which satisfies the risk-return expectations of shareholders and financial managers. Because each of the foregoing is an option to the financial manager, financial planning may devolve into managing a portfolio of options.

Financial planning requires forecasting, but there is more to the story than that. Because every forecast is likely to be imprecise, the deviations around the forecast caused by both avoidable and unavoidable surprises must be planned for. During the financial planning process, financing and investment decisions are analyzed for their impact on the future welfare of the enterprise. Once this impact has been determined, alternative investments and financing schemes are formulated and goals are set.

Ordinarily financial planning is concerned with the long term, although short-term financing and investment decisions are a part of this process. At all times financial planning focuses on *all* the investment and financing decisions of a firm.

Financial Planning Models: To achieve the goals of financial planning, corporate financial models, ranging from very simple to complex systems, are often used. One of the major flaws of corporate financial models is their lack of finance theory. Consequently, a system of incorporating finance theory should be found. The appendix to this chapter provided such a system, a linear programming model called LONGER. This rather complete model indicates what may be accomplished when corporate financial planning considers the impacts of various alternative strategies. What a financial manager seeks is the net contribution to the value of the firm which is equal to the base-case net present value adjusted for the value of a project's marginal contribution to borrowing power--to give effect to the tax shelter--as well as the addition of the marginal cost of equity which is sold to finance a project.

WORKED EXAMPLES

PROBLEM 1: PRO FORMA FINANCIAL STATEMENTS

The financial statements of Book Ends, Inc., are set forth in Table 28-1. As the financial manager of the company, your task is to set up a pro forma set of statements for 1988. The following assumptions are to be used:

1. Sales are forecast to increase by 20 percent.
2. No new stocks will be issued.
3. The following coefficients are used:

$$a_1 = CGS \div REV = 0.87$$
$$a_2 = \text{interest rate} = 10 \text{ percent}$$
$$a_3 = \text{tax rate} = 46 \text{ percent}$$
$$a_4 = \text{depreciation rate} = 10 \text{ percent}$$
$$a_5 = \text{payout ratio} = 50 \text{ percent}$$
$$a_6 = NWC \div REV = 16 \text{ percent}$$
$$a_7 = FA \div REV = 64 \text{ percent}$$

Table 28-1
1988 FINANCIAL STATEMENTS FOR BOOK ENDS, INC. (ALL FIGURES IN $1000s)

INCOME STATEMENT

Revenue (REV)	$4250
Cost of goods sold (CGS)	3655
Earnings before interest and taxes	$ 595
Interest (INT)	170
Tax at 46 percent (TAX)	$ 425
Net income (NET)	196
	$ 230

BALANCE SHEET

Assets:	
Net working capital (NWC)	$ 680
Fixed assets (FA)	2720
Total assets	$3400
Liabilities:	
Debt (B)	$1700
Book equity (EQ)	1700
Total liabilities	$3400

SOLUTION

To solve this problem, compare the forecast results with those of the most recent year. The setup takes two steps.

First, fill in each of the statements below with as much data as you can, starting with the income statement. It helps to use the equations contained in Table 28-3 of the Brealey and Myers text.

PRO FORMA INCOME STATEMENT, BOOK ENDS, INC. ($1000s)

Revenue	$5100.0
Cost of goods sold	4437.0
Earnings before interest and taxes	$ 663.0
Interest	
Earnings before taxes	
Taxes (46 percent rate)	
Net income	

The balance sheet may be completed as follows:

BALANCE SHEET, BOOK ENDS, INC.

	1985	1984	CHANGE
Assets:			
Net working capital (NWC)	$ 816	$ 680	$136
Fixed assets (FA)	3264	2720	544
Total assets	$4080	$3400	$680
Liabilities:			
Debt (D)	$	$1700	$
Book equity (E)		$1700	
Total liabilities	$4080	$3400	$680

And the sources and uses of funds statement looks like this:

SOURCES AND USES OF FUNDS BOOK ENDS, INC.

Sources:	
Net income	$
Depreciation	326.4
Operating cash flow	
Borrowing	
Stock issues	0
Total sources	$____
Uses:	
Increase in net working capital	$136.0
Investment	870.4
Total dividends	____
Total uses	$____

The following gaps exist:

Income statement:

1. Interest (INT)
2. Earnings before taxes
3. Taxes (TAX)
4. Net income (NET)

Balance sheet:

5. 1988 debt (D)
6. 1988 equity (E)
7. Change in debt (ΔD)
8. Change in equity (ΔE)

Sources and uses of funds statement:

9. Net income (NET)
10. Operating cash flow
11. Borrowing (D)
12. Total sources
13. Total dividends (DIV)
14. Total uses

A careful look at that list of 14 items reveals that many are self-determining, once some other information is available. What information? The change in debt (ΔD), that's what, and this is estimated in one of two ways. One may use the formula for change in debt, solve that, and then add the results to the prior year's debt of $1700. Here is the step-by-step process.

$$
\begin{aligned}
\Delta D &= \Delta NWC + INV + DIV - NET - DEP - SI \\
&= \$136 + \$870.4 + 0.5\ NET - NET - \$326.4 - 0 \\
&= \$680 - 0.5\ NET \\
&= \$680 - 0.5(REV - CGS - INT - TAX) \\
&= \$680 - 0.5[\$5100 - \$4437 - 0.1D - 0.46(REV - CGS - INT)] \\
&= \$680 - 0.5[\$663 - 0.1D - 0.46(\$5100 - \$4437 - 0.1D) \\
&= \$680 - 0.5[\$663 - 0.1D - 0.046D(\$663 - 0.1D)] \\
&= \$680 - 0.5(\$663 - 0.1D - \$305.0 + 0.046D) \\
&= \$680 - 0.5(-0.054D + \$358.0) \\
&= \$680 + 0.027D - \$179.0 \\
&= \$501.0 + 0.027(\Delta D + 1700) \\
&= \$501.0 + 0.027\Delta D + \$45.9 \\
&= \$547.9 + 0.027\Delta D \\
0.973\Delta D &= \$547.9 \\
\Delta D &= \$562.1 \\
D &= \Delta D + D_{-1} \\
&= \$562.1 + \$1700 \\
&= \$2263.2
\end{aligned}
$$

Debt financing (ΔD) is $562.1 and total debt (D) is $2262.1, which means that total equity is

$$
\begin{aligned}
E &= \text{total assets - D} \\
&= \$4080 - \$2262.1 \\
&= \$1817.9
\end{aligned}
$$

Additional equity is $117.9($1817.9 - $1700).

The second solution is to find the amount of debt (D) which will be outstanding at the end of 1988. The change (ΔD) is obtained by taking the difference between that and the amount outstanding at the beginning of the period [D_{-1}] of $1700. The equally tedious calculations are set forth below.

$$
\begin{aligned}
D &= \Delta D + D_{-1} \\
&= \Delta D + \$1700 \\
&= \Delta NWC + INV + DIV - NET - DEP - SI + \$1700 \\
&= \$136 + \$870.4 + 0.5\,NET - \$326.4 - 0 + \$1700 \\
&= \$2380 - 0.5\,NET \\
&= \$2380 - 0.5(\$5100 - \$4437 - INT - TAX) \\
&= \$2380 - 0.5(\$663 - INT - TAX) \\
&= \$2380 - \$331.5 + 0.5\,INT + 0.5\,TAX \\
&= \$2048.5 + 0.5\,INT + 0.5\,TAX \\
&= \$2048.5 + 0.5(0.1D) + 0.5[0.46(REV - CGS - INT)] \\
&= \$2048.5 + 0.5D + 0.5[0.46(\$663 - 0.1D)] \\
&= \$2048.5 + 0.05D + 0.5(\$305.0 - 0.046D) \\
&= \$2048.5 + 0.05D + \$152.5 - 0.023D \\
&= \$2201.0 - 0.027D \\
0.973D &= \$2201.0 \\
D &= \$2262.1
\end{aligned}
$$

and

$$
\begin{aligned}
\Delta D &= D - D_{-1} \\
&= \$2262.1 - \$1700 \\
&= \$562.1
\end{aligned}
$$

which is precisely what we obtained before.

Armed with that information, the statements may then be completed. Begin by completing the balance sheet, at least the debt portion. Then complete the income statement, now that you know the total amount of debt is $2262.1, because you can put in the amount of interest to be paid. After you do that, the remainder of the income statement is straightforward. If you take half of the net income as retained earnings and add that to the prior year's equity of $1700, the new equity results. Completing the sources and uses of funds statements is the last step in this process.

PROBLEM 2: LONGER

Book Ends, Inc., will use LONGER to estimate how much to invest or borrow in the coming year. The firm faces the following conditions:

1. Available investment opportunities can absorb $500,000.
2. The expected cash flows are perpetual.
3. The internal rate of return on the cash flows is 10 percent.
4. The market capitalizes cash flows of this nature at 12 percent.
5. The firm plans to finance half of the new investment with debt.
6. The firm has $400,000 in cash.
7. Excess cash will be paid out as dividends.

8. Additions to debt and equity are expected to be permanent.
9. The company's marginal tax rate is 50 percent.

Set up a graphical solution to this problem, making sure you explain each part of the graph.

SOLUTION

This is a linear programming problem, the solution to which begins with setting up the basic equation as well as the constraints imposed by the financial management of the firm. Begin by letting x equal the new investment and y equal new borrowing, both expressed as dollars. Next, use the Modigliani-Miller valuation formula, such that

$$V = V_0 + T_c D$$

where V_0 = market value of existing assets, if they were all-equity financed
T_c = marginal corporate tax rate
D = amount of outstanding debt (does not include borrowing for the new project)

$T_c D$, then, is the present value of the tax shield arising from debt financing. So,

$$V = V_0 + 0.5D - 0.167x + 0.5y$$

We want to find what x and y will be. Because V_0 and D are fixed, we may safely ignore them. We want to solve the following:

Maximize: $-0.167x + 0.5y$ (called the objective function)

Subject to: $x \le \$500,000$ (100 percent invested)

$y \le 0.5x$ (amount of debt issued)

$x \le y + \$400,000$ (balance to be financed)

The graphical solution is contained in the figure below. The steps in the solution are as follows:

1. Make each of the constraints equal to their limits, that is $x = \$500,000$, $y = 0.5x$, and $x = y + \$400,000$.
2. Graph each of the constraints by solving for the indicated function.
3. The three graphed lines establish the boundary of the feasible set of solutions but do not find the optimal solution.
4. Set the maximization function equal to V, the value of the investing and borrowing decision, such that $V = -0.167x + 0.5y$.
5. To find the slope of the function, first set V equal to zero. The slope of the function is

$$\text{Slope} = \frac{\text{rise}}{\text{run}}$$

6. The solution works out thus:

$$V = -0.167x + 0.5y$$
$$0 = -0.167x + 0.5y, \text{ or } x = 3y$$

When $y = 0, x = 0$
When $y = 1, x = 3$

Figure 28-1

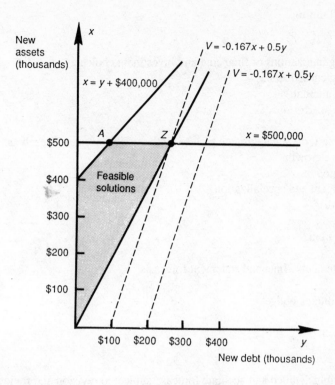

$$\text{Slope} = \text{rise/run} = \Delta x / \Delta y$$

where Δx and Δy mean change in x values and change in y values. For every two units of increase (rise) in x, there is one unit of increase (run) in y.

Increasing values of the objective function are given by shifting in a southeasterly direction (that is, increasing y and decreasing x), while keeping its slope equal to 3. We want to shift the line as far as possible in this direction until it only just touches the feasible region. This gives the point Z as the optimal solution, with $y = \$250,000$, $x = \$500,000$, and an adjusted net present value from the investment equal to $\$41,667$ (or $\$41,500$, if you rounded the ratio of 9 percent to 12 percent).

SUMMARY

Why Do It?

1. Because financing and investment decisions interact

2. To avoid surprises

3. To think ahead

4. To help set goals

5. Not to minimize risks but to find a method of selecting and coping with them

What Is Financial Planning?

1. A process of:
   a. Analyzing interactions of financing and investment choices
   b. Projecting consequences
   c. Selecting alternatives
   d. Measuring performances

2. Focuses on long-term and aggregate picture, with possible scenarios, such as:
   a. Aggressive growth
   b. Normal growth
   c. Retrenchment and specialization
   d. Divestiture

What Goes into the Plan?

1. Pro forma statements--financial statement forecasts

2. Capital expenditures budget

3. Planned financing

4. Two essentials
   a. A reasonably detailed and accurate forecast, subject to revision and review
   b. An ever-elusive search for the optimal financial plan

5. Financial planners manage portfolios of options (the plan is a set of options)
   a. Strategic: the grand scheme, "tell me where you want to go"
   b. Tactical: execution of the strategy, "and I will tell you how to get there"

Financial Planning Models

1. Simulations: trace financial consequences of various actions.
   a. Simple, practical, easy, and cheap.
   b. May produce so many numbers as to confuse rather than enlighten.

2. Models contain no finance.
   a. Built mainly on accounting systems.
   b. Lack benchmarks of achievement which financial theory provides.

3. D'Ambrosio and Hodges's first law:

   Good financial theory is essential to good financial policy. (How do you like that, Brealey and Myers?)

4. No model satisfies all financial goals and needs.

LONGER

1. Differs from other models in that it optimizes.

2. Based on finance theory.

3. Assumes well-functioning capital markets.

4. Object: to maximize firm's net present value.

5. Relies on value additivity.

6. Posits MM's notion that the chief advantage of debt is as a tax shield.

7. A linear programming model.

8. May be made as complicated as one chooses.

9. Shadow price: marginal cost of each constraint in the linear program.
   a. Show what relaxing each constraint adds to NPV.
   b. The shadow price on the investment limit of a new project: measures its adjusted present value.

LIST OF TERMS

Adjusted present value	**Net present value**
Financing decisions	**Pro forma financial statements**
Investment decisions	**Shadow price**
LONGER	

EXERCISES

Fill-in Questions

1. One of the purposes of financial planning is to avoid _____.
2. Financial planning brings together the _____ and _____ choices open to the firm.
3. Forecast financial statements are called _____ statements and are used to anticipate the future and link the present with the past.
4. The value of capital projects which have important financing side effects is called

   _____.
5. A _____ is defined as the change in the objective per unit change in the constraint.
6. When evaluating an investment decision using linear programming, a shadow price of 0.2 on the investment limit means that if we were to invest an additional dollar, _____ would increase by _____.

Problems

1. What-Not, Inc.'s financial statements are set forth below.

Revenues	$5000
Cost of goods sold	4500
Earnings before interest and taxes	$ 500
Interest	120
Earnings before taxes	$ 380
Taxes	171
Net income	$ 209

Assets:	
Net working capital	$ 500
Fixed assets	2000
Total assets	$2500
Liabilities:	
Debt	$1500
Book equity	1000
Total liabilities	$2500

The financial manager estimates that sales next year will increase by 15 percent. The board of directors has decided not to issue more shares in light of the currently weak equity markets. The additional assumptions about the coefficients of the model to be used to determine how much must be borrowed are:

$$a_1 = CGS \div REV = 0.90$$
$$a_2 = \text{interest rate} = 8 \text{ percent}$$
$$a_3 = \text{tax rate} = 45 \text{ percent}$$
$$a_4 = \text{depreciation rate} = 8 \text{ percent}$$
$$a_5 = \text{payout ratio} = 40 \text{ percent}$$
$$a_6 = NWC \div REV = 10 \text{ percent}$$
$$a_7 = FA \div REV = 40 \text{ percent}$$

a. Set up the pro forma financial statements for the coming year.
b. If the depreciation rate were 18 percent instead of 8 percent, would the amount borrowed change?
c. If the payout ratio were increased to 60 percent, how much additional borrowing would be required?
d. What effect would a change in the coefficient a_1 have if it were 88 percent? If it were 95 percent?

2. What-Not, Inc will use LONGER to estimate how much to invest or borrow in the coming year. The firm faces the following conditions:
a. Available investment opportunities absorb $5 million.
b. The expected cash flows are perpetual.
c. The internal rate of return on the cash flows is 12 percent.
d. The market capitalizes cash flows of this nature at 15 percent.
e. The firm wishes to finance 60 percent of the new investment with debt.
f. The firm has $4 million in cash.

g. Excess cash will be paid out as dividends.

h. Additions to debt and equity are permanent.

i. The company's marginal tax rate is 50 percent.

Set up the graphical solution to this problem. Label all relevant points. Explain, in words, the nature of the graph and the story it tells

Essay Questions

1. "When you come right down to it, let's face it, good management provides for both expected and unexpected events and bad management does not. All this should be reflected in financial planning. After all, there is such a thing as contingency planning, ya know." Evaluate this statement in light of the principles of finance of which you are aware.

2. You have just been hired by the corporate strategy group of a large firm. The firm's outlook is uncertain. The vice-president for finance asks you to present a brief statement of how each of the following policies may affect your firm: aggressive growth, normal growth, retrenchment, and divestiture. Begin your answer by explaining what each of those terms means.

3. How does financial planning differ for a firm with generous operating cash flows, modest dividend payout policies, and only a handful of investment opportunities as compared with one that has considerably less operating cash flow because of rapid expansion, also has a moderate dividend payout policy, has stretched its borrowing power virtually to the limit, and is confronted with many investment opportunities?

4. Is it really possible that an investment may have no net present value and still be undertaken by firms simply to enter markets that heretofore were untapped? What financial sense, if any, does that make?

5. How is linear programming used in financial planning?

ANSWERS TO EXERCISES

Fill-in Questions

1. surprises
2. investment; financing
3. pro forma
4. adjusted present value
5. shadow price
6. net present value; 20 cents

Problems

1. a. Before working with the equations in worked problem 1, the partially completed pro forma
        financial statements are as follows:

PRO FORMA INCOME STATEMENT, WHAT-NOT, INC.

Revenues	$5750
Cost of goods sold	5175
Earnings before interest and taxes	$ 575
Interest	
Earnings before taxes	
Taxes	
Net income	

PRO FORMA BALANCE SHEET, WHAT-NOT, INC.

	THIS YEAR	LAST YEAR	CHANGE
Assets:			
Net working capital	$ 575	$ 500	$ 75
Fixed assets	2300	2000	300
Total assets	$2875	$2500	$375
Liabilities:			
Debt	$	$1500	$
Book equity		1000	
Total liabilities	$2875	$2500	$ 375

SOURCES AND USES OF FUNDS, WHAT-NOT, INC.

Sources:	
Net income	$
Depreciation	184
Operating cash flow	
Borrowing	
Stock issues	0
Total sources	
Uses:	
Increase in net working capital	$ 75
Investment	484
Total dividends	
Total uses	

Using either of the equations in worked problem 1 results in new debt of $1721, or $231 more than last
year. The completed statements follow.

	THIS YEAR	LAST YEAR	CHANGE
Assets:			
Net working capital	$ 575	$ 500	$ 75
Fixed assets	2300	2000	300
Total assets	$2875	$2500	$ 375
Liabilities:			
Debt	$1731	$1500	$ 231
Book equity	1144	1000	144
Total liabilities	$2875	$2500	$ 375
Revenues		$5750	
Cost of goods sold		5175	
Earnings before interest and taxes		$ 575	
Interest		138	
Earnings before taxes		437	
Taxes		196	
Net income		240	
Sources:			
Net income		$ 240	
Depreciation		184	
Operating cash flow		$ 424	
Borrowing		231	
Stock issues		0	
Total sources		$ 655	
Uses:			
Increase in net working capital		$ 75	
Investment		484	
Total dividends		96	
Total uses		$ 655	

b. Yes, the equations in worked problem 1 indicate that, with $41 less debt being issued and $41 more in equity being retained, the revised payout ratio is now 24 percent, given the strictures of the model.

c. $22

d. In the 88 percent case the following happens:

New debt: $152, which is $79 less than the case in a.

New equity increases by $79 to $1223.

Net income increases to $244.

In order to increase equity from $1000 last year to $1223 this year, $233 of the $244 of net income must be retained; the payout ratio is then 4.5 percent.

In the 95 percent case, $57 additional debt over the case in a results, so that much less equity is needed. Working through the income statement results in a payout ratio of 63 percent.

Figure 28-2

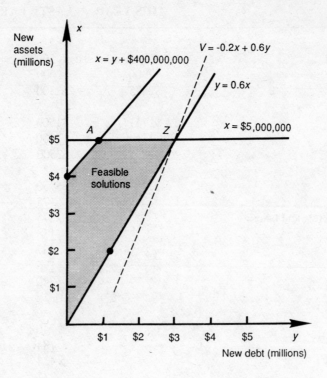

CHAPTER 29
SHORT-TERM FINANCIAL PLANNING

INTRODUCTION

The analysis of short-term financial decisions is the major topic of this chapter. The topic is important for it is at the heart of short-run bill-paying ability. Firms finance their operations from short- and long-term sources. As a rule of thumb, however, short-term assets are financed from short-term sources, and long-term assets are financed from long-term sources.

WHAT TO LOOK FOR IN CHAPTER 29

This chapter's focus is on how financial managers come to grips with cash and working capital problems. Although short-term financial decisions almost always involve short-lived assets, note the linkage between short- and long-term financing decisions arising from a firm's cumulative capital requirements. Ordinarily financial managers try to obtain capital sources whose maturities coincide with the need for the funds. For example, some minimum level of working capital is needed permanently in the business and is financed from permanent sources, whereas working capital that is needed only temporarily is financed from short-lived sources.

Sources and Uses of Funds and Cash: To trace changes in cash and net working capital, sources and uses of cash and sources and uses of funds statements, respectively, are produced. Note that profits and cash flows are not the same and that short-term liquidity measures are frequently used, most notably the current and quick ratios.

Cash Budgeting: A cash budget is a weekly, monthly, or quarterly forecast of cash inflows and outflows. The budget indicates deficient or excessive cash balances, and financing plans are formulated based on it.

Short-Term Financial Planning: Financing decisions are incorporated in the firm's short-term financial plan. We can get the flavor of these plans by considering a narrow range of alternatives, such as unsecured bank borrowing, stretching payables, and financing through a commercial finance company. In practice the range is much richer.
Financial plans are the best guess a financial manager can make. By trial and error each proposed plan is evaluated for its compatibility and costs. Note that simulation and optimization models help but rely heavily on the reality of their underlying assumptions.

WORKED EXAMPLES

PROBLEM 1: SOURCES AND USES OF CASH AND FUNDS
Table 29-1 contains the balance sheets and income statement for Up-Beat Music, Inc. Complete a statement of sources and uses of cash and sources and uses of funds for 1988.

Table 29-1
Up-Beat Music, Inc.

Balance Sheet	1987	1988	Sources and Uses Impact
Current assets			
Cash	15	31	16
Marketable securities	5	0	–5
Inventory	25	17	–8
Accounts receivable	20	35	15
Total current assets	65	83	18
Fixed assets			
Gross investment	75	85	–10
Less depreciation	–15	–17	2
Net fixed assets	60	68	–8
Total assets	125	151	26
Current liabilities			
Bank loans	10	15	5
Accounts payable	35	30	–5
Total current liabilities	45	45	0
Long-term Debt	15	20	5
New worth (equity and retained earnings)	65	86	21
Total liabilities and net worth	125	151	26

Income Statement	1988	
Sales	300	
Operating expenses	245	
	55	
Depreciation	–2	2
	53	
Interest	–3	
Pretax income	50	
Tax at 34 percent	–17	
Net income	33	33
Note:		
Dividend	12	–12
Retained earnings	21	21

SOLUTION

The object of analyzing both these statements is to determine how management derived the funds and cash to finance its operations during this period. Because such information may be valuable for future financial planning, the method for composing such statements is important. To determine the sources and uses of cash, the differences between the two balance sheet dates as well as the cash generated from operations must be analyzed.

• *Step 1:* Compare the differences in each balance sheet account.

• *Step 2:* Determine whether the differences between each balance sheet increase or decrease the cash or funds of the firm.

• *Step 3:* Under the caption "Sources", list all the items which increased the amount of cash or funds. Under the caption "Uses," list all the items which decreased cash or funds.

• *Step 4:* Sum up both sources and uses.

• *Step 5:* Take the difference between sources and uses to determine the net changes in the cash position of the firm.

Applying these steps to Up-Beat Music, Inc., the right-hand column of Table 29-1 indicates the impact each change has on the uses and sources of funds, plus or minus. These results are then summarized, as in Table 29-2, along with the similar pluses and minuses from the income statement.

As you review the pluses and minuses of those statements, remember this: anything that increases the sources of funds is a plus; anything that uses funds is a negative. For example, a reduction of accounts payable is a use of funds, because funds were needed to pay off the payables.

Table 29-2	**Up-Beat Music, Inc.**

Sources and use of funds and cash

Sources of funds	
Sold marketable securities	5
Reduced inventories	8
Increased bank loan	5
Issued long-term debt	5
Cash from operations:	
Net income	33
Depreciation	2
Total sources	58
Uses of funds	
Increased accounts receivable	15
Invested in fixed assets	8
Reduced accounts payable	5
Dividends	12
Total uses	40
Change in cash balance	18

PROBLEM 2: CHANGES IN NET WORKING CAPITAL
What changes in net working capital took place in problem 1?

SOLUTION

Tracing these changes in terms of their impact on net working capital results in the data contained in Table 29-3.

Table 29-3	Up-Beat Music, Inc.

Changes in net working capital

Sources:

Issued long-term debt	5
Cash from operations:	
Net income	33
Depreciation	2
Total	40

Uses:

Invested in fixed assets	8
Dividends	12
Total	20

Changes in net working capital	20

Because it is the difference between current assets and current liabilities, *changes* that result in net working capital stem from factors other than the current assets and short-term liabilities; they stem from long-term financing and investment decisions as well as from current operations.

PROBLEM 3: CURRENT AND QUICK RATIOS

For each year, calculate the two most commonly used liquidity ratios for Up-Beat Music using data from problem 1.

SOLUTION

The first liquidity ratio, the current ratio, is calculated by dividing the current assets by the current liabilities. To calculate the acid test, or quick ratio, we use only the most liquid of all the company's short-term assets, cash, marketable securities, and receivables, and relate that result to the sum of the current liabilities. The ratios for the two years are as follows:

Current ratio = current assets/current liabilities

1987	1988
= $65/$45	= $65/$45
= 1.44	= 1.44

Quick ratio = (cash + marketable securities + receivables)/current liabilities

1987	1988
= ($15 + 5 + $20/$45)	= ($13 + 0 + $35)/$45
= $40/$45	= $48/$45
= 0.89	= 1.07

PROBLEM 4: CASH BUDGET

Section A of Table 29-4 contains the 1988 sales forecast for Up-Beat Music, Inc.:

Table 29-4

Cash budget for Up-Beat Music, Inc.
(in millions)

Section A				
Sales forecast (in million)	First Quarter	Second Quarter	Third Quarter	Fourth Quarter
Sales	92.5	80.5	135.8	165.2

Section B				
Sales and collections forecast (in million)	First Quarter	Second Quarter	Third Quarter	Fourth Quarter
Receivables at start of period	17.0	17.7	15.9	24.2
Sales	92.5	80.5	135.8	165.2
Collections				
Sales in current period (85 percent)	78.6	68.4	115.4	140.4
Sales in last period (15 percent)	13.2	13.9	12.1	20.4
Total collections	91.8	82.3	127.5	160.8
Receivables at end of period	17.7	15.9	24.2	28.6

Section C Cash budget				
Sources of cash				
Collections on accounts receivable	91.8	82.3	127.5	160.8
Other	6.0	10.0	0.0	0.0
Total sources	97.8	92.3	127.5	160.8
Uses of cash				
Payments on accounts payable	84.0	36.0	48.0	80.0
Labor, administrative, and other expenses	35.0	35.0	35.0	35.0
Capital expenditures	20.0	10.0	0.0	0.0
Taxes, interest, and dividends	9.0	9.0	9.0	9.0
Total uses	148.0	90.0	92.0	124.0
Sources minus uses	-50.2	2.3	35.5	36.8

Section D

Calculation of short-term financing needs

Cash at start of period	13.0	-37.2	-34.9	0.6
Changes in cash balance (sources – uses)	-50.2	2.3	35.5	36.8
Cash at end of period	-37.2	-34.9	0.6	37.4
Minimum operating cash balance	10.0	10.0	10.0	10.0
Cumulative short-term financing needs	-47.2	-44.9	-9.4	27.4

Use the following assumptions to construct a cash budget for the company:

1. 85 percent of sales are realized in cash in the quarter sales are made.

2. The remaining 15 percent of sales are collected in cash in the following quarter.

3. The sales prior to the forecast first quarter were $88.3 million.

4. Receivables carried into the first quarter were $17 million.

5. Accounts payable are to be paid on time.

6. All labor and administrative expenditures are paid when due.

7. The capital expenditures are those indicated in the budget below.

8. The firm's financial manager feels "comfortable" with a cash cushion of $10 million.

SOLUTION

Your task is to complete the cash budget for 1988. You accomplish this task in the following steps:

1. Formulate a statement of expected receivables.

2. Formulate a cash budget in which the expected cash sources and cash uses are combined, with the end result being an estimate of the quarterly cash deficiency or excess.

3. Sections B, C, and D of Table 29-4 contain the results.

SUMMARY

Short-Term Financial Planning

1. Needed to ensure solvency.

2. Focus on working capital, all the current assets: cash, marketable securities, receivables, and inventories.

3. Inventory management: production manager has comparative advantage over financial manager in determining how much to invest in inventories in order to minimize stockouts, storage costs, risks of spoilage and obsolescence, and the opportunity costs of tying up money in inventories.

The Long and Short-term Financing Connection

1. Capital requirements
   a. Tend to accumulate over time, mostly irregularly.
   b. Financed from either long- or short-term capital sources.

2. Usually maturities of assets and financing are matched.

3. Seasonal requirements and a comfort level of surplus cash are usually financed from short-term sources.

The Movement of Cash and Working Capital

1. Sources and uses of cash statements: tell us where cash came from and how it was used.

2. Depreciation: a source of cash.

3. Changes in net working capital: captured by the sources and uses of funds statement.

4. Cash cycle: trace the changes in working capital.

5. Two summary measures of current assets and current liabilities.
   a. Current ratio = current assets/current liabilities
   b. Quick ratio = cash + marketable securities + receivables/current liabilities

Cash Budgeting

1. Estimate cash inflows:
   a. Prior receivables
   b. Present sales
   c. Estimated collections
   d. Sales of assets
   e. Tax refunds

2. Estimate cash outflows
   a. Payments on accounts payable (stretch them)
   b. Labor, administrative, and other expenses
   c. Capital expenditures
   d. Taxes, interest, and dividends

3. The difference is the net inflow, from which is estimated the amount that must be financed, including a minimum cash balance.

4. Develop a short-term financing plan.
   a. Large cash flows may result because of seasonal considerations
   b. The cash budget is a best guess, and the uncertainty of its elements should be evaluated.

The Short-Term Financial Plan

1. Financial managers have two major options for financing short-term cash deficiencies:
   a. Borrow from banks, perhaps an unsecured line of credit with a compensating balance.
   b. Stretch out payments (may be costly).

2. Some important questions:
   a. Is the cash reserve too large?
   b. Are the current and quick ratios satisfactory?
   c. What are the intangible costs of stretching payables, such as lost discounts?
   d. Does the plan produce a financially sound result?
   e. Is long-term financing needed and not short-term?
   f. What about adjusting operating and investment plans?
   g. What about selling receivables to a commercial finance company?

3. Answers to any combination of the above, through trial and error, will produce a suitable plan.
   a. Optimization models help.
   b. Simulations work out the what-if conditions.
   c. All models stand and fall on the accuracy of the financial manager's assumptions.

LIST OF TERMS

Cash budget
Compensating balance
Current assets
Current liabilities
Current ratio
Line of credit
Matching maturities

Net working capital
Quick ratio
Sources and uses of cash
Sources and uses of funds
Stretching Payables
Working capital

EXERCISES

Fill-in Questions

1. The concept of _____ is at work when short-lived assets are financed from short-term sources and long-lived assets are financed from long-term sources.
2. A forecast of cash inflows and cash outflows is called a _____.
3. Changes in _____ are captured by the sources and uses of cash statement, whereas the sources and uses of funds statement captures changes in _____.
4. The percentage of a loan that must be retained on deposit is called a _____.
5. Working capital consists of _____, _____, and _____, whereas net working capital is the difference between _____ and _____.
6. The ratio of all the current assets to current liabilities is called the _____ ratio, whereas the _____ ratio relates the sum of _____, _____ and _____ to current liabilities.
7. A prearranged maximum borrowing capability at specified interest rates is known as a _____.
8. Not paying bills when they are due is called _____.

Problems

1. Work out a short-term financial plan for Up-Beat Music, Inc. Use the data from the worked examples.

2. Using the balance sheets and income statement Table 29-5 for Up-Beat Music, Inc., work out a complete sources and uses of cash and a sources and uses of funds statement for 1986.

Table 29-5
YEAR-END BALANCE SHEETS FOR UP-BEAT MUSIC, INC., IN MILLIONS

	1987	1988
Current assets:		
Cash	$ 13	$ 2
Marketable securities	0	$ 5
Inventory	17	22
Accounts receivable	35	48
Total current assets	$ 65	$ 77
Fixed assets:		
Gross investment	$ 85	$ 85
Less depreciation	-17	-19
Net fixed assets	68	66
Total assets	$133	$143
Current liabilities:		
Bank loans	$ 15	$ 13
Accounts payable	30	37
Total current liabilities	$ 45	$ 50
Long-term debt	$ 20	$ 18
Net worth (equity and retained earnings)	68	75
Total liabilities and net worth	$133	$143

INCOME STATEMENT FOR 1988 FOR UP-BEAT MUSIC, INC., IN MILLIONS

Sales	$320
Operating expenses	-289
	$ 31
Depreciation	- 2
	$ 29
Interest	- 3
Pretax income	$ 26
Tax at 50 percent	13
Net income	$ 13
Cash dividends	$ 6

3. Using the data for 1988 contained in problem 2, answer the following:
   a. The company's current liabilities were _____.
   b. The company's current assets were _____.
   c. The company's current ratio was _____.
   d. The company's quick ratio was _____.
   e. The company's net working capital was _____.

4. Table 29-6, Section A, contains revised 1988 data for Up-Beat Music.

Table 29-6
Cash budget for Up-Beat Music, Inc.
(in millions)

Section A

New Data (in millions)	First Quarter	Second Quarter	Third Quarter	Fourth Quarter
Sales forecast	85.0	75.0	100.0	150.0
Other sources of cash	5.0	6.0	7.0	10.0
Accounts payable	72.0	63.0	76.0	84.0
Labor, administrative and other expenses	42.0	42.0	42.0	42.0
Capital expenditures	15.0	0.00	5.0	0.00
Taxes, interest and dividends	19.0	19.0	19.0	19.0

In addition, the following assumptions are made:
   (1) 87 percent of sales are realized as cash in the quarter in which they are made.
   (2) The remaining 13 percent of sales are collected as cash the following quarter.
   (3) Sales prior to the first quarter of this forecasting period were $130.
   (4) Receivables carried into the first quarter were $17 million.
   (5) All accounts payable are paid when due.
   (6) All labor and administrative expenses are paid when due.

Construct a revised cash budget for 1988 and work out a financing scheme for Up-Beat Music, Inc.

1986 CASH BUDGET FOR UP-BEAT MUSIC, INC., IN MILLIONS

	FIRST QUARTER	SECOND QUARTER	THIRD QUARTER	FOURTH QUARTER
Sources of cash:				
Collections				
Other	$ 5.00	$ 6.00	$ 7.00	$10.00
Uses of cash:				
Accounts payable	72.00	63.00	76.00	84.00
Labor, administrative,				
and other expenses	42.00	42.00	42.00	42.00
Capital Expenditures				
Taxes, interest, and dividends	19.00	19.00	19.00	19.00
Total uses				
Sources minus uses				
Short-term financing requirements:				
Cash at start of period				
Change in cash balance				
Cash at the end of period				
Minimum operating cash balance				
Cumulative short-term financing requirement				

Essay Questions

1. What is meant by matching maturities?

2. What rationale can you give for the statement, "We think that firms with a *permanent* cash surplus ought to go on a diet!"

3. How might a financial manager trace changes in cash and working capital?

4. Put in words the value of a cash budget. Do you see the value of a cash budget applying to yourself?

5. What impact does a compensating balance have on (1) the cost of bank borrowings and (2) the amount that must be borrowed?

ANSWERS TO EXERCISES

Fill-in Questions

1. matching maturities
2. cash budget
3. cash; working capital
4. compensating balance
5. cash; receivables; inventories; current assets; current liabilities
6. current; quick; cash; marketable securities; and receivables
7. line of credit
8. stretching payables

Problems

1. Several schemes may be developed, although each of them must provide for covering the deficits developed in the cash budget.

2. From the balance sheet:

Cash	-11
Marketable securities	+ 5
Inventory	+ 5
Accounts receivable	+13
Total current assets	+12
Gross investment	0
Depreciation	+ 2
Net fixed assets	+ 2
Total assets	+10
Bank loans	- 2
Accounts payable	+ 7
Total current liabilities	+ 5
Long-term debt	- 2
Net worth	+ 7
Total liabilities and net worth	+10

From the income statement:

Depreciation	+ 2
Net income	+13
Cash dividends	- 6
Retained earnings	+ 7

Sources and uses of funds and cash:

Sources:	
Depreciation	$ 2
Net income	13
Increased accounts payable	7
Total sources	$ 22
Uses:	
Bought marketable securities	$ 5
Increased inventories	5
Increased receivables	13
Decreased bank loans	2
Reduced long-term debt	2
Dividends	6
Total uses	$ 33
Reduction in cash	$ 11

3. (a) $50; (b) $77; (c) $77/$50 = 1.54; (d) ($2 + $5 + $48 − $22)/$50 = 1.10; (e) $77 − $50 = $27

4.

Table 29-6 (cont'd)

Cash budget for Up-Beat Music, Inc.

Section B

Sales and collections forecast (in millions)	First Quarter	Second Quarter	Third Quarter	Fourth Quarter
Receivables at start of period	17.0	11.1	9.7	12.9
Sales	85.0	75.0	100.0	150.0
Collections				
Sales in current period (87 percent)	74.0	65.3	87.0	130.5
Sales in last period (13 percent)	16.9	11.1	9.8	13.0
Total collections	90.9	76.4	96.8	143.5
Receivables at endof period	11.1	9.7	12.9	19.4

Section C
Cash budget

Sources of cash				
Collections on accounts receivable	90.9	76.4	96.8	143.5
Other	5.0	6.0	7.0	10.0
Total sources	95.9	82.4	103.8	153.5
Uses of cash				
Payments on accounts payable	72.0	63.0	76.0	84.0
Labor, administrative, and other expenses	42.0	42.0	42.0	42.0
Capital expenditures	15.0	0.00	5.0	0.0
Taxes, interest, and dividends	19.0	19.0	19.0	19.0
Total uses	148.0	124.0	142.0	145.0
Sources minus uses	-52.1	-41.6	-38.2	8.5

Section D
Calculation of short-term financing needs

Cash at start of period	2.0	- 50.1	- 91.7	-129.9
Changes in cash balance (sources – uses)	- 52.1	- 41.6	- 38.2	8.5
Cash at end of period	- 50.1	- 91.7	-129.9	-121.4
Minimum operating cash balance	8.0	8.0	8.0	8.0
Cumulative short-term financing needs	- 58.1	- 99.7	-137.9	-129.4

It should be obvious that if the present conditions persist, permanent additions to working capital are in order. Chances are retained earnings or a stock sale is best for this company. Short-term financing does not seem to be in order because of the seeming chronic deficiency in cash flows.

CHAPTER 30
CREDIT MANAGEMENT

INTRODUCTION

As you study the nuts-and-bolts issues of credit management, remember that no clear-cut, scientific guidelines by which to make credit decisions exist. Reasonably sound financial decisions, however, will result if financial managers follow these steps: (1) determine the terms of sale, (2) determine the evidence of indebtedness, (3) determine the creditworthiness of customers, (4) determine how much credit should be extended to each customer, and (5) monitor each account after credit has been extended.

WHAT TO LOOK FOR IN CHAPTER 30

As you study this chapter, look for the five considerations outlined in the preceding section.

Terms of Sale: The terms of sale indicate the method by which customers pay for goods and services. Most goods and services are sold on credit, usually with a cash discount being offered if payment is received within a short period of time, but with the entire amount nonetheless due at the end of a specified time period.

Commercial Credit Instruments: A variety of commercial credit instruments expedite the terms of sale. The chief commercial credit instrument is the open account, which is simply a record on the books of the firm indicating that credit has been extended. Depending on the nature of the business and one's customers, other commercial credit instruments may be used, such as promissory notes, commercial drafts, bank acceptances, and letters of credit.

Credit Analysis: Ordinarily credit analysis precedes credit extension. To that end, financial managers may hire the services of a credit agency, such as Dun and Bradstreet, but that may not be enough. Financial ratio analysis is another method of checking customers' creditworthiness. Yet another method of analyzing the creditworthiness of customers is numerical credit scoring and risk indexes.

The Credit Decision: After the foregoing steps have been taken, the credit decision is made. In essence every credit decision estimates the present value of the difference between revenues to be received and cost expended for credit sales.

Note that no credit manager can pursue the credit search without limit; after all, there is a cost of searching for additional information. Usually the probability of default as well as the size of the order, when compared with the gain from not extending credit, form the bases for the analysis. Repeat orders, however, cannot be ignored without hazard. To cultivate prospective business the financial manager must look beyond the immediate order in hand.

A reasonable credit policy will be based on three general principles. First, maximize expected profits and do not minimize the number of bad accounts. Second, concentrate efforts on those accounts most likely to pose a threat to the financial welfare of the firm, either because of their size or because of their doubtful paying ability. Third, repeat orders must be factored into the overall decision because they have a bearing on the total sales and production ability of the firm.

322

Collection Policy: After credit has been extended, a collection policy must be enforced. By aging accounts receivable, those which are delinquent, and the extent to which they are delinquent, may be identified and appropriate measures taken. Another method of collecting accounts receivable is to sell them outright to firms that specialize in this practice. Factors, as they are called, may absorb the entire credit-collection function or parts of it, for a fee. To further assure that accounts receivable will be collected, credit insurance may be bought.

Bankruptcy: What you should look for in this appendix is the general idea of what bankruptcy is and the financial implications it has for those who extend credit to firms or persons that eventually go belly up. In general, financial managers who extend credit to persons or other firms that eventually become bankrupt cannot expect to receive much relative to their claim.

WORKED EXAMPLES

PROBLEM 1: CASH DISCOUNTS
Find the effective annual cost of forgoing taking cash discounts for each of the following terms of sale: 2/10, *n*/30; 5/20, *n*/45; 2/10, *n*/60; 5/20, *n*/60.

SOLUTION
The object is first to determine the effective cost of the loan arising from not taking the cash discount. For convenience let's deal in increments of $100 of sales and let's take the case of 2/10, *n*/30. Recognize that during the first 10 days you obtain a "free ride" on the seller's credit, (although it is not cost-free, the cost of the free ride most probably being built into the sale price). Also note that if you do not take the cash discount, in effect you are borrowing the difference between the total amount billed, $100, and the amount of the cash discount, $2, which, of course is $98; it costs you $2 each time you borrow the $98. You are borrowing the $98 for 20 days. If you repeat this process throughout the year, you will borrow 18.25 times because there are 18.25 20-day periods in a 365-day year (365 ÷ 20). (Sometimes for convenience and by convention, a 360-day year is used.)

Now for the calculations. The cost of the 20-day, $2 loan is

$$\text{Per period cost of loan} = \text{dollar cash discount/dollar amount of loan}$$
$$= \$2/\$98$$
$$= 0.0204 = 2.04 \text{ percent}$$

You are paying 2.04 percent for each of the 18.25 periods. The effective annual cost is the compound return on the 2.04 percent, namely,

$$\text{Effective annual cost of foregoing cash discounts} = [(1 + \text{per period rate})^{\text{number of periods per year}} - 1] \times 100$$
$$= [1 + 0.0204]^{18.25} - 1] \times 100$$
$$= [(1.0204)^{18.25} - 1] \times 100$$
$$= (1.4456 - 1) \times 100$$
$$= 0.4456 \times 100 = 44.56 \text{ percent}$$

which is very expensive by anyone's standards. Note that it is incorrect to estimate the cost of not taking the discount by merely estimating the cost as 2 percent ($2 ÷ $100) and multiplying that by the number of periods to obtain an answer of 36.5 percent (2 percent x 18.25), because that procedure ignores the effective amount that is borrowed and the compounding effect of the foregone interest.

The calculations for the other terms of sale are as follows:
5/20, *n*/45:

$$\text{Per period cost of loan} = \$5/\$95$$
$$= 5.26 \text{ percent}$$

$$\text{Effective annual cost} = [(1.0526)^{(365 \div 25)} - 1] \times 100$$
$$= [(1.0526)^{14.6} - 1] \times 100$$
$$= (2.1137 - 1) \times 100 = 111.37 \text{ percent}$$

2/10, *n*/60:

$$\text{Per period cost of loan} = \$2/\$98$$
$$= 2.04 \text{ percent}$$

$$\text{Effective annual cost} = [(1.0204)^{(365 \div 50)} - 1] \times 100$$
$$= [(1.0204)^{7.3} - 1] \times 100$$
$$= (1.15884 - 1) \times 100 = 15.88 \text{ percent}$$

5/20, *n*/60:

$$\text{Effective annual cost} = [(1 + \text{per period cost})^{\text{number of periods}} - 1] \times 100$$
$$= [(1 + 0.0526)^{(365 \div 40)} \times 100$$
$$= [1.0526]^{9.125} - 1] \times 100$$
$$= (1.5964 - 1) \times 100$$
$$= 0.5964 \times 100 = 59.64 \text{ percent}$$

PROBLEM 2: ALTMAN'S Z-SCORE

Use Altman's multiple discriminant analysis results to estimate the Z-scores for each of the firms listed below.

	A	B	C	D
EBIT	$ 200	$ 600	$ 50	$ 5
Total assets	400	400	400	400
Sales	400	1900	1200	200
Market price per share	20	100	50	5
Number of shares	100	100	100	100
Book value of debt	100	100	100	100
Retained earnings	50	100	25	50
Working capital	100	200	10	10

SOLUTION

The setup for this answer is as follows:

$$
\begin{aligned}
Z = \ & 3.3(\text{EBIT/total assets}) + 1.0(\text{sales/total assets}) \\
& + 0.6(\text{market value of equity/book value of debt}) \\
& + 1.4(\text{retained earnings/total assets}) \\
& + 1.2(\text{working capital/total assets})
\end{aligned}
$$

The solution for firm A is

$$Z = 3.3(\text{EBIT/total assets}) + 1.0(\text{sales/total assets})$$
$$+ 0.6(\text{market value of equity/book value of debt})$$
$$+ 1.4(\text{retained earnings/total assets})$$
$$+ 1.2(\text{working capital/total assets})$$

$$= 3.3(\$200/\$400) + 1.0(\$400/\$400)$$
$$+ 06.[(\$20 \times 100)/\$100] + 1.4(\$50/\$400) + 1.2/(\$100/\$400)$$
$$= (3.3)(0.5) + (1.0)(1.0) + (0.6)(20) + (1.4)(0.125) + (1.2)(0.25)$$
$$= 1.65 + 1 + 12 + 0.175 + 0.3$$
$$= 15.125$$

For firms B, C, and D the solutions are:

Firm B:

$$Z = 3.3(\$600/\$400) + 1.0(\$1900/\$400)$$
$$+ 0.6[(\$100 \times 100)/\$100] + 1.4(\$100/\$400) + 1.2(\$200/\$400)$$
$$= 4.95 + 4.75 + 60 + 0.35 + 0.6$$
$$= 70.65$$

Firm C:

$$Z = 3.3(\$50/\$400) + 1.0(\$1200/\$400)$$
$$+ 0.6[(\$50 \times 100)/\$100] \qquad + 1.4(\$25/\$400) + 1.2(\$10/\$400)$$
$$= 0.4125 + 3.0 + 30.0 + 0.0875 + 0.03$$
$$= 33.53$$

Firm D:

$$Z = 0.04125 + 0.5 + 3.0 + 0.175 + 0.03$$
$$= 3.74625$$

PROBLEM 3: EXPECTED CREDIT DEFAULT

What-Not, Inc.'s credit manager studied the bill-paying habits of its customers and discovered that 92 percent of them were prompt payers and 8 percent were slow payers. The records also showed that 18 percent of the slow payers and 3 percent of the prompt payers subsequently defaulted. The company now has 1500 accounts on its books, none of which has yet defaulted. What is the total number of expected defaults, assuming no repeat business is on the horizon?

SOLUTION

To solve this problem, first categorize the number of prompt and slow payers. They are

$$\text{Prompt payers} = 1500 \times 0.92 = 1380$$
$$\text{Slow payers} = 1500 \times 0.08 = 120$$

Next multiply the probability of default for each class to obtain the expected number for each class.

Prompt payers: $1380 \times 0.03 = \quad 41.4$
Slow payers: $120 \times 0.18 = \quad \underline{21.6}$
$$63.0$$

A total of 63 accounts (4.2 percent of the total) may be expected to default.

PROBLEM 4: EXPECTED PROFIT OF CREDIT EXTENSION . . .

Given the data in problem 3, revenues from sales of $2000, and cost of the sales of $1740, what is the expected profit (loss) from extending credit to slow payers?

SOLUTION

$$
\begin{aligned}
\text{Expected profit} &= p \times \text{PV(revenues} - \text{cost)} - (1 - p)(\text{cost}) \\
&= 0.82(\$2000 - \$1740) - 0.18(\$1740) \\
&= \$213 - \$313 \\
&= -\$100
\end{aligned}
$$

Clearly, at this level of credit it is not profitable to extend credit to slow payers.

PROBLEM 5: WITH A PRICE INCREASE

Estimate how much What-Not would have to increase prices to make it just worthwhile to extend credit to slow payers in problem 4.

SOLUTION

This problem is solved by setting the entire equation equal to zero and solving for revenues. The answer is

$$
\begin{aligned}
0.82(\text{revenues} - \$1740) - \$313 &= 0 \\
0.82 \text{ revenues} - \$1740 &= 0 \\
0.82 \text{ revenues} &= \$1740 \\
\text{Revenues} &= \$2122
\end{aligned}
$$

At average revenues of about $2122, a price increase of 6.1 percent, the firm is likely to just break even from extending credit to all customers.

PROBLEM 6: EXPECTED PAYOFF OF CREDIT SEARCH: I

Is it worthwhile for the credit manager of What-Not, Inc. to engage in a credit search to determine whether customers are slow or prompt payers if the cost of search is $12, the probability of identifying a slow payer is 0.02, and the expected loss from a slow payer is $100?

SOLUTION

To answer this, set up the problem in this way

$$
\begin{aligned}
\text{Expected payoff from credit check} &= \text{probability of identifying a slow payer} \times \text{gain from not extending} \\
&\qquad \text{credit} - \text{cost of credit check} \\
&= (0.02 \times \$100) - \$12 \\
&= \$2 - \$12 = -\$10
\end{aligned}
$$

It is not worthwhile to engage in the credit check.

PROBLEM 7: EXPECTED PAYOFF OF CREDIT SEARCH: II

At what level of sales per customer would the credit manager in problem 6 be indifferent?

SOLUTION

If the expected loss from a slow payer were six times as large, the credit check pays. This occurs when a customer requires credit amounting to $600.

Set expected payoff from credit check = $(0.02 \times X) - \$12$ equal to zero and solve for X.

PROBLEM 8: IMPACT OF REPEAT ORDERS

We expect that one of our slow-paying customers in problems 3-7 will subsequently place a repeat order. If the customer pays on the first order, we estimate a probability of 0.95 of no default on the second order. How do we evaluate the original extension of credit?

SOLUTION

Let's take this in steps. First, calculate the expected profit on the initial order.

$$\text{Expected profit on initial order} = p_1 \times \text{PV(revenues} - \text{cost)} - (1 - p_1)\text{PV(cost)}$$
$$= (0.82 \times \$260) - (0.18 \times \$1740)$$
$$= -\$100$$

Second:

$$\text{Next year's expected profit on repeat order} = p_2 \times \text{PV(revenues} - \text{cost)} - (1 - p_2)\text{PV} \times \text{(cost)}$$
$$= (0.95 \times \$260) - (0.05 \times \$1740)$$
$$= \$247 - \$87$$
$$= \$160$$

Third:

Total expected profit = expected profit on initial order + probability of payment and repeat order x PV of next year's expected profit on repeat order
$$= -\$100 + 0.82 \, \text{PV}(\$160)$$

Fourth, assuming investments of comparable risk are expected to return 10 percent, the total expected profit (present value) is

$$\text{Total expected profit} = -\$100 + [(0.82)(\$160)]/1.1$$
$$= -\$100 + \$119$$
$$= \$19$$

SUMMARY

Focal Points of Credit Management

1. Terms of sale

2. Evidence of indebtedness

3. Credit analysis

4. The amount of credit to be extended

5. Collection procedures

Terms of Sales

1. Some sales do not require credit extension.

2. Cash discounts: commonplace, varied, and usually determined by industry practices.

Commercial Credit Instruments

1. Define the amount of credit.

2. Open account, a bookkeeping entry.

3. Formal documents: commercial drafts and irrevocable letters of credit.

Credit Analysis

1. Different credit is extended to different classes of buyers.

2. To screen accounts: rely on credit agencies, credit bureaus, bank, and financial ratio analysis.

3. Numerical credit scoring may help.

4. Multiple discriminant analysis is likely to yield better results.

5. Altman's Z-score.

$$Z = 3.3(\text{EBIT/total assets}) + 1.0(\text{sales/total assets})$$
$$+ 0.6(\text{market value of equity/book value of debt})$$
$$+ 1.4(\text{retained earnings/total assets})$$
$$+ 1.2(\text{working capital/total assets})$$

Deciding Who Gets Credit and How Much

1. If repeat orders are unlikely:
   a. Compare additional revenues from extending credit with additional costs.
   b. Expected profit = p x PV(REV – cost) – (1 – p)PV(cost)
   c. Adjust for the additional cost of a credit search.

2. If additional business is likely:
   a. Often pays to accept an order with an initial high probability of nonpayment.
   b. The additional business may add incrementally more than the potential loss.

3. A couple of general principles:
   a. Concentrate on maximizing expected profit, not on minimizing risky customers.
   b. Concentrate on large and doubtful accounts, not on small or clearcut losers.
   c. Look for the possible payoffs from repeat business.

What Happens When They Don't Pay?

1. Monitoring credit sales is the first step in the collection process.

2. Aging accounts receivable:
   a. Signals the customers to be dunned.
   b. May indicate accounts to be turned over to a collection agency.

3. Factor: assumes almost all the collection functions, for a fee.

4. The risk of noncollection may be passed off to an insurance company by buying credit insurance.

Belly Up

1. The ultimate in financial distress: bankruptcy.

2. State and federal laws govern whether and to what extent a firm will be liquidated or reorganized.

3. Pecking order of who-gets-what is established:
    a. Shareholders rarely get anything.
    b. Creditors receive only a fraction of what's due them.

4. Puzzle: Why do firms sometimes petition for bankruptcy when their equity still has a positive value?
    a. Tax loss is a valuable asset.
    b. When a firm is reorganized it is difficult to determine whether all parties to the reorganization will receive what they are entitled to.
    c. Shareholders and junior creditors play for time in the hope of receiving a windfall.
    d. There is a gun aimed at the heads of senior creditors since postpetition creditors have priority over them. They may settle for less than you would otherwise expect.

LIST OF TERMS

Aging of receivables	**Multiple discriminant analysis**
Cash discount	**Open account credit**
Factor	

EXERCISES

Fill-in Questions

1. _____ are often used to induce customers to pay their bills before the end of the free payment period.
2. When the credit terms are 2/10, n/30, this means that customers are entitled to a _____ percent cash discount provided they pay within the first _____ days, but in any event the entire bill must be paid in _____ days.
3. A financial manager who fails to take a cash discount on terms of 2/10, n/30 incurs an effective annual cost of _____ percent.
4. Granting credit depends on whether the _____ profit from doing so is greater than the _____ profit from refusing.
5. If the probability of identifying a slow-paying customer is 0.06, the customer places an order of $60, and the gain that results from not extending the credit is $7, the expected payoff of the credit check is _____.
6. If the probability of detecting a slow payer is 0.07 and a customer places an order for $500, and the gain from not extending credit is $18, the expected payoff from the credit check is _____.
7. Ordinarily a credit manager (does, does not) _____ subject each customer to the same credit analysis. Rather, efforts should be concentrated on the (large, small) _____ and doubtful orders.
8. A firm, usually part of a commercial bank, which purchases accounts receivable is called a _____.
9. The statistical procedure known as _____ was used to estimate the likelihood of financial failure.
10. Most trade credit is _____ credit rather than CBD or COD.

11. Financial managers are said to be _____ when they classify their credit sales according to the percentage of the total that pay their bill in 1, 2, 3, and more than 3 months.

Problems

1. Find the effective annual cost of not taking the cash discounts on the following terms of trade: 3/10, n/30; 3/10, n/45; 3/10, n/60; 4/10, n/30; 5/10, n/30; 6/10, n/30. What general phenomena seem to be at work?

2. Use Altman's multiple discriminant analysis to estimate the scores for each of the following companies:

	1	2	3	4
EBIT	$ 200	$ 400	$ 600	$ 800
Total assets	1000	1200	1400	1600
Sales	2000	2400	2800	3200
Market price per share	40	48	56	64
Number of shares	50	100	150	200
Book value of debt	400	500	600	700
Retained earnings	400	500	600	700
Working capital	600	600	600	600

3. If-Not, Inc.'s credit manager studied the bill-paying habits of its customers and found that 90 percent of them were prompt payers and the remainder were slow payers. She also discovered that 22 percent of the slow payers and 5 percent of the prompt payers subsequently defaulted. The company has 2000 accounts on its books, none of which has yet defaulted. Calculate the total number of expected defaults, assuming no repeat business is on the horizon.

4. Given the data in problem 3, revenues from sales of $1300, and the cost of sales of $1100, what is the expected profit or loss from extending credit to slow payers?

5. Estimate the average level of revenues that makes it just worthwhile to extend credit to slow payers in problem 4.

6. Is it worthwhile for the credit manager of If-Not, Inc. to engage in a credit search to determine whether customers are slow or prompt payers if the cost of each search is $11, the probability of identifying slow payers is 0.06, and the expected cost of a slow payer is $55? Show all calculations.

7. At what sales level would the credit manager in problem 6 be indifferent? Show all calculations.

8. Say there is a 0.92 probability that a repeat customer of If-Not, Inc. will not default. How should the credit manager evaluate the original extension of credit to a customer who has been identified as a slow payer but also as certain to place a repeat order?

Essay Questions

1. In what general way do financial managers proceed to analyze the creditworthiness of a potential customer? Would such analysis be different from that applied to present customers?

2. What role does financial ratio analysis play in credit evaluation? Explain both the advantages and disadvantages of financial ratio analysis.

3. What special role does numerical credit scoring play in evaluating credit risks? Explain fully.

4. What are Z-scores and how are they used in credit analysis?

5. "All I know," says the financial manager of What-Not, Inc., "is sometimes it simply does not pay to continue a credit investigation of customers. There comes a time when you just stop looking." Evaluate this statement and set forth the analytical framework in which it applies.

6. "I don't know about other financial managers, but as the credit manager of What-Not, Inc., I consider maximization of profits, concentration on dangerous accounts, and repeat orders to be the most influential on my credit decisions." Evaluate this statement.

ANSWERS TO EXERCISES

Fill-in Questions

1. cash discounts
2. 2; 10; 30
3. 44.6
4. expected; expected
5. $3.40
6. -$17
7. does not; large
8. factor
9. multiple discriminant analysis
10. open account credit
11. aging receivables

Problems

1. 3/10, *n*/30

    Per period cost = dollar cash discount/dollar amount of loan
    = $3/$97 = 3.093 percent

    Number of periods = 365/20 = 18.25

    Effective annual cost = $[(1 + .0309)^{18.25} - 1] \times 100$
    = 74.26 percent

3/10, *n*/45

$$\text{Effective annual cost} = [(1 + 0.309)^{10.43} - 1] \times 100$$
$$= 37.36 \text{ percent}$$

3/10, *n*/60

$[(1.0309)^{7.30} - 1] \times 100 = 24.88$ percent

4/10, *n*/30

$[(1.0417)^{18.25} - 1] \times 100 = 110.77$ percent

5/10, *n*/30

$[(1.0536)^{18.25} - 1] \times 100 = 154.86$ percent

6/10, *n*/30

$[(1.0638)^{18.25} - 1] \times 100 = 209.17$ percent

---

2. $Z = 3.30(0.20) + 1.00(2.00) + 0.60(5.00) + 1.40(0.40) + 1.20(6.60) = 6.94$
               $Z = 1.10 + 2.00 + 5.76 + 0.58 + 0.60 = 10.04$
               $Z = 1.41 + 2.00 + 8.40 + 0.60 + 0.51 = 12.93$
               $Z = 1.65 + 2.00 + 10.57 + 0.61 + 0.45 = 15.68$

3. Prompt payers   = $2000 × 0.9 = $1800
   Slow payers   = $2000 × 0.1 = $200

   (Prompt × probability) + (slow × probability) = ($1800 × 0.05) + ($200 × 0.22)
                                                = $90 + $44
                                                = $134

4. Expected profit = $0.78($1300 - $1100) - 0.22($1100) = -86

5. $0.78(\text{REV} - $1100) - $242 = 0$
              REV   = $1410

6. Expected payoff = $(0.06 × $55) - $11 = -$7.70$

7. $0.06x - $11 = 0; x = 183.33

8. Total expected profits = $-$86 + 0.78($76) = -$26.72$

CHAPTER 31
CASH MANAGEMENT

INTRODUCTION

You know that efficient management of a firm's resources tends to maximize the value of the enterprise. Cash management is as important to the value and survival of the firm as the management of any of the firm's assets and liabilities. The object of efficient cash management, as always, is to ensure the solvency of the enterprise and to add to the value of the firm.

WHAT TO LOOK FOR IN CHAPTER 31

Efficient cash management is the focus of this chapter. Financial managers knowingly forgo the interest return on invested money in exchange for liquidity. The object of cash management is to insure the proper balance between too little and too much cash (liquidity) and to implement an efficient collection and disbursement system.

Cash as Inventory: Because cash is another raw material needed to carry on the functions of a firm, several inventory models are used to solve the problem of how much cash or cash substitutes to keep on hand. In the Baumol model the three variables of concern are the interest foregone from holding cash, the fixed administrative expenses of buying and selling highly marketable securities, and the rate of cash disbursement. The Miller-Orr model's major variables are the transactions costs in highly marketable securities, the variation in day-to-day cash flows, and the interest rate. The value of these models, as of all models, rests with insights they provide us regarding the important variables to consider.

Cash Collection and Disbursement Systems: Float arises because of the difference in the dates when checks are received for payment of goods and services and when they are cleared. Financial managers estimate the net float between checks written and checks received and adjust cash balances accordingly. To minimize the amount of float working to the financial manager's disadvantage, speeding up collections is necessary, with concentration banking, wire transfers, and lock-box systems being the most prominent. To maximize the amount of float working to the financial manager's advantage, slowing down the rate at which cash moves out of the business is necessary, with mailing checks at the very last moment and paying for goods and services by drafts being commonplace.

Your Friendly Banker: Good bank relationships are essential to efficient cash management. Nothing makes a banker happier than large deposits of cash. To ensure his or her happiness, a banker often requires financial managers to maintain compensating balances, in return for which a number of services are provided "free."

WORKED EXAMPLES

PROBLEM 1: INVENTORY MODEL
Because of the unusual success of *Principles of Corporate Finance*, Everyman's Bookstore finds its demand doubled to 200 copies a year, its cost of money tied up in inventory increased to $1.20 per book, and the fixed, clerical, and handling expenses increased to $2.10 per order. You are asked to determine the optimal order size Q.

SOLUTION
The formula for the solution to this problem is

$$Q = \sqrt{(2 \times \text{sales} \times \text{cost per order})/\text{carrying cost}}$$

Filling in the relevant numbers,

$$Q = \sqrt{(2 \times 200 \times \$2.10)/\$1.20}$$

$$= \sqrt{\$840/\$1.20}$$

$$= \sqrt{700}$$

$$= 26.46 \text{ books}$$

Because fractional books cannot be ordered the optimal order size is 26 books. This implies that orders will be placed about 7.7 times a year (200 books ÷ 26 books), or once about every 47 days (365 ÷ 7.7 times).

The equilibrium between the cost and benefits of ordering in this magnitude is further demonstrated by determining the marginal reduction in order costs and comparing them with the marginal carrying costs.

Marginal reduction in order costs $= (\text{sales} \times \text{cost per order})/Q^2$
$= (200 \text{ books} \times \$2.10)/(26.46)^2$
$= \$420/700.13$
$= \$0.60$

Marginal carrying costs $= \text{carrying cost per book}/2$
$= \$1.20/2$
$= \$0.60$

Marginal reduction in order costs $= \text{marginal carrying costs}$
$\$0.60 = \$0.60$

PROBLEM 2: BAUMOL MODEL
On the assumption that cash is merely another inventory that must be replenished from time to time, Baumol extended the inventory ordering model to cash management. As the financial manager of What-Not, Inc. you want to use the model to determine how frequently you should sell your U.S. Treasury bills in order to cover day-to-day cash outflows, which average $100,000 a month, or $1.2 million a year. If the annual rate of return on your bills is 8.5 percent, and it costs $50 each time you sell bills, what is the optimum number of times per year that you should sell the bills?

SOLUTION

To solve this problem, determine the optimum amount of money that will be needed. Using Baumol's formula, the results are as follows:

$$Q = \sqrt{(2 \times \text{annual cash disbursements} \times \text{cost per sale of Treasury bills})/\text{interest rate}}$$

$$= \sqrt{(2 \times \$1,200,000 \times \$50)/0.085}$$

$$= \sqrt{\$120,000,000/0.085}$$

$$= \sqrt{\$1,411,764,706}$$

$$= \$37,573.46$$

The optimal amount of bills to be sold is $37,573, rounded to the nearest dollar. Because $100,000 per month is needed, you should sell Treasury bills 2.66 times ($100,000 ÷ $37,573) a month, or about 32 times a year (2.66 x 12).

PROBLEM 3: BAUMOL MODEL

As financial manager of What-Not, Inc. you forecast that you will need new cash at the rate of $2 million per year. You estimate the cost of money at 12 percent and that temporary excess cash balances may be invested at 9 percent. Say also you must pay $5000 every time you obtain new money, no matter how much is raised. How often should you go to the market for capital?

SOLUTION

To solve this problem, you may use the Baumol cash management model, with a twist. First solve for Q, the optimal quantity of cash:

$$Q = \sqrt{(2 \times \$2,000,000 \times \$5,000)/0.12 - 0.09}$$

$$= \sqrt{\$20,000 \text{ million}/0.03}$$

$$= \sqrt{\$666,667 \text{ million}}$$

$$= \$816,496.58$$

The total amount needed is $816,497. Note that the denominator of the equation takes into account that cash not needed immediately will earn a positive rate of return and therefore has the impact of increasing the amount of money that should be obtained.

To determine the interval at which you should "take a trip to the capital markets," given the optimal quantity of money needed, divide the optimal quantity Q by the total amount needed ($2 million). The results are

$$\text{Interval} = Q/\text{total needed per annum}$$
$$= \$816,497/\$2,000,000$$
$$= 0.408 \text{ year}$$

335

To determine the time interval in days between successive trips to the capital markets, multiply this by 365 days, to obtain

$$\text{Interval (years) x 365 days}$$
$$0.408 \times 365 = 149 \text{ days}$$

You should go to the capital markets for funds once every 149 days.

PROBLEM 4: MILLER-ORR MODEL

Now you are to determine the upper and lower cash balance limits using the Miller-Orr model of cash management. A minimum cash balance of $15,000 makes you comfortable, given that the variance of daily cash flows is $9,000,000 or the equivalent of a daily standard deviation of $3000. Additional information is (1) daily interest rate is 0.0236 percent and (2) the transaction cost for each sale or purchase is $25.

SOLUTION

The lower limit LL is already established for you at $15,000. The spread between the upper and lower limit is determined by the following formula:

$$\text{Spread} = 3(0.75 \text{ x transaction cost x variance of cash flows/interest rate})^{.33}$$

Filling in the numbers, we obtain

$$
\begin{aligned}
\text{Spread} &= 3(0.75 \times \$25 \times \$9,000,000/0.000236)^{.33} \\
&= 3(0.75 \times \$25 \times \$9,000,000/0.000236)^{.33} \\
&= 3(\$168,750,000/0.000236)^{.33} \\
&= 3(\$715,042,370,000)^{1/3} \\
&= 3(\$8942.19) \\
&= \$26,826.57 \\
&\quad \text{or about } \$26,827.
\end{aligned}
$$

The next step is to calculate the upper limit, using this formula:

$$
\begin{aligned}
\text{Upper limit} &= \text{lower limit} + \text{spread} \\
&= \$15,000 + \$26,827 \\
&= \$41,827
\end{aligned}
$$

The next step is to calculate the return point, using this formula:

$$
\begin{aligned}
\text{Return point} &= \text{lower limit} + (\text{spread}/3) \\
&= \$15,000 + (\$26,827/3) \\
&= \$15,000 + \$8942 \\
&= \$23,942
\end{aligned}
$$

The *decision rule* which emanates from these calculations is: *When cash balances reach the $41,820 level, invest $17,878 ($41,820 - $23,942) in marketable securities; when cash balances fall to the lower limit of $15,000, sell $8942 ($23,942 - $15,000).* In both instances the return point is achieved by this decision rule.

PROBLEM 5: PLAYING THE FLOAT

As you continue to manage the cash of What-Not, Inc., you discover that there is a time lag among the dates on which you write, mail, and pay bills; the dates when the checks are received by the drawees of your checks, and the interval between the dates your checks are deposited in the drawees' checking accounts and the dates on which they are finally cleared. On the date they are cleared, you know that your checking account will be reduced by the amount of each check, but you estimate that you have on average 2 days before this is likely to happen. If on average you send out $50,000 worth of checks a day and the average return obtainable in the year is 0.02 percent daily, what is the annual dollar return obtainable from investing the "unused" portion of your checking account?

SOLUTION

The average daily float is $100,000 (2 days x $50,000 per day). This will earn $20 ($100,000 x 0.00002) per day, $7300 ($20 x 365 days) per year.

However, if your accounts receivables also contain a 2-day time lag before your checking account is credited with payments, and if daily receipts average $30,000, what then is the dollar advantage of playing the float?

The solution lies in determining the net collection float, the difference between the payables float, arising from having written checks against your checking account, and the collections float, arising from checks received but not cleared. In this instance the net collection float is $20,000 ($50,000 - $30,000). If all else stays the same, you will now earn $4 per day, or $1460 a year. This process continues to be profitable up to the point where the total costs equal the total revenues to be gained from doing it.

SUMMARY

The Rationale

1. Cash pays no interest, which is bad. Cash provides liquidity, which is good.

2. Liquid balances are needed to run day-to-day business affairs.

3. Cost of holding cash equals interest foregone from investing it.

4. Costs of having insufficient cash outweigh those of holding cash.

5. Object: to have "just the right amount."

6. Cash may be viewed as an inventory to be built up and depleted as needed.

7. Inventory models are often invoked to help solve the cash management problem.

Cash as an Inventory

1. Two costs of holding inventories: carrying and ordering.

2. At the margin order costs are reduced when larger and larger orders are placed, but carrying costs rise.

3. Object: to order the needed cash such that marginal reduction in order cost equals marginal carrying cost.

4. The formula:

$$Q = \sqrt{\frac{2 \times \text{annual cash disbursements} \times \text{cost per sale of Treasury bills}}{\text{interest rate}}}$$

5. Baumol's model:
    a. Cash is depleted and replenished at a fixed rate.
    b. Determines both the optimal amounts of cash to replenish and the frequency.
    c. High interest rates imply low Q.
    d. If cash is used at a high rate, high Q.
    e. If cost of selling securities is high, high Q.

6. Miller-Orr model:
    a. Object: cash is now viewed as coming and going randomly.
    b. Establish upper and lower bonds at which to deplete and replenish the cash inventory.
    c. The steps:
       (1) Set lower acceptable limit.
       (2) Estimate the variance of cash flows.
       (3) Analyze the interest rates and transaction costs of each purchase or sale of securities.
       (4) Compute upper limit and the return point.

    Spread $= 3(0.75 \times \text{transaction cost} \times \text{variance of cash flows/interest rate})^{.33}$

    d. Use predictable flows to manage the unpredictable set.
    e. Performed better than a set of financial managers but not better than rules of thumb.

7. Raising cash by borrowing
    a. Borrowing rate likely to exceed lending rate.
    b. The trade-off: between holding minimum cash and investing the balances and borrowing to cover unexpected needs.
    c. The rule:

Probability of borrowing $=$ cost of cash balances/cost of borrowing

Cash Management in Large Corporations

1. Large sums involved so that it ordinarily pays to spend lots of time managing cash.

2. Working-fund accounts handle both disbursements and collections.

Cash Collection Systems

1. Payment float: arises when checks are issued but have not cleared

2. Collection float: arises when a check is received but has not cleared

3. The object: to maximize the net payment float or minimize the net collection float

4. Speeding collections
    a. Concentration banking:
       (1) Bank is close to customers and checks are likely to clear faster.
       (2) Administrative, banking, and transfer costs arise.
    b. Lock-box systems:
       (1) Close to source of checks received, so they clear faster.

(2) Bank handles collection and clearing, for a fee.

(3) Linear programming models exist to determine the optimal number of lock boxes.

5. Controlling cash going out.
   a. Draw checks on remote banks.
   b. Pay at the very latest moment.

Bank Relations

1. Compensating balances go a long way toward cultivating "friendly" bankers.

2. NOW and similar interest-bearing accounts will not necessarily change cash management; they only complicate it somewhat.

LIST OF TERMS

Carrying costs	**Order cost**
Concentration banking	**Payment float**
Float	**Playing the float**
Lock-box system	**Transaction costs**
Marginal carrying costs	**Variance of cash flows**
Marginal reduction in order cost	

EXERCISES

Fill-in Questions

1. Cash provides (more, less) _____ liquidity than securities.
2. In equilibrium the marginal value of cash liquidity is equal to the marginal value of the _____ foregone on investments.
3. The two costs of holding inventory are _____ cost and _____ cost.
4. The optimal order size results when the _____ reduction in order cost is equal to the _____ carrying cost.
5. The main cost of holding cash is _____.
6. The (higher, lower) _____ the interest rate, the higher the optimum amount of Treasury bills sold.
7. In the Miller-Orr cash model, the three factors which determine the extent to which cash wanders randomly between upper and lower bounds are _____, _____, and _____.
8. The value of checks that have been written but have not yet cleared is called _____.
9. _____ banking requires customers to make payments to a local bank rather than directly to the company.
10. Renting a post office box to which customers make payments and from which the bank collects the payments is known as the _____ system of cash management.

Problems

1. What-Not, Inc. has $2 million invested in Treasury bills yielding 8 percent per annum; this will satisfy the firm's need for funds during the coming year, in addition to the cash it has on deposit, of course. If it costs $50 to sell these bills, regardless of the amount, how much should be withdrawn at a time?

2. If What-Not, Inc. needs $167,000 a month, under the conditions of problem 1, how frequently should the financial manager sell off Treasury bills?

3. If the interest rate obtainable on Treasury bills were to decrease to 7 percent, as compared with the 8 percent in problem 1, what bearing would this have on the answers to problems 1 and 2?

4. The financial manager of What-Not is explaining why it does not pay to hold more cash than is needed. The company currently has a total of $5 million in cash but estimates that it will need only $1.5 million during the next 3 months. If the cost of transacting in each is the same, what daily dollar return may the financial manager expect if the annual returns on marketable securities are as follows:

U.S. Treasury bills	9.55 percent
Federal agencies	9.75
Negotiable time CDs	10.00
Commercial paper	9.90
Bankers' acceptances	9.80

5. The demand for Principles of Corporate Finance exceeded everyone's wildest expectations, with the result that the demand for the book at Everyman's Bookstore increased to 400 copies a year. Concomitantly, the cost of money tied up in the inventory increased to $1.40 a book, whereas the fixed and clerical expense increased to $2.20 per order. What is the optimal order size?

6. Running Everyman's Bookstore is not without its financial headaches. After all, some books sell very rapidly, whereas others, equally important to the entire product line of books, move very slowly. A cash-management problem arises, and the owner has programmed the Miller-Orr model into her microcomputer. Using historical data, she finds that the variance in daily dollar cash flows is $4 million. She thinks it might be worthwhile to invest temporary excess cash balances, especially now that annual interest rates for a money fund are 9.2 percent, without a transaction cost, although the cost of her time is $5 per transaction. She feels that the lower cash limit that makes her comfortable is $3000. She then plugs this information into her microcomputer. Give the answers she would obtain for each of the following questions: (a) the lower limit, (b) spread, (c) upper limit, (d) return point, (e) decision rule. Show all calculations and explain fully.

7. The owner of Everyman's Bookstore finds that typical terms of sale in the book industry are 2/30, n/90 and that book companies are very slow to clear her checks. The average elapsed time between the time she mails her check for payment of books and the time they clear her bank is 10 days. She averages $4000 a day of checks that have not cleared her checking account. On the other hand, 60 percent of her average daily sales of $8000 is paid in cash, 20 percent by check, and 20 percent by credit card. Assume that the credit cards and check sales clear at the average rate of 3 days. If she obtains a daily rate of return of 0.015 percent, what is the annual dollar return obtainable from investing the unused portion of her checking account?

Essay Questions

1. What rationale can you give for holding cash, especially when it is considered that no interest is earned? Explain fully.

2. In Baumol's model the higher the interest rate one uses the lower the quantity Q of cash is optimal. Explain why this is so.

3. Put in words the essence of the Miller-Orr model.

4. Explain how float may work either for or against a business firm.

5. The financial manager of the Whozits Company, Inc. is contemplating establishing a lock-box system. She asks you to perform an analysis of the number of lock boxes which she should consider in order to make the system as profitable as possible. What answers might you provide her?

ANSWERS TO EXERCISES

Fill-in Questions

1. more
2. interest
3. carrying; ordering
4. marginal; marginal
5. the interest foregone
6. lower
7. transaction costs; variance of cash flows; the interest rate
8. float
9. concentration
10. lock-box

Problems

1. $Q = [(2 \times 2,000,000 \times \$50)/0.08]^{.50} = \$50,000$

2. $\$167,000/\$50,000 = 3.34$ times per month; once every 9 days (30/3.34)

3. $Q = [(2 \times 2,000,000 \times 50)/.07]^{.50} = \$53,452$; 3.12 times per month; every 9.6 days = every 10 days

4. Treasury bills = $(0.0955/360) \times \$3.5$ million = \$928.47

Federal agencies	947.92
Negotiable time CDs	972.22
Commercial paper	962.50
Banker's acceptances	952.78

5. $Q = [(2 \times 400 \times 2.20)/1.40]^{1/2} = (1760/1.40)^{1/2} = 35.46 = 35$

6. Lower limit = \$3000

$$
\begin{aligned}
\text{Spread} &= 3(0.75 \times \text{transaction cost} \times \text{variance/interest rate})^{.33} \\
&= 3[0.75 \times 5.00 \times \$4,000,000/(0.092/365)]^{.33} \\
&= (3(\$15,000,000/0.0002521)^{.33} \\
&= 3 \times \$3903.967 \\
&= \$11,711.90
\end{aligned}
$$

$$
\begin{aligned}
\text{Upper limit} &= \text{LL} + \text{spread} = \$3000 + \$11,712 = \$14,712
\end{aligned}
$$

$$
\begin{aligned}
\text{Return point} &= \text{lower limit} + (\text{spread}/3) \\
&= \$3000 + (\$11,712/3) \\
&= \$6,904
\end{aligned}
$$

Decision rule: When cash balances reach $14,712, invest $7808 in money funds; when cash falls to $3000, sell $3904.

7. Revenues from payables

$4000 x 0.00015 x 10 days x 360 =	$2160.00
Cost of receivables =	
$8000 x (0.20 + 0.20) x 0.00015 x 3 days x 360 =	518.40
Annual net gain =	$1641.60

CHAPTER 32
SHORT-TERM LENDING AND BORROWING

INTRODUCTION

Financial managers invest temporary excess cash balances in short-term securities. When financial managers have a shortfall of cash, they borrow, usually short-term if the deficiency is expected to be temporary. Efficient financial management therefore requires a working knowledge of the short-term securities in which financial managers may invest and the major aspects of borrowing short-term funds.

WHAT TO LOOK FOR IN CHAPTER 32

This chapter brings together both the major instruments of short-term lending and borrowing and the ways in which financial managers use them. Some of their major characteristics are:

1. The marketplace in which the instruments of lending and borrowing are traded is known as the money market.
2. Short-term debt is usually less risky than corporate bonds.
3. The method of calculating yields on most money-market investments is different from that on other types of investment, because they are sold at a discount from their face value, the difference between the purchase price and the discount being the interest earned.

Government Instruments: The dominant money-market instruments are U.S. Treasury bills, which have maturities of 90, 180, 270, and 360 days and are sold at auction either competitively or at the average price of successful competitive bids. Next in importance are United States government agency securities. Although they are not backed by the full faith and credit of the United States government, their quality is impeccable. Next in order of quality are short-term securities of states and other municipalities. Because interest income is exempt from federal income taxation, municipals are very desirable for investors in a high marginal income tax bracket.

Deposits: Although they are insured up to $100,000 by the Federal Deposit Insurance Corporation and similar agencies for non-bank financial institutions, regular commercial time deposits are not typically thought of as money-market investments, are not sold at a discount from face value, and are not negotiable. Negotiable deposits at commercial banks are called certificates of deposit and have denominations of $100,000 or more, a minimum maturity of 30 days, and a maximum maturity of 270 days. Time deposits of dollars with foreign banks or foreign branches of United States banks are called Eurodollar investments.

Commercial Paper: Although still very, very high quality, commercial paper is another notch down in quality from the money-market investments already discussed. Commercial paper is issued directly by only the best-known, largest, and safest companies. Considerable cost savings are obtainable by issuing commercial paper.

Banker's Acceptances: Banker's acceptances are demands written on a bank which, when accepted, become negotiable money-market instruments. When the bank accepts them, they become high-quality and the returns on them are slightly more than those available on Treasury bills.

Repurchase Agreements: Repurchase agreements are frequently used for investing overnight monies because they are loans secured by a government security dealer and because they are highly liquid.

Floating-Rate Preferred Stock: A recent innovation, these securities take advantage of the preferentially low tax to corporations of dividend income (about 7 percent). The rates are typically tied to the prime lending rate.

Short-Term Borrowing: When companies are short of cash, often they go to banks where they borrow on either an unsecured or a secured basis. Some unsecured loans are self-liquidating, for the sale of goods and services for which the loan was made provides the cash to repay the loan; some are used for interim financing, being replaced when long-term financing is arranged. Frequently a line of credit, which specifies the limit of monies to be borrowed, is arranged.

Secured bank loans usually require collateral, either receivables or inventory. Although almost all trade accounts receivable are acceptable collateral for loans, not all kinds of inventory are. The more one borrows the more one is charged for loans, until a point is reached at which no more borrowing is possible - credit rationing is invoked.

Term Loans: Term loans are a final way in which firms finance their short-term needs, even though their duration is as long as 8 years. Often term loan interest rates vary with the prime rate. A revolving credit, which enables the firm to borrow up to an assured amount over a period of as much as 3 years, is frequently found.

WORKED EXAMPLES

PROBLEM 1:

Beautiful Boats Corporation is preparing for the summer boating season and finds that it will need additional funds in December to build up inventory. The amount needed is $2 million and the company's bank has offered to make a loan at 10 percent annually provided the company maintains a 20 percent compensating balance. The manager of a competing bank, when he dropped in to purchase a boat, indicated that he would lend the company the needed monies for 11 percent with no compensating balance. Which bank is making the better offer? Explain fully. Would your answer be different if Beautiful Boats normally maintained a $50,000 cash balance?

SOLUTION

The compensating balance is $400,000 ($2,000,000 x 0.2). The amount of interest charted is $200,000 ($2,000,000 x 0.1). The amount of funds actually available for use is $1.6 million and the dollar cost of using that sum is $200,000. The cost of the loan is 12.5 percent annually ($200,000 divided by $1,600,000).

If the financial manager normally kept an average of $50,000 on deposit, the amount normally available for use increases to $1.65 million and the cost per annum is 12.12 percent ($200,000 divided by $1,650,000).

In any event the 11 percent loan without the compensating balance is the better deal.

PROBLEM 2:

Beautiful Boats Corporation decides to take out a term loan in the amount of $5 million at a cost of 1 percent above the prime rate of interest. If the prime rate varies from 12, 13, 9, 7, and 6 percent per year in each of the years during which the loan is outstanding, what is the dollar interest cost of the loan? Assume the entire loan is paid off at the end of the fifth year.

SOLUTION

$5 million x 0.12 = $ 600,000
$5 million x 0.13 = $ 650,000
$5 million x 0.09 =   450,000
$5 million x 0.07 =   350,000
$5 million x 0.06 =   300,000
                    $2,350,000

PROBLEM 3:

Compare the loan in problem 2 with a loan which has a fixed 15 percent per year interest cost but which is payable in equal annual installments.

SOLUTION

The formula for determining the annual payment on this loan is

$$\frac{i}{[1 - (1 + i)^{-n}]}$$

where i = rate of interest
n = number of repayment periods

Completing the formula

$$\frac{0.15}{[1 - (1 + 0.15)^{-5}]}$$

and solving, we obtain a factor of 0.2983156, which, when multiplied by the amount of the loan, $5 million, produces the annual payment of $1,491,578. Multiplying the annual payments by 5, the number of payments, we obtain $7,457,890. The total amount paid on the loan is $7,457,890 and the difference between that and the amount of the loan, $5 million, is the amount of interest paid, $2,457,890.

PROBLEM 4:

If a 90-day Treasury bill is quoted at a discount of 9.5 percent, at what price must it be selling? Show calculations.

SOLUTION

The general formula is

Percent discount = [(100 – price)/100] x (360/91)

Inasmuch as we wish to find price, we make that our unknown, x, and solve for it. Thus we have

0.095 = [(100 – x)/100] x 3.956044

Solving for x, we obtain 97.5986, which means that a $10,000 Treasury bill sells for $9759.86.

PROBLEM 5:

What is the annual simple interest return on the Treasury bills discussed in problem 4? What is the effective compound rate of return?

SOLUTION

The relative wealth earned over the 91-day period is given by

$$100/97.5986 = 1.0246$$

or a return of 2.46 percent. When this result is multiplied by (365/91), the annual simple interest return is determined. Thus

Simple annual return = 2.46 percent x (365/91)
= 9.87 percent

The effective compound annual return is 10.24 percent and was found using this formula:

$$(1.0246)^{365/91}$$

SUMMARY

Short-Term Lending

1. Money market: market for short-term investments

2. Less default risk than long-term instruments

3. Calculating the yield on money-market investments
   a. Pure discount securities
   b. Have to adjust yields for discounts

4. U.S. Treasury bills
   a. 90, 180, 270, or 360-day maturities
   b. Impeccable quality

5. Agency securities: extremely high-quality, but lack full faith and credit backing of United States government

6. Short-term tax exempts: income is tax-exempt; lesser quality

7. Bank time deposits and certificates of deposit
   a. Small risk of default; guaranteed up to $100,000
   b. Certificates of deposit (CDs): large-denomination ($100,000 or more) negotiable time deposits.

8. Eurodollar investments: loans of dollars on deposit with foreign banks or foreign branches of United States banks

9. Commercial paper
   a. Issued by large, well-known firms of impeccable credit standing
   b. Maturities: 270 days or less
   c. Reduces borrowing costs up to 1.5 percentage points

10. Banker's acceptances: a bank's IOU to pay a given sum at a future date.

11. Repurchase agreements: RPs, repos, buy-backs, 1-day loans

*Floating-Rate Preferred Stock

1. Dividend income taxed to corporations at about 7 percent effective rate

2. Rate tied to general level of interest rates, to avoid volatility risk of long-term fixed-rate securities.

3. Lower yields, usually

Short-Term Borrowing

1. Unsecured loans: self-liquidating; bridge loans:
   a. Line of credit: may borrow at any time up to a specified limit; generally requires periodic cleanup.
   b. Interest rate tied to prime rate.

2. Loans secured by receivables:
   a. Loan up to 80 percent of value
   b. With recourse: borrower is liable for deficient uncollectable accounts.
   c. Not to be confused with factors, who buy receivables.

3. Loans secured by inventory:
   a. Standardized, nonperishable goods serve as collateral.
   b. Warehouse goods in a public or field warehouse.
   c. Floor planning (automobile).

Term Loans

1. One to 8 years; fixed rate; compensating balance; usually unsecured.

2. Revolving credit: legally assured loan for a specific period, usually 3 years; a put option to sell debt to bank on fixed terms.

LIST OF TERMS

Balloon payments	Line of credit
Banker's acceptances	Money market
Commercial paper	Money market fund
Discount securities	Revolving credit
Floor planning	Self-liquidating loans
Interim financing	Trust receipt

EXERCISES

Fill-in Questions

1. In general the default risk for money-market securities is (greater, less) _____ than it is for long-term debt.
2. Money-market investments are _____ securities.
3. When Treasury bills are selling at a discount, their yield (is, is not) _____ the same as the discount.
4. Noncompetitive bids for Treasury bills are filled at the (lowest, average) _____ price of the successful competitive bids.

5. The income from securities of states and other municipalities are (exempt, nonexempt) _____ from federal income taxes.

6. Time deposits are invariably insured by the Federal Deposit Insurance Corporation up to _____.

7. Negotiable certificates of deposit come in denominations of _____ or more.

8. Commercial paper rates usually are (below, equal to, greater than) _____ the prime rate charged by banks.

9. A bank loan which enables a financial manager to borrow up to a preestablished limit is known as _____.

10. A loan collateralized by receivables, but giving the bank the right to require the firm to meet any deficiencies in collection of the receivables to repay the loan is said to be a loan (with, without) _____ recourse.

11. The major difference between a factor loan and the typical receivables loan of commercial banks is that the former (does, does not) _____ buy the receivables whereas the latter (does, does not) _____.

12. An automobile dealer usually employs _____ in order to finance inventory. As evidence of this arrangement, the automobile dealer signs a _____, which is redeemed when the automobiles are sold.

13. The principal form of medium-term debt financing is called _____.

Problems

1. What-Not's bank has offered to lend the firm $5 million at an annual rate of 12 percent, provided the company maintains a compensating balance of 25 percent. Because the financial manager does not think this is the best deal he can obtain, he approached a competitor bank and it offered him a $5 million loan at 15 percent annually with a 10 percent compensating balance. Which is the better deal, expressed on an annual basis?

2. What would be the better deal, if the company in problem 1 usually kept on deposit an average of $100,000?

3. What-Not decided to take out a 5-year $10 million term loan whose rate of interest is 2 percent above the prime rate. If the prime rate is 12, 13, 14, 15, and 11 percent in each of the years the loan is outstanding, what is the dollar amount of interest paid?

4. How does the loan in problem 3 compare with a 16 percent loan, payable in equal annual installments? What is the dollar difference in interest paid?

5. If 90-day Treasury bills were selling at a discount of 8.53 percent, at what price must the bills have been selling?

6. What is the annual simple interest of the bills discussed in problem 5? The annual compound rate of return?

7. From a current issue of the *Wall Street Journal* gather the money-market rates listed in Figure 32-1 of the text. What changes do you observe and to what do you ascribe them?

Essay Questions

1. Briefly describe the money market and the investments that are traded there.

2. What does it mean when we say: "Money-market investments are pure discount securities"?

3. Discuss the following statement: "Because the middle man is eliminated, or at least most of his functions are eliminated, when commercial paper is issued, there is a significant reduction in the cost of funds when commercial paper is used."

4. What is meant by a self-liquidating loan? Interim financing? Line of credit?

5. What provisions are typically found in a line of credit? Explain why you think they are there.

6. What characteristics should be possessed by assets that are used as collateral for inventory loans?

ANSWERS TO EXERCISES

Fill-in Questions

1. less
2. discount
3. is not
4. average
5. exempt
6. $100,000
7. $100,000
8. below
9. a line of credit
10. with
11. does; does not
12. floor planning; trust receipt
13. term loans

Problems

1. Bank 1

$5,000,000 x 0.25 = $1,250,000;
$5,000,000 x 0.12 = $600,000;
Cost = $600,000/$3,750,000 = 16 percent

Bank 2

$5,000,000 x 0.15 = $750,000;
$5,000,000 x 0.10 = $500,000;
Cost = $750,000/$4,500,000 = 16.7 percent

2. Bank 1: $600,000/$3,875,000 = 15.5 percent
Bank 2: $750,000/$4,600,000 = 16.3 percent

3. $10 million x 0.12 = $1.2 million
$10 million x 0.13 = 1.3 million
$10 million x 0.14 = 1.4 million
$10 million x 0.15 = 1.5 million
$10 million x 0.11 = 1.1 million
$6.5 million

4. Payment = {(0.16/[1 − (1.16)$^{-5}$]} $10,000,000 = $3,054,094

    $3,054,094 x 5 = $15,270,469 (total payments);
    $15,270,469 − $10,000,000 (loan) = $5,270,469 (total interest)

5. $$
\begin{aligned}
0.0853 &= [(100 - x)/100] \times (360/91) \\
0.0853 &= [(100 - x)/100] \times 3.956044 \\
8.53 &= (100 - x)3.956044 \\
&= 395.6044 - 3.956044x \\
387.0744 &= 3.956044x \\
97.843806 &= x
\end{aligned}
$$

6. (100 − 97.843806) x 4 = 8.62 percent
    (1.0220371)$^{365/91}$ = 9.14 percent

CHAPTER 33
MERGERS

INTRODUCTION

Mergers are evaluated in the same way as any other investment: as long as the merged firms are worth more combined than when alone, the net present value of the fusion is profitable and shareholders are better off. Mergers, amicable and hostile, are widespread. It behooves financial managers to know when and under what conditions it pays to merge with another firm.

WHAT TO LOOK FOR IN CHAPTER 33

Mergers are evaluated in the same way as any other investment decision, the decision rule remaining the same: if the investment (acquisition) adds more value to the firm than its costs, it should be undertaken. When evaluating the net present value of an acquisition, a financial manager must evaluate the potential gains from the merger, the estimated cost, and the division of these gains between the two companies' shareholders. The problem lies in finding acquisitions that fill that bill of particulars. The three merger categories are: horizontal integration, in which two firms in the same line of business are merged; vertical integration, in which firms which either consume another firm's output or supply its raw material are merged; and conglomerates, in which companies in unrelated businesses are combined.

The chief economic gains from an acquisition, and therefore increases in the value of the firm, arise from economies of scale, for when they are present, two firms are likely to be worth more together than apart.

Motives That Make Sense: Economies of scale may be found in all three types of mergers. Other merger motives include eliminating inefficiencies, using heretofore unused tax shields, using surplus funds, and combining complementary resources.

Motives That Do Not Make Sense: Contrariwise, diversification, bootstrapping, that is, attempting to increase earnings per share which are not based on the productivity of the assets employed, and allegedly lower financing costs do not hold up well as reasonable reasons for a merger.

Merger Costs: The cost of a merger is a premium that the buying firm pays for the selling firm over the value of a selling firm's value as a separate entity. Given the efficiency of markets in which publicly held stocks are traded, companies selling below their intrinsic value are not likely to be found. The costs of cash deals are straightforward. When stock is used to finance an acquisition, the apparent cost is equal to the difference between the number of shares exchanged times the value per share and the dollar value of the acquired firm. But this may not be the true cost, because the acquired firm's value as a separate entity may not be reflected in the value of its shares, the acquiring firm's value as a separate entity may not be the value of its shares, and most likely, the acquired firm's shareholders may receive some of the gains from the merger by virtue of becoming partners in the merged firm. Remember: when cash is used, the cost of the merger is unaffected by the merger gains; when stock is used, the cost depends on the gains because the gains are shared with the acquired firm's owners.

350

Merger Mechanics: Next, you studied the mechanics of mergers and saw that any large acquiring firm must pay heed to federal anti-trust laws, the foremost of which is the Clayton Act of 1914, which, focuses on the intent to lessen competition substantially or to create a monopoly. Also part of the mechanics is the form of the acquisition. A strictly defined merger, for example, takes place when the liabilities and assets of the selling company are transferred and absorbed by the buying company. Consolidations arise when two or more firms come together under the mantle of a new firm. Some tax considerations enter into the evaluation of mergers because some acquisitions are taxable and others are tax-free. In the former case shareholders are viewed as having sold their shares, and are taxed accordingly, whereas in the latter instance shareholders are viewed as exchanging their shares for new ones, there being no taxes recognized at the time of the fusion. The final mechanical aspect of merging is the way in which the accounting books are kept. Two systems exist: a purchase of assets acquisition in which the assets are acquired for amounts usually in excess of their book value, thereby giving rise to goodwill; and a pooling of interest method whereby the firm's separate balance sheets are merged. The evidence suggests that regardless of which accounting technique is used, acquiring firms do no better under one system as opposed to another.

Some Tactical Considerations: Many mergers are agreed to amicably. Sometimes a proxy fight is engaged in to acquire another firm, giving rise to tender offers, arbitrage, and greenmail. Defensive tactics to ward off unfriendly suitors include poison pills and asset or liability restructuring. It is unclear whether an incumbent management wishes merely to perpetuate itself or acts in the best long-run interest of shareholders when it fights a potential acquisition.

Corporate Restructuring: The large spate of merger activity in the 1980s has given rise to extensive restructuring of corporations. Management leveraged buyouts and divesting corporate assets were and continue to be commonplace.

Merger Waves and Profitability: Mergers come in waves, selling companies gain from mergers, and it is unclear whether acquiring companies benefit as much as the sellers. Notwithstanding, no financial manager can ignore without peril the many problems of pulling off a merger successfully.

WORKED EXAMPLES

PROBLEM 1: NPV AND COST OF MERGER
Sink, Inc. plans to merge with Swim Corp. The capital market places a value on Sink of $7.875 million and Swim is valued at $500,000, when they are evaluated separately. After the merger, economies of scale will result in additional cash flows, the present value of which is $250,000. What is the net present value (NPV) of the merger? The cost? Sink will buy Swim for $600,000 in cash. Sink has 150,000 shares outstanding.

SOLUTION
The NPV is obtained by taking the difference between the gain from the merger and the cost.

$$\begin{aligned}
\text{Cost} &= \text{cash} - PV_{Swim} \\
&= \$600,000 - \$500,000 \\
&= \$100,000
\end{aligned}$$

$$\begin{aligned}
\text{NPV} &= \text{gain} - \text{cost} \\
&= [(PV_{Sink + Swim}) - (PV_{Sink} + PV_{Swim})] - (\text{cash} - PV_{Swim}) \\
&= [(\$7,875,000 + \$500,000 + \$250,000) - (\$7,875,000 + \$500,000)] - \\
&\quad (\$600,000 - \$500,000) \\
&= (\$8,625,000 - \$8,375,000) - \$100,000 \\
&= \$250,000 - \$100,000 \\
&= \$150,000
\end{aligned}$$

PROBLEM 2: GAINS IN SHAREHOLDER WEALTH

How did the shareholders of Sink and of Swim make out on the merger?

SOLUTION

To determine how shareholders make out from a merger, begin by recognizing that the cost of the merger is a gain to Swim's shareholders; they capture $100,000 of the $250,000 gain. The NPV calculated above is the gain to Sink's shareholders. It works out this way:

Net gain to acquiring firm's shareholders = overall gain to the combination – gain captured by acquired firm's shareholders

$$= \$250,000 - \$100,000$$
$$= \$150,000$$

As a check, use this formula:

$$
\begin{aligned}
NPV &= \text{wealth with merger} - \text{wealth without merger} \\
&= (PV_{Sink + Swim} - \text{cash acquisition outlay}) - PV_{Sink} \\
&= [(\$7,875,000 + \$500,000 + \$250,000) - \$600,000] - \$7,875,000 \\
&= \$8,625,000 - \$600,000 - \$7,875,000 \\
&= \$150,000
\end{aligned}
$$

PROBLEM 3: BOOTSTRAPPING

Now say that Sink, Inc. is considering the acquisition of Float Company. The data for this deal are set forth in Table 33-1. Assuming there are no economic gains from the merger, complete the third column of that table.

SOLUTION

The third column is completed. Because there are no economic gains from the merger, the combined values (line 6) of the two firms (PV of Sink and Float combined) is simply the sum of their separate PVs. Because Sink is selling at a higher multiple of earnings per share, it purchased Float with half again as many shares as Float had outstanding, making for a total of 225,000 after the merger. The firm's total earnings is the sum of the two entities. When both total earnings and total value are divided by the number of outstanding shares, lines 1 to 3 may be completed. Note that earnings per share increase as well as the current earnings per dollar invested (line 7), but that nothing else changes. Such bootstrapping is a myth and does not create value.

TABLE 33-1 IMPACT OF MERGER ON MARKET VALUE AND EARNINGS PER SHARE OF SINK, INC.*

	SINK, INC. (PREMERGER)	FLOAT COMPANY	SINK, INC. (POSTMERGER)
1. Earnings per share	$ 3.50	$ 3.50	$ 4.67
2. Price per share	$52.50	$26.25	$52.50
3. Price-earnings ratio	15.00	7.50	11.25
4. Number of shares	150,000	150,000	225,000
5. Total earnings	$525,000	$525,000	$1,050,000
6. Total market value	$7,875,000	$3,937,500	$11,812,500
7. Current earnings per dollar invested in stock (line 1 divided by line 2)	$0.067	$0.133	$0.089

*Because of rounding, not all the numbers are exact.

PROBLEM 4: MERGER COST

Now, suppose that just before the merger of Sink and Swim, the following conditions prevailed:

	SINK	SWIM
Market price per share	$52.50	$20.00
Number of shares	150,000	25,000
Market value of firm	$7,875,000	$500,000

The problem is to determine the cost of the merger, assuming all the conditions in problems 1 and 3 continue to hold. Also assume that the market bids up the price of Swim's stock to $22 after the merger announcement.

SOLUTION

The answer is exactly what we obtained in problem 1, that is, before the merger. After the announcement the numbers work out this way:

$$
\begin{aligned}
\text{Cost} &= (\text{cash} - \text{MV}_{\text{Swim}}) + (\text{MV}_{\text{Swim}} - \text{PV}_{\text{Swim}}) \\
&= [\$600,000 - (\$22 \times 25,000)] + [(\$22 \times 25,000) - \$500,000] \\
&= (\$600,000 - \$550,000) + (\$550,000 - \$500,000) \\
&= \$50,000 + \$50,000 \\
&= \$100,000
\end{aligned}
$$

We see (surprise!) that the total cost is the same as before, although its two components have changed.

PROBLEM 5: MERGER COSTS WHEN SHARES ARE EXCHANGED

Now let's say Sink, Inc. wishes to estimate the cost of a merger that entails an exchange of 11,429 (rounded to nearest full share) instead of $600,000 in cash. What are the apparent and true costs of the merger?

SOLUTION

The apparent cost is straightforward.

$$
\begin{aligned}
\text{Apparent cost} &= \text{(number of shares x market price per share)} - PV_{Swim} \\
&= (11{,}429 \times \$52.50) - \$500{,}000 \\
&= \$600{,}000 - \$500{,}000 = \$100{,}000
\end{aligned}
$$

which is what we obtained in all previous cases.

The true cost is determined by the amount of the new value the Swim shareholders obtain in the deal. That is, we have to determine what x is.

$$
\begin{aligned}
x &= \frac{\text{new shares issued to acquired firm's shareholder}}{\text{(outstanding shares of acquiring firm + new shares issued to acquired firm's shareholders)}} \\[6pt]
&= 11{,}429/(150{,}000 + 11{,}429) \\
&= 11{,}429/161{,}429 \\
&= 0.0708 = 7.08 \text{ percent}
\end{aligned}
$$

Sink, Inc. gives up slightly more than 7 percent of its claim on the total value of the merged firm. Now we proceed to determine the true cost of the merger in this way:

$$
\begin{aligned}
\text{True cost} &= x PV_{Sink + Swim} - PV_{Swim} \\
&= 0.0708(\$7{,}875{,}000 + \$500{,}000 + \$250{,}000) - \$500{,}000 \\
&= 0.0708(\$8{,}625{,}000) - \$500{,}000 \\
&= \$610{,}650 - \$500{,}000 \\
&= \$110{,}650
\end{aligned}
$$

PROBLEM 6: POOLING OF INTEREST AND PURCHASE OF ASSETS ACCOUNTING

The book value balance sheets of Sink, Inc. and Swim Corp. are set forth at the top of Table 33-2. What would the ending balance sheets look like after the merger using both pooling of interest and purchase of assets accounting methods?

SOLUTION

Section 2 of the table contains the answer.

TABLE 33-2 PURCHASE OF ASSETS VS. POOLING OF INTEREST ACCOUNTING METHODS FOR MERGER OF SINK WITH SWIM IN MILLIONS

1. INITIAL BALANCE SHEETS

SINK, INC.					SWIM CORP.		
NWC	$1.0	$1.4	D		NWC	$0.1	$0.1	D
FA	2.5	2.1	E		FA	0.2	0.2	E
	$3.5	$3.5				$0.3	$0.3	

2. POOLING OF INTEREST

PURCHASE OF ASSETS
(PURCHASE PRICE – $600,000)

SINK, INC.					SINK, INC.		
NWC	$1.1	$1.5	D		NWC	$1.1	$1.5	D
FA	2.7	2.3	E		FA	2.7		
	$3.8	$3.8			Goodwill	0.4	2.7	E
						$4.2	$4.2	

SUMMARY

Estimating the Economic Gains and Costs of Mergers

1. Present values add.

2. Economic gain results only if the two firms are worth more together than separately.

$$\text{Gain} = PV_{AB} - (PV_A + PV_B)$$
$$\text{Cost} = \text{cash} - PV_B$$

3. Acquired shareholders capture some of the gain, which is part of the cost of the merger.

$$NPV = \text{gain} - \text{cost}$$
$$NPV = PV_{AB} - (PV_A + PV_B) - (\text{cash} - PV_B)$$
$$NPV = \text{wealth with merger} - \text{wealth without merger}$$

Sensible Motives for Mergers

1. Economies of scale: natural goal of horizontal mergers

2. Economies of vertical integration: coordination and administration; technology

3. Eliminate inefficiencies

4. Unused tax shields

5. Use of surplus funds

6. Combining complementary sources

Some Dubious Reasons for Mergers

1. Diversification: shareholders diversify for themselves, probably more cheaply and efficiently.

2. Bootstrapping: comeuppance occurs when earnings growth slows.

3. Lower financing costs: iffy unless it lowers the chance of financial distress.

Estimating the Cost of a Merger When Financed by Cash

1. Cost: The premium paid to selling firm over its value as a separate entity.

$$\text{Cost} = (\text{cash} - MV_B) + (MV_B - PV_B)$$
$$= \text{premium paid over market value of B} + \text{difference between market value of B and its value as a separate entity}$$

Estimating the Cost of a Merger When Financed by Stock

1. Apparent cost may not equal true cost.

$$\text{True cost} = xPV_{AB} - PV_B$$

2. Cash deals: cost unaffected by merger gains.

3. Stock deals: cost depends on gains because they are shared.

The Mechanics of a Merger

1. Mergers and antitrust law
   a. The statutes: (1) Sherman Act; (2) Clayton Act; (3) Federal Trade Commission Act
   b. The actions: conspiracy in restraint of trade; unfair competition; acts to lessen competition or tend to create a monopoly

2. The form of acquisition
   a. Merger: buyer assumes all the assets and all the liabilities of seller
   b. Acquisition of stock
   c. Acquisition of assets

3. A note on merger accounting:
   a. Purchase of assets: add together two firms' balance sheets.
   b. Pooling of interests: may pay more for assets than recorded on books, giving rise to goodwill.
   c. Nothing happens to cash flows.
   d. In efficient capital markets, accounting treatments should make no difference.

4. Some tax considerations
   a. Taxable acquisitions: shareholders viewed as having sold shares and taxed accordingly; firm assets are revalued with new depreciation schedules
   b. Tax-free acquisition: selling shareholders viewed as exchanging shares for new ones of like kind and quality; firm taxed as if two firms had always been together.

Merger Tactics

1. Many mergers are amicable; some are hostile.

2. Proxy fights arise, via tender offers.

3. Arbitrageurs speculate on the prospects of the proxy fight.

4. Management may contest takeover bids.
   a. Need to invoke defensive tactics, often before a takeover attempt occurs.
   b. May wish to extract a higher bid price.
   c. May be motivated to protect its jobs.

Corporate Restructuring

1. Cash-rich companies may be forced to pay that cash to shareholders or forced to diversify into areas beyond its present competence, if acquired by another firm.

2. Management buyouts occur, usually by issuing large sums of debt.

3. Often certain assets are sold off to make acquisition less attractive.

Merger Waves and Profitability

1. Mergers come in waves, but we do not know why.

2. Selling companies gain from mergers; average premium is about 20 percent in the case of mergers and 30 percent in the case of tenders.

3. Not clear that acquiring companies gain.

4. Postmerger integration problems: Overestimate value of some assets; people; administrative.

LIST OF TERMS

Amalgamation (consolidation)
Apparent cost of mergers
Bootstrapping
Clayton Act of 1914
Complementary resources
Conglomerate mergers
Consolidation (amalgamation)
Economic gains from the merger
Economies of scale

Federal Trade Commission Act of 1914
Horizontal mergers
Pooling of interest accounting
Proxy
Purchase of assets accounting
Sherman Act of 1890
Tender offer
True cost of mergers
Vertical mergers

EXERCISES

Fill-in Questions

1. If two merged firms are worth more together than apart, an _____ gain results.
2. A _____ merger is one that takes place between two firms in the same line of business; a _____ merger is one in which the buyer expands forward or backward to the ultimate consumer or the supplier of raw materials; and a _____ merger involves companies in unrelated lines of business.
3. Bootstrapping (does, does not) _____ result in real gains created by a merger and there (are, are not) _____ increases in the two firms' combined value.
4. The (true, apparent) _____ cost of a merger between two firms may exceed the (true, apparent) _____ cost, if the stock prices, observed (before, after) _____ the merger is announced do not reflect the merger gains or their division between the two firms' stockholders.
5. The _____ Act focuses primarily on restraint of trade; _____ Act focuses primarily on unfair competition; and the _____ focuses primarily on acts that tend to lessen competition substantially or create a monopoly.
6. Strictly defined, a merger refers to the case in which the assets and liabilities of the selling company are transferred to the buying company and the (selling, buying) _____ company disappears as a separate entity.
7. When two companies are combined into a single new company, a _____ is said to have taken place.
8. The right to vote someone else's shares is called a _____.
9. _____ is a general offer made directly to a firm's shareholders to buy their stock at a specified price.
10. When a merger takes place and two firms' separate balance sheets are added together, this is called a _____ from an accounting standpoint.
11. When the accounting technique used to give evidence to a merger gives rise to goodwill, it is safe to assume that a _____ method of accounting was used.

Problems

1. Use the data for the three separate firms in Table 33-3 to answer the following questions. Answer each question independent of all other questions.
   a. What are the cost and net present value of the combination of What-Not, Inc. and If-Not, Inc., if, as a result of the merger, the economies expected are $400,000 and What-Not, Inc. plans to pay $3 million in cash for If-Not?
   b. If What-Not acquires If-Not for $3 million in cash, how will the shareholders of each make out on the deal?
   c. If What-Not, Inc. merges with Why-Not, Inc. there are no economic gains from the merger, and $1.2 million in stock is paid for Why-Not, demonstrate the bootstrapping effect of the merger.

TABLE 33-3 DATA FOR WHAT NOT, INC., IN MILLIONS

	WHAT-NOT, INC.	IF-NOT, INC.	WHY-NOT, INC.
Earnings per share	$4	$2	$2
Price per share	$64	$28	$12
Price-earnings ratio	16	14	6
Number of shares	200,000	100,000	200,000
Total earnings	$800,000	$200,000	$200,000
Total market value	$12,800,000	$2,800,000	$2,400,000
Book values:			
NWC	$1.1	$0.4	$0.3
FA	2.8	1.0	0.8
D	2.0	0.7	0.3
E	1.9	0.7	0.8

d. Calculate the apparent and true costs of the merger between What-Not, Inc. and If-Not, Inc., assuming expected economies of $400,000 and the shareholders of If-Not receive one share of What-Not for every two shares they hold.

e. Show the results of accounting for the merger between What-Not, Inc. and If-Not, Inc., using both pooling of assets and a purchase of assets methods, where If-Not is acquired for $3 million.

Essay Questions

1. Explain why buying another company is just like any other investment decision financial managers make.

2. Explain how unused tax shields may be beneficial to an acquiring firm.

3. Set forth some doubtful reasons that are used to explain mergers, and explain why you selected those that you did.

4. It has been and still is argued that mergers are consummated in order to diversify a firm. Evaluate the diversification motive for mergers.

5. Is it true that mergers tend to lower financing costs?

6. Why do you think mergers come in waves, and why do you think that the crest of the waves coincides with high stock prices?

7. Who gains more from a merger, the selling company or the acquiring one? Explain the reasons why you think one gains more than the other. Is it possible that neither gains? Explain.

8. Many financial managements contest takeovers. Why do you think this is the case, and what techniques do they employ?

ANSWERS TO EXERCISES

Fill-in Questions

1. economic
2. horizontal; vertical; conglomerate
3. does not; are not
4. true; apparent; before
5. Sherman Act; Federal Trade Commission; Clayton Act of 1914
6. selling
7. consolidation (amalgamation)
8. proxy
9. tender offer
10. pooling of interest
11. purchase of assets

Problems

1. (a)

$$\text{Cost} = \text{cost} - PV_{\text{If-Not}}$$
$$= \$3,000,000 - \$2,800,000$$
$$= \$200,000$$

$$
\begin{aligned}
NPV &= \text{gain} - \text{cost} \\
&= [PV_{W+I} - (PV_W + PV_I)] - (\text{cash} - PV_I) \\
&= [(12.8 + 2.8 + 0.4) - (12.8 + 2.8)] - (3.0 - 2.8) \\
&= (16 - 15.6) - 0.2 \\
&= 0.4 - 0.2 \\
&= 0.200 = \$200,000
\end{aligned}
$$

(b)

Net gain to acquiring firm = average gain to combination – gain captured by acquired firm

What's gain = $400,000 - $200,000 (If's gain) = $200,000

What's gain

$$
\begin{aligned}
NPV &= \text{wealth with merger} - \text{wealth without merger} \\
&= (PV_{W+I} - \text{cash outlay}) - PV_W \\
&= [(12.8 + 2.8 + 0.4) - 3)] - 12.8 \\
&= (16 - 3) - 12.8 = 13 - 12.8 = \$200,000
\end{aligned}
$$

(c)

Number of shares used to buy Why-Not = value of Why-Not ÷ market price per share of What-Not
$$= \$2,400,000/\$64$$
$$= 37,500 \text{ shares}$$

Total shares outstanding after merger = 200,000 + 37,500
$$= 237,500$$

BOOTSTRAPPING EFFECTS OF THE MERGER BETWEEN WHAT-NOT, INC. AND WHY-NOT, INC.

	WHAT-NOT, INC. (PREMERGER)	WHY-NOT, INC.	WHAT-NOT, INC. (POSTMERGER)
1. Earnings per share	$4.00	$2.00	$4.21
2. Price per share	$64	$12	$64
3. Price-earnings ratio	16	6	15.20
4. Number of shares	200,000	200,000	237,500
5. Total earnings	$800,000	$200,000	$1,000,000
6. Total market value	$12,800,000	$2,400,000	$15,200,000
7. Current earnings per dollar invested in stock	$0.0625	$0.1667	$0.0658

(d)

$$\text{Apparent cost} = (\text{number of shares x market price per share}) - PV_I$$
$$= (50,000 \text{ x } \$64) - 2.8$$
$$= 3.2 - 2.8 = \$400,000$$

True cost

$$x = \text{new shares issued to acquired firm's stockholders/outstanding shares of acquiring firm + new shares}$$
$$= 50,000/200,000 + 50,000 = 50,000/250,000 = 0.2$$

$$\text{True cost} = (x)(PV_{W+I}) - PV_I$$
$$= 0.2 \text{ x } 16.0 - 2.8$$
$$= 0.4 = \$400,000$$

(e)

PURCHASE OF ASSETS VS. POOLING OF INTEREST OF WHAT-NOT, INC. AND IF-NOT, INC.

1. INITIAL BALANCE SHEETS

    WHAT-NOT, INC

NWC	$1.1	D	$2.0
FA	2.8	E	1.9
	$3.9		$3.9

    IF-NOT, INC.

NWC	$0.4	D	$0.7
FA	1.0	E	0.7
	$1.4		$1.4

2. POOLING OF INTEREST

    WHAT-NOT, INC

NWC	$1.5	D	$2.7
FA	3.8	E	2.6
	$5.3		$5.3

    PURCHASE OF ASSETS

    WHAT-NOT, INC.

NWC	$1.5	D	$2.7
FA	3.8		
Goodwill	2.3	E	4.9
	$7.6		$7.6

CHAPTER 34
INTERNATIONAL FINANCIAL MANAGEMENT

INTRODUCTION

Three additional problems are tacked onto financial decision making when firms operate in international markets: (1) financial managers must contend with more than one currency; (2) interest rates differ from country to country; and (3) financial managers must analyze international investments differently from national investments. As you know now, even international investments are subject to the rigour of net present value: If an international investment adds more value to the firm than it takes away, accept it.

WHAT TO LOOK FOR IN CHAPTER 34

The foreign exchange market is the place in which foreign currencies are traded. Spot rates, which are rates of exchange on foreign currencies for immediate delivery, and forward rates, which are rates of exchange in foreign currencies deliverable in the future, form the basis for dealing in foreign currencies.

Four Fundamental Relations: Four fundamental relations add insight to foreign exchange markets: (1) those dealing with different rates of interest on different currencies; (2) differences between forward and spot rates of the same currencies; (3) determination of next year's expected spot rates of exchange between two currencies; and (4) rates of inflation between two foreign countries and their impact of exchange rates. All four are interdependent because: differences in interest rates between two currencies are equal to differences in expected inflation rates, which in turn are equal to expected changes in spot rates, which themselves are equal to differences between forward and spot rates of the same currency, which, finally, are equal to differences in interest rates between two different currencies. All of which is to say that the system for analysis is about as self-contained as one can imagine. These relations arise because the real rate of return on invested capital among all countries tend to equilibrate even though nominal interest rates may differ. The interest rate parity theory, the expectations theory of forward rates, the law of one price, and capital market equilibrium are the concepts underlying the solutions to the four fundamental relations.

Currency Risk: Most financial managers hedge their foreign investment exposures. Financial managers may insure themselves against currency risk by selling foreign currencies forward against the currencies they presently have.

International Investment Decisions: Not surprisingly you will find that overseas investments are evaluated by discounting estimated cash flows at the opportunity cost of capital, and positive adjusted NPV projects are accepted. Two ways exist to calculate net present value. One converts the foreign currency into the domestic one, and discounts the cash flows at the domestic opportunity cost of capital. This method requires a forecast of foreign exchange rates. The other method discounts foreign investments at the foreign country's cost of capital and converts the result into the domestic currency.

The Cost of Capital for Foreign Investment: As you ruminate about this unresolved issue, remember that first principles tell us to use rates of return on comparable-risk assets. Remember also that diversification is valuable and international diversification may be even more valuable. In general, it is wiser to adjust estimated cash flows for foreign risks than to adjust the discount rate.

Financing Foreign Operations: When financing foreign operations, financial managers have three options: (1) export capital from the domestic country; (2) borrow foreign currencies; and (3) borrow wherever interest rates are lowest. It should not be surprising to know that financial managers use all three. Taxes play an important role in how international investments are financed. Minimizing the taxes paid in both domestic and foreign countries is advisable, and double tax agreements tend to mitigate, but not obviate, this matter.

Political Risk: If foreign governments change the rules after you have made your investments, "all bets are off." To mitigate this potential problem make someone else a party to the investment and financing decisions.

WORKED EXAMPLES

PROBLEM 1: FOREIGN EXCHANGE DISCOUNT OR PREMIUM
Using Figure 34-1, calculate the Monday forward discount or premium for the dollar against each of the following currencies: British pound; Canadian dollar; French franc; Japanese yen; and West German mark.

SOLUTION
To answer this problem, calculate the per period rate of discount or premium and then multiply by the number of periods in the year to approximate the annual discount or premium. For example, taking British pound, 90-day futures, we obtain

Forward discount (premium) = [(futures exchange rate - spot exchange rate) ÷ spot
exchange rate] x 100
= [(1.8607 - 1.8610) ÷ 1.8610] x 100
= -0.016 percent.

The per period forward discount is -0.016 percent. The annual rate is -0.19 percent [(360/30) x -0.016 percent].

The annual rate for 90-day futures is

Forward discount = (360 days ÷ 90 days) x [(1.8575 - 1.8610) ÷ 1.8610] x 100
= 4 x -0.188071 = -0.75 percent.

And the annual 180-day forward rate is

Forward discount = (360 ÷ 180) x [(1.8509 - 1.8610) ÷ 1.8610] x 100
= -1.09 percent

The comparable rates for the other currencies are set forth in Table 34-1.

Table 34-1 Forward Discounts (Premiums), Percent

Days	British Pound	Canadian Dollar	French Franc	Japanese Yens	Swiss Franc	W. German Mark
30	-0.19	-0.63	-1.30	4.15	4.65	4.60
90	-0.75	-0.94	-1.30	3.75	4.34	4.28
180	-1.09	-1.10	-1.41	3.63	4.31	4.19

364

Figure 34-1
Reprinted by permission of *The Wall Street Journal*, © Dow Jones & Company, Inc. (1987). All rights reserved.

FOREIGN EXCHANGE

Monday, December 28, 1987

The New York foreign exchange selling rates below apply to trading among banks in amounts of $1 million and more, as quoted at 3 p.m. Eastern time by Bankers Trust Co. Retail transactions provide fewer units of foreign currency per dollar.

Country	U.S. $ equiv. Mon.	U.S. $ equiv. Thurs.	Currency per U.S. $ Mon.	Currency per U.S. $ Thurs.
Argentina (Austral)	.2857	.2857	3.50	3.50
Australia (Dollar)	.7170	.7160	1.3947	1.3966
Austria (Schilling)	.08711	.08711	11.48	11.48
Belgium (Franc)				
Commercial rate	.02998	.02935	33.35	34.07
Financial rate	.02985	.027924	33.50	34.20
Brazil (Cruzado)	.01422	.01432	70.30	69.82
Britain (Pound)	1.8610	1.8315	.5373	.5460
30-Day Forward	1.8607	1.8312	.5374	.5461
90-Day Forward	1.8575	1.8280	.5384	.5470
180-Day Forward	1.8509	1.8214	.5403	.5490
Canada (Dollar)	.7663	.7653	1.3050	1.3067
30-Day Forward	.7659	.7649	1.3057	1.3074
90-Day Forward	.7645	.7635	1.3080	1.3097
180-Day Forward	.7621	.7611	1.3122	1.3139
Chile (Official rate)	.004302	.004302	232.43	232.43
China (Yuan)	.2687	.2687	3.7220	3.7220
Colombia (Peso)	.003815	.003815	262.14	262.14
Denmark (Krone)	.1587	.1594	6.3025	6.2750
Ecuador (Sucre)				
Official rate	.004049	.004049	247.00	247.00
Floating rate	.004728	.004728	211.50	211.50
Finland (Markka)	.2472	.2482	4.0450	4.0290
France (Franc)	.1845	.1818	5.4215	5.5020
30-Day Forward	.1843	.1816	5.4255	5.5060
90-Day Forward	.1839	.1811	5.4370	5.5215
180-Day Forward	.1832	.1829	5.4550	5.4685
Greece (Drachma)	.007752	.007752	129.00	129.00
Hong Kong (Dollar)	.1288	.1288	7.7650	7.7650
India (Rupee)	.07752	.07698	12.90	12.99
Indonesia (Rupiah)	.0006061	.0006061	1650.00	1650.00
Ireland (Punt)	1.6285	1.6280	.6143	.6141
Israel (Shekel)	.6441	.6441	1.5525	1.5525
Italy (Lira)	.0008511	.0008382	1175.00	1193.00
Japan (Yen)	.008097	.007937	123.50	126.00
30-Day Forward	.008125	.007964	123.07	125.57
90-Day Forward	.008173	.008009	122.36	124.86
180-Day Forward	.008244	.008078	121.30	123.80
Jordan (Dinar)	2.9155	2.9155	.0343	.0343
Kuwait (Dinar)	3.6590	3.6590	.2733	.2733

Country	U.S. $ equiv. Mon.	U.S. $ equiv. Thurs.	Currency per U.S. $ Mon.	Currency per U.S. $ Thurs.
Lebanon (Pound)	.002146	.002146	466.00	466.00
Malaysia (Ringgit)	.4008	.4007	2.4950	2.4955
Malta (Lira)	3.1477	3.1447	.3180	.3180
Mexico (Peso)				
Floating rate	.0004545	.0004545	2200.00	2200.00
Netherland (Guilder)	.5563	.5461	1.7977	1.8310
New Zealand (Dollar)	.6605	.6520	1.5140	1.5337
Norway (Krone)	.1569	.1570	6.3750	6.3700
Pakistan (Rupee)	.05714	.05714	17.50	17.50
Peru (Inti)	.03030	.03030	33.00	33.00
Philippines (Peso)	.04824	.04824	20.73	20.73
Portugal (Escudo)	.007502	.007519	133.30	133.00
Saudi Arabia (Rival)	.2666	.2666	3.7505	3.7505
Singapore (Dollar)	.5020	.5025	1.9920	1.9900
South Africa (Rand)				
Commercial Rate	.5110	.5110	1.9569	1.9569
Financial Rate	.3225	.3200	3.1007	3.1250
South Korea (Won)	.001258	.001258	795.10	795.10
Spain (Peseta)	.009029	.009042	110.75	110.60
Sweden (Krona)	.1686	.1689	5.9300	5.9220
Switzerland (Franc)	.7743	.7567	1.2915	1.3215
30-Day Forward	.7773	.7596	1.2865	1.3165
90-Day Forward	.7827	.7648	1.2776	1.3076
180-Day Forward	.7910	.7727	1.2642	1.2942
Taiwan (Dollar)	.03509	.03509	28.50	28.50
Thailand (Baht)	.03969	.03969	25.19	25.19
Turkey (Lira)	.001012	.001012	987.82	987.82
United Arab (Dirham)	.2723	.2723	3.673	3.673
Uruguay (New Peso)				
Financial	.003660	.003660	273.23	273.25
Venezuela (Bolivar)				
Official rate	.1333	.1333	7.50	7.50
Floating rate	.03396	.03396	29.45	29.45
W. Germany (Mark)	.6256	.6144	1.5985	1.6275
30-Day Forward	.6280	.6168	1.5924	1.6214
90-Day Forward	.6323	.6209	1.5816	1.6106
180-Day Forward	.6387	.6271	1.5657	1.5947
SDR	1.40817	1.38971	0.710140	0.719576
ECU	1.29097	1.26534	......	......

Special Drawing Rights are based on exchange rates for the U.S., West German, British, French and Japanese currencies. Source: International Monetary Fund.

ECU is based on a basket of community currencies. Source: European Community Commission.

z-Not quoted

PROBLEM 2: EQUILIBRIUM FORWARD RATE

As the financial manager of What-Not, Inc. you have $10 million to invest for 1 year and are considering United States or British loans. Say the United States interest rate on 1-year loans of this size is 9 percent, the current spot rate on the British pound is that shown in Figure 34-1, and the rate of interest on 1-year investments in Britain is 8.5 percent. What forward rate of exchange is needed to make you indifferent between investing in United States and British 1-year loans?

SOLUTION

To solve this problem, the schematic which depicts the interrelationships among differences in interest rates, expected differences in inflation rates, the expected change in spot rates, and differences between forward and spot rates is necessary. The formulas are as follows:

$$\text{Difference in interest rates} = \frac{(1 + r_\$)}{1 + i_£} \tag{1}$$

$$\text{Expected differences in inflation rates} = \frac{E(1 + i_\$)}{E(1 + i_£)} \tag{2}$$

$$\text{Expected changes in spot rates} = \frac{E(S_{\$/£})}{S_{\$/£}} \tag{3}$$

$$\text{Differences between forward and spot rates} = \frac{f_{\$/£}}{S_{\$/£}} \tag{4}$$

Because everything depends on everything, and more strongly, everything *equals* everything, each equation may be set equal to any other, so that

Differences in interest rates = expected differences in inflation rates = expected changes in spot rates = differences between forward and spot rates

In this case you are interested in equations (1) and (4), because you are dealing with differences in interest rates, equation (1), and differences between forward and spot rates, equation (4). Right? Right! So we have

Difference in interest rates = differences between forward and spot rates

$$\frac{1 + r_\$}{1 + r_£} = \frac{f_{\$/£}}{S_{\$/£}}$$

Filling in the available data, we have

$$\frac{1 + 0.09}{1 + 0.085} = \frac{f_{\$/£}}{1.8610}$$

$$1.0046 = \frac{f_{\$/£}}{1.8610}$$

$$f_{\$/£} = 1.8525$$

The equilibrium 1-year forward rate on British pounds is 1.8525.

PROBLEM 3: IMPLIED RETURNS

If the West German expected inflation rate is 4 percent, that of the United States is 5 percent, and 1-year West German loans return 6 percent, what is the implied rate of return on United States 1-year loans?

SOLUTION

From the set of equations set forth in the solution to problem 2 we find that equations (1) and (2) are to be used to solve this problem. The setup follows:

Difference in interest rates = expected differences in inflation rates

$$\frac{1 + r_\$}{1 + r_{DM}} = \frac{E(1 + i_\$)}{E(1 + i_{DM})}$$

$$\frac{1 + r_\$}{1.06} = \frac{1.05}{1.04}$$

$$r_\$ = 7.02 \text{ percent}$$

PROBLEM 4: ESTIMATED INFLATION RATE

Using the data in Figure 34-1 for the spot rate, assuming the 1-year forward Swiss franc rate is 0.7950, and assuming an expected 1-year inflation rate in Switzerland of 3 percent, what is the implied United States inflation rate for the coming year?

SOLUTION

Equations (2) and (4) are used to solve this problem.

Expected differences in inflation rates = differences between forward and spot rates

$$\frac{E(1 + i_\$)}{E(1 + i_{SF})} = \frac{f_{\$/SF}}{S_{\$/SF}}$$

$$\frac{1 + i_\$}{1.03} = \frac{0.7950}{0.7743}$$

$$i_\$ = 5.75 \text{ percent}$$

PROBLEM 5: DOUBLE-TAX

What-Not, Inc has two operating subsidiaries in two mythical countries, Myth 1 and Myth 2. What-Not's United States corporate tax rate is 34 percent and those for Myth 1 and Myth 2 are 25 and 42 percent. Both Myths have a double-tax agreement with the United States. If What-Not earns $1 million before taxes in both countries, what taxes are paid in the United States and overseas, if all net income is remitted in the form of cash dividends?

SOLUTION

	Myth 1 Tax - 25.00%	Myth 2 Tax - 42.00%
Profits before tax	1,000,000	1,000,000
Foreign country tax	250,000	420,000
Net profits	750,000	580,000
United States tax	340,000	340,000
Less double tax relief (maximum 34%)	250,000	340,000
U.S. tax payable	90,000	0
Available for dividend	660,000	580,000

SUMMARY

The Foreign Exchange Market

1. Exchange rate: the ratio of the number of domestic currency units needed to buy one unit of a foreign currency

2. Spot rate of exchange: price of currency for immediate delivery

3. Forward rate of exchange: price of currency for future delivery

Some Basic Relations

1. Figure 34-2 indicates general relationship

Figure 34-2 Basic Relations

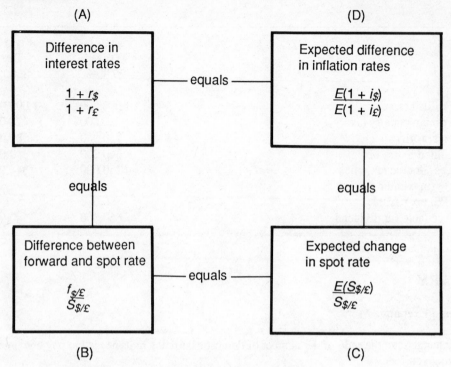

2. Interest rates and exchange rates (boxes A and B of Figure 34-2):
   a. Interest rate parity: interest rate differential must equal the differential between the forward and spot exchange rates.
   b. Seems to hold when taxes and government regulations are absent.

3. The forward discount and changes in spot rates (boxes B and C):
   a. Expectations theory of exchange rates: the percentage difference between forward rates and today's spot rates equals the expected change in spot rates.
   b. On average forward rate equals future spot rate, although it is an exaggerated estimate of future changes.

4. Changes in the exchange rate, and inflation rates (boxes C and D)
   a. Law of one price: similar goods are priced roughly the same in each country.
   b. Changes in domestic prices must be matched by changes in the price of the domestic currency.
   c. Estimated differences in relative inflation rates are rough estimates of changes in spot rates of exchange.

5. Interest rates and inflation rates (boxes D and A):
   a. Capital tends to flow to its highest and best use.
   b. In equilibrium expected real return on capital is the same in different countries.
   c. Money rate of interest will reflect expected inflation.
   d. Differences in money rates are equal to expected differences in inflation rates.

Insuring against Currency Risks

1. Future payments may be insured by selling the foreign currency forward.

2. Can separate each problem from its financing scheme.

3. Brealey and Myers favor insurance over speculation.
   a. Low cost and simple.
   b. To speculate, one needs information superior to all other market participants.

4. Four lessons:
   a. Forward rates may tell you how to allow for exchange risk in contract pricing.
   b. Insurance is worth having (expectations theory).
   c. May insure by selling forward or by borrowing foreign currency and selling spot (interest rate parity theory).
   d. Converts the foreign currency into the domestic one, and discounts the cash flows at the domestic opportunity cost of capital.

International Investment Decisions

1. Same procedures and criteria as for any investment
   a. Discount estimated cash flows at the return obtainable on comparable-risk assets
   b. Accept all projects with positive NPVs

2. Two methods:

	METHOD 1	METHOD 2
Step 1	Estimate future cash flow in foreign currency	Estimate future cash flow in foreign currency
Step 2	Convert to dollars (at forecasted exchange rates)	Calculate present value (use foreign currency discount rate)
Step 3	Calculate present value (use dollar discount rate)	Convert to dollars (use spot rate)

   a. Method I requires exchange rates forecast; Method II does not.
   b. If Method I is used, use consensus forecast.
   c. Foreign country inflation rate is likely to loom large in the decision.
   d. Let the differences in country interest rates be your proxy to the difference in inflation rates.
   e. Both methods produce the same results as long as we assume the parity relationships of Figure 34-1.
   f. If a forecast of exchange rates is in the cards, against which Brealey and Myers advise, Method I should be used.

The Cost of Capital for Foreign Investment

1. The risk-reward trade off of overseas investments must be evaluated.

2. No clear-cut answers.

3. Risk is mitigated by diversification, and international diversification is particularly appealing.

4. No precise answer to the opportunity cost of capital for foreign investments question.

5. Smarter to adjust cash flows (probabilistically) for political or other foreign risk considerations than to adjust the discount rate.

Financing Foreign Operations

1. Pay for foreign investments in three ways:
   a. Export domestic capital.
   b. Borrow in foreign country.
   c. Borrow where interest rates are lowest.

2. Some risks
   a. Exported capital is exposed to devaluation risk. Borrow foreign currency to avoid this exchange risk.
   b. Law of one price works fairly well and hence insulates us from this exchange risk somewhat, not perfectly.
   c. Trying to borrow at the lowest nominal rate is likely to reveal that real rates are about the same.

3. Tax and the financing method
   a. Choice of financing depends on how subsequently generated funds are to be used.
   b. Tax considerations make the choice important.
   c. Double taxation agreements help.

4. Political risk:
   a. Make it painful for future or incumbent foreign governments to engage in untoward acts.
   b. Finance from the World Bank.
   c. Borrow from intermediaries and guarantee the loan contingent on the government living up to its part of the deal.
   d. Use a consortium of large banks that the foreign government does not wish to alienate.

5. Interactions of investment and financing decisions
   a. An international investment project cannot be separated from its method of financing.
   b. Many international investment projects have numerous financing side effects.
   c. Still, go back to first principles by establishing the base case NPV, and adding to or a subtracting from that the present value of financing side effects.

LIST OF TERMS

Eurocurrency market	Interest rate parity theory
Expectations theory of exchange rates	Forward market
Floating rates	Law of one price
Spot rate of exchange	

EXERCISES

Fill-in Questions

1. An American company importing from Japan (buys, sells) _____ yen, whereas a Mexican company buying American goods (buys, sells) _____ pesos.
2. Exchange-rate quotations for the price of a currency for immediate delivery is known as _____.
3. Financial managers who buy and sell currency for future delivery do it in the _____ market for foreign currencies.

4. If a financial manager loses interest when making a loan in terms of sterling but gains when she sells sterling forward at a higher price than she paid for it, the interest rate differential and the annual forward discount must be equal according to the _____ theory.

5. The _____ theory of exchange rates says that the percentage difference between forward exchange rates and spot exchange rates is equal to the expected change in the spot rate.

6. When the price of a foreign currency is always equal to the ratio of foreign and domestic prices of goods, the _____ is at work.

7. The law of one price suggests that changes in the spot rate of exchange may be approximated by estimated differences in relative_____ rates.

8. The theory that states that the sterling rate of interest covered for exchange risk should be the same as the dollar rate is called the _____ theory.

9. The European international market for short-term loans that are virtually free of government regulation is called the _____ market.

10. The expectations theory of forward rates says that on average the (spot, forward) _____ rate is equal to the (present, expected)_____ spot rate.

Problems

1. Using the data contained in Figure 34-1, calculate the Thursday (Friday was Christmas Day) forward discount or premium for each of the following currencies: British pound; Canadian dollar; French franc; Japanese yen; Swiss franc; and West German mark. Compare your calculations with those in worked problem 1. What differences do you observe? Are they what you expected? Why or why not? Explain fully.

2. Using the data below, complete the answers that are left blank. Show all calculations.

	A	B	C
$r_\$$, percent	10	10	9
$r_£$, percent	12		9
$E(i_\$)$, percent	7	7	
$E(i_£)$, percent			7
$E(S_{\$/£})$		2.300	
$S_{\$/£}$	2.219	2.200	
$f_{\$/£}$			2.400

3. What-Not, Inc.'s two foreign operating subsidiaries face 32 and 52 percent corporate tax rates, whereas the domestic company is confronted with a 34 percent United States corporate tax rate. Double-tax agreements are in effect. The financial manager wants you to determine the estimated dividends available for shareholders, if the money each subsidiary earns is repatriated as cash dividends. What would you say to her? Show whatever calculations you may make.

Essay Questions

1. How does international financial management differ from domestic financial management?

2. The Brealey and Myers text identifies four problems with which financial managers must contend when dealing in foreign countries. What are they? Give a one-paragraph explanation of each. Also provide a one-paragraph discussion of how a financial manager should comport the financial affairs of his enterprise when confronted with each of these conditions.

3. How are money rates of interest in each country related to their respective real rates of interest? Additionally, how are money rates of interest among countries related to the real rates of interest among the same set of countries? What implications do your answers have for efficient financial management?

4. What does it mean to repatriate funds and what potential problems might financial managers encounter when dealing with foreign countries?

5. When making international investment decisions, what analytical framework must a financial manager employ to determine the correct discount rate? Explain fully.

ANSWERS TO EXERCISES

Fill-in Questions

1. buys; sells
2. spot rate of exchange
3. forward
4. interest rate parity
5. expectations
6. law of one price
7. inflation
8. interest rate parity
9. Eurocurrency
10. forward; expected future

Problems

1.

Table 34-2 Forward Discounts (Premiums), Percent

Days	British pound	Canadian dollar	French franc	Japanese yens	Swiss franc	W. German mark
30	-0.20	-0.63	-1.32	4.08	4.60	4.69
90	-0.76	-0.94	-1.54	3.63	4.28	4.23
180	-1.10	-1.10	1.21	3.55	4.23	4.13

2. Col. A: $E(i_£) = 8.95$ percent; $E(S'_{\$/£}) = 2.1796$; $f_{\$/£} = 2.1794$
   Col. B: $r_£ = 5.22$ percent; $E(i_£) = 2.35$ percent; $f_{\$/£} = 2.30$
   Col. C: $E(i_\$) = 7.00$ percent; $E(S'_{\$/£}) = 2.40$; $S_{\$/£} = 2.40$

3.

	Myth 1 Tax - 32.00%	Myth 2 Tax - 52.00%
Profits before tax	1,000,000	1,000,000
Foreign country tax	320,000	520,000
Net profits	680,000	480,000
United States tax	340,000	340,000
Less double tax relief (maximum 34%)	320,000	340,000
U.S. tax payable	20,000	0
Available for dividend	660,000	480,000

CHAPTER 35
PENSION PLANS

INTRODUCTION

Private pension plans are very important to society and assume greater and greater financial importance to most corporations. Financial managers must understand them for they are important assets and liabilities to be managed.

WHAT TO LOOK FOR IN CHAPTER 35

Most pension plans are defined benefit plans in which specified sums of money are paid to eligible employees when they retire. The dollar amount of a person's pension is based on either a career-average or a final-average formula, the latter becoming more and more prevalent with the advent of recent high levels of inflation. The Employee Retirement Income Security Act (ERISA) is the federal legislation which provides, among other things, for the eventual full vesting of pension benefits and which established the Pension Benefit Guarantee Corporation which guarantees the payment of fully vested but unfunded pension liabilities.

Pension Plan Balance Sheet: Pension Plan liabilities arise from past as well as future services of employees. The present value of the pension plan consists of the fund's current value plus the present value of future contributions. The present value of expected benefits for past services and the expected present value of future services are added to obtain the total pension liabilities. If the present value of the fund assets is less than the present value of accrued benefits, an unfunded accrued benefit arises. Changes in the value of pension fund securities, employee turnover, increased pension benefits, and changes in assumed actuarial discount rates all influence the total amount of pension benefits that must be met out of corporate income.

The Pension Benefit Guarantee Corporation (PBGC) insures most of the money in private pension funds. The PBGC must also approve of plan terminations and it may refuse permission unless a firm is bankrupt. Pension liabilities in excess of plan assets are now recorded on balance sheets.

Managing the Pension Fund: Pension funds are managed either by insurance companies or through a trust, which in turn hires professional money managers. The PBGC largely protects employee's pensions. Tax laws encourage firms to engage in tax arbitrage by selling bonds to fund a pension plan, and having the pension plan invest totally in bonds. The bond interest expense to the corporation is tax deductible and the interest income to the pension fund is exempt from taxes as it is earned. Through simulations, a pension fund's total risk and expected rate of return may be estimated.

Measuring Fund Performance: Financial managers must know the elements of pension fund performance measurements, because that performance may significantly influence the amount of future pension fund liabilities. The internal rate of return, sometimes called the dollar-weighted rate of return, is often used to measure performance, but the time-weighted rate of return is preferred because it gives equal weight to each unit of time as well as to the cash flows into and out of the pension fund. When evaluating pension fund performance, two dimensions are looked at: what the pension fund would have earned were it a benchmark, completely unmanaged, market portfolio; and the portfolio manager's ability to pick stocks.

WORKED EXAMPLES

PROBLEM 1: ESTIMATED PLAN DEFICIT

If the present value (PV) of What-Not, Inc.'s pension fund is $4.5 million, the PV of contributions for future services is estimated at $3.5 million, the PV of expected benefits from past service is $6.5 million, and the PV of expected future service cost is $7.5 million, estimate the deficit of pension plan assets. Also indicate what you, as the firm's financial manager, should allocate to the fund if you wish to amortize the deficit over the next 15 years, assuming that you obtain a 9 percent annual compound return on your investments.

SOLUTION

To estimate the deficit today, take the difference between the sum of the present value of the pension fund and the contributions the firm anticipates making during the next 15 years and the sum of the present values of the expected benefits, from both past service and future service.

> Deficit = (PV pension fund + PV of future contributions) – (PV of benefits from past service + PV of expected future service costs)
> = ($4.5 million + $3.5 million) – ($6.5 million + $7.5 million)
> = $8.0 million – $14 million
> = -$6 million

To amortize this deficit's present value by the end of the fifteenth year, use the annuity method to determine how much should be set aside in each year, assuming the rate of return on the contributed monies is 9 percent compounded annually. Using a hand-held calculator, the answer is $744,353, or $744,000 a year for convenience. Using Appendix Table 3, the answer is $6 million ÷ 8.061 = $744,325 annually.

PROBLEM 2: TAX ARBITRAGE

"Hey look," one of the directors of What-Not, Inc. says to you, "recently I attended a finance lecture series and one of the finance profs argued the case for tax arbitrage of pension plans. The deal sounded too good to be true. Is this yet another fancy academic dream that goes nowhere in practice?" What is your response to this director? Assume a marginal tax rate of 34 percent, a pension liability of $20 million a year in perpetuity and a required market rate of return of 10 percent.

SOLUTION

The place to begin is to determine how many bonds the firm must float in order to cover pension liabilities. It works out to be:

> Borrow = $20 million/0.10
> = $200 million

Because the pension contribution is a tax-deductible expense, the $200 million has an after-tax cost of:

> (1 – 0.34) x $200 million = $132 million

Next, the pension fund invests the $200 million contribution in corporate bonds at the then prevailing rate of 10 percent, for a tax-exempt income of $20 million, which is used to pay the annual pension liability.

This scheme contrasts with paying the pensions when due with $20 million, only part of which is shielded, (1 – 0.34) x $20 million = $13.2 million to be exact. The net cash gain to the corporation is the difference between what it borrows and the after-tax cost of the pension contribution, that is, $200 million – $132 million = $112 million.

And there you have it, almost by magic. Leverage remains unchanged and shareholders are made better off because their cash flow stream has been enhanced. After that demonstration you should say: Voila!

PROBLEM 3: FUND PERFORMANCE

What-Not, Inc.'s financial manager is a trustee of the company's pension plan which is managed by the outside firm of Make Money & Co. To prepare for a meeting with the portfolio manager, she is reviewing the following information of the equity portion of the fund. What analysis should the financial manager make, so that she may ask intelligent questions?

	Returns, %	
Year	What-Not, Inc.'s Pension Plan	Standard & Poor's 500 Composite
1969	-11.9	-8.5
1970	9.3	4.0
1971	9.9	14.3
1972	18.5	19.0
1973	-13.3	-14.7
1974	-23.8	-26.5
1975	45.0	37.3
1976	23.0	24.0
1977	-12.9	-7.2
1978	2.8	6.4
1979	21.2	18.7
1980	35.0	32.4
1981	-12.0	-5.3
1982	25.0	21.5
1983	55.2	22.6
1984	5.0	6.3
1985	28.7	31.8
1986	22.6	18.7
1987	13.1	12.0
Average	12.65	10.88
Standard deviation of return	21.24	17.20
Beta	1.14	1.00
Average Treasury bill rate: 1969 - 1987	7.48%	

SOLUTION

The first step is to determine the fund risk premium.

Fund risk premium = average fund return – average rate of interest
= 12.65 percent – 7.48 percent
= 5.17 percent

It is apparent that being in equities during this time was smart. To see how smart, let's go on.

The second step is to determine the rate of return obtainable on a benchmark portfolio; she wants to know the return "any dummy could have obtained if he had merely bought and held the market portfolio as represented by the Standard & Poor's 500 Composite Stock Index," to put it in her words. The benchmark portfolio is obtained by multiplying the risk premium on the market portfolio by the beta of What-Not's equity portfolio.

$$
\begin{aligned}
\text{Benchmark portfolio's risk premium} \; &= \; \text{beta of fund x risk premium on} \\
&\qquad \text{the market} \\
&= \; 1.14 \text{ x } (10.88 \text{ percent} - 7.48 \text{ percent}) \\
&= \; 1.14 \text{ x } 3.40 \text{ percent} \\
&= \; 3.88 \text{ percent}
\end{aligned}
$$

It still looks good, because the dummy, or benchmark, portfolio would not have been a better performer than the managed portfolio.

Next let's calculate the alpha of the pension fund to find out how good the portfolio manager was at picking stocks.

$$
\begin{aligned}
\text{Alpha} \; &= \; \text{gain from picking stocks} \\
&= \; \text{fund risk premium} - \text{benchmark portfolio's risk premium} \\
&= \; (r - r_f) - \beta(r_m - r_f) \\
&= \; (12.65 \text{ percent} - 7.48 \text{ percent}) - 1.14(10.88 \text{ percent} - 7.48 \text{ percent}) \\
&= \; 5.17 \text{ percent} - 1.14(3.88 \text{ percent}) \\
&= \; 5.17 \text{ percent} - 3.88 \text{ percent} \\
&= \; 1.29 \text{ percent per year}
\end{aligned}
$$

The portfolio return arose from the manager's ability to pick stocks. But the gain indicates that the risk of the fund portfolio is greater than the risk of the Standard & Poor's 500. If it were not, the alpha would be zero because there is no stock picking in the benchmark portfolio. To illustrate this, construct a second benchmark portfolio which has both the same risk as the market portfolio and some unique risk. By taking the ratio of the standard deviation of the portfolio to the standard deviation of the market portfolio, and then multiplying by the market risk premium, a benchmark portfolio, which has the same riskiness as the market and some unique risk too, is constructed. Armed with that information we can obtain the clues we need to tell us about the manager's skills in picking stocks. Set it up this way.

$$
\begin{aligned}
\text{Net gain from picking stock} \; &= \; \text{fund risk premium} - \text{risk premium on second} \\
&\qquad \text{benchmark portfolio} \\
&= \; (r - r_f) - \sigma/\sigma_m(r_m - r_f) \\
&= \; (12.65\% - 7.48\%) - [(21.24 \div 17.20)(10.88\% - 7.48\%)] \\
&= \; 5.17\% - (1.23 \text{ x } 3.88) \\
&= \; 5.17\% - 4.77\% \\
&= \; 0.40\% \text{ per year}
\end{aligned}
$$

By constructing the portfolio as she did, the portfolio manager actually gained a small fraction of a return from picking stocks. As a matter of fact, managing pension funds is far more complex than this little example demonstrates. Nonetheless, our financial manager is now equipped with some insight regarding the manager's abilities during this period. Whether they will persist remains to be seen, and continues to be one of her many responsibilities. Let's see how this analysis works out in the next problem.

PROBLEM 4: FUND PERFORMANCE, AGAIN

Recognizing that the period of analysis is short, what analysis should be made of What-Not, Inc.'s pension fund portfolio manager during the last 5 years for which there are data?

SOLUTION

The setup is the same as it is in problem 2. The average return on the Standard & Poor's 500 was 18.3 percent; the average return on the pension fund was 24.9 percent; the average return on Treasury bills was 7.1 percent; and the standard deviations of the index and the fund were 9.8 and 19.2 percent. During this period the fund's beta was 1.28. The calculations are as follows.

1. Fund risk premium = 24.92% – 7.10% = 17.82%

2. Benchmark portfolio risk premium = [1.28 x (18.30% – 7.10%)] = 14.34%

3. Alpha = 17.82% – 14.34% = 3.48%

4. Net gain from picking stocks = {17.82 – [(19.19 + 9.80) x 14.34]} = -10.25%

The first moral is clear: the total nineteen years does not tell us much about the last five years. The second moral: So she looks like a great portfolio manager, but she assumed a portfolio risk which is more than twice as risky as What-Not's pension portfolio. Although you were not asked to calculate it, a dollar invested in the non-managed Standard & Poor's 500 Composite index grew to $1.86 at the end of 1987. A dollar in the What-Not pension fund grew to $1.87, and yet the portfolio was at least twice as risky.

The financial manager is likely to start thinking about replacing the present portfolio manager. Surely the portfolio manager's fees are difficult to justify in light of the inability of the manager to add value to the portfolio beyond some simple-minded scheme.

SUMMARY

Introduction

1. Increasingly important asset and liability to be managed

2. ERISA

Types of Pension Plans

1. Defined benefit.

2. Negotiated.

3. Inflation adjustments.

4. ERISA specifies vesting.

The Pension Plan Balance Sheet

1. Actuary's central role.

2. Liabilities: past and future service.

3. Assets: present value of pension fund plus present value of contributions.

4. Valuing liabilities:

Pension liabilities = PV of expected benefits for past service (or PV of accrued benefits or PV of vested accrued benefits) + PV expected future service costs.

5. Valuing the pension fund:

$$\text{Unfunded liability} = \text{PV(accrued benefit)} - \text{PV(fund assets)}$$

6. Valuing future contributions: find normal costs by using accrued-benefit cost, projected-benefit cost, or level cost methods.

7. Estimating the deficit: experience losses (amortized over 15 years); supplemental liability (amortized over 30 years).

8. Another look at the pension plan balance sheet:
   a. Discount rate is most difficult decision.
   b. Changing actuarial rates changes earnings.

9. ERISA, fund contributions, and pension insurance:
   a. PBGC.
   b. Unfunded pension liabilities have prior legal claim.
   c. Companies in financial distress have a put option against PBGC.

Plan Terminations

1. One way for a financially unhealthy company to walk away from large financial obligations, except for the presence of PBGC.

2. Healthy companies may terminate with approbation of PBGC and recapture past funding.

Accounting for the Pension Plan

1. Recent accounting regulations require that unfunded pension liabilities be recorded on the balance sheet.

2. New regulations are an important first step in pension accounting.

Managing the Pension Fund

1. Funding: either insurance companies or trust funds (more common, 70%)

2. Risk and pension funds
   a. Value of fund does not increase as risk increases.
   b. PBGC reduces participant's risk.
   c. Shareholders bear pension fund risk.

3. Taxes and pension fund policy:
   a. Black-Tepper: borrow and use proceeds to fund pension plan.
   b. Tax arbitrage a firm's two cash flows, interest expense, which is tax-deductible, and fund interest income, which is tax-exempt.
   c. Firm borrows at corporate after-tax bond rate and fund earns the pretax corporate bond rate.

    d.   Total leverage stays the same.

    e.   Shareholders' wealth increases.

Measuring Fund Performance

1. Estimating returns
    a.   Dollar weighted: equally weights each cash flow; no regard to timing; internal rate of return
    b.   Time-weighted: accounts for the timing of cash flows

2. Performance yardstick: objective is to differentiate between returns ascribable to market-related factors and returns ascribable to fund manager's skill.

3. Steps
    a.   Fund risk premium:
         = average fund return − average rate of interest
$$= r - r_f$$
    b.   Benchmark portfolio measures risk premium of unmanaged fund:
         = Beta x risk premium on market
$$= \beta(r_m - r_f)$$
    c.   Gain from picking stocks (alpha):
         = fund risk premium − benchmark portfolio's risk premium
$$= (r - r_f) - \langle (r_m - r_f)$$
    d.   Net gain from picking stocks:
         = fund risk premium − risk premium on second benchmark portfolio with equal risk
$$= (r - r_f) - \sigma/\sigma_m(r_m - r_f)$$
    e.   Some cautions:
        (1) Difficult consistently to outperform benchmark.
        (2) Unusual performance may be due to chance.
        (3) Real estate and foreign investments confound the performance measurement problem.

LIST OF TERMS

Alpha	Pension Benefit Guarantee Corporation
Career average	Risk premium
Defined benefit plan	Stock selection
Dollar-weighted rate of return	Tax arbitrage
Employee Retirement Income Security Act	Time-weighted rate of return
ERISA	Unmanaged portfolio
Experience losses	Vesting
Final average	

EXERCISES

Fill-in Questions

1. The federal legislation which governs pension funds is called _____, the acronym for which is _____.

2. A retirement plan which offers employees a firm promise of so many dollars a month from age 65 or a specified proportion of their final salary is called a _____.

3. The two plans most commonly employed to determine the amount of pension benefits are _____ and _____. The _____ plan pays a pension equal to a specified percentage of the employees' compensation in each year that they were a member of the plan, whereas the _____ plan bases its pension payments on the average of the last given set of years of service. The _____ pension compensation scheme is a better hedge against inflation than the _____ compensation scheme.

4. The _____ part of the retirement plan entitles members to part or all of their pension benefits, no matter what.

5. The two principal liabilities of a pension plan arise from _____ and _____ services, and are expected to be covered from _____ and _____.

6. The greater the rate of return on the pension fund, the (greater, less) _____ future contributions will be, and the (greater, less) _____ will be reported earnings.

7. Pension fund losses resulting from a difference between expectations and experience are called _____, whereas losses in the present value of a pension fund arising from such items as increased pension benefits are called _____.

8. The internal rate of return, when used to measure pension fund performance is called the _____ rate of return.

9. The _____ rate of return is preferred to a dollar-weighted rate of return because it gives equal weight to each unit of time.

10. A corporation that sells bonds and funds its pension with the proceeds has engaged in _____ because the interest is tax deductible in the first instance and nontaxable in the second.

11. The risk premium is the return premium a pension fund receives for assuming risk and is equal to the difference between the fund's total return and the _____.

12. The total risk premium on a pension fund consists of two components: premium on an _____ and _____.

13. If the risk premium on the market portfolio is 10 percent and the beta of an unmanaged portfolio is 1.2, the benchmark portfolio's risk premium is _____.

14. The gain from stock selection is called _____ and is measured as the difference between _____ and _____.

Problems

1. The present value of Book Ends, Inc.'s pension fund is $32.5 million; the present value of expected future service costs is $64.0 million; the present value of contributions for future services is estimated at $59.8 million; and the present value of expected benefits from past service is $42.2 million. Estimate the deficit of pension plan assets. What sums of money should the financial manager allocate annually, if she wishes to amortize the deficit over the next 10 years? 15 years? 20 years? Assume that the financial manager expects to obtain an 11 percent compound annual rate of return on all invested funds.

2. Tax arbitrage must be a good deal, because it is a form of subsidized financing and that is always preferred to nonsubsidized financing. Demonstrate just how good a deal tax arbitrage is for What-Not, Inc. using the following data.

Marginal tax rate:	34 percent
Pension liability (perpetuity):	$15 million
Market rate of return:	10 percent

382

3. The financial manager of Book Ends, Inc. is also a trustee of the company's pension fund. She is attending the quarterly trustees' meeting at which, among other things, the investment manager that runs the trusteed money, We, Can, Pickum & Co., Inc., is presenting its yearly review of pension fund performance. She is presented with the information in the following table, and immediately proceeds to analyze it. What quantitative measures should she use as a first pass at the data? Show all calculations.

	Returns, %	
Year	Book End Inc.'s Pension Plan	Standard & Poor's 500 Composite
1969	-8.8	-8.5
1970	5.2	4.0
1971	15.4	14.3
1972	18.9	19.0
1973	-12.2	-14.7
1974	-27.7	-26.5
1975	35.3	37.3
1976	26.6	24.0
1977	-14.0	-7.2
1978	7.3	6.4
1979	12.3	18.7
1980	37.9	32.4
1981	-7.3	-5.3
1982	22.1	21.5
1983	50.6	22.6
1984	7.0	6.3
1985	33.2	31.8
1986	20.5	18.7
1987	10.1	12.0
Average	12.23%	10.88%
Standard deviation of return	20.18	17.20
Beta	1.10	1.00
Average Treasury bill rate:1969 - 1987	7.48%	

4. How did the firm, We, Can, Pickum & Co., Inc., perform during the first 9 years for which there are data? During the last 10 years? Assume the Treasury bill rate for the past 10 years averaged 8.5 percent a year and that for the first 9 years it was 6.01 percent. Use the following data:

	Book Ends, Inc.	S & P 500
First 9 years		
Average return %	4.30	4.63
Standard Deviation	21.21	20.61
Beta	1.05	
Last 10 years		
Average return %	19.37	16.51
Standard deviation	17.21	11.84
Beta	1.33	

Essay Questions

1. Why is the study of pension funds important to financial managers?

2. What are the sources for pension liabilities, how are these liabilities financed, and how might they affect the company's income statement? The value of the firm? To what extent should the financial manager worry about these factors? Why?

3. What are the implications of poor investment performance of a pension fund for a company's pension liabilities?

4. If the actuary does not allow for wage inflation in calculations of required contributions to a pension fund, and subsequent labor negotiations insist on wage adjustments, how might the firm's financial plans be affected?

5. The typical pension fund is sponsored by a corporation. Organizationally, a set of trustees is appointed to administer the trust established by the plan sponsor, the corporation. Under the 1974 Employee Retirement Income Security Act (ERISA), the trustees are charged with the responsibility to act as a prudent investor would act under similar circumstances. If the financial manager is one of the trustees, as they invariably are, what does this say about the knowledgeability and information set that a financial manager must now acquire?

6. What does a financial manager need to know about pension fund performance and its implications for efficient financial management of a firm?

7. Why is the internal rate of return inappropriate for measuring pension fund performance? Is your answer in any way similar to the inappropriateness of using yield to maturity to evaluate a bond?

8. Outline the steps financial managers should take to evaluate the performance of their company-sponsored pension funds. Indicate why you chose the steps you did.

9. "Any dummy can obtain the rate of return on the market portfolio. In order to induce me to hire a professional money manager to oversee my pension fund, he must demonstrate his ability to achieve rates of return in excess of that of the market rate of return." This statement was made at a recent board of directors meeting of What-Not, Inc. How would you respond to this financial manager's comment? Explain fully.

ANSWERS TO EXERCISES

Fill-in Questions

1. Employee Retirement Income Security Act; (ERISA)
2. defined benefit plan
3. career-average; final-average; career-average; final-average; final-average; career-average
4. vested
5. past; future; the present value of the pension fund; the present value of future contributions
6. less; greater
7. experience losses; supplemental liability
8. dollar-weighted
9. time-weighted
10. tax arbitrage
11. risk-free interest rate
12. unmanaged fund; reward for stock selection
13. 12 percent
14. alpha; fund risk premium; the benchmark portfolio's risk premium

Problems

1.

Deficit = (PV of pension fund + PV of future contributions) − (PV of past services +
PV of future services)

= ($32.5 + $59.8) − ($42.2 + $64.0)

= -$92.3 + $106.2

= $13.9 million

ANNUAL AMOUNTS		
10 yr.	$2,360,000	($13.9 million/5.889)
15 yr.	1,933,000	
20 yr.	1,746,000	

2.

Borrow: $15/0.10	= $150 million
After-tax cost: (1 − 0.34) x $150	= $99
Pension income: 0.10 x $150	= $15
Net gain from tax arbitrage: $150 − $99	= $51

If the tax rate had been 46 percent, as it was prior to the Tax Reform Act of 1986, the tax advantage would have been $69 million.

3. Fund risk premium = 12.23% − 7.48% = 4.75%

Benchmark portfolio risk premium = 1.10 x (10.88% − 7.48%) = 3.74%

Alpha = 4.75% − 3.74% = 1.01%

Net gain from picking stocks = {4.75% − [(20.18 ÷ 17.20) x (10.88% − 7.48%)]} = 4.75% − 3.99% = 0.76%

4.

Book Ends, Inc.	First 9 years	
Average fund performance		4.30%
Average interest rate		6.10%
Beta		1.05
Average market performance		4.63%
Fund standard deviation		21.21
Market standard deviation		20.61
Fund risk premium =	-1.80%	
Benchmark portfolio risk premium =	1.54%	
Alpha =	-0.26%	
Net gain from picking stocks =	-0.21%	

Book Ends, Inc.	Last 10 years	
Average fund performance		19.37%
Average interest rate		8.50%
Beta		1.33
Average market performance		16.51%
Fund standard deviation		17.21
Market standard deviation		11.84
Fund risk premium =	10.87%	
Benchmark portfolio risk premium =	10.65%	
Alpha =	0.22%	
Net gain from picking stocks =	-4.62%	

CHAPTER 36
CONCLUSION: WHAT WE DO AND
DO NOT KNOW ABOUT FINANCE

INTRODUCTION

So, here we are at the end of what must have seemed a long journey. You have traversed the entire landscape of financial decision making within corporations. Let's bring together the bits and pieces so as to isolate the set of things that we know with reasonable certainty and some of the important things that are still up in the air.

WHAT TO LOOK FOR IN CHAPTER 36

What can one say that is intelligent when one has traversed almost 900 pages of text? One can say several things, that's what. Most of all, what you must ask yourself, and should have been asking yourself all along is: How does a financial manager make rational decisions in light of what we know and, more importantly in some respects, in light of what we do not know? This chapter summarizes the blood and guts issues confronting all financial managers, regardless of the size of their firms.

What We Know: Here is the shopping list of things we know:

1. Net present value is the only proper way by which to evaluate assets. The task of financial managers: Maximize the net present value.

2. The capital asset pricing model tells us that an asset's risk is composed of a market-related component and one indigenous to the firm.

3. We know that firm-related risk may be diversified; so we conclude that only market-related risk counts when making financial decisions.

4. Following therefrom, we know that mergers and acquisitions do not add value unless the combined firm produces greater cash flows than either firm produced when they were independent of each other.

5. We know that security prices react quickly to almost all available information (reflecting fully what is known), and hence present prices are the best estimate of true value.

6. Financial managers, therefore, should make their decisions on the *assumption* that capital markets are mostly efficient most of the time.

7. We know that the discount rate used to evaluate investment projects is an opportunity cost, a rate of return, and is measured by returns on investments of comparable risk.

8. We know that the assets of comparable risk are found in security markets.

9. We know that the risk of comparable assets is measured by beta, which captures the nondiversifiable risk facing investors.

386

10. We know option theory will loom large in financial decision making, because all decisions represent options--claims--on some specific event, a series of cash flows or an option to default on the debt, for example.

11. Because of the value-additivity principle, we know that the particular way in which the income of a firm is split between its creditors and owners does not influence the total value of the firm, and Modigliani and Miller, bless their souls, continue to hold forth.

Is It All Peaches and Cream? The above litany of things we know gives the illusion that financial decision making is an open-and-shut case. You should have a healthy skepticism for such a simplistic view of the finance world. The list of things we do not know is, and always will be, far larger than the list of things we do know. (Quick, which Brealey and Myers' law is that?) And as if that were not enough, we will learn new and better ways to cope with what we already know, the capital asset pricing model being a case in point.

What We Do Not Know: "Well then," you are probably saying, "what are the things we do not know, or about which we have some serious questions?" Here we go:

1. We know that financial managers make financial decisions but we do not know precisely how they make them. We know how they should make them; but the process they actually use eludes us, especially when it comes to strategic financial planning.

2. We know that net present value is the only proper way to evaluate investment opportunities, but we do not have many insights about how to discover investments that add more value to the firm than they take away.

3. We know that the expected return on comparable-risk assets should be used to evaluate investment opportunities, but we do not know how to estimate, with the degree of assurance we would like, the beta of a firm's investment opportunity set.

4. We can all fall in love with the capital asset pricing model, at least at first blush. But such amorous feelings may well wane after we find out that it is hard to prove or disprove; that statistical tests may be flawed; that results do not seem to square with the model; that, heaven forbid, investors seem to be concerned with diversifiable risk; and that not all investors have the same outlook for their financial rewards.

5. The evidence is fairly convincing that the markets for financial assets, at the minimum, are fairly efficient, but a disquieting set of evidence has emerged in recent years that suggests that they may not be nearly as efficient as we once thought.

6. And what about management? Is it an off-balance sheet liability? Does management always work with the value additivity principle (law of conservation of value) uppermost in its mind?

7. What about all the new securities issued in the past ten years or so? Why so many and to what reasonable purpose are they put? We know they are there; we do not have a complete explanation for them.

8. We cannot say for certain whether capital structure decisions are important. We constantly observe different capital structures for firms of the same risk class. Are financial managers telling (signaling, a candidate for being the buzzword of the day, much as a beta is) us something we should know?

9. And dividend policy controversies are likely to go on and on. We know the theory says that dividend policy does not count, for the value of the firm is unaffected by it. Yet so many different dividend policies exist, policies inexplicable by taxes and such, that we must ponder this knotty problem even more than before.

10. And what of liquidity? We do not have too many intelligent things to say about working capital management because we do not have a complete and rigorous theory of liquidity as applied to financial managers of business firms.

11. Even mergers are not explicable by what we know. The valued-additivity principle tells us that no new values are created from mergers unless the cash flows of the combined firms exceed the sum of the cash flows of the two firms when viewed separately. Why then are there so many mergers?

SUMMARY

"Yikes," you may say, "that's really discouraging. I wish I had read this chapter first. It would have saved me tons of time studying all the other stuff that preceded it." Take heart, have faith, be stout, and forge ahead, knowing that to chronicle the problem areas confronting financial managers is merely to recognize that no field of study has all the answers, not even finance. Use what we know as an engine for discovery. Know also that so much of our theory, as neat as it is, translates into the *art* of financial management. Most of all, this is not the end of your studies; it is merely the beginning of your understanding of the world of corporate finance. Such is the nature of education. Such is life. One would be surprised were it otherwise.